014560439 Liverpool Univ

The Cambridge Companion
Human Rights Law

D0626628

Human rights are considered one ⌐. ⌐⌐⌐ ⌐⌐⌐ ⌐⌐oughts of the early
twenty-first century. This book presents in an authoritative and
readable form the variety of platforms on which human rights law is
practised today, reflecting also on the dynamic inter-relationships that
exist between these various levels. The collection has a critical edge.
The chapters engage with how human rights law has developed in its
various subfields, what (if anything) has been achieved and at what cost,
in terms of expected or unexpected side-effects. The authors pass
judgment about the consistency, efficacy and success of human
rights law (set against the standards of the field itself or other external
goals). Written by world-class academics, this *Companion* will be
essential reading for students and scholars of human rights law.

Conor Gearty is Professor of Human Rights Law at the London School of
Economics and Political Science. He is a specialist in European and UK
human rights law, as well as in terrorism law and civil liberties, on each of
which subjects he has written extensively. He is also a barrister and a
founding member of Matrix Chambers from where he continues to practise.

Costas Douzinas is Professor of Law and Director of the Birkbeck
Institute for the Humanities. In his many books, and the talks he has
given around the world, he has developed a position on human rights
that seeks to retain the radical and emancipatory power of the term and
practice without however accepting the arid and self-interested
arguments of the powerful (of both the scholarly and political variety).

WITHDRAWN FROM STOCK

The Cambridge Companion to
Human Rights Law

Edited by

Conor Gearty
London School of Economics and Political Science

and

Costas Douzinas
Birkbeck College, University of London

CAMBRIDGE
UNIVERSITY PRESS

CAMBRIDGE UNIVERSITY PRESS
Cambridge, New York, Melbourne, Madrid, Cape Town,
Singapore, São Paulo, Delhi, Mexico City

Cambridge University Press
The Edinburgh Building, Cambridge CB2 8RU, UK

Published in the United States of America by Cambridge University Press, New York

www.cambridge.org
Information on this title: www.cambridge.org/9781107016248

© Cambridge University Press 2012

This publication is in copyright. Subject to statutory exception
and to the provisions of relevant collective licensing agreements,
no reproduction of any part may take place without the written
permission of Cambridge University Press.

First published 2012

Printed and bound in the United Kingdom by the MPG Books Group

A catalogue record for this publication is available from the British Library

Library of Congress Cataloguing in Publication data
The Cambridge companion to human rights law / edited by Conor Gearty
and Costas Douzinas.
    p. cm.
Papers presented at a conference at Birbeck College in London in November 2011 – Preface.
Includes bibliographical references.
ISBN 978-1-107-01624-8
1. Human rights – Congresses.   I. Gearty, C. A.   II. Douzinas, Costas, 1951–
K3239.8.C36   2012
341.4′8–dc23

2012023178

ISBN 978-1-107-01624-8 Hardback
ISBN 978-1-107-60235-9 Paperback

Cambridge University Press has no responsibility for the persistence or
accuracy of URLs for external or third-party internet websites referred to
in this publication, and does not guarantee that any content on such
websites is, or will remain, accurate or appropriate.

Contents

Preface

This study was planned and brought to fruition over the past couple of years. It has been the source of many thoroughly enjoyable excuses for conversation between the two of us, and also provided the platform for a quite extraordinarily energetic and creative conference at Birkbeck College in London in November 2011. Our idea for the conference was to bring together not only the contributors to this volume but also to a sister volume that we are editing. The result was a four-day event marked by papers that combined strong interdisciplinary engagements with fascinating multidisciplinary styles. Like blindfolded wine tasters we played the game of telling discipline from style without checking first who the speaker was and we were not often wrong – our lawyers, a good proportion of this volume's contributors, did not let us down, demonstrating that good lawyers can always engage with the world outside without sacrificing the analytical strengths that have made them excellent in their own field in the first place.

Human rights law has migrated from a little-known corner of international law to the whole of law and to the entirety of social relations. To collate a compendium on human rights law is an impossible task. A compendium is a 'shortcut across a mountain' and by extension a shortening, an abridgment, an abbreviation. Can such heavy concepts as those entailed in human rights law be shortened or abridged? A compendium must be a shortcut to the most weighty matter, to gains saved over centuries. Can there be a shortcut for human rights law? In this sense, we freely acknowledge that the present collection is caught in a paradox that can be resolved only partially. We have done our best in the selection of contributors to capture the international nature of our subject and the vibrancy of current debates within it. Of course we would have liked an even wider range of writers, from more places and different backgrounds, but the demands of space precluded this.

We are grateful to the Leverhulme Trust for funding the conference, the Birkbeck Law School, the LSE Department of Law and the Birkbeck Institute for the Humanities for their support in hosting the conference and to

Critique: The International Journal of Critical Legal Thought and managing director of the publishing house *Birkbeck Law Press*. Costas has written extensively on legal and political philosophy, human rights, aesthetics, literature, art and critical theory. His books include *Postmodern Jurisprudence* (1991); *The End of Human Rights* (2000); *Critical Jurisprudence* (2005); *Nomos and Aesthetics* (1996); *Human Rights and Empire* (2007); *Philosophy and Resistance in the Crisis* (forthcoming 2013). He has edited the collection *Law and the Image*; *Adieu Derrida*; *The Idea of Communism*; *New Critical Legal Studies*. His books have been translated into twelve languages.

Conor Gearty is Professor of Human Rights Law at the London School of Economics and Political Science, a founding member of Matrix Chambers and a fellow of the British Academy. He has published many books on human rights, civil liberties and terrorism, most recently *Debating Social Rights* (2011, with Virginia Mantouvalou) and *Essays on Human Rights and Terrorism* (2008). His publication on the internet *the rights future* (see www.therightsfuture.com) appeared in 2011 and his *Liberty and Security* will be published by Polity Press at the start of 2013. As a practising barrister he has appeared in cases in the Administrative Court, the Court of Appeal and the House of Lords.

Anna Grear is Associate Professor of Law at the University of Waikato, New Zealand. She is a legal theorist whose work focuses largely upon questions related to law's construction of the human being and of the human relationship with the world, broadly conceived. In human rights theory, her work has primarily focused upon questions concerning international human rights subjectivity and the politics of dis/embodiment. Her book *Redirecting Human Rights: Facing the Challenge of Corporate Legal Humanity* was published in 2010.

Patrick Hanafin is Professor of Law at Birkbeck Law School, Birkbeck College, University of London, where he also directs the Law School's Centre for Law and the Humanities. His research engages with questions of law and biopolitics, law and literature, human rights and citizenship, and the construction of community and identity in constitutional discourse. He has been a Visiting Professor at the School of Law at the University of Porto, Portugal and at the Law Faculty at the University of Pretoria, South Africa.

Chris Himsworth has been teaching and researching in public law at the University of Edinburgh since the mid 1970s. Latterly he has been Professor of Administrative Law and is now Emeritus Professor at the University. He has written widely in the fields of administrative law, local government, devolution and human rights and has had a particular interest in Scottish devolved government and inter-governmental relationships within the UK.

Florian Hoffmann is currently the Franz Haniel Chair of Public Policy and a Deputy Director of the Willy Brandt School of Public Policy at the University of Erfurt, Germany. Prior to joining the School in 2010 he taught at the London School of Economics and Political Science and the Catholic University of Rio de Janeiro (PUC-Rio). He works at the interface between law and politics, with a special interest in international law and human rights.

Samuel Moyn is Professor of History at Columbia University, where he has taught since 2001. Most recently, he is the author of *The Last Utopia: Human Rights in History* (2010); he is also editor of *Humanity*, a new interdisciplinary journal. He has served as Visiting Professor of Law at Harvard and Yale University, and is now at work on the trajectory of human rights in the last several decades.

Manfred Nowak is Professor of International Law and Human Rights and Scientific Director of the Vienna Master of Arts in Human Rights at the University of Vienna. He is also Director of the Ludwig Boltzmann Institute of Human Rights, and served for many years as UN Expert on Enforced Disappearance, as Judge at the Human Rights Chamber for Bosnia and Herzegovina, and as UN Special Rapporteur on Torture 2004–10. He has authored more than 500 publications in the fields of constitutional, administrative and international law with a focus on fundamental and human rights.

Gerd Oberleitner is Senior Lecturer at the Institute of International Law and International Relations at the University of Graz, Austria. He was Lecturer in Human Rights at the London School of Economics and Political Science and Visiting Scholar at the School's Centre for the Study of Human Rights, the European Inter-University Centre in Venice and the Université du Québec à Montréal. His publications include *Global Human Rights Institutions: Between Remedy and Ritual* (2007).

Gerard Quinn is Professor of Law at the National University of Ireland, Galway and director of its Centre for Disability Law and Policy. He led the delegation of Rehabilitation International at the negotiations during the Working Group session of the UN Ad Hoc Committee that negotiated the UN Convention on the Rights of Persons with Disabilities. He is a former member of the Irish Human Rights Commission and a former Vice President of the European Committee on Social Rights (Council of Europe).

Margot E. Salomon is Senior Lecturer at the Centre for the Study of Human Rights and Law Department, London School of Economics and Political Science.

She specialises in international human rights law and global economic justice and has consulted and published widely on the topic. Recent publications include *Global Responsibility for Human Rights: World Poverty and the Development of International Law* (2007) and 'Deprivation, Causation, and the Law of International Cooperation', in M. Langford *et al.* (eds.), *Global Justice, State Duties* (2012).

Martin Scheinin is Professor of Public International Law at the European University Institute in Florence, Italy. In 2005–11 he served as the first UN Special Rapporteur on the promotion and protection of human rights and fundamental freedoms while countering terrorism.

Gerry Simpson holds the Sir Kenneth Bailey Chair of Law at Melbourne Law School. He is a Visiting Professor of Public International Law at the London School of Economics and Political Science and Open Society Fellow at the State University of Tbilisi in Georgia. His latest book, The *Margins of International Law*, will be published in 2012.

Acronyms and abbreviations

ACESCR	American Convention on Economic, Social and Cultural Rights
ACHR	American Convention on Human Rights
APC	African, Pacific and Caribbean
ART	assisted reproductive technology
ASEAN	Association of Southeast Asian Nations
ASP	Acts of the Scottish Parliament
BIT	Bilateral Investment Treaty
CAT	Convention against Torture and Other Cruel, Inhuman or Degrading Treatment or Punishment
CCPR	Covenant on Civil and Political Rights
CEDAW	Convention on the Elimination of all Forms of Discrimination against Women
CERD	International Convention on the Elimination of all Forms of Racial Discrimination
CHM	common heritage of mankind
CIDT	cruel, inhuman or degrading treatment or punishment
CPT	European Committee for the Prevention of Torture
CRC	Convention on the Rights of the Child
CRPD	Convention on the Rights of Persons with Disabilities
CRT	Convention on the Rights of the Child
CSW	Commission on the Status of Women
CTITF	Counter-Terrorism Implementation Task Force
DRC	Democratic Republic of the Congo
DRD	Declaration on the Right to Development
ECHR	European Convention on Human Rights and Fundamental Freedoms
ECJ	European Court of Justice
ECOSOC	Economic and Social Council
ECtHR	European Court of Human Rights
GATT	General Agreement on Tariffs and Trade
HRA	Human Rights Act (UK)

IACHR	Inter-American Court on Human Rights
ICC	International Criminal Court
ICESCR	International Covenant on Economic, Social and Cultural Rights
ICISS	International Commission on Intervention and State Sovereignty
ICJ	International Court of Justice
ICTR	International Criminal Tribunal for Rwanda
ICTY	International Criminal Tribunal for the Former Yugoslavia
IIA	International Investment Agreement
ILO	International Labor Organization
INTERFET	International Force for East Timor
JCPC	Judicial Committee of the Privy Council
MP	Member of Parliament (Westminster)
MSP	Member of the Scottish Parliament
NATO	North American Treaty Organisation
NGO	non-governmental organisation
NIEO	New International Economic Order
NIO	New Informational Order
NPM	national preventive mechanism
OAS	Organisation of African States
OAS	Organization of American States
OAU	Organisation of African Unity
OECD	Organisation for Economic Cooperation and Development
OHCHR	Office of the High Commissioner of Human Rights
OPCAT	Optional Protocol to the Convention against Torture
PPP	purchasing power parity
PSNR	principle of permanent sovereignty over natural resources
PTSD	post-traumatic stress disorder
R2P	responsibility to protect
SHRC	Scottish Human Rights Commission
SNP	Scottish National Party
TNC	transnational corporation
UDHR	Universal Declaration of Human Rights
UN	United Nations

UNCAT	UN Convention against Torture and Other Cruel, Inhuman or Degrading Treatment or Punishment
UNCLOS	UN Convention on the Law of the Sea
UNDP	UN Development Programme
UNHCR	UN High Commissioner for Refugees
UPR	Universal Periodic Review
WARM	World Association for Reproductive Medicine
WTO	World Trade Organization

considers the limitations in 'conceptions of personhood'[2] that flow out of the work of those philosophers (principally here Alan Gewirth and James Griffin) who seek to impose a rational approach to human rights, above the messiness of history and the contingent meaning of words. Douzinas argues that the '"correct interpretation" of the capacity for rational action has been and still is a strategy used to exclude people'.[3] Gerard Quinn's Chapter 2 (with Anna Arstein-Kerslake), 'Restoring the "human" in "human rights"' is a case-study in challenging the consequences of such exclusion. Their central concern is with the UN Disability Convention but they see the success of this agreement in its having been able to reach far beyond the conventional, autonomous-based approach to personhood to force the kind of fresh understanding that not only gives new life to what it means to be human but embraces as well the relational, personal aspects of humanity: what matters is what it means for this person here and now and not 'persons' in general. As Quinn and Arstein-Kerslake observe (and this is what they see as the key breakthrough), the Convention 'starts with what it means to be a human being ... [rather than] with a menu of rights to be mechanically tailored to yet another thematic group'.[4] This chapter ends on a startling note of concern about the future, perhaps even the present, with genetic manipulation offering new opportunities to mould humanity, often under cover of the human rights of (potential) parents: 'humans cannot be reduced to an essence, that we are who we are because of our interaction in community (something that does not come pre-packaged) and that while cognitive ability complicates our existence it does not destroy our humanity.'[5]

As a starting observation about our book, therefore, this *Companion* asks its readers to think hard about what humanity entails, and in doing so to be open to fresh accounts of what this might involve: no closed list of human rights is to be found in a schedule to this volume, worked on by teams of research assistants in pursuit of definitiveness. The 'human' in 'human rights law' entails openness, fluidity, an earthy resistance to the certain. Douzinas' Chapter 3 shows how damaged this idea of the human has been by its being reluctantly added in by those liberal writers who have always been far more interested in (and arguably dominated by) the separate notion of rights. All this takes us inevitably to politics, and it is a further goal of our *Companion* that it should engage with rather than affect to rise above the noise, the scheming and the abuses of power that mark out how we interact with each

---

[2] *Ibid.*, p. 60.   [3] *Ibid.*, p. 65.   [4] See p. 38.   [5] *Ibid.*, p. 54.

other on issues of general importance. To use a Dworkinian term, human rights should give us an 'attitude' within the world of politics – but (we would say) no automatic over-lordship sitting outside it. This is part of what the 'humanity' in 'human rights' necessarily entails. If Quinn and Arstein-Kerslake show us one vision of the human to have flowed from a successful reorientation on a global stage, Patrick Hanafin in Chapter 10 reveals another, on a smaller canvass (Italy) perhaps, but involving a framing of humanity that also has universal import – the legal recognition of the embryo with all that this involves, not only for those who would wish to bring pregnancies to an end ('the right to privacy' or more dramatically 'to control over one's own body') but also – the main thrust of the chapter – with laws on assisted reproduction.

Hanafin tells a classic human rights story about a '"manifesto law" which has for its real objective the upholding of a traditionalist idea of family formation'[6] and which in turn provokes a political resistance on the part of important sectors in Italian society which leads in turn 'to a very gradual rewriting of the Act through judicial intervention'.[7] For Hanafin it is in 'such acts of citizen resistance [that] we witness how rights can become something other than dead letters enunciated but never enacted'. Such 'engagements can be seen as enactments of what Étienne Balibar has called a "right to politics"'.[8] Interestingly, efforts to close down politics here have been unsuccessful, with the European Court of Human Rights (ECtHR) having refused a definitive intervention (*S H and others* v. *Austria*, extensively discussed by Hanafin). His concluding remark can be generalised into another of this *Companion*'s main ideas: 'The example of Italy provides both a warning to those who think reproductive autonomy should be taken for granted and also provides examples of how collective citizen action is essential in the establishment and maintenance of reproductive rights.' What the human is matters as much as what 'rights' and 'law' entail – and is similarly in our own hands.

Understanding rights

Can this idea of having a 'right' to something possibly mean anything at all? And – to mimic the exam question – if so, what can it be? A number of our chapters take on this key issue directly. For Douzinas in Chapter 3,

---

[6] See p. 193.   [7] *Ibid.*, pp. 193–194.   [8] *Ibid.*, p. 194.

philosophical attempts to create solid foundations fail in two related ways. They either identify human rights with rights *tout court*, inflating and cheapening their currency, or they turn rights into the main building block of an anaemic morality leaving no space for critique or dissent. The privileging of agency or personhood as the master principle of human rights not only detracts from the human (as we have seen) but serves also to promote civil and political rights at the expense of economic and social well-being. The result is a human rights law that is found wanting so far as important struggles for equality, dignity and social justice are concerned. Douzinas wants instead to celebrate the absence of solid foundations, over-riding rational justifications and conclusive definitions, the absence in other words of all that many deem essential. It is the gaps that flow from this that make the tensions between lawyers, philosophers and campaigners creative, serving to re-define the meaning and extending the scope of human rights, opening them to new groups, uses and practices.

In his search for 'Foundations beyond Law', Florian Hoffmann in Chapter 4 sees precisely these 'undetermined' others, outsiders, 'strangers, women, heathen, savages, barbarians' as being the lost groups who allow those inside the circle to claim universal equality and the identity of same-ness. For Hoffman as much as for Douzinas, the rights that make up human rights are an essentially contested concept. While human rights *law* needs a foundation or justification, the *moral* discourse of rights has no purchase on reality without the enforcement that only the law can give. Despite the religious and moral provenance of the idea of human rights, their positivi-sation has been necessitated by the need for moral foundations while also making possible the pensioning off of exactly this idea. To Hoffmann, human rights are 'no static concept, no jigsaw puzzle with neatly fitting pieces, but a dynamic and highly adaptive process'. Each discourse has its part to play, contributing 'a certain functionality to the process; law pro-vides facticity, moral discourse normativity and culture habit', and it is out of their 'continuous recombination' that emerges 'the infinite diversity of attitudes towards and uses of human rights' which we see in the world around us.[9]

So politics are unavoidable here too. Anna Grear in Chapter 1 tells us about the Universal Declaration of Human Rights (UDHR), that great mani-festo of humanity (an 'iconic matrix'[10]) that aspires to rise above politics

---

[9] See p. 96.   [10] See p. 19.

and law, 'framing the project' as her chapter title puts it. But of course this is impossible. Capturing well the intended spirit of this volume as a critical friend to its subject, Grear is distinctly non-hagiographic in her engagement with this and other 'human rights breakthroughs': to her 'international human rights law, in both theory and practice, is riven with contradictions, disputations, rival framings and oppositional accounts'.[11] But she defends her approach as essential to the right kind of progress, not the Whiggish predictability of the rise of the good but something altogether more compelling: 'Human rights emerge from [these] critical accounts as "ideas" (albeit powerful, world-shaping ideas) which are revealed as being semantically elusive "placeholder[s] in a global conversation that allows a constant deferral of the central defining moment in which rights themselves will be infused with substance"'.[12] Such an outcome is by no means necessarily bleak: 'Hope lies, perhaps, in the idea that international human rights law has not yet exhausted the critical energy of human rights as an endlessly recursive interaction concerning inclusions and exclusions in which every inclusion necessarily creates new, unforeseen exclusions, and in which every lived exclusion births new claims for inclusion.'[13] The 'perhaps' here is a warning against the kind of absolutism into which human rights warriors are too easily drawn, but it remains a positive note nonetheless.

The necessity of law

Law, morality, politics and culture contribute in their different ways to the understanding and practise of human rights, but they do not form a perfect pyramid with a moral *Grundnorm* at the bottom. Law at least has a kind of tangibility as a beacon of ethical truth in an otherwise choppy sea of moral and political uncertainty. This is what gives the third of our triad of foundations, human rights *law*, so much force in our field. The temptation is always to lure law into more truth than its structure can bear, an enticement that this *Companion* resists while always recognising the potency of the idea with which it is dealing. Grear introduces the subject with her

[11] *Ibid.*, p. 24.
[12] *Ibid.*, p. 25. citing A. Ely-Yamin, 'Empowering Visions: Towards a Dialectical Pedagogy of Human Rights' (1993) 15 (4) *Human Rights Quarterly* 640–85 at 663.
[13] *Ibid.*, p. 34.

mapping out of the 'carnivalistic'[14] excitement of the post-Second World War growth of international human rights law. Chaloka Beyani in Chapter 9 takes up this story, covering the global tale but also identifying the various ways in which this big idea has managed also to take regional shape, as localised versions of a shared perspective on the world. Beyani's concern is to describe these 'regional drivers of the universal'[15] and also at the same time to argue for their importance as more effective deliverers of content than are all those international instruments which are more concerned with aspiration than the kind of dull engagement with delivery that law generally (and rightly) thinks of as its especial strength.

Gerd Oberleitner's study of the enforceability of international human rights law in Chapter 13 takes this last point on directly, or to put it in his succinct way, 'Does enforcement matter?' To Oberleitner, understanding the complex challenge of effectively enforcing human rights necessitates borrowing from other ideas within the law family, principally those of enforcement, compliance control and dispute settlement. Understanding what is to be gained from 'enforcement' requires us first to know what our goal in calling for this is: what do we seek to achieve when we 'enforce' human rights? Is it the protection of individual victims from violence? Financial damages for victims of past violations? Or is it grander, long-term changes in domestic laws and practice perhaps; the eradication of extreme poverty; the creation of a just social order? To Oberleitner, 'the improvement of the human rights situation is not an isolated process but is closely linked to larger economic and democratic developments in a given state' and it is exactly for this reason that it is 'imperative that an expansion of enforcement mechanisms does not conceal human rights as the larger political and societal project that they are'.[16] In a way that echoes a further goal of ours in bringing these essayists together, we learn (once again, albeit in this fresh context) that things – even things seemingly so clear as human rights law – are not as simple as they appear, and – if it is true understanding (rather than the lure of false certainty) that we are after – nor should they be.

Conor Gearty and Chris Himsworth in Chapters 11 and 12 carry the human rights law theme into the national and sub-national spheres. Gearty's particular concern is with working out how the idea of a set of

---

[14] *Ibid.*, p. 21, citing U. Baxi, *The Future of Human Rights* (Oxford University Press 2006) 46.
[15] See p. 189.   [16] See p. 267.

human rights truths can function within a democratic system of government that by its very definition (happy dependence on electoral whim) is wedded to the contingent. To Gearty, the answer lies not in positioning courts as guarantors of rights in opposition to elected governments but rather in seeing these judicial guardians as democratically mandated invigilators on behalf of human rights, able to warn but not to override. He sees the UK Human Rights Act (HRA) as having marked a point at which serious work has finally begun in properly re-integrating human rights within the political sphere, the disastrous nature of earlier experiments with supposed apolitical judicial supremacism (e.g. the USA) having proved impossible even for advocates of 'law's empire' to have continued to ignore. Himsworth's chapter complements Gearty's in taking the human rights idea further into the lower reaches of the law, well past the universal and further even than the regional, and in Himsworth's case past the national, into local or devolved administration. The findings, drawn from a close study of the Scottish scene, are remarkable: 'Far from providing a stable environment in which human rights protection might take its place alongside other opportunities for diversity in subsidiarity, the conditions of constitutional autonomy defined by the combination of devolution under the Scotland Act with the much longer-standing separateness of the Scottish legal system have produced a fluidity and antagonism which have come to be most prominently characterised by the iconic lightning conductor of human rights adjudication.'[17] To the question, 'Is there no end to the politics of human rights, even in human rights law?', the answer appears to be 'Of course not; how could there be?' In their different ways all our contributors stand for the better grasping of this simple point, or (to put it another way) the truth behind the necessary uncertainty of all the other (human rights) truths.

Some paradoxes of human rights law

So much, then, for the triad of ideas upon which the *Companion* depends for its coherence. In putting things in the way that we have done thus far, we are led to a core paradox, that of a subject (human rights and flowing out of it human rights law) whose contingent political power depends on the

[17] See p. 247.

denial of this contingency in favour of a foundationalism that it knows neither can – nor should – exist. Paradox is never far away in any critically engaged discussion of human rights. A paradox, from *para-* 'contrary to' and *doxa* 'dominant view' is what is 'contrary to expectation or orthodoxy'. In logic, a paradoxical proposition is true and false at the same time or an impasse in an inquiry, often arising as a result of equally plausible yet inconsistent premises. *Paradoxology* on the other hand means 'marvellous speaking' or the 'narrating of marvels'. At its best human rights law is a marvellous discourse and practice that does not follow orthodoxy.

We have already embraced the widest manifestation of the paradox in our discussion of Beyani, Gearty and Himsworth: while the concept of right is in some sense universal, the content of human rights law differs from place to place. This should be no surprise. The 'human', like the 'natural' and the 'God-given', claims to transcend parochial and historical limitations but the law is inevitably temporally and spatially located. Law offers stability and predictability, legal problems have right answers and clear outcomes. Humanity on the other hand as aspiration or inspiration is open-ended and mobile, it looks back to history and tradition and forward to a time of justice and peace. In this sense, human rights law or a law that incorporates human rights has installed in its midst the demands of a justice which is as Grear has suggested always still to come. In this way human rights law incorporates the principle of its own self-transcendence. This sense of a dynamic, fast-moving and paradoxical constellation permeates our *Companion*.

For Upendra Baxi in Chapter 8 the paradox takes the form of discovery as opposed to invention and of universal normativity against the tradeoffs, negotiations and compromises that legal observance by governments necessarily involves. Did (the principles of) human rights exist before their declaration, in which case were they simply unconcealed or discovered? Or are they a creation or invention of modernity? The American and French revolutions 'declared' or re-stated natural rights because they had been 'concealed' or distorted during the ages. In this narrative, the law of human rights is an immanent part of history, despite being abused and concealed. If human rights or their principles existed prior to their legislation, as many liberal philosophers claim, then they are eternal, synchronic, universal. Accusations of partiality or Eurocentrism must therefore be wrong: the founding philosophical and legislative fathers were simply the mouthpieces of the world spirit. If, on the other hand, human rights were created *ab novo* and introduced into law and politics by their 'founding fathers', the historical context of their emergence conditions their nature and action. Discovery or invention, immanent or imposed, ahistorical or historically determined – this is the foundational dilemma at the heart of rights. If invented, rights are products of secular theology, commands of an all-powerful legislator. Their provenance colours their reception and opens them to accusations of partiality. If immanent or discovered, rights are the modern markers of reason or nature and their propagation and spread becomes part of humanity's mission. There is a pragmatic dimension to this that we need to add to Baxi's treatment of his large subject, for to critics of human rights juridicalisation he has this question: how else in the moment of 'concrete universality' may 'the morality of duty be translated into practices of arresting the abuse of public power?'[18]

The point about alternatives (or their absence) is a broad one, and it is in this context that paradox can emerge as signalling a route to progress. Joanne Scott writes in her classic study of women in the French revolution that the 'rights of man' had 'only paradoxes to offer' to women. Scott takes the phrase from a letter by Olympe de Gouges, the French feminist who published the *Declaration of the Rights of Woman and Citizen* in 1791, at the beginning of the 'human rights movement'. De Gouges argued that 'if women are entitled to go to the scaffold, they are entitled to go to the assembly'.[19] For Scott, the paradox of de Gouges' declaration went beyond the 'conflict between universal principle and exclusionary practice … to the need both to accept and refuse "sexual difference"'.[20] The French and American revolutionary declarations present the subject and beneficiary of rights as an abstract human being. The rights-holder is the 'man' of the rights of man, 'everyone' or 'anyone'. And yet, once we turn from the abstractions of law to real people with flesh and blood a different picture emerges. The 'everyone' of the universal human subject is shadowed by the various categories of exclusion and marginalisation. More optimistically, and in a way that, as we have seen Hoffmann in Chapter 4 echoes, the French philosopher Jacques Rancière has given a succinct description of the paradoxical way rights move from the inner circle of privileged beneficiaries to the excluded beyond.[21] Double standards get ironed out, old paradoxes get replaced by new contradictions,

---

[18] See p. 168.

[19] Jacques Rancière, 'Who is the Subject of the Rights of Man?', in I. Balfour and E. Cadava (eds.), 'And Justice for All: The Claims of Human Rights' (2004) 103 (2/3) *The South Atlantic Quarterly* 303.

[20] J. W. Scott, *Only Paradoxes to Offer* (Cambridge, MA: Harvard University Press, 1996) 3–4.

[21] Rancière, 'Who is the Subject' 19.

and the dynamic restlessness of human rights forces it into new battles with abuses of power, and so the process goes on.

We should not forget that this is a human rights *law Companion*, and that third of our triad of organising words takes us to a further paradox inherent in our study: the necessary interdisciplinarity of this most law-oriented of subjects. Human rights needs law in order to function while at the same time needing as well to transcend law in order to make itself interesting and fresh, to have in other words something of value to say. Many chapters in this volume explicitly draw on the strengths offered by other fields while remaining true to their disciplinary focus. Abdullahi An-Na'im directly confronts the question in Chapter 5, which commences our section devoted to the inter-connectedness of human rights. To An-Na'im, whose concern here is with the study of human rights, the paradox of localism (already mentioned) is compounded by the residual colonialism of so much of this local content and by the inevitable dependence on state power to make rights real. The exposure of 'inherent ambiguities and tensions in the concept [of human rights] that need clarification and mediation' is something that we should not so much fear as embrace as evidence that we are on the right path to progress. In asking 'how can interdisciplinarity escape the limitations of disciplinarity by maintaining its flexibility and indeterminacy, while being focused and effective in fulfilling its mandate' and, further, in questioning how 'interdisciplinarity [is] different from multidisciplinarity, and how [can we] achieve its value-added in practice',[22] An-Na'im is demonstrating that enquiry is a core part of discovery, that arrival must be preceded by travel and destinations need to be sought before they can be found. If there is a manifesto for this *Companion*, then, it might be the idea with which An-Na'im starts his exploration of the power of interdisciplinarity (albeit in a more specific context) that of 'imagining the unimaginable and retrieving the irretrievable'.

Nightmares and dreams

We have already heeded Baxi's warning to the sceptics to be on guard against the question 'so what would you do?' Nowhere is the need for our subject clearer and the scepticism of the well-meaning quieter than in

---

[22] See p. 111.

relation to the human rights work being done in the fields of torture, anti-terrorism and war crimes. Here are three worlds of gloomy evil in which human rights stands not so much for what can be achieved but rather for the human in the face of terrible abuse, the chance of being woken from a nightmare. Manfred Nowak's comment at the start of his Chapter 16 on the first of these practices is shocking: 'having carried out the mandate of UN Special Rapporteur on Torture for six years and having conducted fact-finding missions to eighteen countries in all world regions as well as three joint studies with other special procedures, I have come to the conclusion that *torture is practised in more than 90 per cent of all countries and constitutes a widespread practice in more than 50 per cent of all countries*'.[23] Nowak is convinced of the utility of a human rights approach: '[t]he right protected by the prohibition of torture, cruel, inhuman or degrading treatment or punishment under international human rights law is the *right to personal integrity and human dignity*, which is also closely related to the prohibition of slavery.'[24] And as to why things have gone so terribly wrong, why there is 'this tremendous implementation gap between the noble aspiration to protect human dignity and the sobering reality on the ground',[25] by way of explanation Nowak points to 'retributive philosophies of criminal justice, a lack of empathy for those behind bars (detention is in most countries a "privilege" of the poor, the marginalised and the oppressed), corruption in the criminal justice system (police, prosecutors, judges and prison officials), and a lack of access of the poor to justice'.[26] As with Baxi and his call to control the abuse of power, good human rights scholarship is not afraid of structural causes for the abuses that it details – in Nowak's case the disparity in wealth that is silent in so many standard accounts of human rights but remains a pervasive (albeit neglected) explanation for much that human rights scholars and activists alike deplore.

Martin Scheinin's Chapter 15 on 'Resisting panic' is energetically upbeat about the impact of human rights law in shaping global and regional responses to the notorious Al Qaeda attacks of 11 September 2001. (And it is worth noting that Gearty in Chapter 11 makes the same point in passing about the UK HRA.) There is a constant tension in human rights between the terrible nature of the stories told and the spirited and energetic way in which human rights advocates (scholars and activists alike) devotedly believe that

---

[23] See p. 307. (Emphasis in original.)   [24] *Ibid.*, p. 325. (Emphasis in original.)
[25] *Ibid.*, p. 326.   [26] *Ibid.*

things can be different and better. Both a scholar and a UN 'player' (in his six-year role as Special Rapporteur on counter-terrorism and human rights), Scheinin brings to his study a degree of optimism about human rights, which he describes as the '*main* form of resistance'[27] to the governmental (and UN) excesses that followed the terrible events of 11 September. His ten reasons for optimism, the 'positive trends'[28] that he outlines, are a reminder that in human rights struggles there are victories as well as defeats, highs as well as lows, and that defensive manoeuvres to avoid extreme abuse can sometimes succeed.

Margot E. Salomon's Chapter 14 on economic injustice in the world and the so far ineffectual role of human rights in countering it may be read as a necessary antidote to Scheinin by those who find misery more to their taste. Certainly of all the chapters in the book, Salomon's message is bleakest: 'An audit of development and international law over fifty years points to stark conclusions: that international law in this area serves certain interests and not others and that the nature and scale of poverty and under-development globally are in large part a result of the choices of those states at the top.'[29] But this chapter's offering of 'reasons to be cynical'[30] – while perhaps justified in Salomon's field – is not a feature of the *Companion* as a whole. And even Salomon is not an incorrigible pessimist: 'The juridical re-imagining of the role and parameters of a contemporary international law of human rights that the right to development asserts in the interest of global justice are not to be dismissed lightly. However ... it seems that it will only ever be part of an unfinishable story.'[31] Even here with our subject at its lowest point we are back with the dynamic quality that makes human rights law so compelling.

Turning now to war crimes, Gerry Simpson in Chapter 6 tracks the common origins of international criminal and international human rights law, narrating a story of the growth of the former field through a reading of the origins of humanity in 'enemies of mankind' (pirates, tyrants and aggressors) and 'crimes against humanity' (war criminals) – this time the paradox of humans cast outside humanity in the defence of universal humanity. Simpson is concerned not to allow us to consign such readings to ancient history; the successes of the present moment have given us 'a sort of punitive humanitarianism that conjoins war, humanity and punishment'[32] and which warns us as well against too complacent a disjunction between human rights

---

[27] See p. 304. (Emphasis in original.)   [28] *Ibid.*, p. 295.   [29] See p. 291.   [30] *Ibid.*
[31] *Ibid.*   [32] See p. 131.

and violence. Simpson's chapter provokes this thought: have things changed for human rights in the last decade with the increasing attacks on the principle of sovereignty, a breaking down of An-Na'im's concern about state power? The list is long. Criminal trials of political and military leaders for war crimes and crimes against humanity, economic and diplomatic sanctions on states for violations of human rights, human rights conditionalities on aid and trade agreements, finally, the use of force in humanitarian wars (the subject of Simon Chesterman's Chapter 7) have all eaten away at national sovereignty, the modernist cornerstone of international law. The law of human rights has undertaken enthusiastically the task of saving people from their evil governments. Simpson writes at the time of the opening of the last trial of four senior officers of the Pol Pot regime in Cambodia. He details the ways in which judicial proceedings have been used in order to punish gross human rights violations.

The hybrid international and national Cambodian court is part of the difficult emergence of international criminal justice that culminated with the creation of the International Criminal Court (ICC). Yet the Cambodian case underlines the founding contradiction at the heart of the international order. We need at this juncture to recall Oberleitner's challenging Chapter 13 about the (lack of) enforcement of international human rights law. Chesterman reminds us that when Vietnam intervened in Cambodia to free the long-suffering victims of the killing fields from the Khmer Rouge genocidal regime, the USA and its Western allies, still reeling from the defeat in the hands of the Vietnamese, furiously denounced the action as a violation of Cambodia's sovereignty. Despite the quick Vietnamese victory, which freed the Cambodian people from the Pol Pot regime, the West went on recognising the Khmer Rouge as the legitimate government of the country for many years. The legality and usefulness of humanitarian wars is limited, Chesterman concludes. Despite the development of the doctrine of a 'responsibility to protect' (R2P) vulnerable populations, the principle of non-intervention survives and humanitarian interventions remain controversial.

The compendiousness of human rights law

What then of the 'gain or profit through saving' of human rights law? Does it justify itself and therefore (in its primary sense as an abridgement) this

Companion? And what too of the Baxi question as to what would you do? Samuel Moyn's examination in Chapter 17 of the use of international law for the protection of human rights is especially challenging in this regard. He concludes that the record is mixed, more so than the vibrant energy and optimism of our contributors – emblems now of the wider movement – would suggest. To Moyn, wearing perhaps the clothes of an old-fashioned advocate of change who refuses to accept that since his ideas are unrealisable human rights is the only option, the promoters of international action are 'pessimist reformers'. They are horrified with the state of the world but they don't believe that radical correction is possible. If evil rules and there is no alternative, the marginal improvements of international law are the most we can hope for. This postmodern melancholia however undermines belief and action for radical change. The international law of human rights sees its function as offering redemption from evil. But this modesty forecloses the radical potential of human rights to create a world of social justice and peace. In other words for all its wonders human rights stop us talking about bigger questions, those of power, justice and poverty.

If this is true generally, it is a trap into which this *Companion* has been determined not to fall. Of course there are limitations to human rights, not only those identified by Moyn but by many of our other contributors as well. But with Moyn we grab these problems and use them as our raw material for future success, sometimes seeking to reshape human rights, and sometimes (when the time is right?) moving beyond the language altogether. But right now what better term do the custodians of the human spirit have to hand? It might be said again that human rights have only paradoxes to offer. But recalling a central theme both of this Introduction and of our *Companion* as a whole, it is precisely in paradox that the vitality and vibrancy of our field is revealed. Like life, which is full of contradictions, it is paradoxes, dilemmas and aporias that move human rights practice on. When lawyers, campaigners and dissidents mobilise these conflicts and tensions – between international and national law; between the claims to universality and the exclusions of particularity; between law and justice – then we can see the potential of the future and the dues of humanity shining like a strong sun through the hackneyed house of law.

Part I

All kinds of everyone

'Framing the project' of international human rights law: reflections on the dysfunctional 'family' of the Universal Declaration

Anna Grear

'Frames are principles of selection, emphasis and presentation composed of little tacit theories about what exists, what happens, and what matters.'[1]

'To frame is to select some aspects of a perceived reality and make them more salient in a communicating text.'[2]

The task of 'framing the project' of international human rights law is daunting to say the least. First, there is the sheer enormity and complexity of the international human rights law 'project': adequately mapping the subject and its key related issues is impossible in a whole book, let alone a short chapter.[3] Secondly, it is daunting because of the sense of epistemic responsibility involved. Every framing inevitably involves selection – if not pre-selection – through the conscious (and/or unconscious) placing of focus upon features or factors considered to be significant and/or valuable.[4] As Gitlin puts it, framing is a way of choosing, underlining and presenting 'what exists, what happens and what matters'. In this sense, the founding document (or as Entman might put it, the inaugural 'communicating text') of international human rights law (the Universal Declaration of Human Rights, UDHR)[5] functions as a particularly potent form of framing, for it selects aspects of perceived reality, making them not just salient but symbolically central to the entire philosophical, moral, juridical order designated by the term 'international human rights law'.

Framings, it should be noted, are inescapable – and are always an exercise of epistemic closure or limitation in the sense that frames tend to

---

[1] T. Gitlin, *The Whole World Is Watching: Mass Media in the Making and Unmaking of the New Left* (Berkeley, CA and London: University of California Press 1980) 6.

[2] R. M. Entman, 'Framing: Toward Clarification of a Fractured Paradigm' (1993) 43 (4) *Journal of Communication* 51–8 at 52.

[3] Joseph and McBeth point out in their editorial introduction to the *Research Handbook on International Human Rights Law* (Cheltenham: Edward Elgar 2010), for example, that it is 'simply impossible to capture' all the relevant issues 'in a single book' (at xiii).

[4] Not always for reasons that should count as valuable.

[5] GA Res. 217(111) of 10 December 1948, UN Doc. A/810 at 71 (1948).

draw attention to selected aspects of a perceived 'something' at the expense of a host of other candidates for attention producing, in the process, a set of muted or even invisible 'others' – a whole range of unfocused-upon factors, features or (for the primary purpose of the discussion here) subjectivities.

Framing choices in international human rights law are particularly influential. International human rights law can be understood as deploying a power verging on the 'anthropogenetic' – that is to say, the power precisely to 'name' (and thus discursively to 'create') the 'human' itself. For some readers, this claim may seem counter-intuitive. After all, the international human rights law edifice is usually understood to rest upon the foundation of a notion of the pre-existing 'natural' human being. While, however, there is a certain complex truth in the idea that the UDHR and its normative progeny deploy the 'human being' as a foundational category, it is also the case, as we shall see in the course of the reflections that follow, that the 'human' of international human rights law is, in fact, a highly complex construction taking the form of a 'universal' human subject which has been observed, as we shall see, to (re)produce a range of 'others' as marginalised subjects. Thus, much as a family photograph might reveal the unconscious favouritisms or oversights of the parent holding the camera, the framing of international human rights law's universal subject suggests a degree of dysfunction or fracture attending the 'human family' evoked by the aspirational text of the UDHR.

This argument, however, will have to wait awhile. In 'framing the project' of international human rights law for the purposes of a *Companion* we must surely first introduce at least a rudimentary outline of the project drawn from mainstream, traditional accounts and so provide an account of the project's broad textual self-enunciation and institutional structure.

Framing the project: traditional accounts

Traditional accounts of the international human rights law project converge to locate it in a rich amalgam of natural law, positive law and an unprecedented international 'consensus' 'on substantive norms with high moral voltage'[6] at the end of the Second World War. It is generally agreed that the

---

[6] B. De Sousa Santos, *Towards a New Legal Common Sense: Law, Globalization and Emancipation* (London: Butterworths 2000) 260.

1945 UN Charter[7] effectively brought human rights into the sphere of international law – in the process achieving the simultaneous internationalisation of human rights and the birth of the 'human individual' as a subject, rather than an object, of international law.[8] This development is generally attributed with authoritatively establishing the idea, in normative terms at least, that ensuring respect for human rights should no longer be entrusted solely to the power of the nation state. Ever since the relatively sparse first enunciation in the UN Charter of an international order of human rights, the UN has been widely seen as being instrumental in an apparently ceaseless and expanding process of international human rights standard-setting through an almost kaleidoscopic proliferation of instruments and treaties.

Of all these instruments and treaties, however, one stands out as the iconic matrix from which all international human rights standards take their symbolic and juridical life: the UDHR. The UDHR is widely understood to be the foundation of international human rights law, possessing immense symbolic and rhetorical power and exerting a virtually ineluctable normative traction. It is of note that no state has ever denounced the UDHR, from the moment of its adoption (in 1948) right up until the present day. The UDHR was affirmed, in fact, along with the universality and indivisibility of human rights, by the Vienna Declaration and Programme of Action[9] in 1993, and it remains the normative fulcrum for the international human rights law project, a status consistent, arguably, with its own inaugural self-enunciation as a 'common standard of achievement for all peoples and all nations'.[10] Since its formulation, the influence of the UDHR has been impressive. It has been praised for giving life to an entire generation of post-colonial states, for providing the rights-centred template for a host of new constitutional documents, and as though this were not enough, it is also credited with being the normative source of over 200 international human rights instruments.[11] The centrality of the UDHR as the frame within which the international human rights project unfolds, therefore, is

---

[7] Charter of the UN, 1 UNTS XVI, 24 October 1945.

[8] See T. Buergenthal, 'The Normative and Institutional Evolution of International Human Rights' (1997) 19 (4) *Human Rights Quarterly* 703–23.

[9] UN Doc. A/CONF.157/23 (1993) of 25 June 1993, endorsed by GA Res. 48/121 of 14 February 1994, [2].

[10] UDHR, Preamble.

[11] G. Robertson, *Crimes Against Humanity: The Struggle for Global Justice* (London: The New Press 2006) 35.

indisputable, its practical influence undeniable: As Donnelly puts it, '[f]or the purposes of international action, "human rights" means roughly "what is in the Universal Declaration of Human Rights"'.[12]

Traditional accounts of international human rights law also emphasise a series of phases or stages of standard-setting[13] that reflect (and for the purposes of this discussion at least) pre-figure critiques of the UDHR. The initial vigour of the standard-setting activities reflected by the drafting of the UDHR cooled noticeably in the light of Cold War politics, producing a marked lull in the production of human rights documents, unbroken until the 1965 adoption of the International Convention on the Elimination of all Forms of Racial Discrimination (CERD),[14] a development which quite naturally reflected the concerns of the newly decolonised nations which were then swelling the ranks of UN membership and beginning to influence the preoccupations of the international community.[15]

In 1966, there was a fresh phase of general or universal standard-setting through which the rights of the UDHR found further enunciation in two international legal documents, in narrow chronological order, the International Covenant on Economic, Social and Cultural Rights (ICESCR)[16] and the International Covenant on Civil and Political Rights (ICCPR).[17] The dichotomous separation between these two 'categories' of rights is often traditionally explained as reflecting a Cold War ideological rift, but for many the separation also reflects perceived differences between the categories of rights in terms of their relative justiciability, putative operation as primarily 'negative' or 'positive' rights and relative enforceability.[18] Together, the UDHR, the ICESCR and the CCPR are referred to as the 'International Bill of Rights', and are supplemented, further expressed (or implicitly criticised – depending on one's chosen frame) by further standard-setting exercises. All of this has resulted in a proliferation of

---

[12] J. Donnelly, *Universal Human Rights in Theory and Practice* (Ithaca, NY: Cornell University Press, 2003) 22.

[13] See Buergenthal, 'The Normative and Institutional Evolution' n. 8 above.

[14] Opened for signature 7 March 1966, 660 UNTS 195 (entered into force 4 January 1969).

[15] Joseph and McBeth, editorial introduction.

[16] Opened for signature 16 December 1966, 993 UNTS 3 (entered into force 3 January 1976).

[17] Opened for signature 16 December 1966, 999 UNTS 171 (entered into force 23 March 1976).

[18] B. Turner, 'Human Vulnerabilities: On Individual and Social Rights', http://web.gs.emory.edu/vulnerability/zpdfs/turnerpub.pdf (date of last access 13 July 2011).

international human rights treaties, focusing upon either specific rights (such as the UN Convention against Torture and Other Cruel, Inhuman or Degrading Treatment or Punishment, UNCAT[19]) or (perhaps more critically for present purposes) on *specific rights-holders* (such as the Convention on the Elimination of all Forms of Discrimination against Women, CEDAW[20]).

This almost 'carnivalistic'[21] expansion in the number of international UN human rights treaties has been accompanied, at different times and rates, by the incremental spread and maturation of a set of regional international human rights regimes: the European Convention of Human Rights and Fundamental Freedoms (ECHR[22]) (adopted in 1950, which embraces only civil and political rights); the American Convention on Human Rights (ACHR[23]) (which excluded economic and social rights but later gave them normative space in the form of a separate protocol); The African Charter on Human and People's Rights (Banjul Charter[24]) (adopted by the Organisation of African Unity, OAU, in 1981 – embracing all categories of right in one culturally distinctive document). There is also a neonate and culturally distinctive Arab and Muslim regional system (expressed in the Arab Charter on Human Rights,[25] adopted by the Council of the League of Arab States in 1994 and which entered into force in 2008).[26] No matter to what degree such human rights regimes operate at differing stages of juridical and institutional maturity and reflect radically differing regional and cultural commitments and histories, it is notable that they all, without exception, explicitly affirm their normative continuity with the iconic UDHR.

---

[19] Opened for signature 10 December 1984, 1465 UNTC 85 (entered into force 26 June 1987).

[20] Opened for signature 18 December 1979, 1249 UNTS 13 (entered into force 3 September 1981).

[21] U. Baxi, *The Future of Human Rights* (Oxford University Press 2006) 46.

[22] Convention for the Protection of Human Rights and Fundamental Freedoms, 213 UNTS 222 (entered into force 3 September 1953), as amended by Protocols Nos. 3, 5, 8 and 11 (entered into force on 21 September 1970, 20 December 1971, 1 January 1990 and 1 November 1998, respectively).

[23] American Convention on Human Rights, OAS Treaty Series No. 36, 1144 UNTS 123 (entered into force 18 July 1978).

[24] African Charter on Human and Peoples' Rights (adopted 27 June 1981, entered into force 21 October 1986) (1982) 21 ILM 58 (African Charter).

[25] League of Arab States, Arab Charter on Human Rights, 22 May 2004, reprinted in (2005) 12 *International Human Rights Reports* 893 (entered into force 15 March 2008).

[26] See M. Amin Al-Midani and M. Cabanettes (trans.) and S. M. Akram, 'The Arab Charter on Human Rights 2004' (2006) 24 (2) *Boston University International Law Journal* 147–64.

Framing the project: critical accounts

The UDHR and the international human rights system, as has already been implied, is also subject to a range of critiques, some of which are now well embedded within mainstream human rights scholarship and debate. The most famous of these reflects cultural relativist arguments deconstructing the 'universalism' of human rights, arguments which emerge from a range of alternative framing positions, including, most notably, 'Asian values', Islam and postmodernism.[27] Within such discursive accounts, there is a closely related and oft-repeated accusation that the UDHR is an instrument of 'Western cultural imperialism', a mere Trojan horse for the imposition of 'Western' commitments upon 'non-Western' cultures. This critique is intimately related to the idea that the UDHR is Eurocentric in both origin and formulation.[28]

Such critiques, in turn, are addressed by defences of international human rights universalism resting on a variety of claims. It is argued, for example, that the UDHR Drafting Committee was more internationally diverse than is often assumed,[29] and that the values in the UDHR reflect at least a thin convergence or 'justificatory minimalism'[30] centred upon on values viewed as being common to or at least conceptually derivable from many, if not most, great human philosophical and religious traditions.[31] Donnelly argues, for example, that 'Christians, Muslims, Confucians, and Buddhists;

---

[27] See, for examples of discussions canvassing relevant and related arguments, K. Engle, 'Culture and Human Rights: The Asian Values Debate in Context' (2000) 32 (2) *Journal of International Law and Politics* 291–333; H. Samuels, 'Hong Kong on Women, Asian Values and the Law' (1999) 21 (3) *Human Rights Quarterly* 707–34; A. J. Langlois, *The Politics of Justice and Human Rights: South East Asia and Universalist Theory* (Cambridge University Press 2001); K. Dalacoura, *Islam, Liberalism and Human Rights*, 3rd edn (London: I. B. Tauris 2007); M. Ignatieff, 'The Attack on Human Rights' (2001) 80 *Foreign Affairs* 102–16; Z. Arslan, 'Taking Rights Less Seriously: Postmodernism and Human Rights' (1999) 5 *Res Publica* 195–215.

[28] For example, see M. Matua, 'Savages, Victims and Saviours: The Metaphor of Human Rights' (2001) 42 (1) *Harvard International Law Journal* 201–46.

[29] J. Morsink, *The Universal Declaration of Human Rights: Origins, Drafting and Intent* (University of Pennsylvania Press 2002) 21.

[30] J. Cohen, 'Minimalism About Human Rights: The Most We Can Hope For?' (2004) 12 (2) *The Journal of Political Philosophy* 190–213 at 213.

[31] A range of perspectives related to this can be found in H. Kung and J. Moltmann, *The Ethics of World Religions and Human Rights* (London and Philadelphia, PA: SCM Press, 1990). See also J. Donnelly, '*Human Dignity and Human Rights*' (2009), Swiss Initiative to Commemorate the 60th Anniversary of the Universal Declaration of Human Rights: *Protecting Dignity: An*

Kantians, Utilitarians, Pragmatists, and neo-Aristotelians; liberals, conservatives, traditionalists, and radicals, and many other groups as well, come to human rights from their own particular path'.[32] Moreover, the *de facto* universality implied by the almost global international recognition of the UDHR is also cited as evidence of its contemporary legitimacy as a common standard of achievement for all peoples. It is pointed out, furthermore, that the Vienna Declaration and Programme of Action affirms universalism, construing it as a value capable of respecting cultural variation and specificity while at the same time retaining for it an important primacy in order to defend against culturally derived violations of the minimum standards set forth by international human rights norms.[33] In this sense, as Donnelly has argued, we can understand international human rights norms to be 'relatively universal'.[34]

There exist, of course, a range of other critiques – some of which are related to those already noted. The criticism, for example, that civil and political rights are incipiently favoured over economic and social rights within the institutional mechanisms of international human rights law,[35] a fact taken to reflect a fundamental ideological privileging of liberal constructs of rights descended from the commitments of the 'West', remains painfully apt, particularly in the contemporary globalised context.[36] It has been argued, relatedly, that the entire international human rights law project stands discursively colonised by the project of neoliberal capitalism and the hegemonic power of transnational corporations (TNCs) within the international legal order.[37] Such arguments can be linked to earlier

Agenda for Human Right, www.udhr60.ch/report/donnelly-HumanDignity_0609.pdf (date of last access 15 June 2011). See also J. Donnelly, 'Human Rights and Human Dignity: An Analytic Critique of Non-Western Conceptions of Human Rights' (1982) 76 (2) *The American Political Science Review* 303–16.

[32] Donnelly, 'Human Dignity and Human Rights' 7.

[33] See Part 1, para. 1 of the Vienna Declaration.

[34] J. Donnelly, 'Cultural Relativism and Universal Human Rights' (1984) 6 (4) *Human Rights Quarterly* 400–19 at 419. But see also the critique of this offered by M. Goodhart, 'Neither Relative Nor Universal: A Response to Donnelly' (2008) 30 (1) *Human Rights Quarterly* 183–93.

[35] See, for an introduction to the depth of the challenge, D. Beetham, 'What Future for Economic and Social Rights?' (1995) 43 (1) *Political Studies* 41–60.

[36] See the excoriating critique of the imperatives of neoliberal globalisation and their deleterious effect upon the realisation of socio-economic rights offered by Baxi, *The Future of Human Rights*.

[37] See Baxi, *The Future of Human Rights*; S. Gill, 'Globalisation, Market Civilization and Disciplinary Neoliberalism' (1995) 24 *Millennium Journal of International Studies* 399–423; A. Grear, *Redirecting Human Rights: Facing the Challenge of Corporate Legal Humanity* (Basingstoke: Palgrave Macmillan 2010).

imagination forwards, but is ever-deferred, always 'not yet'. Meanwhile, their meaning, as critical accounts stress, remains contestable, semantically unsettled, radically porous, open to co-option, colonisation and, importantly, never, ever above the interplay of power relations.

One contingent re-framing

We have already noted the centrality of the iconic UDHR to the entire edifice of human rights law and mentioned its production of a universal human rights bearer. As I have earlier suggested, a central paradox of international human rights law rests on the construction of this universal 'human subject'. Despite the fact that the UDHR clearly enshrines its rights as belonging to all members of the 'human family', to 'everyone', it is far from clear that all human beings as concrete beings find themselves fully embraced or represented by the universal human rights subject. In fact, there is arguably a dysfunction or fracture at the heart of the 'human family' of the UDHR – and it is this observation that forms the inspiration for this particular framing of the international human rights law project.

It is clear on various accounts, including its own, that the UDHR attempts to respond to the need to protect the human being understood *qua* human being. If we combine the emphasis of the UDHR preamble with the language of Article 2, this inclusive aspiration becomes clear: the invocation of terms such as 'everyone' and 'the human family' are supported by the *explicit de-legitimation* of forms of discrimination based upon any putative distinctions or sub-divisions between human beings:

Everyone is entitled to all the rights and freedoms set forth in this Declaration, *without distinction of any kind*, such as race, colour, sex, language, religion, political or other opinion, national or social origin, property, birth *or other status*. Furthermore, no distinction shall be made on the basis of the political, jurisdictional or international status of the country or territory to which a person belongs, whether it be independent, trust, non-self-governing or under any other limitation of sovereignty [emphases added].

It is clear from this that no putative basis for distinction, even those centred upon the nation state itself, should form a legitimate basis for the denial of human rights. This emphasis is unsurprising in so far as certain scholarship has revealed the central concern driving the drafters of the Declaration to be an explicit reaction to the bio-centric, racist and species-segmenting abuse of state power by the Nazi state[43] (which was itself conceived of as a species-specific entity: as an 'Aryan' organic body of which Hitler was the head).[44] This argument, emerging from Morsink's careful analysis of the records of the deliberations of the Drafting Committees,[45] is lent further plausibility by the preamble's immediate reference to the 'barbarous acts that have outraged the conscience of mankind'. Although, inevitably, this view is contested, it seems relatively clear that the affirmation of the fundamental commonality of the human race was a conscious aim of the drafters and that the UDHR explicitly emphasises the unacceptability of selective segmentations and discriminatory practices and violations, whether those were primarily driven by awareness of Nazi laws and practices or were also responding to wider socio-historical patterns and trajectories.

The UDHR aspiration for human familial inclusion and the explicit rejection of discrimination based on sub-divisions in the human family is accompanied, it will be argued here, by an enduring paradox consisting in the directly contradictory (re-)production, within international human rights law, of an entire range of outsider or marginalised subjectivities. The puzzle of this contradictory state of affairs seems to hinge on a fundamental contradiction inherent in the figuration of the abstract form of human nature deployed as the 'universal' subject of rights.

Linking the abstract human being of the UDHR with the abstract man of the earlier French Declaration, Douzinas argues that '[o]nce the slightest empirical or historical material is introduced into abstract human nature, once we move from the declarations onto the concrete embodied person, with gender, race, class and age, human nature with its equality and dignity retreats rapidly'.[46] We should pause to note, moreover, the *patterned nature of the specificities* in relation to which equality and dignity retreat. Such *patterned retreat* in the face of embodied empirical and historical particularity is especially troubling for the international human rights law project for, as Otto suggests, such critique '*goes to the heart* of the post-World War

---

[43] J. Morsink, 'World War Two and the Declaration' (1993) 15 *Human Rights Quarterly* 357–405 at 357.

[44] See Morsink on 'Hitler's Organic State and Articles 1 and 2' (1993 15 *Human Rights Quarterly* 359–66); A. Hitler, *Mein Kampf* (R. Manheim, trans.) (Boston, MA: Houghton Mifflin 1971) 150.

[45] Morsink, 'World War Two' 357.   [46] Douzinas, *The End of Human Rights* 96.

II discourse of universal human rights which, *as its most fundamental premise*, purports to apply *equally, without distinction*, to *"everyone"* [(Article 2 UDHR)]. [Despite this t]he allegedly universal subject of human rights law ... reproduces hierarchies, including those of [gender], race, culture, nation, socio-economic status and sexuality.'[47]

It seems that the universal human rights subject installed at the heart of the international human rights law project appears to (re-)produce the very hierarchies and discriminatory patterns that the UDHR itself explicitly rejects. This presents, clearly, something of a conundrum, and despite the proliferation (as we have already seen) of a range of 'identity'-inclusive documents, such as CEDAW, patterns of marginalisation remain obdurately real and installed within international human rights law. The evidence for the reality and impact of these marginalised subjectivities emerges from various critical positions and sources, but it is worth nothing that even at the origins of the UDHR, marginalisation was an historically real problem. For example, women, in particular, were marginalised (almost explicitly) in the very drafting process: the Commission on the Status of Women (CSW) had to fight hard just to achieve a shift away from the language of the rights of 'all *men*' towards the rights of 'all human beings'. This limited concession, moreover, entailed the explicit rejection of the explicitly sexuate and inclusive formulation sought by the CSW – that of 'all people, men and women'.[48] It is of note that the masculine pronoun remains stubbornly dominant throughout the text of the UDHR, which is also completely silent on the issues of gendered violence and reproductive rights. Critics have noted, moreover, that women's equal rights are semantically tied to the context of the family (Article 16 UDHR) and that there is a problematic further muting of women's rights claims through the traditional liberal public/private divide (which famously reserves the public domain for men while relegating women to the 'private' domestic sphere) – itself a profound barrier to genuine female rights enjoyment – and uncritically installed at the heart of the international human rights law project.[49]

---

[47] D. Otto, 'Disconcerting "Masculinities": Reinventing the Gendered Subject(s) of International Human Rights Law', in D. Buss and A. Manji (eds.), *International Law: Modern Feminist Approaches* (Oxford: Hart 2005) 105–29 at 105–6. (Emphasis added.)

[48] See J. Morsink, 'Women's Rights in the Universal Declaration' (1991) 13 *Human Rights Quarterly* 229–56.

[49] For more, see F. Beveridge and S. Mullally, 'International Human Rights and Body Politics', in J. Bridgeman and S. Millns (eds.), *Law and Body Politics: Regulating the Female Body* (Aldershot: Dartmouth 1995) 240–72.

In a sense, the *very need* for CEDAW and other treaties directed at particular groups or 'identities' of rights-claimant reflects the existence of marginalised and hierarchically constructed subjectivities within international human rights law. It is precisely the felt/lived sense of exclusion, hierarchical marginalisation or invisibility that has driven women and a range of other marginalised 'others' to seek the specific enumeration of their rights. This dynamic strongly suggests the (re)production within international human rights law of what we can with a high degree of accuracy label as '*non-universal* human subjectivities' (those deemed inherently *incapable* of representing all humanity).

The evidence suggests, though, that the existing universal, far from being universal in reality, despite its claim to be inclusively representative, is a radically 'non-universal universal', an abstract construct enacting familiar exclusions historically linked to certain much-criticised conceptual and ideological features of Western thought.[50] In short, the philosophical foundations of the universal human subject enact a certain kind of 'tilt'. This point is not without its irony. It has been noted by Morsink that the urgent ethical humanitarian sensibility driving the UDHR drafters was such that 'they did not need a philosophical argument in addition to the experience of the Holocaust'[51] in order to justify the UDHR. Yet, despite their ethical humanitarian energy, their moral outrage and high degree of empathy with victims of human violation, the drafters of the UDHR, in attempting to inaugurate a new age of international, ethical and juridical concern predicated upon the important concept of inclusive universality, turned (naturally enough perhaps) to the pre-existing formula of abstract universalism enshrined within Western philosophy, and in particular, to the iconic French Declaration of the Rights of Man and the Citizen.

The universal subject or 'man' of the French Declaration has, of course, its own philosophical foundations and antecedents. Its formulation, for example, is radically continuous with the philosophical, political and rights-based discursivity of John Locke, and with earlier philosophical assumptions concerning the primacy of 'man's nature' as being quintessentially 'rational'. The rational man of the French Declaration, as Douzinas' argument above implies,[52] is the direct progenitor of the universal 'human

---

[50] See Grear, *Redirecting Human Rights* Chapters 3, 4 and 5.
[51] Morsink, 'World War Two' 358.
[52] Douzinas, *The End of Human Rights* 46 and related text.

being' of the UDHR. In fact, there are extensive continuities between the UHDR and the earlier Declaration. Marks has argued that the proclamation of rights in the French Declaration had a 'major impact on the form and content of the UDHR proclaimed 160 years later, and subsequently, on the current codex of internationally recognized human rights'.[53] The assertion that all 'men are born and remain free and equal in rights' (Article 1 of the French Declaration) becomes, in Article 1 UDHR, the statement that all 'human beings are born free and equal in dignity and rights' – an almost identical formulation, as Hunt suggests, but for the exchange of 'human beings' for 'men'.[54] The drafters of the UDHR, reached out, then, for the pre-existing symbols of a rich human rights imaginary at the heart of which stood an abstract universal.

The abstract universal 'man'/'human being' is conceived of as being essentially 'neutral' – as representative of all humanity. Closer inspection, however, reveals this 'neuter' universal to be a cipher that is never neutral, never empty, because its essential rationality comes laden with philosophical and ideological provenance – most especially a long-standing co-imbrication of rationality and maleness. Inevitably, then, this abstract universal is gendered. (We have already noted the related struggle of the CSW to change the language from 'men' to that of 'human beings' in the UDHR drafting process.) If we pause to reflect once more on the fact that, as Douzinas points out, 'universal' dignity and equality rapidly retreat once the abstract human subject takes on materiality or concrete form, we can begin to grasp the essence and implications of the problem. The universal seems to be constructed as neutral, yet the retreat of dignity and equality is precisely along the well-worn conduits of discriminatory species segmentation so familiar in our long human history of inequalities, diminutions, degradations, marginalisations, oppressions and violences.

The marginalised subjectivities revealed by such realities suggest, just as a photographic negative might, the precise contours of the construct covertly privileged by the neuter-impossibility of the 'universal *one*' of human rights.

---

[53] S. P. Marks, 'From the "Single Confused Page" to the "Decalogue for Six Billion Persons": The Roots of the Universal Declaration of Human Rights in the French Revolution' (1998) 20 *Human Rights Quarterly* 459–514 at 460.

[54] L. Hunt, *The French Revolution and Human Rights: A Brief Documentary History* (New York: Bedford/St Martin's Press 1996) 3. The text of the American Declaration of Independence (1776) declares 'all men' to be 'created equal, [and] endowed by their Creator with certain unalienable Rights, [and] among these are Life, Liberty and the pursuit of Happiness'.

The marginalisation of 'women, humans of colour, children, humans with disabilities, humans who are older or poor, and those with different sexual orientations'[55] – those with long histories of exclusion – including indigenous peoples – point ineluctably towards a hidden 'insider' – the 'one' who is most definitely '*not*' any of these. It is as if a great invisible figure inhabits the universal. The figure revealed by the patterned retreat of particularity in international human rights law emerges from the ebb, as 'natural man' or 'natural human being' – in 'his' materialisation, however, bearing a predictable set of particularities. 'He' (for this is a construct not a living man (despite the fact that some groups of men have clearly benefited from their (incomplete) correspondence with its contours)) emerges as the male, the property-owning, the European and the white.[56] To claim this is simply to insist that international human rights law, in this particular regard, is no real exception to the history of rights struggles before it, although this paradox is all the more troubling in international human rights law, where the issue is both more complex (the UDHR explicitly denounces discrimination) and *more telling* (*for the same reason*).

History is where ideology breaks cover.[57] The paradoxes of the universal are reflected in a long history of rights settlements, history revealing a pattern – not just in the UDHR – of rights being born of visceral, critical reactions against a violently uneven status quo or an immense injustice – followed by their institutional crystallisation, at which point their radical potential is muted or foreclosed,[58] captured by the power of pre-existing elites (albeit not completely – thankfully the critical energy of rights is never entirely exhausted in the process). Even in revolutionary France, where rights-talk was at its most universalistic and liberationist, the initial institutional settlement strongly reflected the priorities of the powerful: the 'rights of man' were granted, paradigmatically to the male, rational property-owning citizen – notwithstanding vigorous and open debate concerning the rights of slaves, Calvinists, Jews and homosexuals and the attempts by some women to gain rights to active political citizenship.[59]

---

[55] D. Nibert, *Animal Rights, Human Rights: Entanglements of Oppression and Liberation* (Oxford: Rowman & Littlefield 2002) 4.

[56] Douzinas, *The End of Human Rights* 100.

[57] See M. Horwitz, 'Comment: The Historical Contingency of the Role of History' (1981) 90 *Yale Law Journal* 1057–9.

[58] N. Stammers, 'Social Movements and the Social Construction of Human Rights' (1999) 21 *Human Rights Quarterly* 980–1008.

[59] Hunt, *The French Revolution*.

By the time of the UDHR, as the text itself reflects, there was a widely accepted awareness of just such past discriminatory patterns – yet – as we have seen – discriminatory patterns remained installed in the drafting process itself (almost explicitly, concerning gender), and remain problematically installed within the cognitive and ideological architecture of the abstract 'universal subject' of international human rights. A key challenge related to these patterns concerns a tendency in abstractionism towards (incomplete) disembodiment. The construct of the universal human being simply does not do justice to the full complexity, the sheer fleshy variability and multiple forms, colours, shapes and sex/genders of the embodied human personality in all its vulnerability. The thin 'non-universal universal' cannot do justice to the 'thick' humanity of the entire human family. There is, quite simply, no adequate protection in the UDHR for the human being *qua* human being, a fact representing a profound ethical failure lying at the heart of the most putatively humanitarian of rights regimes.

Lest readers think this statement too strong, let us pause to reflect with Arendt in *The Origins of Totalitarianism* on the fact that human rights 'based on the assumed existence of a human being as such broke down at the very moment when those who professed to believe in [them] were for the first time confronted with people who had lost all other qualities and specific relationships – except that they were still human'.[60] This breakdown concerns, paradigmatically, 'the refugee' – the very figure who should most embody any *international* human rights subjectivity genuinely founded upon the radical presence of the human being *qua* human being *as such*. Yet Article 14 UDHR, examined closely, fails to guarantee the refugee the right to enter another country, producing a lacuna signalling the radical failure of the promise of the universal in the stark light of the very moment when the promise of full inclusion in the 'human family' of the UDHR is most necessary: for those otherwise juridically naked, radically dislocated human beings fleeing war, economic privation, environmental devastation or tyranny. Article 14 arguably announces, or *amplifies*, the dysfunction lying at the heart of international human rights law concerning the discrepancy between the avowedly universalist aspirations of the UDHR and the fractured reality of its patterned (re-)production of marginalised subjectivities.

In Arendt's terms, the fact that the UDHR fails to embrace the embodied vulnerable particularity of the human being *qua* human being, and the fact

---

[60] H. Arendt, *The Origins of Totalitarianism* (New York: Harcourt 1971) 299.

that the UDHR 'family' remains haunted by international human rights law's multiple 'others', signals a 'void' at the heart of international human rights law. This 'void' (and its historical and contemporary resonances) amply suggests, moreover, dark intimations of the radically differential distributions of life and death in the well-defended patterns and practices of injustice now characterising our global age of corporate capital predation.[61] Indeed, the spectre of deepening climate injustice and its (as-yet) differential distribution of privation, immiseration, cultural destruction and radical human dislocation[62] points, if anything, to the continuing salience of Arendt's lament.

What use then, we might ask, are international human rights, if they fail precisely at the point where they are called upon in the very name of the juridically naked, embodied, vulnerable humanness so poignantly exposed? Was achieving this very nakedness not the precise aim of the Nazi programme of stripping away both citizenship and legal personhood – a process which assiduously preceded the procedurally regulated extermination of Jews and other victims in the camps of the Third Reich and which, through the imposition of 'juridical death' opened the way for the practices of Holocaust so foundational, on one reading at least, to the inception of the UDHR as an outraged reaction to it?[63]

How, then, are we to answer this call for human rights meaning? Arguably, human rights break their promise when they fail to be bearers of outrage and compassion. It is arguably at the very moment of experienced 'nakedness', in the face of the 'void' itself, in the 'felt' gap between the 'now' and the 'not yet', in the savage contradiction between human rights promise and human rights betrayal, which the illimitable energy and paradox of human rights returns. For it is in the very experiential realities of the betrayal of the promise of the universal, in the viscerally felt failures of inclusion, in the embodied, lived senses of marginalisation, exclusion or excision that human energies surge back into the space of human rights failure, articulating new words, breathing (literally) a pain that re-awakens

---

[61] See Baxi, *the Future of Human Rights*; Gill, 'Globalisation'; Grear, *Redirecting Human Rights*; F. Pearce and S. Tombs, *Toxic Capitalism: Corporate Crime and the Chemical Industry* (Aldershot: Dartmouth 1998).

[62] See, e.g., L. Westra, *Ecoviolence and the Law* (Ardsley, NY: Transnational Publishers 2004); L. Westra, *Environmental Justice and the Rights of Ecological Refugees* (London: Earthscan 2009); L. Westra and B. E. Lawson (eds.), *Faces of Environmental Racism: Confronting Issues of Global Justice* (Lanham, MD: Rowman & Littlefield 2001).

[63] Morsink, 'World War Two' 358.

human rights as an endless contestation concerning the constitution of the 'human family'. Hope lies, perhaps, in the idea that international human rights law has not yet exhausted the critical energy of human rights as an endlessly recursive interaction concerning inclusions and exclusions in which every inclusion necessarily creates new, unforeseen exclusions, and in which every lived exclusion births new claims for inclusion. Perhaps in this sense, we can render legible the 'void' of international human rights law, with Rancière, as being precisely that fragile but persistent space of hope in which international human rights are 'the rights of those who have not the rights that they have and have the rights that they have not'.[64]

Further reading

Baxi, U., *The Future of Human Rights* (Oxford University Press 2008)
    Human Rights in a Post-Human World: Critical Essays (Oxford University Press 2009)
Beveridge, F. and Mullally, S., International Human Rights and Body Politics', in J. Bridgeman and S. Millns (eds.), *Law and Body Politics: Regulating the Female Body* (Aldershot: Dartmouth 1995) 240–72
Donnelly, J., *Universal Human Rights in Theory and Practice* (Ithaca, NY and London: Cornell University Press 2003)
Douzinas, C., *The End of Human Rights* (Oxford: Hart 2000)
    Human Rights and Empire: The Political Philosophy of Cosmopolitanism (Abingdon: Routledge–Cavendish 2007)
Evans, T., *Human Rights Fifty Years On* (Manchester University Press 1998)
Gearty, C., *Can Human Rights Survive?* (Cambridge University Press 2006)
Grear, A., *Redirecting Human Rights: Facing the Challenge of Corporate Legal Humanity* (Basingstoke: Palgrave Macmillan 2010)
Harding, C., Kohl, U. and Salmon, N., *Human Rights in the Market Place: The Exploitation of Rights Protection by Economic Actors* (Aldershot: Ashgate 2008)
Holmes, H. B., 'A Feminist Analysis of the Universal Declaration of Human Rights', in C. C. Gould (ed.), *Beyond Domination: New Perspectives on Women and Philosophy* (Totowa, NJ: Rowman & Allanheld 1984) 250–64
Hunt, L., *The French Revolution and Human Rights: A Brief Documentary History* (New York: Bedford/St Martin's Press 1996
    Inventing Human Rights: A History (New York: W. W. Norton 2007)
Ishay, M., *The History of Human Rights: From Ancient Times to the Globalization Era*, 2nd edn (Berkeley, CA: University of California Press 2008)

---

[64] J. Rancière, 'Who is the Subject of the Rights of Man?' (2004) 103 *South Atlantic Quarterly* 297–310 at 302.

Morsink, J., 'Women's Rights in the Universal Declaration' (1991) 13 *Human Rights Quarterly* 229–56 'World War Two and the Declaration' (1993) 15 *Human Rights Quarterly* 357–405

Otto. D., 'Violence against Women: Something Other Than a Human Rights Violation?' (1993) 1 *Australian Feminist Law Journal* 159–62
  'Disconcerting "Masculinities": Reinventing the Gendered Subject(s) of International Human Rights Law', in D. Buss and A. Manji (eds.), *International Law: Modern Feminist Approaches* (Oxford: Hart 2005) 105–29

Steiner, H. J., Alston, P. and Goodman, R., *International Human Rights in Context: Law, Politics, Morals* (Oxford University Press 2007)

Turner, B., *Vulnerability and Human Rights* (Pennsylvania State University Press 2006).

2 Restoring the 'human' in 'human rights': personhood and doctrinal innovation in the UN disability convention

Gerard Quinn with Anna Arstein-Kerslake

'What is needed nowadays is that as against an abstract and unreal theory of State omnipotence on the one hand, and an atomistic and artificial view of individual independence on the other, the facts of the world with its innumerable bonds of association and the naturalness of social authority should be generally recognized, and become the basis of our laws, as it is of our life.'[1]

Recovering the human

'Human rights' – here are two words expressing two different normative domains. Most simply assume that the two are mutually reinforcing, mutually implicated by each other, coterminous and coeval. Everywhere in the world, first-year law students are routinely told that we enjoy human rights simply because we are human. The question of whether there are any essential criteria of being human or of 'personhood' and, if so, what they are, is left dangling as if solved by the conjuncture of 'human' with 'rights'. That is, rights-talk tends to cloud our view of what it means to be human. And rights tend to impute a certain view of humanity – one that is not necessarily tied to observable reality. Another result is the absence of any clear toeholds in the slippery debate about whether there are any non-human 'persons' (e.g. animals or even the earth) and, if so, whether they are the proper subject of rights.

The core argument of this chapter is that we have to retrieve some autonomous meaning from what it means to be 'human' in order to refresh our conception of rights and to make it fit for purpose in contemporary society. Put another way, my central proposition is that the essentially political or instrumental purpose of rights, which one cannot and indeed

---

[1] J. N. Figgis, *Political Thought from Gerson to Grotius 1414–1625: Seven Studies* (New York: Harper Torchbooks 1960) 206, cited in R. Pound, 'Mechanical Jurisprudence' (1908) 8 *Columbia Law Review* 605, 609.

should not gainsay and which is clearly observable throughout history, has exerted a subtle but powerful undertow on what we mean to be human. True, rights-talk is supposed to be (or is commonly explained as) non-instrumental, inhabiting the pure ether of deontology. But in an important sense human rights and a particular vision of the political community are holograms – see one and you see the other. One often gets the feeling, however, that this architecture is more important than the rights and specifically the human values that they are supposed to serve. In order to bring rights back to the human condition, in order to make them both honour and serve that condition, it is necessary first to dissolve them, as Holmes would have it, in cynical acid in order to wash away political encrustations and reveal the deeper relationship between the two.[2]

One suspects that something precious has been lost or repressed by the dominance of an inevitably political conception of 'rights' over the 'human' domain. Or, to put this another way, that the essentially political character of rights has suppressed powerful trace elements of what it means to be human. In the result human rights seem to commit us to an exaggerated caricature (a 'myth system') of the human condition: the rational, self-directing, wholly autonomous individual possessing moral agency unto him/herself. The spatial image at play is that of the masterless man freely choosing his/her own conception of the good and wandering purposively in an anomic no-man's land interacting (or not) freely with others and opting (occasionally) to engage with and influence public power. Rights are primarily concerned with the intersection between this masterless man and power – especially public power. In as much as rights have a perspective on personhood and human flourishing it tends to be agnostic. Rights-talk itself is impoverished by this disconnect. Important rights such as the right to participate are seen less as an essential ingredient for self-realisation and more as a desiccated form of civic virtue.

Our own everyday experiences are strikingly at odds with the 'myth system'. Even behavioural economics openly accepts the fallacy of the rational man and rational action as the basis of analysis.[3] The interesting thing about the UN Convention on the Rights of Persons with Disabilities (CRPD) adopted in 2006 is that it forces to the surface many of these

---

[2] O. W. Holmes, Jr, 'The Path of the Law' (1897) 10 *Harvard Law Review* 457, 462.

[3] E.g. H. A. Simon, 'A Behavioral Model of Rational Choice' (1955) 69 *Quarterly Journal of Economics* 9.

suppressed suspicions about the disconnect between 'rights' and the human condition. The disability convention is of much more general interest beyond disability. Indeed, I have previously spoken of it as an instrument that is not even mainly about disability.[4] It is primarily about the latest iteration of a cosmopolitan theory of justice that happens to be grounded on disability. The point is that it adds to that theory – it stretches it and potentially enriches it.

The import of the CRPD to the broader human rights community is, I suggest, twofold. First of all, it starts with what it means to be a human being. That is to say, it does not start with a menu of rights to be mechanically tailored to yet another thematic group. It really does pivot on a three-dimensional view of the reality of life as a person with a disability. Largely, this was down to the very active involvement of civil society groups during the negotiations.[5] What this brought to the surface was an insistence on the capacity of all persons with disabilities to forge their own destinies, a frank acknowledgement of shared personhood and of the myriad of supports – formal and informal – that we all rely on to help us forge our own pathways and the critical importance of participation and the ethic of belonging that it instils. In effect, it is built on a much more three-dimensional view of the human condition and of human flourishing than would have been possible by simply working backwards from the logic of rights. In a sense it represents a rejection of the 'mechanical jurisprudence', which Roscoe Pound inveighed against in the modern context of human rights.[6]

Secondly, and I argue as a consequence of the above, the CRPD pushes the boundaries of established human rights doctrine. For example, in it one will find a more concrete move than hitherto toward intersectionality – that much-debated but little-understood idea about the endless plasticity of human identity and how the interaction of these identities compounds the experience of discrimination (Articles 6 and 7). In it one will find an innovative right to live independently and be included in the community (Article 19). Identity is forged largely by human interaction – the very thing denied many people with disabilities. In it one will find a myriad of active participation rights that in their own way open up pathways to aspects of the lifeworld (the economy, society, the cultural sphere). Added to this is the innovative right to

---

[4] G. Quinn, 'Rethinking Personhood: New Directions in Legal Capacity Law and Policy', Lecture, Vancouver: University of British Columbia, 29 April 2011.

[5] See V. Ilagan, 'Statement on Behalf of the International Disability Caucus at the 5th Session of the United Nations Ad Hoc Committee' (4 February 2005).

[6] See generally R. Pound, 'Mechanical Jurisprudence' (1908) 8 *Columbia Law Review* 605.

be actively involved (not merely consulted) in any public policy process that affects the person (Article 4.3). What is the point of a convention that helps one challenge bad laws if one can't change the underlying process that produces these laws in the first place? In it one will find a novel approach to economic, social and cultural rights, one which does not entrap persons with disabilities in a welfare cage on a pretence of placing them on a pedestal but rather is turned around to sub-serve human flourishing. Present as well in the CRPD is a broader concept of equality that self-consciously embraces accumulated disadvantage through time.[7] Acknowledging disadvantage is one thing – but the CRPD seeks to reverse it by creating opportunities to participate and for self-realisation in community.

All of this was made possible because of a much more nuanced understanding of what it means to be human and specifically a person with a disability. This was impossible to avoid on the ground of disability. The question of the foundations of personhood could be – and was – postponed in other treaty-drafting processes. No one seriously doubted that women were human, that racial minorities were human, that immigrants and refugees were human. Of course there was a debate about when is a child a child in the drafting of the Rights of the Child Convention.[8] But that had nothing to do with any intellectual exercise to identify the essential criteria of personhood (leaving to one side the propriety of 'essentialism' when it comes to personhood) – and had more to do with the narrower political goal of ensuring that unborn persons count as persons.

But what of the personhood of people with disabilities – especially those with profound intellectual disabilities? Is it to be said that the distance between their observable lives is so far from the 'myth system' of the 'masterless man' that they do not count as human, are not the fitting subjects of a theory of justice and are not to be allowed to stand to benefit from rights? The Nazis certainly thought so.[9] And one is tempted to say that many in the human rights community tended to think so until recently and regarded persons with disabilities – especially those with intellectual disabilities – in

---

[7] O. M. Arnardóttir, 'A Future of Multidimensional Disadvantage Equality?', in O. M. Arnardóttir and G. Quinn (eds.), *The UN Convention on the Rights of People with Disabilities: European and Scandinavian Perspectives* (Dordrecht: Martinus Nijhoff 2009) 41, 47–54.

[8] *See* P. Alston, 'The Unborn Child and Abortion Under the Draft Convention on the Rights of the Child' (1990) 12 *Human Rights Quarterly* 156.

[9] E. Colombo, Italian Minister for Foreign Affairs, Preface to M. R. Savile, *The Disabled Persons and the International Organizations* (Rome: International Documentation Ent. 1981).

terms of a social welfare cushion that provided for their basic needs but often at a cost of their segregation form the mainstream. Does a significant distance from the 'myth system' disqualify one as a person?

The flashpoint in the disability convention – literally and figuratively – was the drafting of Article 12 that is innocuously entitled 'equal recognition before the law'. The ultimate text was the result of several quite different impulses. Like most controversial pieces of internationally negotiated text it has its fair share of constructive ambiguity. On balance it tips states away from a 'deficits-oriented' perspective on disability and towards one that views fragility as a universal aspect of the human condition and remediable with sufficient supports (not necessarily supports provided for by the state or on a statutory basis). Few – including the author – saw at the time how the evolving text of Article 12 had the potential to zip open some deep contradictions in human rights-talk about personhood and what its implications for human rights might be more generally.

For it turns out that the disability convention in general and Article 12 in particular forces us to expose the 'myth system' of personhood in human rights-talk. For one thing, it forces an understanding that human personhood is not atomised but in fact shared. We are all both a support and threat to each other and almost always at the same time. It turns out that personhood and human flourishing imply a certain degree of interdependence as well as independence. Through this convention we can see that personhood implies a certain vision of the community that frames the process of individuation. This approach to personhood brings to the fore the insight of the ancients which is that the freedom that is most worth having is the right to belong, to contribute, to be seen as belonging and to be valued as part of something beyond oneself.[10]

I need now to probe the deeper theory of personhood that is encapsulated in the story of Article 12 and how it, in effect, stumbled upon and knocked over one of the foundation stones of human rights thinking. To do this I must place some of the doctrinal innovations of the CRPD in the context of the revolution of Article 12. These innovations have the potential to refresh human rights thinking in general and not just in the specific field of disability. Before looking at Article 12 in more detail we need now to examine approaches to personhood that precede the breakthroughs of the CRPD.

---

[10] See Sir E. Barker, *The Political Thought of Plato and Aristotle* (Mineola, NY: Dover 2009) (1st edn 1959).

Personhood: a contested ideal

Rights are for humans. But which humans count? On balance and throughout the world, one tends to qualify as a human 'subject', or as a 'person' before the law, as a sentient being capable of exercising moral agency, provided one is rationally capable of apprehending the world, rationally able to process information, rationally able to understand the consequences of one's actions for self and others, rationally capable of choosing between alternative courses of action and possessed of sufficient communicative ability to be able to rationally transmit one's will and preferences to others.[11] Note the implicit assumption that cognition is the 'essence' of personhood. Once you have sufficient cognition then a wide liberty is afforded even to do things that will inevitably result in harm. A certain dignity of risk is afforded to those deemed cognitively capable even though they may proceed to repeat the same mistakes (e.g. enter bad marriages). The same wide dignity of risk is not permitted to those with less cognitive ability. There a protective impulse takes over – one laden down with centuries of paternalism.

Protecting people against themselves or others is not inherently bad. Indeed, Article 16 of the CRPD contains an innovative provision securing to persons with disabilities the right to protection against violence, exploitation and abuse on an 'equal basis with others'. In play is a radical re-balancing of protection versus the autonomy of the individual. In the past persons with disabilities were stripped of the right to make decisions for themselves in order to protect them even though alternative adult protection systems would have done a more effective job. But do we really protect people by removing their right to make their own decisions? The evidence suggests otherwise.[12]

The stakes are high. The right to make decisions for oneself – to chart one's own life path – without interference from third parties or the state is considered the foundation stone and greatest achievement of liberal legal and political philosophy. It flows from one's recognition as a person before the law. It enables individuals to direct their own destiny in accordance with

---

[11] This focus on cognition and rationality in granting legal personhood can be seen in functional tests of capacity, as is demonstrated in the England and Wales Mental Capacity Act 2005.

[12] B. J. Winick, On Autonomy: Legal and Psychological Perspectives (1992) 37 *Villanova Law Review* 1705, 1755–68.

their wishes, preferences and conceptions of the good life. It is thus seen as critically instrumental in ordering an open and free society based on individual conscience and freedom.

The concept of 'legal capacity' is simply the legal tool by which people exercise their moral agency in the world. When exercised as a sword, it affords persons the right to make decisions for themselves in all spheres of life and, crucially, to have those decisions respected by others. This applies in spheres including the intimate sphere (right to marry, found a family, adopt children), the social sphere (social inclusion in the life of the community) and the political sphere (the right to vote, to hold office and pursue office). It also applies in the economic sphere where most of us lead our lives through a myriad of private transactions (the right to conclude contracts, to control banking transactions, to own, rent and manage one's own property). In this sense it is a portal to the exercise of a wide range of rights. When exercised as a shield, legal capacity also functions to fend off others who might purport to make decisions on our behalf, even when well intentioned. It includes a right against forced treatment and an authority to give or refuse consent to various treatments, interventions or procedures, whether medical or otherwise.

It follows that the loss of legal capacity can be catastrophic for any individual, a form of 'civil death'.[13] Its loss typically leads to decisions being made for one by a third party (so-called 'substitute decision-making') whether informally, through limited guardianship (tied to a particular set of decisions or for a particular period of time) or, in its most extreme form, through plenary guardianship (covering all aspects of one's life). Such substitute decisions are supposedly made in one's 'best interests' with appropriate procedural safeguards (eliminating conflict of interest) and substantive safeguards (no right to make certain kinds of decisions). In the past the effectiveness of safeguards against abuses was highly questionable.[14] Unfortunately, the loss of legal capacity might prove to be self-perpetuating since it can be difficult to restore capabilities that have become degraded through lack of use. The persons affected include, in the main, those with intellectual disabilities, persons with mental illness or problems and even persons with communicative disabilities. The cohort is set to grow,

---

[13] W. Blackstone, *Commentaries on the Laws of England*, Vol. 1, 442–5 (Oxford: Clarendon Press 1765).

[14] For an analysis of guardianship regimes in Eastern Europe see Mental Disability Advocacy Centre's (MDAC) series of reports, titled *Guardianship and Human Rights*.

especially as the world and Europe ages.[15] There remain many laws, practices and policies throughout the world (including in Europe) that unduly restrict the legal capacity of persons with disabilities to make decisions for themselves.

It is important to recall that persons with disabilities were not the only ones to suffer 'civil death' in the past. The merger of a women's legal capacity and even personhood with that of her husband and which was rationalised in part by a misplaced paternalism – amounted to a form of slavery that took centuries to roll back.[16] Women are now full persons before the law with the right to hold and dispose of property, enter contracts and otherwise control their personal destinies. This is crystallised in Article 15 of the UN Convention on the Elimination of all Forms of Discrimination against Women (CEDAW, 1987) – which brooks no exception to the legal capacity of women. If paternalism has no place in the context of gender it is generally given some latitude with respect to children on a theory that they lack capacity to make many decisions for themselves (at least up to a certain age). Although true, this is always counter-balanced with a sense that there is an obligation (usually falling on parents in the first instance) to positively nurture the capacities of children and to gradually empower them to make decisions for themselves. This is done (or at least ideally done) using the social capital of the family and the natural supports that occur in the community in which children grow up. Paternalism for children, in this sense, is justified as a gradually diminishing phenomenon that evaporates as the system of background support succeeds in imparting the skills and insights needed to exercise autonomy. It is to be noted that paternalism in the disability field was never generally accompanied by any such ameliorating philosophy. It was probably assumed that, unlike children, no improvement in capabilities could be expected over time with respect to those with certain disabilities.

At least at the level of ideas, persons with disabilities – and especially those with intellectual disabilities – are now beginning thanks to the CRPD

---

[15] European Commission (Economic and Financial Affairs), *The 2012 Ageing Report: Underlying Assumptions and Projection Methodologies*, 20, http://ec.europa.eu/economy_finance/publications/european_economy/2011/pdf/ee-2011-4_en.pdf

[16] In England and Wales, one of the last vestiges of this 'civil death' upon marriage was not removed until 1973 with the enactment of the Domicile and Matrimonial Proceedings Act, which abolished the rule that, upon marriage, a woman's domicile was automatically considered to be her husband's, regardless of whether the couple had subsequently received an order of judicial separation.

to emerge into full legal personhood. Article 12 is closely analogous to Article 15 of CEDAW. Ninety-five states around the world have ratified CRPD so far. The USA has signed and ratification is pending before the US Senate. To grasp the revolutionary potential of the new paradigm represented by Article 12 we need now to explore a little more two of the more traditional approaches to capacity in this field specifically and then to contrast these with a third 'modern' one.

The first 'status-based' approach entails an assessment of legal capacity on the basis of purely medical diagnosis of cognitive impairments. In other words, having a particular disability (usually pivoting on a loss of cognitive capacity or mental illness) was treated in law as being tantamount to a loss of legal capacity. There was no sense that one might retain residual decision-making capacity at least with respect to a certain kind of decision despite cognitive incapacity. In a way this is similar to how married women – *qua* married women – submerged their personhood into that of their husband in centuries past.

The second, 'outcome-based approach' takes into account a person's prior decisions or pattern of decisions, and then assesses these in terms of their conformity to 'normal' or 'societal values'. If there is a wide deviance, then the person is regarded as lacking mental capacity, and is therefore vulnerable to losing legal capacity. Likewise, if a person makes a series of improvident decisions (e.g. to buy an expensive box set of movies rather than to eat) or if a pattern of flawed decision-making can be identified (repeatedly falling in love with the 'wrong' kind of person), then this pattern of 'bad' decisions exposes the individual to a potential loss of legal capacity. In other words, within this approach the law works backwards from a perception of 'bad' decisions to an assumption of a lack of underlying legal decision-making capacity.

But it is now clear that one's status as a cognitively impaired person does not necessarily lead to a conclusion concerning one's legal capacity to make decisions about one's own life. As a matter of principle the 'outcome-based approach' is objectionable because it flagrantly contradicts one of the goals of the 'rule of law' which is to create maximum space for the expression of one's own conception of the good – as long as it is lawful and does not detract from a like liberty in others.[17] It is also objectionable from a practical perspective because even if society is entitled to treat a pattern of bad

---

[17] See J. Rawls, *A Theory of Justice* (Cambridge, MA: Harvard University Press 1971) 235–43.

decisions as *prima facie* evidence of a lack of legal capacity, it does not necessarily follow that a pattern of bad decisions alone provides a secure basis on which to adjudge mental incapacity and hence legal incapacity.

It was because of the slow but inexorable rise of awareness about the drawbacks of these two traditional approaches that a third emerged in the1990s. This has been labelled the 'functional approach'.[18] Perhaps its single best exemplar is the elegantly crafted Recommendation (99) 4 of the Committee of Ministers of the Council of Europe on '*principles concerning the legal protection of incapable adults*' (1999). This approach assesses mental capacity (and ultimately legal capacity) on an 'issue-specific' basis in terms of the actual, rather than assumed, functional capability of the individual to make a particular category of decision at a specific point in time. This requires decision-making capacity to be assessed with respect to particular kinds of decisions rather than across the board. Therefore, a decision about a person's mental capacity in relation to one matter (for example, the capacity to make financial decisions) will not necessarily determine their capacity on other matters (for example, the capacity for sexual relations or health decisions), and a person might lack capacity one day, but regain it later (depending perhaps on the trajectory of a mental illness, the effectiveness of treatment and the quality of social supports).

Significantly, this more modern 'functional approach' rejects the idea that there are 'incapacitated persons'. Rather, persons may have incapacities with respect to particular sets of decisions, but only if that is what the evidence demonstrates. The 'functional approach' assumes that people have functional capability to make decisions but concedes that 'substitute decision-making' can be allowed, albeit under a narrowly reduced set of circumstances and with safeguards.

The 'functional approach' seemed intuitively sound and it was certainly an improvement on the previous models. Why change it? It is to be noted that all three approaches share some basic characteristics. First of all, they effectively share a medical approach. Psychiatrists are often called on for expert testimony on one's capacity to manage everyday affairs even though their training is on diagnosis and treatment. The traditional deference given to such reports by courts inevitably means that for all this talk of function,

---

[18] A. Dhanda, 'Legal Capacity in the Disability Rights Convention: Stranglehold of the Past or Lodestar for the Future?' (2006–7) 34 *Syracuse Journal of International Law and Commerce* 429, 431–2.

determinations on capacity are effectively status-based.[19] Secondly, all three approaches focus on mental capacity as the *sine qua non* for legal capacity. And mental capability is understood almost exclusively (and narrowly) as cognitive ability. So in a sense all are referable back to the 'myth system' of human rationality. Thirdly, all three approaches tend to focus on decision-making capacity in a *synchronic* sense – that is, at the particular point in time of making a decision. None appears to take an interest in decision-making in a broader or *diachronic* sense. Fourthly, none appears to factor into their decision-making the fact that most 'ordinary' people actually rely on a wide variety of supports, social cues and the benefits of social capital to give context, meaning and direction to their choices. Co-decision rather than purely individual decisions is actually the norm. If a person – any person – is cut off from these social cues for identity and decision (e.g. through institutionalisation) and if the 'mystic chords of memory'[20] that connect people to one another are shredded then it is no surprise that decision-making capacity is damaged. And fifthly, none speaks directly to the need to provide supports to augment residual capacity and assist such people in the making of decisions about themselves.

The stage was therefore set for a wholly new approach in the CRPD – one that can only take root if it is seen to be based on a very different conception of personhood. It is the making of this breakthrough that marks the provision out as of exceptional importance.

Article 12 of the CRPD: more a 'revolution' than an 'evolution'

The issue of legal capacity was always going to be central in the new convention. As has already been observed, one of the main problems in the disability field has been that persons with disabilities have been treated more as 'objects' (to be managed, cared for or controlled) than as 'subjects' (capable of directing their own lives).[21] In a sense Article 12 is one weapon among others in a convention that is intended to roll back the

---

[19] See, e.g., Mental Disability Advocacy Centre (MDAC), *Guardianship and Human Rights in Bulgaria* (2008).

[20] A. Lincoln, *First Inaugural Speech* (Washington 1861).

[21] G. Quinn and T. Degener, 'The Moral Authority for Change: Human Rights Values and the Worldwide Process of Disability Reform', in Gerard Quinn *et al.* (eds.), *Human Rights and*

manifestations of control, especially in the form of overly broad civil commitment laws and laws that permit forced treatment. Article 12.1 states the obvious, which is that persons with disabilities have a right to recognition everywhere before the law. What is interesting is the need to state the obvious. Article 12.2 is to the effect that persons with disabilities enjoy the right to exercise legal capacity 'on an equal basis with others' and in 'all spheres of life'. It is unclear who those 'others' (the comparators) are. Article 12.3 – the core of Article 12 – is to the effect that states shall provide support where needed to enable people with disabilities to exercise their legal capacity. This marks a decisive move away from a deficits-oriented guardianship paradigm that at the first sight of a decision-making deficit removes the legal right to make decisions and shifts instead to a supports paradigm that uses the fact of a deficit to explore ways in which supports can be put in place to enable capacity to grow and be exercised. Article 12.4 provides an extensive list of safeguards which some states interpret as rationalising a functionalist approach (which would allow for at least some guardianship or substitute decision-making)[22] while others interpret Article 12.4 as only applying to a support model of legal capacity and not any form of substitute decision-making regime. Article 12.5 makes it plain that the right to exercise legal capacity applies to one's own financial affairs.

In a sharp break with the past, Article 12 seems to call for an almost irrefutable presumption of legal capacity. In effect, it separates out mental capability (which may vary) from the right to legal capacity that remains constant. It enjoins states to respond to the fragility of mental capacity with supports to enable persons to exercise their legal capacity.

The idea that persons with even severe cognitive disabilities may, despite their disabilities, retain full legal capacity might appear counter-intuitive. Yet a settled body of opinion has crystallised since 2006 which now tips our understanding of Article 12 decisively in the direction of a support model – one that augments capacity rather than displaces it at the first sign of a human

Disability: The Current Use and Future Potential of United Nations Human Rights Instruments in the Context of Disability (Geneva: OHCHR 2002) 9.

[22] For example, upon ratification, Canada entered the following declaration and reservation: 'Canada recognises that persons with disabilities are presumed to have legal capacity on an equal basis with others in all aspects of their lives. Canada declares its understanding that Article 12 permits supported and substitute decision-making arrangements in appropriate circumstances and in accordance with the law. To the extent Article 12 may be interpreted as requiring the elimination of all substitute decision-making arrangements, Canada reserves the right to continue their use in appropriate circumstances and subject to appropriate and effective safeguards' (11 March 2010).

deficit. For example, in a 2009 report the Office of the UN High Commissioner for Human Rights has stated its view that legal incapacity regimes that are based directly or indirectly on disability are incompatible with the convention. It specifically endorsed the move to a support paradigm.[23]

Of course, the Office is not the body that officially interprets the convention – but its word is exceptionally weighty in the international legal order. The relevant treaty monitoring body, the UN Committee on the Rights of Persons with Disabilities, is already drawing conclusions on state reports based very much on a positive understanding of Article 12. The Committee has recently considered the reports of Spain and Tunisia – both countries that still operate guardianship systems for people with disabilities that remove or restrict the person's right to make decisions. In both cases, the Committee expressed concern 'that no measures have been undertaken to replace substitute decision-making by supported decision-making in the exercise of legal capacity'.[24] With respect to both countries, the Committee recommended that the states concerned 'review the laws allowing for guardianship and trusteeship, and take action to develop laws and policies to replace regimes of substitute decision-making by supported decision-making, which respects the person's autonomy, will and preferences'.[25] The Committee is currently working on its own general Comment on Article 12 (effectively laying out in depth its considered views on the interpretation of Article 12). Given the tone and content of the Committee's conclusions so far, the General Comment will likely be an extended commentary on what the supported decision-making paradigm might look like rather than focus on the case for moving from a deficits model to a supports model.

The European Court of Human Rights (ECtHR) has already invoked the CRPD as an aid in interpreting states' obligations under the European Convention on Human Rights (ECHR) itself (even against states like Switzerland that have not signed the CRPD).[26] The jurisprudence of the

---

[23] UN OHCHR, *Thematic Study on Enhancing Awareness and Understanding of the Convention on the Rights of Persons with Disabilities*, para. 45, UN Doc. A/HRC/10/48 (26 January 2009).

[24] *Consideration of Reports Submitted by States Parties under Article 35 of the Convention: Concluding Observations, Tunisia*, Committee on the Rights of Persons with Disabilities (CRPD), 5th Sess., UN Doc. CRPD/C/TUN/CO/1 (11–15 April 2011) 4.

[25] *Consideration of Reports Submitted by States Parties under Article 35 of the Convention: Concluding Observations, Spain*, Committee on the Rights of Persons with Disabilities (CRPD), 6th Sess., UN Doc. CRPD/C/ESP/CO/1 (19–23 September 2011) 5.

[26] *Glor v. Switzerland*, 13444/04 ECtHR (Sect. 1) (2009).

ECtHR is moving in a positive direction with respect to Article 12. Referring specifically to Article 12, the Court's recent judgment in *Stanev* v. *Bulgaria* (January 2012) shows that it is scrutinising existing guardianship laws ever more closely.[27] This case involved a man who was unable to challenge his detention and degrading treatment in a social care facility without the consent of his guardian, leading the court to find that guardianship regimes such as Bulgaria's violated the right to a fair trial under Article 6 of the ECHR. The High Commissioner for Human Rights in the Council of Europe – Thomas Hammarberg – issued his own Issues Paper on legal capacity reform in Europe in February 2012. It also strongly endorses the modern view of Article 12.[28]

Normative developments in this area are not confined to the UN or Europe. The relevant monitoring committee of the Inter-American Convention on the Elimination of All Forms of Discrimination against Persons with Disabilities has issued its own General Observation on the interpretation of that convention in light of Article 12.[29] It states its view that Article 12 'implies a change of paradigm away from substitution of a person's will ... to the new paradigm based on decision-making with support and safeguards' and 'the support envisaged by the convention as "appropriate" focuses on abilities (more than disabilities) and on elimination of obstacles in the environment so as to facilitate access and pro-active inclusion in social life'.[30]

In short, this trend in favour of the move to the support paradigm as the chief departure point in the drafting of fresh legislation is palpable. How can one make sense of this 'revolution'? How can it be communicated – convincingly – to others?

The point about the revolution is that it does not work unless one abandons cognition as the essence of personhood. Nothing in the convention pivots on the 'myth system' of the rational and masterless man. In fact it depends rather on a frank acknowledgement of the reality and complexity

---

[27] *Stanev* v. *Bulgaria*, 36760/06 ECtHR [GC], para. 72 (2012).

[28] T. Hammarberg, *Who Gets to Decide? Right to Legal Capacity for Persons with Intellectual and Psychosocial Disabilities*, Issue Paper commissioned by the Council of Europe Commissioner for Human Rights, Comm. DH/Issue Paper (2012) 2 (20 February 2012).

[29] General Observation of the Committee for the Elimination of All Forms of Discrimination against Persons with Disabilities on the need to interpret Article I.2(b) in fine of the Inter-American Convention on the Elimination of All Forms of Discrimination against Persons with Disabilities in the context of Article 12 of the UN Convention on the Rights of Persons with Disabilities, OEA/ Ser.L/XXIV.3.1, CEDDIS/doc.12(I-E/11) rev. 1 (4–5 May 2011) 6.

[30] *Ibid.*, 5.

of human existence. It chimes better with reality than the myth system, a reality that is increasingly being revealed in other walks of scholarship. Contemporary neuroscience, for example, demonstrates how the concept of the mind is in fact a relational idea – it evolves in association with others.[31] Of course the very possibility of this interaction is the very thing denied to most persons with intellectual disabilities. And contemporary clinical psychology questions not merely the permeability between cognition and emotion but even the division itself between the two.[32] Will and preferences are more important than cognition.

Connectedness, involvement, participation: all hold the key to flourishing. They link us to the myriad of informal supports we inevitably get from human interaction. Re-connecting people to social capital in their own communities is one of the keys to human flourishing especially with respect to persons whose social connectedness is paper thin – which would certainly include older persons. Using rights to re-engineer this connectedness is the key to the CRPD.

Children of the revolution: other innovations in the disability convention

The adoption of a much more holistic conception of personhood in the disability convention led to, or facilitated, other conceptual innovations elsewhere in the document. It certainly makes them more explicable than if recounted as the mechanical application of general rights to disability.

The much-vaunted concept of 'intersectionality' is important here. It rests on an understanding that the human condition cannot be neatly refracted into discrete identities or labels and that the cumulative and multiplying effect of these identities is somehow not adequately captured in traditional protections against discrimination in existing human rights instruments. The more holistic conception of personhood in the CRPD created space for a broader posture to intersectionality than in other instruments. Preambular paragraph e in the CRPD acknowledges that disability itself is an evolving concept and a function of the interaction of the person with the

---

[31] See A. Damasio, *Self Comes to Mind: Constructing the Conscious* Brain (New York: Knopf Doubleday 2010).
[32] See J. Lehrer, *How We Decide* (Boston, MA: Houghton Mifflin Harcourt 2010).

environment. Preambular paragraph *q* recognises that women and girls with disabilities are at greater risk than are others with disabilities. Article 6 goes on to recognise that women and girls with disabilities are subject to multiple forms of discrimination and obliges states to take appropriate measures to deal with these exposures to risks. Likewise, Article 7 focuses on the special vulnerabilities of children with disabilities. The CRPD is not a perfect instantiation of intersectionality.[33] But it at least makes a stab in the right direction. It remains to be seen how the committee overseeing the convention will approach this; hopefully it will assist in the growth of a concept of intersectionality that at least has some roots in the CRPD.

The right to live independently and be included in the community (Article 19) likewise stems from this broader conception of personhood. This includes a right to choose where to live, with whom and on what basis. To a certain extent community embeddedness augments capacity. Inappropriate institutionalisation in the past shredded this natural connectedness with community and played a part in degrading decision-making capacities. A home isn't just bricks and mortar. It is 'an extension of and mirror for the living body in its everyday activity' and powerfully facilitates the 'materialization of identity'.[34] There is therefore a symbiotic link between augmenting legal capacity and achieving meaningful de-institutionalisation.

Protecting persons with disabilities against violence, exploitation and abuse and restoring decision-making power to them to live the life they want to lead is not enough. The many spheres of human interaction – the things that make life worth living and that add the essential ingredients for personhood to flourish – need to be opened up. That is why the various rights of access and participation in the CRPD are so important. Article 9 deals with a general right of accessibility. Article 29 deals with access to the political world for persons with disabilities. This is very important since persons with disabilities typically lack political impact (despite their large numbers). Article 30 deals with access to, and participation in, cultural life, recreation and sports. It contains a number of unusual features. These access rights are rounded out by Article 13 in the context of the justice system. The point, though, is that these rights are not calibrated merely to

---

[33] See generally D. Schiek and A. Lawson (eds.), *European Union Non-Discrimination Law and Intersectionality: Investigating the Triangle of Racial, Gender and Disability Discrimination* (Farnham: Ashgate 2011).

[34] I. M. Young, *Intersecting Voices: Dilemmas of Gender, Political Philosophy and Policy* (Princeton University Press 1997) 150.

give people access to spheres hitherto foreclosed or to influence power – they are provided to enable self-transformation and valorisation of the individual.

It has been remarked elsewhere that the concept of equality in the convention is itself innovative.[35] It takes explicit account of cumulative disadvantage as well as intersecting or multiple discrimination. This nudges us to reframe the issue of legal capacity away from decision-making at a particular point in time into a much deeper enquiry about disadvantage – and especially the absence of networks of inclusion and social connectedness. It is to be noted that a failure to afford an individual 'reasonable accommodation' itself amounts to discrimination (the definition of discrimination in Article 2). The main point though is that it is palpably not enough to frame equality narrowly in the context of disability. In this sense the CRPD does not so much bring out something that is peculiar to disability as it makes plain something that applies to all humanity.

Another innovative feature of the CRPD lies in the way in which it co-mingles civil and political rights with economic, social and cultural rights. The convention is concerned not only to expand human freedom but also – and very self-consciously – to put in place the conditions of that freedom. So, for example, it is no longer enough just to respond to diminished mental capability with substitute-decision making. A more substantive and structural response is now called for. This is interesting because – rhetoric to one side – it brings out the truth in the much-vaunted thesis of the interdependence of rights. It does so not by repeating ritualistic or mechanical incantations of interdependence but by tailoring social supports to enable a broader conception of personal freedom to become a reality.

Conclusion: implications for the broader human rights field

Traditional human rights thinking tends not to get beyond a fixation on power and the intersection between the individual and power. It rests on demonstrably unrealistic ideal pictures of the human condition. The disability convention shows that by inverting the normal logic and focusing first on human flourishing it is possible to craft rights to more

[35] See O. M. Arnardóttir, 'A Future of Multidimensional Disadvantage Equality?', in O. M. Arnardóttir and G. Quinn (eds.), *The UN Convention on the Rights of People with Disabilities: European and Scandinavian Perspectives* (Dordrecht: Martinus Nijhoff 2009) 41, 47–54.

self-consciously embed the conditions for human flourishing. This revolutionary step rests on a new attitude toward personhood – one that does not give primacy to cognition or rationality. People are not just formulaic 'rights-bearers'. They have dreams – big and small – and they live and thrive in communities. Rights-talk has to reach this if it is to be relevant.

The doctrinal innovations in the CRPD – intersectionality; the right to live independently and be included in the community; an expansive right to participate; a deeper theory of equality; and a more nuanced approach to economic, social and cultural rights that ties them explicitly to a freedom agenda – are all explicable once one understands this move toward a deeper conception of personhood and flourishing. These innovations can and should be translated across to existing human rights conventions.

Perhaps their portability is most easily seen if the current process for drafting a thematic convention on the rights of older people gets seriously underway.[36] Enhancing the capacity of older people to remain in charge of their own lives is beyond doubt important. Having appropriate community supports in place obviates the need for the institutionalisation of older people. Embedding a right to participate would help stitch back together the threads of social connectedness that naturally fray through time. And arranging social support to enable an active life would seem a much better use of largesse than warehousing people out of sight and out of mind. This is a revolution worth exporting not just because the technical innovations of the CRPD ratchet up doctrine but because it resolutely starts first with what it means to be human and then only secondly with the rights that can enable flourishing. It is the way that Article 12 makes this possible that marks the provision out as unexpectedly revolutionary.

I end on a broader note. There is another reason why this surprising turn towards personhood in the disability convention may well turn out to be crucial in the coming years. The USA enacted the world's first piece of legislation prohibiting the discriminatory use of genetic information: the Genetic Information Non-Discrimination Act 2008. The primary intention was to enhance public confidence in the developing science of genetics by assuring people of redress when the resulting information is misused. Similar European legislation is probably not far off. Valuable though this is, it skirts the raw edge of a much deeper problematic: how or whether to regulate the use of

---

[36] Resolution to Establish an Open Ended Working Group on Ageing, United Nations General Assembly, 65th Sess, UN Doc. A/RES/65/182 (4 February 2011).

the new genetic and other medical technology to manipulate human characteristics and design (if that be the right word) human beings. Can and should
characteristics that we currently think of as constitutive of our very identity be
screened out of our blueprint? Can and should our mental faculties be aug-
mented? Can and should more tolerable colleagues in the workplace and more
effective fighters in the army be designed? The next generation of human
rights thinkers and activists will not be able to avoid these questions. Perhaps
one important toehold in the almost inevitable slide down this nightmarish
slippery slope will be provided by the core idea of the disability convention:
that humans cannot be reduced to an essence, that we are who we are because
of our interaction in community (something that does not come pre-packaged)
and that while cognitive ability complicates our existence it does not destroy
our humanity.

Further reading

Bach, M. and Kerzner, L., 'A New Paradigm for Protecting Autonomy and the
    Right to Legal Capacity', Paper prepared for the Law Commission of
    Ontario (October 2010) 7–8, www.lco-cdo.org/disabilities/bach-kerzner.
    pdf

Cognitive Disability and Its Challenge to Moral Philosophy, E. Feder Kittay and
    L. Carlson (eds.) (Oxford: Wiley–Blackwell 2010)

Dhanda, A., 'Legal Capacity in the Disability Rights Convention: Stranglehold of the
    Past or Lodestar for the Future?' (2006–7) 34 *Syracuse Journal of International
    Law and Commerce* 429–62 at 431–2

Essential Principles: Irish Legal Capacity Law, Amnesty International Ireland, the
    Centre for Disability Law and Policy (Galway *et al.* : NUI 2012)

European Yearbook of Disability Law, Vol. 1, G. Quinn and L. Waddington (eds.)
    (Oxford: Intersentia 2009)

Flynn, E., *From Rhetoric to Action: Implementing the UN Convention on the Rights of
    People with Disabilities* (Cambridge University Press 2011)

Quinn, G., 'Personhood and Legal Capacity: Perspectives on the Paradigm Shift of
    Article 12 CRPD', Paper presented at the Conference on Disability and Legal
    Capacity under the CRPD (Boston, MA: Harvard Law School) 20 February 2010
    'Rethinking Personhood: New Directions in Legal Capacity Law and Policy',
    Lecture (Vancouver: University of British Columbia, 29 April 2011)

Report on Hearings in Relation to the Scheme of the Mental Capacity Bill, Houses
    of the Oireachtas, Joint Committee on Justice, Defence, and Equality
    (May 2012) (31/JDAE/005), www.oireachtas.ie/parliament/media/michelle/
    Mental-capacity-text-REPORT-300412.pdf

Symposium: The United Nations Convention on the Rights of Persons with Disabilities (Spring 2007) 34 *Syracuse Journal of International Law and Commerce* 2

Thematic Study on the Structure and Role of National Mechanisms for the Implementation and Monitoring of the Convention on the Rights of Persons with Disabilities, Office of the UN High Commissioner for Human Rights, Human Rights Council, 13th session (A/HRC/13/29) (22 December 2009)

UN Convention on the Rights of Persons with Disabilities – European and Scandinavian Perspectives, O. M. Arnardóttir and G. Quinn (eds.) (Dordrecht: Martinus Nijhoff 2009)

UN Convention on the Rights of Persons with Disabilities – Multidisciplinary Perspectives, J. Kumpuvuori and M. Scheinin (eds.) (Helsinki: The Centre for Human Rights of Persons with Disabilities in Finland (VIKE) 2009)

Who Gets to Decide? Right to Legal Capacity for Persons with Intellectual and Psychosocial Disabilities, Council of Europe Commissioner for Human Rights (20 February 2012)

3 The poverty of (rights) jurisprudence

Costas Douzinas

When, in 1983, I ran the first-ever human rights course in my Law School only four brave and idealistic students registered, making me almost abandon the exercise. I told these pioneers that human rights are the conscience of law, practised by a few idealistic lawyers and invoked by dissidents and rebels. How different things look today. If only thirty years ago rights were the repressed conscience of the profession, they have now become its dominant rhetoric. No law student graduates without having taken a specialist course in human rights. Human rights have crept up everywhere in the curriculum. Textbooks on human rights and contract, tort, company, crime, trade, the environment and every other part of the law's empire appear with an alarming regularity. As friends complain, all law teaching today seems to be about human rights. The dissident pioneers have become the established majority, the repressed idealism dominant consciousness, the protest ruling ideology.

'Sooner or later, every discussion of law in contemporary society seems to turn to the subject of rights' opens an influential collection on rights.[1] Liberal jurisprudence has set itself the task to explain and celebrate this amazing turnaround. 'The discourse of rights is pervasive and popular in politics, law and morality' a more recent textbook opens boldly. 'There is scarcely any position, opinion, claim, criticism or aspiration relating to social or political life that is not asserted and affirmed using the term "rights"... It is not enough to hold that a proposal will lead to an improvement in wellbeing or a reduction in suffering, unless it can also be presented as a recognition of someone's rights, preferably their human rights.'[2] According to Robert Nozick's ode to extreme liberalism: 'Individuals have rights and there are things no person or group may do to them (without violating their rights).'[3] Rights are 'side constraints', stops on the pursuit of

---

[1] A. Sarat and T. Kearns, 'Editorial Introduction', in A. Sarat and T. Kearns (eds.), *Legal Rights: Historical and Philosophical Perspectives* (University of Michigan Press 2000) 1.

[2] T. Campbell, *Rights: A Critical Introduction* (London: Routledge 2006) 3.

[3] R. Nozick, *Anarchy, State, Utopia* (Oxford: Blackwell 1974) 1.

the common good, a sentiment echoed in Ronald Dworkin's bravura statement that rights 'trump' governmental policies.[4] Finally, according to John Rawls' rather exaggerated claims, rights are the main tool and target of justice (and therefore of politics) and human rights trigger humanitarian interventions in our postmodern world.[5]

Politics, morality, the law, world order: all revolve around rights. This is a quite impressive achievement in our cynical, 'non-ideological' age. Rights are the ideology after the death of ideologies, the only ideology or 'idolatry', according to Michael Ignatieff, its apologist in chief.[6] Left and right, state and church, globalising imperialists and anti-globalisation protesters all use the language of rights. In our era of 'posts', where the 'end of history' alongside modernity, class, and 'the human' has been proclaimed (rather hastily; Francis Fukuyama, its celebrated proposer, has since admitted that reports of the death of history have been premature[7]), rights are the last universal vocation.

Has the victory and ubiquity of rights ended domination and exploitation, repression and violence? Has law and politics changed so radically in such a short period? Does the invocation of 'rights' mean that the world possesses a common horizon which, when reached, will usher in Kant's promised perpetual peace? This is a comforting idea, daily denied in news bulletins. What is perpetual about our world is the increasing wealth gap between the metropolitan lands and the rest of the world, the yawning chasm in income and chances between the rich and the poor, the mushrooming and strictly policed walls dividing the North from the South, the comfortable middle classes from the 'underclass' of immigrants, refugees and undesirables, those pockets of 'third world' in the midst of the first. If anything, our world looks increasingly more hostile and dangerous. If human rights have triumphed in the world, their victory is drowned in disaster.[8]

This chapter examines the ways in which liberal jurisprudence has dealt with the ascendancy of human rights. Its main exponents have tried to

---

[4] R. Dworkin, *Taking Rights Seriously* (London: Duckworth 1977) xi, 90–4.
[5] J. Rawls, *A Theory of Justice* (Oxford University Press 1972); *The Law of Peoples* (Cambridge, MA: Harvard University Press 1999).
[6] M. Ignatieff, *Human Rights as Politics and Idolatry* (Princeton University Press 2001).
[7] F. Fukuyama, 'After Neoconservatism', *New York Times*, February 19, 2006; 'Why Shouldn't I Change my Mind?', *Los Angeles Times*, April 9, 2006.
[8] C. Douzinas, *The End of Human Rights* (Oxford, Hart 2000) Ch 1.

develop rational justifications for the discourse of rights with limited interest in their practice. As a result, we don't learn much about actual rights by reading liberal jurisprudence, but we learn a lot about its epistemological and ideological priorities. This is an anatomy of rights jurisprudence.

Jurisprudential treatises often use the terms 'rights' and 'human rights' interchangeably. This strange equation helps us understand the provenance of the debate. Samuel Moyn and other historians have recently argued that human rights emerged in the late twentieth century as a response to developments of the period, from the Cold War and decolonisation to the counter-cultural rebellion of the 1960s and its domestication.[9] This revisionist historiography has showed that human rights as a set of legal principles and remedies was born alongside the United Nations and was ambiguously and reluctantly promoted by international legal agreements and remedies. Human rights started acquiring their current caché as late as the 1970s.

Already at that point, John Rawls, Ronald Dworkin and Robert Nozick among others had started developing a jurisprudence of rights which had no place for human rights. In a 1978 political theory bibliography of rights 'next to no authors treated "human rights" as such'.[10] Without missing a beat, however, this fledgling enterprise was transferred from rights to human rights in the 1980s, albeit without much discussion of the process out of which these human rights had emerged.[11] The historical, theoretical and political differences between the two terms and practices were either overlooked or confined to footnotes. This 'inflationary' approach was further exaggerated by the growing tendency of philosophers to present rights as the main component of morality *tout court*. Unlike lawyers who struggle with the contradictions and inconsistencies of the human rights record, moral philosophy seems obsessed with the idea of purifying (human) rights

---

[9] S. Moyn, *The Last Utopia: Human Rights in History* (Cambridge, MA: Harvard University Press 2010); S.-L. Hoffman (ed.), *Human Rights in the Twentieth Century* (Cambridge University Press 2011); M. Mazower, *No Enchanted Place* (Princeton University Press 2009).

[10] Moyn *The Last Utopia*, 215.

[11] Moyn reports that Dworkin introduced the phrase 'human rights' in 1977 'as if he had always been talking about them. When invited by the Colombia University . . . to address the topic . . . Dworkin gave a lecture entitled "Human Rights" but simply rehearsed his analysis of rights as so-called moral trumps', *The Last Utopia* 216. Rawls does not mention human rights in his *Theory of Justice* but uses them extensively in *The Law of Peoples*. Gewirth uses the same arguments for rights in his *Reason and Morality* (University of Chicago Press 1978) and for human rights in *Human Rights: Essays in Justification and Application* (University of Chicago Press 1982).

of empirical 'flaws' and legalistic prevarications. We will examine this jurisprudential tendency through a reading of the work on human rights of two major analytical philosophers, Alan Gewirth and James Griffin.[12]

'There are scarcely any accepted criteria, even among philosophers, for when the term [human rights] is used correctly and when incorrectly. The language of human rights has become seriously debased', Griffin concludes in *Human Rights* (Gr, 199). For Gewirth too, philosophers agree 'in part on the scope and content' of rights but attempts to establish the existence or justification of rights have failed (G, 43).[13] Admitting the failure of moral philosophy to develop a satisfactory theory, Gewirth and Griffin set out to discover a rational foundation for human rights. Unless the philosopher can show that they have 'sound reasons', right claims become 'vocal ejaculations' or 'propagandistic manipulations' (Gr, 45). For Griffin, moral philosophers have devoted little attention 'to substantive arguments that try to prove or justify that persons have rights other than those grounded in positive law. Such arguments would indicate the criteria for there being human rights, including their scope and or content, and would undertake to show why these criteria are correct or justified' (Gr, 41). Despite their central role in moral and political life, human rights have far too little content.

These are apparently serious problems. Whether they have any significance for campaigners, dissidents and lawyers using the rights language in political and legal struggles is an altogether different issue. Whatever philosophers think, human rights have an institutional existence in treaties, bills of rights and courts, and play a central role in popular struggles and campaigns. The term is routinely used by people who have nothing in common. As the Catholic theologian and key draftsman of the Universal Declaration Jacques Maritain put it, 'we can all agree about rights on condition no one asks why'.[14] Normative jurisprudence cannot go down this route, however, because it smacks too much of its great enemies, pragmatism, realism and deconstruction promoted by the likes of Richard Rorty and critical legal studies (Gr, 283, n. 36). Rorty is scathing

---

[12] Gewirth, *Human Rights*; J. Griffin, *On Human Rights* (Oxford University Press 2008). Page references to Gewirth's book in the text take the form (G, 00); to Griffin's (Gr, 00). A strong defence of Gewirth's argument is found in D. Beyleveld, *The Dialectical Necessity of Morality* (University of Chicago Press 1991).

[13] Gewirth dismisses Nozick, Marx, Dworkin and Rawls peremptorily because they all fail to develop a internally consistent moral justification for rights, *Human Rights* 43–5. Griffin attacks the same philosophers for slightly different reasons, *On Human Rights* 20–8.

[14] Quoted in M. A. Glendon, *A World Made New* (New York: Random House 2001) 77.

about the role of rational justifications and prefers instead a 'sentimental education' of rights.[15] Critical legal studies have shown in great detail how moral justifications often disguise power asymmetries and hierarchies.[16]

Gewirth and Griffin hope to save rights from critics, pragmatists and historians and from the mistakes of their peers. Both ground rights on similar conceptions of personhood; both come up with similar lists of rights, although their methods differ. Their human rights treatises are a good example of the strengths and weaknesses of normative jurisprudence.

Rights inflation

Alan Gewirth starts from two widely shared premises. He accepts the rhetorical claim that human rights belong equally to all irrespective of place or time simply because we are human. For Gewirth, as Duncan Ivison puts it, 'if a particular right exists (i.e. of which a morally valid justification can be given), then it must always have existed'.[17] Secondly, human rights are moral rights, indeed the core case of morality. Rights belong to all humans because they are justified by a universally valid moral principle. The job of moral philosophy is therefore to discover or construct such a principle.

This is a good instance of the 'inflationary' theory of human rights. Gewirth identifies universal morality with human rights and equates human rights with rights *tout court*. 'For human rights to exist there must be valid moral criteria or principles that justify that all humans, qua humans, have the rights and hence also the correlative duties. Human rights ... are universal moral rights' (G, 42). The assertion is highly problematic. Natural or human rights did not 'exist' in an enforceable and therefore meaningful way before the eighteenth-century century revolutions. The rhetorical mention of the 'rights of man' in the revolutionary declarations was closely connected with French and American historical conditions and ideological priorities. The contingent character of the emergence of human rights is refuted however through the introduction of the moral axiom. The bulk of the argument therefore must try to unearth or

---

[15] R. Rorty, 'Human Rights, Rationality and Sentimentality', in S. Shute and S. Hurley (eds.), *On Human Rights* (New York: Basic Books 1993).

[16] C. Douzinas and A. Gearey, *Critical Jurisprudence* (Oxford: Hart 2005).

[17] D. Ivison, *Rights* (Stocksfield: Acumen 2008) 30.

construct a moral foundation of rights, which will determine their scope and content.

Gewirth adopts the standard Hohfeldian classification of rights. Human rights are 'entirely or mainly' claim-rights. Claim-rights are realised through the correlative duties of others parasitically created on the back of rights. A right gives a power to its holder by binding the corresponding duty-bearer(s). A right exists when someone can make morally justified and effective demands on others. The right to free speech, for example, imposes duties on those who could restrict its operation ('Congress', in the iconic statement of the First Amendment, 'shall pass no law abridging' the freedom of expression of individuals). For Gewirth, universal human rights are distinct from the more specific 'legal, prudential and intellectual' rights. 'If the existence or having of human rights depended on [legal] recognition, it would follow that prior to, or independent of, these positive enactments no human rights existed' (G, 42).

What kind of moral principle could justify rights in such an ahistorical way? Effective demands on others are created by commandments and rules and are enforced by laws and institutions. Positive law, whether domestic or international, is historically specific and conditioned by the balance of forces and ideological priorities of time and place. Legal rights cannot pass the muster of moral universality. The argument turns therefore on the distinction between moral, legal and human rights. Can universal moral (or human) rights exist historically 'prior' to or independently of their enforcement? The answer confuses somewhat moral justification and institutional setting, universal morality and particular legalities. Claim-rights depend on the simultaneous creation of right-holders and duty-bearers; individual powers intimately rely on the duties of others created, as Gewirth has to admit, by 'institutional, especially governmental, rules'. 'Governmental rules' are laws. The argument that moral/human rights are different from legal rights was introduced a couple of paragraphs before this admission of their intimate reliance on law. Accepting that human rights depend, indeed are created by rules, including of the legal variety, undermines the claim that a valid moral principle justifying the universal applicability of rights exists.

Rights depend on enforceable rules. Rules come into existence in particular historical and institutional contexts. Many cultures and languages did not develop a term for rights until relatively recently. Greek and Roman law did not have legal rights. 'The concept lacks any means of expression in

Hebrew, Greek, Latin and Arabic, classical or medieval, before about 1400, let alone Old English, or in Japanese even as late as the mid-nineteenth century'[18] and Chinese well into the twentieth. In Europe, legal rights emerged as a result of rules initially protecting property. Gewirth accepts that the term 'right' arose towards the end of the Middle Ages but claims that the absence of the term does not mean that the behaviour it covers did not exist. Most schools of moral philosophy disagree. For Onora O'Neill, 'unless obligation-holders are identifiable by right-holders, claims to have rights amount only to rhetoric: nothing can be claimed, waived or enforced if it is indeterminate where the claim should be lodged, for whom it may be waived or on whom it could be enforced'.[19] Raymond Geuss takes a stronger position. A right 'exists' if there is a mechanism to enforce it and adds that this mechanism must be 'backed up by an effective method of implementa- tion'.[20] As Alasdair MacIntyre puts it, at his sarcastic best, when rules are absent, making a claim of right is like offering a cheque in a society that does not recognise money.[21] If such rules don't exist, legal or human rights (in Gewirth's or any other sense) do not exist either. Indeed a main advant- age of rights for liberals is that the remedies in case of non-compliance are initiated by the right-holder herself thus giving the individual an additional significant power.[22] This is, then, Gewirth's paradox: human rights are both universal and dependent on (legal) rules. If they are universal they cannot vary according to historical differentiations; if they are created by rules, they cannot be universal.

Let us turn to the moral justification. Human rights promote personhood or 'normative agency' by protecting the 'goods' of freedom and well-being. The steps of the syllogism look compelling. Since I desire the purposes of my actions, they are 'good' for me. Similarly, the pre-conditions of action are necessary 'goods' for me. These pre-conditions are freedom and well-being; I must 'logically hold' therefore that I have a right to them. Kantianism then kicks in. I must equally accept that all purposive agents have rights to freedom and well-being. *Ergo* human rights and the corresponding duties exist and are mandatory because they are logically the necessary conditions of self-interested action. The rational egotist will be propelled forward at

---

[18] A. MacIntyre, *After Virtue* (London: Duckworth 1989) 67.

[19] O. O'Neill, *Towards Justice and Virtue: A Constructive Account of Practical Reasoning* (Cambridge University Press 1996) 129.

[20] R. Geuss, *History and Illusion in Politics* (Cambridge University Press 2001) 146.

[21] *Ibid.*, 65.   [22] Campbell, *Rights* 2–5.

each stage of the argument by the principle of non-contradiction. But the causal links between good, goods, rights and human rights are rather tenuous.

The moral foundation thus identified determines which rights enter the canonical list. They are defined in the negative and belong to three types: basic, 'non-subtractive' and 'additive'. Basic goods/rights are violated when someone is killed, starved or terrorised. Non-subtractive rights are violated when someone is lied to, cheated, defamed or suffers broken promises. Finally, additive goods suffer when a person's self-esteem is attacked, he or she is denied education, is discriminated against, or when the development of virtues is hindered (G, 56). When someone violates these rights, he is morally wrong and contradicts himself since all morally wrong actions are rationally unjustifiable (G, 57).

Such basic rights include education and sustenance for the starving. Gewirth's *The Community of Rights*, which concentrates on the USA because 'the American experience can be taken to be broadly representative of many other Western countries', extends the minimum welfare entitlements of the poorest to child-care, minimum property and public sector employment.[23] They too derive from the generic rights to freedom and well-being. Gewirth believes that welfare benefits turn into human rights because rational egotists view them as rationally necessary. This well-meaning reasoning is historically complacent and politically naïve. It neglects the fact that throughout history rich individuals and powerful communities have rejected such an extension of rights. Attempts by the oppressed and dominated to assert and fight for rights, the main way through which the scope and reach of rights has grown, are dismissed as too adversarial.[24] It appears that the rational egotist is either too egotistic to care for re-distribution in favour of the poor or too rational to place counter-intuitive logic ahead of her interests. Furthermore, the emphasis on the community of citizenship excludes from consideration the one area where human rights have made a difference. Documented and *sans papiers* immigrants, refugees and aliens receive minimum protection through human, not citizenship rights. A community of rights based on the calculations of rational egotists tends to be ethnically and politically closed.

James Griffin warns that 'we have constantly to remind ourselves of the destructive modern tendency to turn all important matters into matters of

---

[23] A. Gewirth, *The Community of Rights* (Oxford University Press 1996) 111.   [24] *Ibid.*, 122.

rights, especially human rights' (Gr, 95). Gewirth's rights inflation is typical of the tendency. His 'human rights' are a compilation of standard moral norms with minimal welfare additions. Rational morality and human rights are identical in a cyclical way: (human) rights are universal; morality is universal; therefore (human) rights equal morality. And yet every step in the syllogism is problematic. 'I desire x' is quite distinct from the conclusion 'x is good' and 'I have a right to x'. A right may be universalisable, a desire or need is not, this side of a communist society. Eliding desire with rights or the 'good' with my 'goods' is the royal road to relativism. Gewirth could retort that his objects of desire address the most general goods, those of freedom and well-being. But precisely because they are so general they can facilitate all kinds of inflationary individuation and specification. The problem is not so much with the nature of desires that are to be turned into goods/rights but with the process itself. Desire is insatiable, it never stops once its immediate object is achieved. This is the reason why turning 'I desire x' into 'I have a right to x' has been the dominant ideology of neoliberalism and consumer culture.[25]

The same happens when the good, doing the right thing, becomes 'goods'. Goods are objects of individual desire, possessions and triggers of imaginary identifications. Acting the right way has been replaced by a bunch of rights. This is the culmination of what Alasdair MacIntyre has called the 'moral catastrophe' of modernity.[26] The deepening tear in the social fabric, opened by selfish individualism, is being filled by proliferating individual rights. The sliding of the moral good into individual rights empties the self of moral resources. When the organic bonds of community, civility and religion retreat, only external constraints can limit insatiable egotism. As John Kleinig puts it, '[w]here people do love and care for each other, there is no need for rights-*talk*, since what is due to the other will be encompassed within the loving or caring relationship'.[27] A society where individual rights with their adversarial culture have become the main moral source can survive only with the help of criminal law, the police force and extensive surveillance.

The philosophical restraints are harder to pin down. Gewirth realises that his universalism can easily slide into its opposite. Not all desires can become rights, he warns, nor can all goods be good. Rights cannot refer to

---

[25] Douzinas, *The End of Human Rights* Chs 11 and 14.

[26] MacIntyre, *After Virtue* Chs 5 and 6.

[27] J. Kleinig, 'Human Rights, Legal Rights and Social Change', in E. Kamenka and A. Ehr-Soon Tay, *Human Rights* (New York: St Martin's Press 1978) 46. (Emphasis in original.)

'unfounded desires but to truly grounded requirements of agency, the indispensable conditions that all agents must accept as necessary for action' (G, 48). What desires are unfounded, which conditions indispensable? Gewirth sets the bar of admissible desires high by arguing that a Florida vacation, for example, is not such a necessity. But when desire or private 'goods' have become the ground of rights, only the self can decide if they are indispensable or not. If a Florida vacation is necessary to get over some deeply traumatic association, it is indispensable. Conscious and unconscious desires are the opposite of universal goods. Their translation into rights does not lead to a common morality but to social fragmentation. The same opt-out clause appears in the context of the empirical preconditions of normative action. A 'right to x' means that one can 'have or do x'. For Gewirth, the 'ought' includes the 'can', 'only if the capability in question is correctly interpreted'. The right to property, for example, 'correctly interpreted' does not include the capacity to have property.

Let us conclude on this point. For the liberal philosophy of personhood, human rights belong to 'normal' people. The few problem cases, such as children or the mentally ill, will be decided in such a way that their 'generic rights must be proportionate to their ability to exercise them'. But this is a statement of, not an answer to, the problem of 'normality'. The 'correct interpretation' of the capacity for rational action has been and still is a strategy used to exclude people.[28] As Joanna Bourke details, women, blacks, slaves and ethnic minorities have been consistently treated as subhuman because irrational, unintelligent or uncivilised.[29] Today immigrants, refugees and the poor are outside the pale of humanity. A long contemplation on the centrality of personhood ends where it began: persons have rights and rights support persons. It is a 'pure' theory of rights that stays well clear of any empirical matter that could disrupt the perfect philosophical closure.

Rights deflation

For Gewirth, a rational agent accepts, on pain of self-contradiction, that the preconditions of his action are good for him and that these goods are

---

[28] C. Douzinas, *Human Rights and Empire* (London: Routledge 2007).
[29] J. Bourke, *What it Means to be Human* (London: Virago 2011). For the race politics of rights, see E. Darian-Smith, *Religion, Race, Rights* (Oxford: Hart 2010).

universally applicable human rights. Rights support the actions of self-interested egotists. His achievement is to turn the most common critique of rights for individualism and selfishness into their moral foundation. Griffin, too, bases human rights on personhood and reaches similar conclusions. His methodology, however, differs. He concentrates on human rights instead of rights in general. His approach combines institutions and philosophy, 'bottom up' and 'top down' parts. Starting from the routine usage of human rights, the philosopher 'resorts' or ascends to 'higher principles' 'to explain their moral weight ... and to resolve conflicts between them' (Gr, 29). The demotic approach uses international treaties, legal documents and the ordinary speech of 'actually existing' human rights while the philosophical starts from the metaphysics of personhood; the two meet half-way, producing a kind of dialectical synthesis.

While for Gewirth morality must find a rational justification in the teleology of prudential egotism, Griffin believes, in semi-Hegelian fashion, that reason unravels in world history, including the history of human rights. He concludes that the list of rights endorsed by the West, suitably corrected, promotes the principles of personhood. This is a well-known philosophy of history. Humanity is moving inexorably towards its Western destiny. The final stage has not been reached yet by 'some of the tribal societies of the Middle East [which] are not yet ripe for freedom' (tell that to the rebels of Tunis, Cairo, Syria or Bahrain). On the other hand, it would be wrong 'to give up the [Western] moral point of view, as we understand it, in which our idea of human rights' is founded (tell that to the occupiers of Wall Street or the City of London) (Gr, 25–7).

Again the unearthed principle determines the content of rights. 'Human rights have to do with a certain minimum – the minimum necessary for human agency' (Gr, 187). Minimum 'normative agency' includes deliberation, assessment, choice and action. A level of information and education and a bare 'minimum provision of resources and capabilities ... something more than physical survival' are part of the minimum but not much more (Gr, 33). 'We value our human existence, more than happiness' Griffin concludes; human rights are 'protections of this standing'. This rather stringent principle is as abstract as anything Griffin criticises in Hume, Kant or Rawls. A mitigating clause, inelegantly called 'practicalities', is therefore immediately added: practicalities allow features of human nature and of society as 'second nature' to be added to the personhood principle, helping determine the exact content of rights. They introduce 'empirical

information' (therefore historical variability) about the limits of 'understanding and motivation'; improbably however they are universal, 'not
tied to a particular time and place'. These practicalities are sufficiently
specific to turn free speech or property into human rights but not free
press or equality (Gr, 37–9).

It follows that rights promote not 'human *good* or *flourishing*, but merely
what is needed for human *status*' (Gr, 34, emphasis mine). They protect that
'somewhat austere state, a characteristically human life'. This is indeed an
austere definition of self, almost Scrooge-like for anyone who does not
belong to the ranks of the well-off middle classes. For the many millions for
whom the struggle for sheer survival is the only opportunity for exercising
'normative agency', the exalted principles of personhood offer basic subsistence only. Rights allow us to pursue 'our conception of worthwhile life'
(Gr, 34) or to pursue happiness. But we have no right to a worthwhile life, no
right to happiness. The reason for this is clear. Liberty 'can be infringed only
by another agent. If our options are narrowed by acts of nature or *large-
scale economic or social events* not under human control, no one's liberty is
infringed' (Gr, 161, emphasis mine). The 'logical' consequences of this
axiomatic position are clear. Liberty is clearly understood and, correctly
interpreted, must be protected. The 'many' principles of equality (equal
respect, fairness, egalitarianism) on the other hand can be 'easily confused'.
Poor confused equality should be excluded therefore from the list of rights
(Gr, 39). Not even an obligation to 'ensure equal opportunity in the realization of one's conception' exists (Gr, 162).

But the opposite is true. The essence of equality is simple and easily
understood. Everyone counts as one and none as more than one. What
Griffin considers its 'confused' applications are the result of the age-long
attempt to dilute this simple principle. Freedom on the other hand has
always been a much more ambiguous and contested concept. Take
Griffin's example of unacceptable restriction on autonomy: a family
removing its offspring to the bible-belt to stop them from pursuing the
vocation and consolations of philosophy.[30] One does not need to follow the
news closely to know that the current economic and political orthodoxy,
which has imposed radical austerity all over the world and is destroying the

---

[30] The Greek Stoics withdrew from public life precisely in order to practise philosophy. Only
this way they reached *ataraxia* or imperturbability, the precondition of the philosophical
vocation. Perhaps being prevented from studying certain types of philosophy might
contribute to the business of thinking.

welfare state, is a much more radical deprivation of agency and life chances than anything stroppy parents can do. The problems faced by thousands of single parents, for example, unable to provide above bare subsistence to their children are of little concern.

We don't have to search for the reasons for this major omission. Sociology, economics, psychology and the rest of social science have consistently argued that domination (lack of freedom) and oppression (deprivation of well-being) result from the operation of structure and system and not from the singular actions of 'evil' people. The gravest deprivations and constraints on liberty are a consequence of the obscene inequalities created by these 'large-scale economic or social structures', which Griffin excludes from human rights consideration. Human rights are limited to the prevention of physical forms of violence and degradation while the systemic pressures of capitalism and nationalism are largely exempted from their protective umbrella. One could imagine however a social system in which most 'agentic' deprivations of liberty have been removed, but still people are subjected to radical domination and exploitation. The catastrophic effect of aggressive neoliberalism on both liberty and equality are clear to most people but are not evident to the philosophical high table (where many examples are located). This is a serious impoverishment of the human rights potential. Human rights become the late-capitalism ideology of the middle classes.

If we now move to Griffin's list of rights, the claims of reason provide a severe filter for 'actually existing' rights. Only the most basic and formal preconditions of agency pass the muster of moral reason and become worthy rights. For Griffin, the 'confused' status of equality has led to the inclusion of various dubious items in the Universal Declaration of Human Rights (UDHR) and other legal documents. As was to be expected, these 'confused' rights are social and economic. The list is long. Article 25 of the UDHR protects a person's 'standard of living adequate for his and his family's well-being' instead of 'a certain minimum level of well being'; similarly, 'well-being' is an over-generous term covering from the 'lowest to the highest' and must be rationed. It is confused to include the right to 'paid holidays', to 'distributive justice' to 'equal pay for equal work' (Article 23.2 UDHR) or to 'just and favourable remuneration' (Article 23.3 UDHR). The 'right to work' is unacceptable because advanced societies 'are nearing conditions in which a job will not be, even for a large proportion of the population, the necessary means to the end [of material survival]' (*sic*)[31] (Gr, 207). Perhaps this is true within the environs of Oxford Colleges, but not in the Oxford high street. Finally, 'group rights' do not exist because no good moral argument can be found for them. Or, perhaps because those who exercise them challenge oppressions and exploitation on which 'normative agency' thrives. An extension of 'practicalities' to the lives of ordinary people would perhaps undermine the claim to rational universality. Here we reach the limits of the dialectical 'bottom up–top down' approach. Freedom and normative agency trump equality and well-being.

Jurisprudence as ideology

Have Gewirth and Griffin succeeded in saving the 'debased' philosophical coinage of rights? Their quest is based on two premises. First, if morality and rights are rational they are, like the rules of arithmetic, the same for everyone. Secondly, if moral rules and rights are universally valid they are mandatory. These are extravagant claims. The morality of modernity inherited the bulk of its rules from Christianity and adjusted them to accommodate the primacy of the individual. Released from Christian teleology and social hierarchy, the individual has been proclaimed sovereign over his moral universe. But these largely inherited moral rules, deprived of sociological grounding, must be glossed in new shiny colours. Reason was called in to provide the missing link between moral rules and the limited sources of normativity in modernity. The attempt to prove the rational foundation of morality and the accompanying belief that such a proof would create an obligation to obey its rules has become an obsession for liberal jurisprudence and has seriously undermined its utility. Even if some really clever philosopher were to come up with a generally acceptable rational foundation for rights, it would still not generate moral obligations. This is a basic philosophical recognition from Socrates and Phaedra to Hegel and Kierkegaard. Philosophy has taken fully on board Ovid's tragic admission *video meliora proboque: deteriora sequor* (I know the good and approve it; but I follow evil).[32] No rational justification of morality and

---

[31] This does not undermine the wider point that a legal right to work is an unattainable ideal in a market society. Griffin attacks the moral argument for introducing a right to work. He is uninterested in its legal or empirical non-existence and the ideological role it plays in human rights lists.

[32] Ovid, *Metamorphoses* (Oxford Paperbacks 2008) VII, 20.

no moral foundation of rights can account for the way in which rights proliferate at the same rate as their violation.

Philosophical disputations and theoretical debates acquire importance beyond their immediate peer group when they enter public consciousness and condition the *zeitgeist* of an age. Ideas must be publicised, discussed, adjusted to the interests and ideologies of powerful groups before they are eventually adopted as a dominant ideology. Theoretical concepts become ideologically hegemonic when embedded in 'unreflective social practices'.[33] This means that the philosophical discussion of morality and rights must be accompanied by an examination of their practical applications. Philosophy needs the insights of sociology and the practices of law to become real. To this extent, Griffin's methodology is sociologically and historically more propitious than Gewirth's. A dose of positivism is necessary when discussing human rights. But this positivism-lite ends with the same list of human rights as Gewirth, who does not bother with legal niceties. Their main encounter with reality appears in their discussion of their ideal lists of rights.

Gewirth and Griffin use the philosophical analysis to censor and exclude what legal and political practice has already accepted. Gewirth's inflationary tendency becomes Griffin's deflation of rights. In both cases, when the real (actually existing human rights) clashes with the rational (the normative claims of personhood) the real loses out. Moral philosophy examines human conduct. It cannot claim that it is a second-order meta-ethics indifferent to the moral and legal rules and rights that are part of life. The use of a limited conception of personhood to exclude the demands of equality that both legal practice, in its messy way, has developed and moral conduct accepts is highly problematic. The elasticity of human rights placed on a spectrum between the whole of morality and liberal freedoms shows jurisprudence as a highly ideological practice. We can identify the ideological element in their methodology, the most neutral-sounding part of the theories. Gewirth calls his methodology 'prudential' and 'dialectical'. I can only accept human rights if grounded on my own interests (my desires are my 'goods') and on the universality of reason (everyone else desires what I do). 'Normative necessity' is based on the self-interest and rationality of personhood. Or, as Gewirth puts it, his theory is 'deontological' and 'teleological'. Its mandatory aspect is based on the power of reason and the fear of inconsistency. The rational is not real, as in Hegel, but morally obligatory.

---

[33] I. Shapiro, *The Evolution of Rights in Liberal Theory* (Cambridge University Press 1986) 5.

But the very emergence of human rights shows this to be wrong. Their creation was an admission that moral rules, legal rights and reason are not adequate normative resources. The 'teleological' part, on the other hand, is based on the claim that rights are good for the self because they help realise his desires. Self-interest and reason should tell me that rights are necessary and universal. In this sense, the teleology of self-interest becomes the deontology of rights. This identification of deontology and teleology shows that the sharp distinction between rights and utilitarianism liberal jurisprudence draws is largely superficial. When rights and utility clash in the calculations of individuals or power-holders, reasoned morality cannot decide the dispute. Rights and utility are two ways of promoting the centrality of self-interest. Their strong separation may belong to jurisprudence seminars but it does not belong to real life.

We do not need long philosophical treatises on the meaning of personhood to know that economic and social rights are not particularly welcome to liberals. Nor do we need sophisticated analyses to learn that subjectivity (or personhood) is the metaphysical foundation of liberalism. The subject of rights is a being whose rationality, motivation and (self-) reflection follows the protocols and procedures of normative philosophy (she is fully aware of her purposes or 'goods' and consciously refrains from self-contradiction). She plans her action and acts with clear purposes and intentions (the teleology of individualism) following consistent normative commitments and aspirations (its deontology). A typical Cartesian subject, she has power over her will because she has privileged access to the contents of her mind.[34] Transferred to morality, this conception of personhood becomes the basis of methodological and moral individualism: society exists for the promotion of individual purposes. Individuals are the primary unit of moral concern; morality is rights-based and duties derive from rights.

Phenomenology, hermeneutics, structuralism, anthropology and psychoanalysis have convincingly showed the many dimensions of reality irreducibly antithetical to the subject's mastery. Psychoanalysis explains that a level of mental life outside consciousness affects us uncontrollably. The various 'hermeneutics of suspicion' show how social relations taken as natural or normal are the surface only of deeper structures of domination or exploitation. Feminism, critical race theory, queer theory attack the belief in the power of reason and emphasise the centrality of body,

---

[34] C. Douzinas, *The End of Human Rights* Chs 6 and 7.

emotions, gender and sexuality in our identity and destiny. Against the Cartesian project, Hegel's claim of access to absolute knowledge or liberal possessive individualism, human knowledge and power encounter radical limits. Our mental life and beliefs are conditioned by powers and forces outside our control. As a result, the subject is now approached as fragmented rather than whole, vulnerable rather than masterful, its unity dissolved in multiple 'subject positions'.

Following this deconstruction of human omnipotence, the 'person' of rights must be seen as a mask only (as its Latin etymology indicates), a cipher for the empirical individual. 'Humanity' is a virtual category, being 'human' an abstract predication for the real self. The 'I want' of the subject of jurisprudence becomes 'I can' only if a series of empirical preconditions external to the legal speech-act are met. The distance between normative capacity and real-life achievement is the same as that between the recognition of the right to property and the ability of a nurse to buy a flat in central London. In a documentary about the plight of undocumented or *sans papiers* immigrants living an underground life in London Jami, who sleeps rough in parks, addresses people like us who, from our comfortable homes, keep proclaiming 'Human rights, human rights': 'What's the difference between me and them? They are human like me. People like me have two hands, two eyes and two legs. What's the difference between me and them? Human rights, human rights. But where are the human rights for the asylum seekers?'[35] If, as liberal philosophy claims, human rights belong to humans on account of their bare humanity and not of membership of smaller categories such as nation, state or class, Jami and his friends should have at least the minimum consolations of humanity. They have no 'human' rights. Jami's indictment shows that human rights do not 'belong' to humans; they construct humans on a spectrum between full humanity, lesser humanity and the inhuman.

Notes towards a critical jurisprudence of rights

Let us, finally, sketch how a critical ontology and morality of rights might look. Legal rights were creations of early modernity; they are the basic

---

[35] J. Domokos and D. Taylor, 'Asylum Seekers: Britain's Shadow People' 16 March 2009, www.guardian.co.uk/uk/video/2009/mar/16/asylum-seekers-refused-britain.

building blocks of Western law. Rights are individual entitlements but their action is relational, realised through the acts or omissions of others. A property right, the first and still the model right, gives exclusive use and enjoyment of an object to its owner by excluding all others. But property offers more. Only when we depart neo-Kantian jurisprudence in the direction of Hegel that the full contribution of rights emerges. When I take possession of an object, I externalise myself by placing my will onto that object and through it into the world. Property brings me into contact with others and becomes a necessary moment in the dialectics of identity. Desiring the object and taking hold of it is a way of negotiating my desire for (the recognition of) others. Here the law comes in. The simple possession of an object is always under threat. Property becomes safe only through the operation of law. Property rights give legal recognition to the fact of possession. Others now acknowledge my ownership on condition that I acknowledge theirs. Property rights lead to a form of interpersonal recognition in which others respect me through the incarnation of my will in the object protected by law.

Property and legal rights more generally give the self recognition for qualities he shares with others. When I say to a policeman or an employer 'you cannot do this, it is against my rights', I implicitly make three related claims. First, in a rule of law system the law creates and protects equal rights for all and does not allow discrimination against some. Secondly, legal rights make me worthy of respect; they confirm that, like all others, I have free will, moral autonomy and responsibility. Finally, legal recognition gives me self-respect, when I realise that I too am capable of moral action and that, like others, I am an end in myself. Human dignity, respect for others and self-respect are linked with the ability to make moral decisions and to raise legal claims. Legal rights are the way through which I acquire the recognition given to everyone and anyone, irrespective of individual characteristics.

This minimum recognition of abstract humanity is the great achievement of our legal civilisation. But it remains rudimentary and defective. Property and poverty offer a good example of the problem. The recognition offered by the abstract right to property, by the potential to hold property, is clearly inadequate. As Anatole France put it, the law, in its majestic equality, forbids the rich as well as the poor to sleep under bridges, to beg in the streets, and to steal bread. While the poor have equal formal rights and the dignity legal recognition potentially offers, they cannot realise them.

Caught between law's recognition of abstract equality and its indifference towards material inequality and concrete needs, the poor are the best examples of the failings of legal rights as a tool of social justice, something that Hegel fully acknowledged in his theory of *Notrecht* – unlike Kant and his followers.[36]

The law tries to remedy the failings of legal rights through the creation of citizenship rights. Legal rights give recognition to the sameness of humanity, to the attributes that make us all similar. Civil and political rights extend this recognition to bodily integrity and movement and political participation. Finally, social and economic rights acknowledge the differences that give concrete identity to selves and promise a minimum level of resource in order to turn formal rights into material entitlements. But these prerequisites of social justice remain rhetorical statements of aspiration rather than justiciable claims. The 'ought' of the right does not include the 'can' of its realisation. The dominant socio-economic system is largely indifferent to poverty or wealth and income inequalities. Extreme material differentiation (which has now reached epic proportions) and poverty are the driving forces of capitalism as the sweatshops of China and the slums in major cities attest.

A similar analysis applies to the politics identity rights promote. Gender, race or sexuality, the differentiating characteristics that socio-economic rights add to the abstract profile of the legal person, bring her closer to reality. The distance between abstract human nature and concrete characteristics justifies the demand for differential treatment, which respects the specific aspects of identity. But even when group claims are accepted, the individual struggle for recognition is not over. In the continuous conversation with other people and institutions that constructs our identity, rights fall short. It may recognise aspects of my gender, sexuality or ethnicity; it may ban discrimination on these grounds. These are major achievements but their scope is necessarily limited. The law classifies people according to universal categories and general concepts. Generic recognition often becomes misrecognition. Discrimination law propagates a monolithic image of race, for example, that all people of colour are expected to possess. As Tim Murphy puts it, a paradox operates here: 'Anti-discrimination regimes (an end to distinctions!) proliferate the use/visibility of distinctions including in the area of "forbidden" categories – race, sexual orientation,

---

[36] D. Losurdo, *Hegel and the Freedom of Moderns* (Durham, NC: Duke University Press 2004) Ch VII.

age, etc. – "celebrations of difference" (of course). The thematisation and valorisation of diversity – what quickly becomes identity politics – amounts to a construction of identity which resides in difference.'[37] Concrete identities on the other hand are constructed through the contingent and highly mutable combination of many positions, only some of which are generalisable and shared with others. Human rights attempt to stop discrimination against women or gays, but they do not give full recognition to this unique woman or gay unless it takes full account of the long history of material and cultural deprivation that being 'different', 'abnormal', 'not fully human' has inflicted on its victims. This is the reason why the success of anti-discrimination legislation has been so limited despite good intentions. Power and rights appear to be closely linked.

Let us move briefly to morals. As Tom Campbell concludes his 'democratic positivist' theory of rights, the statement 'I have a right to x' and 'it is right to do x' (in one of the various ways that being or doing right can be defined) have become virtually interchangeable. The identification is explained by something called the 'generalisation thesis': rights are created by rules which are, in turn, moral generalisations of what is usually right to do. Such rules are predominantly legal but they include the 'non-legal societal' variety.[38] But rights and right do not coincide. On the contrary, a social morality of individual rights is the morality of exit from ethics. Premodern secular and Christian ethics had a strong sense of the good grounded on the nature of people and communities and a thick set of interpersonal relations. Similarly, Hegelian philosophy built its concept of right out of social relations, reciprocal respect and esteem and the struggle for recognition besides the more formal legal protocols and rights. The contemporary proliferation of rights, however, has swallowed moral entities associated with ethics, such as duty, responsibility and care.

It was Kant who famously reversed the order between good and right: the ancient priority of the good from which moral (and legal) commands flowed, was an example of 'heteronomy' from which the Enlightenment emancipated man. In modernity, the right, what is right according to the law, takes precedence and determines the good. The gap between right and rights appears for the first time; legal rights become the main way through

---

[37] T. Murphy, 'Thoughts on Race Equality and Human Rights', in M. King and C. Thornhill, *Luhmann on Law and Politics* (Oxford: Hart 2006) 73.

[38] Campbell, *Rights* 4–5.

which state law operates while morality is demoted to the status of the private, religious or sexual. Modernity fears and tries to ban the ethics of the good. As a result, the only type of duty the liberal tradition recognises is parasitical upon the exercise of rights. The usual cry of despair of politicians and commentators ('we have many rights; what about responsibilities') is therefore misconceived. In a liberal state, virtue or duty cannot act as independent normative sources. For a social and legal system based on rights, responsibilities are either a support of rights or a perpetual embarrassment.

Kantian moral philosophy attempted to re-link freedom and morality through the overarching operation of reason. Reason's counsel dictates law's form: it must be universal without violating the freedom and autonomy of others. The quest for a rational justification of rights starts here. But the rift modernity opened between right and rights is too deep to be mediated by reasoned self-legislation, form too weak an adhesive. Rights, these creations of (legal or social) rules, promise to reconcile heteronomy and autonomy. They are given by society or law, they are examples of other-derived normativity. But in entitling their bearer to exercise them in pursuit of his interests; in privatising their exercise by enfranchising the individual to initiate their public enforcement; by organising their content in accordance with the desires and needs of their holders, rights offer a modicum of autonomy, of a law given by the self to itself for itself.

This great modern achievement is beset with many practical and theoretical problems. Kant's third antinomy between freedom and necessity survives. Normative jurisprudence returning to the Kantian reconciliation assumes that force can be pacified by form, that law is a non-violent and rationally integrated discourse, that domination (the question of power) has been displaced into technical disputes about law and rights which can be safely entrusted to rules technicians (lawyers and judges). Finally, it assumes that social responses to power asymmetries and domination (the question of social conflict) can be exported to politics in practice and political philosophy in theory. The philosophy of rights insulated itself from political conflict and concentrated its formidable intellectual powers in the business of elaborating the most rationally persuasive and aesthetically pleasing rationalisations of law and rights. Conflict and struggle was simply deposited outside law.

This is a counter-intuitive image of social and individual life and an impoverished version of rights and law. A society that has moved from a conception of the good to different and conflictual 'goods' recognises the existence of all-pervasive conflict. The protection of my various capacities to pursue my individually perceived goods will necessarily clash with the view of others. The moral and legal experience of a society of rights is paradoxical. We are taught to see ourselves as autonomous agents. But the enthronement of individual desire as the motor of the socio-economic and legal world needs strong external, heteronomous limits on insatiable desire. A strong state, a ruthless criminal law and invasive regulation, control of behaviour, discipline and surveillance are not the evil agglomerations of authoritarianism. Rights are not 'trumps' or 'side-constraints' against these unnatural or delinquent extensions of power. Rights both manifest a socio-economic system in which power uses individuals and offer defences against abuses of power. As the autonomous persons of normative juris-prudence we don't want to be controlled by others and rights protect this wish. As empirical people we cannot avoid controlling and manipulating others. Power and morality, sovereignty and rights are not involved in a zero sum game; they are intertwined. Thomas Hobbes who derived his all-powerful sovereign from the most exacting examination of individual rights remains more accurate in his depiction of market society than any of his more faint-hearted liberal epigones.

We must reject therefore many premises of liberal jurisprudence in order to develop a more realistic understanding of rights and the person. The real self is constructed in social relations, in family settings, community belong-ings and country loyalties; she is Burkean and Arendtian, not Lockean and Rawlsian. Her identity develops in a struggle for recognition with others, both intimate and proximate as well as the distanced and strangers; she is Hegelian not Kantian. Finally, the real individual is always involved in relations of domination and conflict with dominant institutions and powerful others.

Despite the philosophical aspirations, no single theory of morality can give a full account of human rights. This is perhaps the reason for their success. The abstract statements of rights can authorise all kinds of contra-dictory applications *in concreto*, theories promote many and even conflict-ing perspectives. The attraction of human rights is that they can be all things to all people; whatever your politics, ideology or beliefs some type of rights theory can be found to accommodate even antagonistic interests, predilections and preferences. If human rights are to deliver their moral promise, we must abandon their inaccurate conception of the person.

A sense of right and of the good beyond individual rights and 'goods' must be reintroduced into our ethics. This is perhaps what is emerging now in the occupied squares and streets of North Africa, Europe and America where people are developing new collective ways of being and acting in the world.

Further reading

Brown, W. and Hallet, J. (eds.), *Left Legalism/Left Critique* (Durham, NC: Duke University Press 2002)

Campbell, T., *Rights: A Critical Introduction* (London: Routledge 2006)

Cheah, P., *Inhuman Conditions: On Cosmopolitanism and Human Rights* (Cambridge, MA: Harvard University Press 2006)

Douzinas, C., *The End of Human Rights* (Oxford: Hart, 2000)

Douzinas, C. and Gearey, A., *Critical Jurisprudence* (Oxford: Hart 2005)

Douzinas, C. and Gearty, C., *The Meanings of Human Rights: The Philosophy and Social Theory of Rights* (Cambridge University Press 2013)

Gewirth, A., *The Community of Rights* (Oxford University Press 1996)

Grear, A., *Redirecting Human Rights: Facing the Challenge of Corporate Legal Humanity* (London: Palgrave Macmillan 2010)

Ivison, D., *Rights* (Stocksfield: Acumen 2008)

Hoffman, S.-L. (ed.), *Human Rights in the Twentieth Century* (Cambridge University Press 2011)

Moyn, S., *The Last Utopia: Human Rights in History* (Cambridge, MA: Harvard University Press 2010)

Sarat, A. and Kearns, T. (eds.), *Legal Rights: Historical and Philosophical Perspectives* (University of Michigan Press 2000)

Shapiro, I., *The Evolution of Rights in Liberal Theory* (Cambridge University Press 1989)

Part II

Interconnections

Florian Hoffmann

For many, the fall of the Berlin Wall and the end of the Cold War marked the triumph of human rights (discourse) and the inauguration of a new era which, in allusion to a term coined by American legal philosopher Ronald Dworkin, could be described as the 'rights' empire'.[1] This 'empire' denoted, of course, not a reality in which all human beings did, in fact, enjoy the state of being represented by human rights, such as a life in dignity, civil and political liberties, the rule of law and democracy, and a (certain) degree of social welfare. Rather, it signified a discursive hegemony that turned human rights discourse into the common currency of a globalising world.[2] In fact, the impressive expansion of the international human rights regime,[3] and the proliferation of new constitutions with ample bills of rights in Central and Eastern Europe, Sub-Saharan Africa and Latin America have turned 'rights-talk' into the predominant instrument for defining and defending personal and collective identities. This does not, of course, allude to the reality behind rights-talk, which remains at best ambivalent, but to the fact that human rights has come to enjoy a near monopoly on emancipatory and utopian discourse in a post-communist and post-industrialist era.

Who owns human rights (discourse)?

Whoever seeks liberation from any type of real or perceived oppression couches his or her claims in the language of human rights. Whoever aspires to live out his or her particular identity also expresses this desire in human rights terms. Individuals and groups across the globe use human rights to articulate their claim for better lives. As such, they have at once become one of the defining discourses of globalised (post)modernity and an expression

---

[1] See R. Dworkin, *Law's Empire* (Cambridge, MA: Belknap Press 1986).
[2] C. Douzinas, *The End of Human Rights* (Oxford: Hart 2000) 1 ff.
[3] See L. Henkin, *The Age of Rights* (New York: Columbia University Press 1990).

of its hubris.[4] In their dominant interpretation they represent the ongoing process of emancipation and differentiation by individuals from social norms and governmental power that has become the hallmark of liberal democracy and market-based capitalism. Yet, they have also been at the heart of critiques of a 'Western' modernity that is seen to over-emphasise liberty over responsibility, individuals over nations, markets and competition over community and solidarity.[5] Indeed, even within the mature Western democracies, rights-based claims to different aspects of individual identity increasingly run up against security-based claims to protect the integrity of a collectively defined 'way of life' against its detractors such as 'criminals', 'terrorists' or simply 'others'.[6]

Rights, in short, remain an 'essentially contested concept' over which both its proponents and its critics continue to argue.[7] And this argument is, essentially, one over foundations – that is, over the authority of different narratives on where human rights come from and what they (ought) to mean to whom. However, this open and open-ended debate on the moral and cultural foundations of human rights is cross-cut by a phenomenon that acts as an independent variable on the discourse, namely that of law and legalisation. Starting, arguably, with *Magna Carta*, which was, itself, modelled on the feudal contract, via the constitutionalisations of the late eighteenth century, and up to their incorporation into international law in the second half of the twentieth century, there is a history of legalising (human) rights that runs parallel to the reflection on their moral and cultural foundation, and yet is distinct from it. Both are linked tautologically, for each refers to the other in order to fill a gap it cannot close by itself. Hence, (human rights) law requires moral or cultural foundations it cannot generate itself, whereas foundational (human rights) discourse seeks the facticity which only legal positivation and institutional enforcement can

---

[4] See, inter alia, the critical essays in M. Gibney (ed.), *Globalizing Rights* (Oxford University Press 2003).

[5] See T. Evans, *Human Rights Fifty Years On* (Manchester University Press 1998).

[6] See C. Gearty, *Can Human Rights Survive?* (Cambridge University Press 2006); R. A. Wilson, *Human Rights in the 'War on Terror'* (Cambridge University Press 2005); see also F. Hoffmann, 'The Dignity of 'Terrorists', in F. Hoffman and F. Mégret (eds.), *Dignity: A Framework for Vulnerable Groups*, Report to the Swiss Initiative to Commemorate the 60th Anniversary of the Universal Declaration of Human Rights (2010) 88.93, www.udhr60.ch/report/HumanDignity_Megret0609.pdf.

[7] W. B. Gallie, 'Essentially Contested Concepts' (1956) 56 *Proceedings of the Aristotelian Society* 167–98.

give it. Indeed, foundational and legal human rights discourse might be interdependent in an even deeper way, as legalisation might well constrain the ways in which foundations can be conceived.[8] Likewise, hard cases in (human rights) law are often only resolved by returning, sometimes under the guise of 'principles' or with reference to the underlying idea of 'human dignity', to moral or cultural narratives.[9] Yet, the operational logics of law and of foundational discourse remain separate and, arguably, ultimately incommensurable. The law cannot 'understand' moral or cultural discourse from within its own logic and vice versa.[10] The difference lies in the foundations of foundation: the foundation of (human rights) law is legality or legal validity, as determined by clearly defined (secondary) rules.[11] The foundation of these, in turn, lies outside of the law and, from its internal perspective, is simply a given.

The foundation of foundational discourse, in turn, is moral legitimacy and cultural significance, the foundations of which lie in the particular narrative through which human rights are reconstructed and which are always contested and contestable by alternative narratives. At the heart of all foundational discourse lies an argument about the potential validity of human rights in different *fora*, whereas legal discourse is premised on a validity that must always already be given. As a result, the question of foundations has always also been a question of ownership. It is a question of who may speak for human rights under what authority. And it has brought forth a long-standing contest between human rights lawyers, foundational thinkers of human rights – moral philosophers, anthropologists, historians, etc. – and simple 'users' of the language, on who is the principal owner of the discourse. By and large, the lawyers can so far be said to have been resoundingly victorious.

On the surface, the reason for this seems almost trivial: positive law enforced by courts simply pits normative power against (possible) truth and insight therein. Once a fundamental right is enshrined in a domestic constitution, once a state becomes party to an international human rights

---

[8] See S. Meckled-García and B. Çali, 'Lost in Translation: The Human Rights Ideal and International Human Rights Law', in S. Meckled-García and B. Çali, *The Legalization of Human Rights* (New York: Routledge 2006) 11–31.

[9] See F. Hoffman and F. Mégret (eds.), 'Introduction', in F. Hoffmann and F. Mégret (eds.), *Dignity: A Framework for Vulnerable Groups* 1–6.

[10] See N. Luhmann, *Law as a Social System* (Oxford University Press 2004).

[11] See H. L. A. Hart *The Concept of Law*, 2nd edn (Oxford University Press 1994).

treaty, the question of foundations, that is, of moral legitimacy or cultural significance, becomes immaterial. All that counts from a legal perspective is whether a particular norm is (legally) valid and then whether it has been complied with or not. Compliance does not depend on (foundational) consent, but only on the obligation to comply that stems from the deontological structure of law.[12] It, incidentally, also does not depend on 'real' compliance, as non-compliance does not render law any less legal but simply constitutes a violation of the law. Nor do human rights lawyers need to concern themselves with the foundations of adherence, that is, the moral, political or other reasons for why a government or a state has adopted a human rights instrument in the first place. The sole referent for human rights lawyers is the valid norm, whether governments and states like it in any particular case or not. This removes all contestability and all ambivalence from human rights discourse, it radically reduces its complexity, and it renders it institutionally decidable and, thus, enforceable.[13] From this, it derives its particular force that consists of isolating human rights both from time – i.e. history – and space – i.e. cross-cultural significance – that is, from their foundations, in general. Indeed, legalisation suspends the essential contestability of human rights and, by reducing them to specific legal claims enforceable in specific institutions, renders them certain and stable. Like all law, human rights law operates through the binary code of legal/illegal or rather violation/non-violation and it secures its integrity by remaining normatively closed, that is, by not self-reflexively thematising its own validity.[14] All of this has given the legal dialect the upper hand over all other human rights dialects making it into a 'Queen's English' of sorts within the human rights community. In fact, it has become a substitute for (non-legal) foundational discourse and is often evoked as a last-resort, trumping argument in broader foundational debates. Indeed, in advocacy situations, most human rights professionals will take human rights law as their starting point, with the latter's facticity being seen as a sort of magical fiat, a pre-ordained ground which is beyond questioning.[15] To be sure, most

---

[12] R. Alexy, *A Theory of Constitutional Rights* (J. Rivers, trans.) (Oxford University Press 2009).

[13] A. Fagan, *Human Rights: Confronting Myths and Misunderstandings* (Cheltenham: Edward Elgar 2009).

[14] G. Teubner, *Law as an Autopoietic System* (Oxford: Wiley–Blackwell 1993).

[15] See F. Hoffmann, 'Facing the Abyss: International Law Before the Political', in M. Goldoni and C. McCorkindale (eds.), *Hannah Arendt and the Law* (Oxford: Hart 2012).

human rights professionals are not naïve and purposely elect to 'speak' human rights legally precisely in order to avoid the contestability and institutional weakness of foundational discourse. Yet, in doing so, they claim superior ownership of the law over human rights, promulgating thereby a human rights law beyond foundations.

Foundations in time and space

Before returning to the relation between (human rights) law and (its) foundations, a brief excursion into human rights in their temporal and spatial dimension is called for. If one lifted the heavy lid the law has placed over the historical and cultural contingency of human rights, what would one see? In terms of history, the two extreme poles of the 'origins debate' are formed by, on one hand, those who consider Stoic ideas on human personality and the Aristotelian concept of *dikaion*, justice, as well as the Judaeo-Christian theological heritage as direct precursors of 'human rights[16] and, on the other hand, those who hold that the concept is 'as modern as the internal combustion engine'.[17] In between, there is a host of candidates for the position of 'founder': by far the most popular are Thomas Hobbes and John Locke, followed at some distance by Hugo Grotius and the Spanish neo-scholastics (Suarez, Vitoria *et al.*), who are, in turn, trailed by William of Ockham, and, to a lesser extent, Jean Gerson, as well as the canon law jurists of the so-called eleventh-century 'Renaissance' of Roman Law. Though subsequent 'points' on the human rights timeline, such as the revolutionary period, idealist thought, and the early human rights 'movement' are usually considered important further stepping stones, the great majority of authors situates the origin of the concept of 'rights' in the seventeenth century or earlier.[18]

Generally, three analytically distinct lines of historical development can be distinguished. Firstly, there is the history of the idea of what is now often termed 'moral rights', i.e. the attribution of innate subjective faculties to

---

[16] See Douzinas, *The End of Human Rights* 23 ff. and, generally, B. Tierney, *The Idea of Natural Rights: Studies on Natural Rights, Natural Law and Church Law 1150–1625* (Atlanta, GA: Scholars Press 1997).

[17] K. Minogue, 'The History of the Idea of Human Rights', in W. Laqueur and B. Rubin, *The Human Rights Reader* (New York: Temple University Press 1979) 3–17.

[18] See C. Gearty, *Are Human Rights Universal?* (London: Cameron May 2008)1 ff.

human beings *qua* their shared humanity; this history comprises the *ius naturalis* of the Middle Ages, the 'natural rights' of the Renaissance and Reformation period, the 'rights of man' and '*droits de l'homme*' of the English, American and French revolutions, the rights language used in the anti-slavery and women suffrage movements, and up to the Universal Declaration of Human Rights (UDHR) and the Nuremberg principles.[19] Secondly, there is the history of the concept of 'legal rights', i.e. claims vis-à-vis others, the community, or the sovereign which are, at least theoretically, held to be enforceable by appropriate institutions; this spans, arguably, the first precursors in classical Roman law, the medieval feudal 'contract' and other fields such as property and legislation, the notorious early rights documents, namely *Magna Carta* of 1215, the Petition of Rights, the (English) Bill of Rights of 1689, the Virginia Declaration and the American Declaration of Independence, both of 1776, and the US Constitution's Bills of Rights of 1791, and the further 'domestication' of rights in subsequent constitution-making; it is primarily a history about the development of what has come to be termed constitutional, fundamental, or basic rights within nation states, though, to some extent it also includes the history of general international law, which has, of course, attempted to transpose the domestic constitutional structure onto an imaginary international society of states.[20] And thirdly, there is the history of what could be called the 'human rights movement', i.e. the self-conscious reference to human rights within the context of different political struggles, and the gradual (moral) 'legitimation' and 'legalisation' of the claims made in these contexts. This history includes the well-known 'constitutive moments' of human rights that ultimately lead to the UDHR, beginning, *inter alia*, with the anti-slavery movement, the struggle for women's rights and universal adult suffrage, and the fight for labour rights and rights of democratic participation. This would also comprise the history of the gradual 'differentiation' of international human rights law into a distinct sub-field of general international law, through such developments as international humanitarian law, international minimum standards for the treatment of aliens, minorities protection, the emergent notion of genocide and crimes

---

[19] See, for an introductory overview of the human rights 'movement', in P. Alston, H. J. Steiner and R. Goodman, *International Human Rights in Context*, 3rd edn (Oxford University Press 2007).

[20] M. Ishay, *The History of Human Rights from Ancient Times to the Globalization Era*, 2nd edn (Berkeley, CA: University of California Press 2008).

against humanity, international trusteeship and decolonisation and the anti-apartheid struggle.[21]

A closer look at the terminological histories of each of these lines of development might provide further clues about the conceptual cornerstones of human rights. The term itself is of recent coinage, having been introduced with the UN Charter and the UDHR. Its predecessors were the 'rights of man' and, of course, 'natural rights' – *ius naturale/lex naturalis*. The former emerged as *droits de l'homme* in French *physiocrat* and *philosophes* circles, and culminated in the revolutionary *Declaration des Droits de L'Homme et du Citoyen* of 1789; the then generic *hommes* – 'hu-man'[22]- having been chosen as a supposedly non-theist alternative to the older 'natural rights'.[23] The Declaration was very widely received, among others by the English radicals, and, most notably by Thomas Paine and his *Rights of Man*, written in reply to Burke's critique of the revolution.[24] Though in their core meaning, the *droits de l'homme* did not fundamentally differ from 'natural rights' in that both expressed subjective claims based on the universal characteristics of human beings, they nonetheless came to have slightly different connotations; indeed, unlike human rights, which now enjoy near terminological hegemony, the 'rights of man' and 'natural rights' were used in parallel in different *fora*. 'Natural rights' remained the term of choice in moral philosophy, whereas the 'rights of man' came to be associated with constitutionalism and political theory. There is, of course, a subtle difference in each term's approach to universality; whereas both evidently allude to the innate faculties of human beings as such, 'natural rights' have a distinctly metaphysical, if not theistic, undertone to them in which 'nature' connotes the necessary and non-contingent character of rights which are

---

[21] A. Neier, *The International Human Rights Movement: A History* (Princeton University Press 2012).

[22] It is, of course, a still persistent myth that the inventors and subsequent users of the generic term 'man' – denoting today's human being – were unaware of its male-centredness; although the modern feminist critique should not be smuggled into the late eighteenth century, it is equally mistaken to ascribe some form of serene innocence to authors of that time; 'man' was then, as now, defined in contradistinction to 'woman', with the prototype of the individual being the former, rather than the latter: see J. Scott, *Only Paradoxes to Offer: French Feminists and the Rights of Man* (Cambridge, MA: Harvard University Press 1996); see also Douzinas, *The End of Human Rights* 97 ff.

[23] See, for example, Condorcet's statement that natural rights belonged to abstract man, as they were 'defined as a sensitive being . . . capable of reasoning and of having moral ideas', cited in Douzinas, *The End of Human Rights* 97.

[24] T. Paine, *The Rights of Man* (Mineola, NY: Dover 1999).

neither creations of, nor subject, to human will;[25] the 'rights of man', in contrast, while still clearly derived from 'natural rights', nonetheless already point to a belonging to a 'community of men', a form of citizenship of humanity, membership in which is simply the primary attribute of 'men', with any metaphysical cause being of secondary importance.

It is, arguably, this incipient distinction between humans and citizens, clearly articulated in the French Declaration, which also marks the gradual differentiation of moral and legal rights conceptions. The rights of 'men' remain on the level of abstract, universalistic morality, whereas those of citizen are linked to a concrete and particular sovereign that defines itself with reference to its populace and territory, and not by reference to divine grace.[26] Although, within the latter sphere, the effective interlinking of what Jürgen Habermas has called (human) rights and popular sovereignty occurred only very gradually, already the original split between 'man' and citizen represented an irreversible turn towards secularisation and positivation. Yet, the roots of legal rights extent further back: as was seen, the idea of special and, importantly, concrete and 'useable' entitlements goes back at least to the late medieval Italian city states, if not, in a more limited way, to the early medieval charters such as the *Magna Carta*. Both contexts illustrate the features of such concrete legal rights: they were ultimately bestowed by, and existed vis-à-vis, a sovereign community, and they contained certain clearly defined entitlements for the members of the group of rights-holders. It is also clear that in parallel with this development, private rights of commerce and economic production already existed throughout the Middle Ages.[27]

It is from these roots that the continental, and especially German, term 'subjective rights' developed, referring to the legal recognition of an inviolable sphere of individual autonomy upon which relations between individuals are premised. This, originally Kantian, 'private law' perspective of rights seems to coincide with the Anglo-American use of the term 'rights', except that the latter essentially constitutes the law as such, and hence has included relations to public, political authority, whereas the former excludes what forms, in continental civil law systems, public and administrative law. However, while the original Kantian conception of (private) law

---

[25] Douzinas, *The End of Human Rights* 85 ff.

[26] Douzinas, *The End of Human Rights* 103, 117.

[27] J. Habermas, *Between Facts and Norms* (Cambridge: Polity 1997) 132.

had as its source the moral conception of individual autonomy, once that conception was lost in the process of modernisation and social differentiation, the source of law came to be located not in individual subjectivity, but in the objective, institutionalised legal order. Subjective rights, hence, became derivative of objective law – objective in the sense of empirically, not deontologically, valid – and lost their connection not only to the moral subject, but also to the natural person, as the legal system came to be seen as self-contained in its own legal fictions or its code. This change in the source of validity of subjective rights corresponds, of course, to the move from a concept of law intimately linked with morality, to a positivist one, in which it is autonomous.[28]

The objectification of subjective rights is, however, also referred to in a different context, namely in relation to the materialization of law in the modern welfare state. Here subjective rights come to be increasingly interpreted not as delimiting a sphere of personal autonomy, but as serving general social interests, which condition their nature and scope.[29] That the positivation of rights in the domestic sphere was intimately linked with the emergence of the sovereign, later liberal, and yet later democratic nation state also meant, of course, that legally, human rights had to take the shape of inter-national ones, conceded by nation states with respect to acts suffered by individuals (and later groups) within their national boundaries. The innovation here was not the often alleged expansion of domestic rights regimes to a supranational one, but the extension of (some) citizenship rights to non-citizens and, only very gradually, the creation of international institutions to serve, in the best of cases, as a last appeal chamber for cases that failed in domestic jurisdictions. The international sphere recognised by the law is, in its classical design, derivative of the national and, thus, in stark contrast with the universal aspirations that the moral conceptions of (human) rights continued to have. The UDHR is, of course, a hybrid creature, speaking to a moral universe of humankind, but having been negotiated and enacted by way of international law, granting moral human rights to all persons irrespective of their citizenship and *qua* their being human, while not imposing any international legal obligations on the states who signed it. To an extent, this ambiguity between moral universality and legal inter-nationality has marked human rights ever since, even in those cases in

---

[28] Habermas, *Between Facts and Norms* 112 ff.
[29] Habermas, *Between Facts and Norms* 113.

which states have consented to positivise them domestically and internationally.[30]

In terms of the spatiality of human rights, universality and relativity are already built into the semantic texture of human rights. Historically, the idea of the universality of rights is probably inseparable from the emergence of the concept of rights as such, though not as a quantitative or geographical attribute, but rather as a qualitative and spatial one. For, as was just seen, the concept of the universality of rights can be linked to the post-feudal, conciliarist and constitutionalist discourse that has accompanied the process of European state formation from the late Middle Ages onwards.[31] Here the *universitas* can be said to refer to that group of people who, by sharing certain essential attributes, constitute a common whole, and who, conversely, 'belong' to that whole. In constitutionalist discourse, which conceptually accompanied the gradual broadening of the personalised feudal relationship into an abstract political community, this sense of universality is expressed in the figure of the citizen: citizenship is, first of all, the 'included-ness' in the political community, and rights are no longer personal claims, but the abstract characteristics of 'the citizen', redeemable vis-à-vis the institutions of political society, i.e. the state.[32] Hence, the network of particularised relationships is transformed into a singular and general one, namely between (individual) citizens and the state. The *universitas* of citizens is qualitative in that it re-conceives individuals in abstraction from their particular social relations with reference to assumed common traits – expressed through the membership rights of citizens – and, conversely, in that it postulates an imaginary whole, the belonging to which entails those traits. It is spatial in that it implies the idea of a limit which divides between those inside and those outside, with those inside being determined by their essential sameness and equality, and those outside being undetermined others, such as, historically, 'strangers', 'women', 'heathens', 'savages', 'barbarians' and the like. Hence, the universe of rights-holders merely refers to a relative space, the contours of which are

---

[30] See W. Sweet (ed.), *Philosophical Theory and the Universal Declaration of Human Rights* (University of Ottawa Press 2003).

[31] See, *inter alia*, H. Berman, *Law and Revolution: The Formation of the Western Legal Tradition* (Cambridge, MA: Harvard University Press 1983) and K. Pennington, *The Prince and the Law 1200–1600: Sovereignty and Rights in the Western Legal Tradition* (Berkeley, CA: University of California Press 1993).

[32] J. Coleman, *The Individual in Political Theory and Practice* (Alderley: Clarendon Press 1996).

determined by that which it pretends not to be, and not to an absolute, and thus geographical, space, namely *the* universe as such.[33]

This relative and particular conception of universality has, of course, been partly overshadowed by a parallel root of the concept of rights' universality, notably that implied in the idea of natural rights. Though the concept of natural rights is complex and multi-layered, it is generally based on the core assumption that individuals are endowed with certain essential characteristics that are independent from their socio-cultural context and that are, thus, shared by all; these 'all' are, consequently, elevated to 'human beings', whose very human-ness is expressed through particular rights. These are conceived of as 'natural' since they are not derivative of, and thus dependent on, human will, but are, in this original conception, God-given; 'God' is, of course, here the creator of everything and everybody and, therefore, the source of the unity of humankind and, indeed, 'nature'. *Prima facie*, this would necessarily imply a more quantitative, if not geographical, notion of universality, since 'the universe' is precisely the particular *place* that contains all of creation, and all of creation *belongs* within it. Hence, on the face of it, this seems to be a similar construction to that of the citizenship figure, only vastly expanded to include not only some, but all human beings. Indeed, this notion of absolute universality, in the modern sense of globality, pervades human rights discourse until today: universality of human rights stands for all-inclusiveness, the presumption of some fundamental sameness of all human beings which makes all belong to (i.e. citizens of) an imaginary universal community.

Yet, even the universality of natural rights, like the universality of citizenship rights, only denotes a relative, and not an absolute space, namely one delimited by a particular world view, or paradigm. It is only in the particular metaphysical assumptions of occidental Greco-Judaeo-Christianity that these specific 'human beings' are universal through their God-createdness and some essential common features, i.e, from a particular *internal* perspective. Although different internal perspectives – and their respective universalities – may be partially equivalent if analysed from an external, sociological point of view, they are, in terms of their inner paradigmatic logic, necessarily incommensurable.[34] Hence, the conception of universality

---

[33] This being, thus, a 'constitutive outside'; for this 'term of art', see E. Laclau, *New Reflections on the Revolution of Our Time* (New York: Verso, 1990) and *Emancipations* (New York: Verso 1996).

[34] See P. Winch, *The Idea of a Social Science and its Relation to Philosophy* (New York: Routledge 2007).

contained in the idea of natural rights is relative to the particular meaning system they refer to. Contrary to common usage, universality is, thus, not an objective and straightforward concept, but is, already on an abstract semantic level, historical and context-specific. Seen from this angle, foundations do not, in fact, provide a foundation, which takes us back to the one foundational non-foundation human rights have, namely law.

Law and its significant others

There are a number of potential fields that come to mind when casually reflecting on where the language of human rights is being used. The most usual suspects would seem to be law, morality, culture, politics, history, sociology, anthropology and religion. Indeed, in most, if not all of the subdisciplines of the social sciences, as well as in a good number of the humanities, the term human rights would seem to be present in some way. Yet, for the present purposes, the most relevant fields will be taken to be the first three, namely law, morality, and culture. The reason for this particular choice is the fact that, when it comes to human rights, many of the other fields can be reduced to one of these three. Hence, references to human rights in religious discourse, for instance, are virtually always in truth either moral or cultural references. Likewise, human rights in political discourse are really references to their legal, moral or, occasionally, cultural nature. Moral discourse will here be taken to encompass references to the rational self-thematisation of political community, i.e. of the relationship of human beings among each other individually and collectively. It denotes, thus, what has occasionally been described as the grand meta-narratives,[35] or the attempt by different groups to rationally reconstruct themselves as political communities, to sketch the world as it ought to be according to some comprehensive, coherent, rational and, thus, (theoretically) universal scheme. Such a moral logic informs virtually all discourses on human rights, attributing to them some purpose or deeper reason for why individuals or groups should have certain types of rights.

The cultural discourse of human rights, in turn, will be taken to refer to those conceptualisations of human rights that have, primarily, cultural

---

[35] See J.-F. Lyotard, *The Postmodern Condition: A Report on Knowledge* (University of Minnesota Press 1984).

significance. This is, of course, a tautological definition, owing to the enormous breadth and controversality of the concept of culture; the latter is due, not least, to the concept's close association, or, indeed, conflation over time with a number of other highly contested terms, such as, *inter alia*, nation, people, civilisation, race and society. It can, generally, be said to have emerged along two opposite conceptual lines, one emphasising difference and relativity, the other sameness and universality.[36] As regards the cultural paradigm of human rights discourse, a definitional starting point would be to take it to be the customs, traditions, habits and practices of individuals and communities in relation to human rights. It is, essentially, fluid and indeterminate, permanently contested and re-defined. It is, nonetheless, distinct from law and morality, as it denotes what, with some caution, could be termed the life-world component of human rights. Whereas law and morality as they are employed here are, by definition, rational discourses, the cultural dimension of human rights would denote the non-rationalised, background notions of human rights that individuals display in day-to-day situations. Law, in turn, will be taken to be a system of behavioural rules which are conceived of as valid both internally, meaning that they follow the criterion of logical consistency, and externally, meaning that they are concretely enforced either by force, the threat of force or simply by the impact of sedimented expectations. As such, it is largely a performative discourse intimately interlinked with institutions and actors.

This strict distinction between law and morality, is, of course, itself a historical construct or, in sociological terms, the symptom of a particular social development. Max Weber notoriously explained law as the rationalised exercise of political power wherein the assumption of the rationality of law is seen as distinct from assumptions or beliefs concerning tradition or religion.[37] This, in turn, is to be seen as part of his already mentioned thesis that the rise of capitalism in Europe after the Reformation led to a steady rationalisation of social relations which caused European societies to re-define themselves on radically different lines. On this account, legitimacy is defined as purely internal to law that, as a concept, merges with its attributed rationality. The importance of this sociological reconstruction of the legal positivist viewpoint lies in this fact, namely that reason is here no longer interpreted as a moral source of (positive) law, as in natural law

[36] See C. Geertz, *The Interpretation of Cultures* (New York: Basic Books 1977).
[37] See Habermas, *Between Facts and Norms* 541.

theories, but that modern law itself is seen as the manifestation of rationality, i.e. that it is the principal distinguishing mark of modern, as opposed to traditional, societies. In Weber's account of modern positive law, legitimacy is not defined as a justificatory and hence extra-legal, i.e. moral, element of law, but it is seen to consist in the very fact that law and morality are totally differentiated and hence uncontaminated by each other. Legitimacy becomes thus simply a predicate of legality. This strictly formalist view of law as value-free rationality was not only always a productive fiction[38] – i.e. a productive misreading of late-nineteenth-century liberal jurisprudence[39] – but it was also contradicted by the evolution of modern law itself, namely in the form of what Weber called its 'materialisation', i.e. its expansion into social regulation and distributive justice. Materialisation was meant to incorporate value judgements based on political morality into law – Weber called it fearfully a 'moralisation' of law – thereby destroying its presumed formal autonomy.[40] With regard to rights it is at this conceptual turning point that, however, occurred in different historical contexts throughout Europe, that a formal view of negative liberal rights is challenged by a substantive view of positive, pro-active ones.

Human rights law beyond foundations

Human rights are, hence, not so much a singular discourse, but a discursive formation in the Foucauldian sense, characterised by 'dispersion, choice, division, [and] opposition'.[41] Within it, the articulation of discursive elements is always only provisional, they never fully succeed in securing meaning. Indeed, a discursive formation may be constituted by several individual discourses that stand in a competitive relation with one another.[42] This does not merely render discursive foundations fundamentally indeterminate, but also unstable, i.e. marked by a permanent and ultimately chaotic movement of the discourses of which they are constituted. While the structural logic of individual discourses

---

[38]   Habermas, *Between Facts and Norms* 553.

[39]   See H. Bloom, *A Map of Misreading* (Oxford University Press 1975).

[40]   See M. Weber, *Economy and Society* (Berkeley, CA: University of California Press 1992) 160 ff.

[41]   See E. Laclau and C. Mouffe, *Hegemony and Socialist Strategy: Towards a Radical Democratic Politics*, 2nd edn (London: Verso 2001).

[42]   T. Purvis and A. Hunt, 'Discourse, Ideology, Discourse, Ideology, Discourse, Ideology . . .' (1993) 44 *British Journal of Sociology* 473–99.

within a discursive foundation may be understood, each such discourse is incapable, on its own, of establishing a semantic unity; instead, it continuously attempts to fill this lack by referring to discursive elements outside itself, which belong to other, competing discourses within the same formation. This 'out-referencing' does not only destabilise the systemic functioning of each discourse but, by interlinking the constitutive discourses within a formation, it creates a dynamic network of cross-references. Indeed, the discursive formation as such never appears in its totality, but rather consists of the successive instantiations of the different inter-linkages of its constitutive discourses. Human rights can be seen as just such a discursive formation, made up of several distinct discourses, and itself constituted by a host of actors, practices and institutions, which do not necessarily speak the same dialect (of human rights), yet provide the space within which human rights discourse unfolds.

Law, morality and culture are alternatives which cannot be translated into each other, but which are completely equivalent in that they cover the same 'thing', if only from different perspectives. That 'thing', human rights, is like a master signified, lurking behind each constitutive paradigm, and yet being signified only by all three of them together. As such, human rights would seem to be a typical case of over-determination,[43] i.e. a symbolic order that is signified by a multiplicity of different, but equivalent, signifiers or sets of signifiers. Each paradigm's attempt at full signification, at capturing the totality of human rights, is undermined by the overflow of meaning of that which is signified. Here we have an example of, as Laclau and Mouffe put it, 'field of identities which never manage to be fully fixed is the field of overdetermination'.[44] Importantly, the over-determined character of human rights entails that the concept is not, as one might assume, structurally pre-determined by three stable sets of signifiers which simply signify 'their' respective bit – notably law, morality, or culture; rather, it emerges as a result of the multiple and cross-cutting, yet continuously failing signification attempts by each paradigm. Hence, on the one hand, the concept of human rights is the master signified which firmly binds the paradigms together in a current of mutual cross-references, and, thus, makes them constitutive of itself. Yet, on the other hand, that which is constituted is not a positivity, some transcendental signified providing a firm, unequivocal ground for human rights, but the symptom of its lack and, hence, of the impossibility of signification.

---

[43] Laclau and Mouffe, *Hegemony and Socialist Strategy* 97.
[44] Laclau and Mouffe, *Hegemony and Socialist Strategy* 111.

Human rights are, thus, not any fixed entity, but emerge as the effects of the continuously failing attempt of signification by each of its different discourses. The concept, therefore, necessarily encompasses all, yet is fully determined by none of them. Law, morality and culture can, hence, be seen as being locked into a chain of mutual allusions that never achieves semantic closure. Human rights are, hence, no static concept, no jigsaw puzzle with neatly fitting pieces, but a dynamic and highly adaptive process. Its elements are not the layers of a scholastic pyramid in which moral foundation form the base, over which comes acculturation and habit and then, at the top, hard legal norms. Rather, each discourse contributes a certain functionality to the process; law provides facticity, moral discourse normativity and culture habit. Out of their continuous recombination grows the infinite diversity of attitudes towards and uses of human rights. Foundational questions are, hence, not beneath or beyond the law, but always engage with it in quite unforeseeable ways.

Further reading

Dembour, M.-B., *Who Believes in Human Rights? Reflections on the European Convention* (Cambridge University Press 2006)

Douzinas, C., *The End of Human Rights* (Oxford: Hart 2000)

Evans, T., *Human Rights Fifty Years On* (Manchester University Press 1998)

Gearty, C., *Are Human Rights Universal?* (London: Cameron May 2008)

Goldoni, M. and McCorkindale, C., *Hannah Arendt and the Law* (Oxford: Hart 2012)

Henkin, L., *The Age of Rights* (New York: Columbia University Press 1990)

Hoffmann, F., 'Shooting in the Dark: Reflections towards a Pragmatic Theory of Human Rights (Activism)' (2006) 41 (3) *Texas International Law Journal* 403–14

   'Human Rights, the Self, and the Other: Reflections on a Pragmatic Theory of Human Rights', in A. Orford (ed.), *International Law and Its Others* (Cambridge University Press 2006)

Ishay, M., *The History of Human Rights: From Ancient Times to the Globalization Era*, 2nd edn (Berkeley, CA: University of California Press 2008)

Meckled-García, S. and Çali, B., *The Legalization of Human Rights* (New York: Routledge 2006)

Pennington, K., *The Prince and the Law 1200–1600: Sovereignty and Rights in the Western Legal Tradition* (Berkeley, CA: University of California Press 1993)

Rorty, R., 'Human Rights, Rationality and Sentimentality', in S. Shute and S. Hurley (eds.), *On Human Rights: The Oxford Amnesty Lectures 1993, 1994* (Oxford University Press 1994)

The interdisciplinarity of human rights 5

Abdullahi A. An-Na'im

The subject of this chapter is the interdisciplinarity of the *study* of human rights, and not of the rights themselves, like freedom of expression or right to health care, in the abstract. A study like this can apply to such matters as the subjective meaning of the right as experienced by the people who claim it and the context in which it is exercised. In my view, however, the study of all aspects of human rights should be for the purpose of informing and facilitating the practical implementation of these rights, rather than as a purely academic exercise. It would therefore follow that the interdisciplinarity of the study of human rights should be directed at guiding policies and struggles for the protection of human rights. As an approach to the study of human rights, reference to interdisciplinarity addresses such questions as what it is, what does it do, and what does it add to disciplinarity and multi-disciplinarity? In other words, the title of this chapter raises questions about the relationship among disciplinarity, *multi*-disciplinarity and *inter*-disciplinarity, that is, how are these concepts related yet different, and what each of them means for the study of human rights in ways that are conducive to effective and sustainable implementation of these norms around the world.

A primary concern with any discourse of human rights is to what extent is it, or can it be, as *globally inclusive* as possible because that is the nature of the subject. As I will explain later, human rights must be by definition universal, if they are to be at all, because they are supposed to be the entitlements of all human beings, equally and without distinction. In other words, the human rights project may be doomed to failure for whatever reason, but if it is to succeed at all, it must be about the universal rights of all human beings. This project has been resisted for a variety of reasons when it was first proposed in the aftermath of the Second World War, and continues to attract strong scepticism.[1] For those like myself who do believe

---

[1] See, e.g., (1947) 49 (4) *American Anthropologist* 539–43; and UNESCO (ed.), *Human Rights, Comments and Interpretations* (London and New York: Allan Wingate 1947). For the persistence of strong scepticism, see A. Vincent, *The Politics of Human Rights* (New York:

in the necessity and possibility of the universality of human rights, the inquiry would be about what does this belief mean and require, whether in theoretical or conceptual terms, or as a matter of political, legal and cultural practice. This commitment to the universality of human rights indicates that discourse about the subject should be as globally inclusive as possible. Therefore, for our purposes in this chapter, discourse about the relevance of 'disciplinarity' and 'interdisciplinarity', as explained below, should also be as inclusive as possible. In other words, the global inclusivity of discourse about interdisciplinarity is necessary because the inquiry is about its relationship to human rights that require such inclusivity by virtue of the inherent universality of these rights. In particular, this concern with inclusivity of discourse about this relationship would apply to the epistemological and methodological assumptions of the underlying ideas of disciplinarity and interdisciplinarity.

Yet, global inclusivity will probably remain an elusive ideal because to be coherent any discourse needs to be conceptually and contextually located and bounded. Participants in any discourse can only speak from their respective subjectivities, which will necessarily be located and bounded in particular ways, including the diverse and competing influences that shape our consciousness, our moral and political commitments, our academic or professional competence and so forth. The paradox here is that inclusivity is about bringing every voice and experience into the conversation, but that is unlikely to happen on equal terms because of the long-standing and continuing impact of European colonialism/imperialism throughout the world. Regarding the subject of this chapter, the experiences and voices of peoples around the world that are supposed to be included in discourse about the relationship between human rights and interdisciplinarity are already influenced by European epistemological and methodological assumptions of the underlying idea of disciplinarity.

To take my own case to illustrate the point, I am an African Muslim from Northern Sudan, the product of a secular British colonial education, and am now living and working in the United States. Depending on how we define the subject, my participation in discourse may be seen as adding only the experience and voice of one person, or as somehow reflecting a combination of the various influences shaping my consciousness and commitments. In either case, however, my experience and voice already include European

Oxford University Press 2010); S. Moyn, *The Last Utopia: Human Rights in History* (Cambridge, MA: Harvard University Press 2010).

influences, while the experience and voice of Europeans are unlikely to be influenced by the epistemological and methodological assumptions of my African/Islamic culture and intellectual history. However, my hybrid sensibility may be more helpful for cross-cultural coherence, thereby facilitating more inclusivity of discourse than an exclusively African and/or Islamic sensibility because people need to share some common ground in order to communicate coherently. Indeed, sensibility that is exclusively indigenous to any place or culture may not be possible in today's globalised world.

I believe it is possible to mediate the paradox of inclusivity of discourse in the post-colonial world through what I call imagining the unimaginable and retrieving the irretrievable.[2] The idea is to imagine how the epistemological and methodological assumptions of formerly colonised peoples might have evolved on their own terms if colonialism had never happened, and then to try to retrieve that imagined continuity into the post-colonial experiences and voices of those peoples. The paradox persists because the processes of imagining and retrieval are already influenced by the same colonial epistemological and methodological assumptions that one is trying to avoid. Still, I believe, this complex paradox can be mediated by diminishing and indigenising those influences. Part of that process, I suggest, is to perceive European influences as part of a continuous narrative of global humanity, rather than a chauvinistic intellectual hegemony. Space does not permit further elaboration on this mediation of paradox in relation to global inclusivity of discourse about interdisciplinarity and human rights, but I believe it useful to bear this concern in mind as we explore the subject of this chapter. As suggested later, the possibility of such mediation should be one of the topics for further research.

In light of these tentative remarks, my basic argument in this chapter is that interdisciplinarity is integral to human rights at a conceptual as well as practical level in defining and implementing human rights norms. I will begin by highlighting the paradox of universality of human rights in order to clarify my concern with the inclusivity of discourse and to note the utility of interdisciplinarity in this regard. In the second section I will discuss the notion of interdisciplinarity in relation to human rights from the same perspective. In the last section, and as indicated a moment ago, I will suggest some topics for further inquiry on the subject of this chapter.

---

[2] A. An-Na'im, *African Constitutionalism and the Role of Islam* (University of Pennsylvania Press 2006) 27–30 and Ch 2.

The paradox and contingency of human rights

Human rights are moral and political entitlements that are due to all human beings equally by virtue of their humanity, and without any distinction on such grounds as race, sex, religion or national origin. In other words, I am entitled to these rights simply for being human, without any other requirement or qualification. I would not include the legal definition and enforcement of human rights in this basic concept because the absence of that legal dimension in any situation is precisely what the concept is intended to challenge and redress. As an external frame of reference for judging how the state treats its own citizens, the existence of human rights must be independent of recognition by the state, although the agency of the state is necessary for practical implementation. To concede that a claim to an entitlement as a human right is valid because the state says so is to defeat the purpose of the concept itself as an independent basis for evaluating state performance. At the same time, the sovereignty, territorial integrity and political independence of the state must be respected in the processes of evaluating state performance. This is an aspect of the paradox and contingency of human rights.

It may be helpful to note here that defining human rights as entitlement of all human beings equally is a normative claim, not an assertion of fact. The same is true about the idea of the human in human rights as a self-determining person, as I will affirm below. Such a normative claim is most needed, and therefore useful as a basis for people's struggle for their human rights, precisely in the face of violation of these rights, not an assertion of their established protection. It is therefore incoherent to argue that consensus does not already exist around human rights as a global political agenda,[3] because factual claims about human rights on a global scale are neither necessary, nor is it possible to verify their truth or fallacy. In other words, we do not have the methodological tools and material resources to empirically 'prove' or 'disprove' the normal claim of human rights. Even if it can, I argue, such an empirical investigation is not necessary. The normative claim of human rights is necessary for those who believe in it, who would then strive to promote sufficient consensus to generate the political will to implement these rights in their own specific context.

---

[3] T. Evans, *Human Rights in the Global Political Economy: Critical Processes* (Boulder, CO and London: Lynne Rienner 2011) 15–16.

Still, it is true and to be expected that the above noted working definition of human rights involves at least two main paradoxes. First, as already noted, since they are supposed to be the rights of all human beings, human rights are by definition universal. But how can human rights norms be universal in the reality of the permanent and profound cultural, religious, ethical and contextual diversity of human societies? Moreover, since national sovereignty is itself the manifestation of the collective right to self-determination, as I will explain later, the second paradox is in expecting states to protect human rights against their own officials. By identifying these (and other) paradoxical aspects of the human rights paradigm I mean to acknowledge them as integral to the human rights paradigm itself, rather than matters of incidental inconvenience that could have been avoided or can be eliminated. I use the term 'paradox' also to indicate that these are features that can and should be mediated, rather than being possible to resolve once and for all.

The effective and sustained implementation and protection of human rights are contingent on the mediation of the double paradox of universality and sovereignty through the promotion of the political will to develop norms and institutions, allocate resources, and so forth. The basic issue here is similar to what happens with the implementation and protection of fundamental constitutional rights at the national level, namely, how to translate normative entrenchment beyond the contingencies of regular politics. The mediation of paradox in both cases (of constitutional rights and human rights) requires the mobilisation of political will to allocate resources, build institutions and motivate the general public to engage in monitoring violations and demanding accountability and remedies. These processes will require legitimacy for the norms and processes among the relevant population, which raises the issue of universality for human rights that are supposed to apply everywhere. I need now to offer some brief elaboration on these remarks.

As a *concept*, human rights are necessarily universal because they are supposed to be the rights of every human being, yet the 'human' in this concept of human rights is particular to her or his identity, beliefs, experiences and context. In terms of *content*, what are these rights and what makes them universal in the reality of permanent and profound diversity among human beings, individually and collectively? How can people of different cultural, religious or philosophical orientation, different social and economic class, education and so forth, agree on what is due to all human beings by virtue of their humanity? There is then the role of *context* in the definition as well as the implementation of human rights in the reality of deeply rooted and structural difference in power relations among and within societies.

The modern human rights paradigm has only emerged and evolved since the mid 1940s. In particular, the articulation and implementation of this paradigm on a global scale that is consistent with the concept itself was mandated by the Charter of the UN and subsequent process of decolonisation during the second half of the twentieth century. Foundational documents like the American Declaration of Independence and the French Declaration of the Rights of Man and the Citizen have contributed to the development of the idea of fundamental rights of citizens, not the rights of human beings as such. Moreover, since the 'human' in human rights is a self-determining human person, rights are not human rights unless they are accepted as such by their human subject, who can then strive to protect them for themselves. This holistic vision cannot be realised all at once in theory or practice, but the project is truly of human rights only to the extent that the theory and practice are designed to realise this people-centred vision in a comprehensive and pragmatic manner.

The human rights paradigm also developed by mediating the above-mentioned paradoxes of assertion of the universality of rights in a reality that is marked both by permanent and profound cultural and contextual difference, and by self-regulation by the state. This second paradox is clearly reflected in the Charter of the UN itself, which calls for international co-operation in the protection of human rights and fundamental freedoms as one of the purposes of the UN (Article 1.3), while at the same time confirming non-intervention in the domestic jurisdiction of states as one of the principles of the UN (Article 2.7). However, the tension between self-determination for individual persons, on the one hand, and collective self-determination for national, cultural, racial or ethnic groups can lead to the violation of the human rights of individuals under the guise of protecting or promoting the collective right to self-determination.[4]

Conversely, the universality of human rights can be the standard by which the legitimacy of state sovereignty can be evaluated. Such possibilities of mediation, however, can only materialise through the agency of people who are sufficiently motivated to risk harsh repression, including

---

[4] Vincent, *The Politics of Human Rights* 95.

threat to life and livelihood, for demanding respect for their human rights. External coercive enforcement of human rights norms is not only illegal under international law, but also unlikely to work, and probably counter-productive in practice. I would therefore emphasise the importance of promoting legitimacy to enhance the sustainable efficacy of human rights norms since coercive enforcement is both unlikely in practice and unacceptable in principle.

The paradox of self-regulation by the state is in the relationship between international human rights norms and institutions, on the one hand, and the territorial sovereignty of states, on the other. According to current international law doctrine, only states can set human rights norms and assume responsibility for the protection of the rights of persons subject to their jurisdiction. Yet, the international law principle of territorial sover-eignty and political independence of states precludes coercive external imposition, except possibly under extremely limited circumstances strictly defined by international treaties that are negotiated and voluntarily ratified by states themselves. A current lawful possibility of coercive enforcement is by the Security Council of the UN under Chapter VII of the UN Charter, when such violations constitute a risk to international peace and security.

The modern state has apparently come to accept commitments to protect human rights as an additional and necessary feature of their entitlement to sovereign equality. While non-intervention remained a central element in the construction of sovereign statehood, legitimacy also demanded evi-dence of a good human rights record.[5] The paradox is in expecting any state to adopt human rights norms to limit its own powers, and then to effectively enforce those limitations against the officials of the same state. This para-dox should also be seen against the broader backdrop of the doctrinal and institutional limitations of international law in general, like its inability to regulate the conduct of non-state actors who violate human rights and humanitarian law principles. While the sovereign state continues to play a role within global politics, newly emerging socio-economic structures have created conditions under which the same sort of harm that is technically called human rights violation when by a state occurs beyond the reach of the state.[6] It can also be argued that the traditional tension between claims of state sovereignty and individual freedoms is now sometimes superseded

---

[5] Evans, *Human Rights in the Global Political Economy* 123.
[6] Evans, *Human Rights in the Global Political Economy* 115–16.

by the tension between the economic imperatives of globalisation and human rights.[7] Yet, over time, the decline in people's participation, coupled with the maintenance of an order in which the governed are increasingly objectified, ensures that people become more accountable to remote globalised centres of authority, rather than those centres being accountable to people.[8]

The premise and rationale of the idea that the 'human' in human rights is a self-determining human being is that the person should defend and protect her/his own rights, yet it is difficult to see how a victim of a human rights violation can have the ability and resources to protect her/his own rights. Whether it is arbitrary detention, suppression of freedom of speech and association, or denial of rights to education, health care or housing, the violation in fact hampers our ability to protect our rights. We need external resources and actors to protect our rights when we are actual victims of violations, yet reliance on external protection of rights is likely to perpetuate our dependency instead of enhancing our self-determination. Whoever provides the resources and acts to protect the rights of others will do so on his/her own terms that are by definition not those of the victims whose rights we purport to protect. When my rights are protected by others, those others get to decide what my rights mean and how they should be protected, and I become the 'object' of their charity, not the autonomous human subject who is protecting her own rights.

This paradox of 'human rights dependency' can be mediated through the promotion of the cultural legitimacy of human rights in various societies in order to motivate and mobilise people to protect their own rights.[9] But the paradox continues, as dependency on external protection can only be diminished over time through the co-operation of internal and external actors. The difficulty here is not only that external actors are unlikely to appreciate the need to submit to internal initiative and leadership, but also that internal 'beneficiaries' are unable to compel external actors to act against those actors' view of which rights they wish to protect and how they wish to do that. Moreover, even if it were practically possible, to require external actors to submit to internal leadership can be problematic when it means requiring external actors to accept attitudes and behaviour within

---

[7] Evans, *Human Rights in the Global Political Economy* 120.

[8] Evans, *Human Rights in the Global Political Economy* 14.

[9] See generally, e.g., A. An-Na'im (ed.), *Human Rights in Cross-Cultural Perspectives: Quest for Consensus* (University of Pennsylvania Press 1992).

the community that they believe to be in violation of, for instance, the rights of women or children.

In any case, the methods for implementing human rights are also conditioned by culture, religion and tradition of the people who hold the right. This is probably why any attempt at 'transplanting' the legal institutions of developed states into traditional cultures, often without any knowledge of existing cultural norms and mores, inevitably fails.[10] The problem is not only that Western imposition of human rights exposes the 'West' to charges of cultural imperialism, which some Western human rights scholars find to be preferable to not attempting to promote the idea of a rights-based society, but that also and quite apart from this, imposition does not work.[11]

In light of the preceding comments, I would argue that interdisciplinarity is integral to every aspect of the theory and practice of human rights. For instance, the mediation of the various paradoxes highlighted above defies simplistic assertions of legal obligation or coercive political tactics. The agency of the self-determining human subject of human rights must be taken seriously at every level of analysis and action. As noted earlier, the imperative of the global inclusivity of the discourse, noted at the beginning, should be taken into account in understanding what interdisciplinarity means and how it works in this context. Yet, for the strategies and policy implications of discourse to be coherent and practically useful, it needs to be conceptually and contextually located and bounded to be coherent. Taking such examples into account, I will now discuss the meaning and implications of interdisciplinarity, its benefits and limitations in relation to human rights law in particular. How can this approach help in the mediation of the paradoxes and tensions at the theoretical level of the universality of human rights and in the process whereby human rights norms are defined and agreed upon? And how can it assist in understanding the role of context in the interpretation and implementation of human rights norms? It should be further noted that interdisciplinarity is also needed at the practical level of developing and implementing policies, evaluating human rights outcomes, choosing legitimate choices among competing claims of rights, and connecting such policies to political stability, economic development, environmental concerns and so forth. An interdisciplinary approach is needed for addressing all such questions.

---

[10] Evans, *Human Rights in the Global Political Economy* 40–1.
[11] Evans, *Human Rights in the Global Political Economy* 38.

Interdisciplinarity of human rights

It may be argued that the value of interdisciplinarity in the study of human rights lies in its flexibility and indeterminacy. To submit the term and concept to a strict definition would 'discipline' it, that is, confine it within a set of theoretical and methodological orthodoxies. 'The very nature of interdisciplinarity, as we understand it, requires that those who engage in it will always be working beyond the edges of what they know how to do well; in conception and methodology, such work cannot become conventional.'[12] Yet, we must at least describe the meaning and implications of the term and concept in order to be able to talk about what it is, or what it can or cannot do. Such a minimalist indication of meaning and scope might begin by trying to clarify what the idea of interdisciplinarity is supposed to counter or redress, namely, the limitations of disciplinarity. This inquiry would include an explanation of disciplinarity, and appreciation of the need for different disciplines in the study of human rights.

Different fields of academic study have developed their own concepts, structure and methods of research that are believed to enable each discipline to contribute to clarifying and addressing relevant issues and concerns. Disciplinary boundaries are believed to be effective in their respective fields because they combine particular methods with agreed-upon knowledge and assumptions. This makes studies more efficient because the terms and conditions of discourse are specified and understood by participants in the discipline. Conversely, it seems to follow, going beyond the boundaries of an established discipline could lead to confusion and miscommunication. It is probably true that the very nature of knowledge today creates a paradox.[13] On the one hand, the volume and intricacy of information creates a need to confine knowledge into disciplines in order to better organise and manage a field of knowledge.[14] On the other hand, being confined can have its drawbacks. The strict boundaries of disciplines do not allow for exploration across disciplines.[15] Since each discipline has its flaws, working with

---

[12] A. Dalke, P. Grobstein and E. McCormack, 'Theorizing Interdisciplinarity: The Evolution of New Academic and Intellectual Communities', http://serendip.brynmawr.edu/local/scisoc/theorizing.html (date of last access 12 July 2011).

[13] M. H. Strober, *Interdisciplinary Conversations: Challenging Habits of Thought* (Stanford University Press 2011) 2.

[14] Strober, *Interdisciplinary Conversations* 2.   [15] Strober, *Interdisciplinary Conversations* 2.

more than one discipline can overcome or minimise the consequences of such flaws, thereby contributing to a greater understanding of inter-related issues and concerns.[16]

Understanding interdisciplinarity in contrast to disciplinarity may indicate that the advantage of the latter are disadvantages of the former, and vice versa. Some would argue from this perspective that interdisciplinarity is redundant because it is just another tool to manage academia, seeking to accomplish the same task that disciplinary studies do, namely, explore areas of knowledge.[17] For those who hold this view, the collapse of disciplines means the collapse of interdisciplinarity as well because interdisciplinarity is said to be the institutional ratification of the logic of disciplinarity.[18] That is, assuming interdisciplinarity becomes a discipline, it is bound to share the problems and limitations of disciplinarity. For its proponents, however, interdisciplinarity 'challenges to revise and potentially transcend the ways in which we understand and employ our own disciplinary terms . . . [it is] a continuing and refreshing counterbalance to the "conventional"'.[19] In other words, even if it becomes a discipline, it would add value to the way we do disciplinary work. If we think of interdisciplinarity as a philosophy and an approach to knowledge and communication, it can still improve on what traditional disciplines can do. That is, the task of interdisciplinarity is to do what strict disciplinarity cannot do by virtue of their disciplinary nature. This is what I mean by the flexibility and indeterminacy of interdisciplinary: the more it can resist being reduced into a rigid discipline the better it can do what disciplines are not supposed to be able to do because of their adherence to disciplinary boundaries, assumptions and methodologies.

As a minimalist working definition, the idea of interdisciplinarity evokes a sense of something different, perhaps more, than disciplinarity, which indicates that it can be understood in relation to, if not in contrast with, disciplinarity. 'Interdisciplinary studies may be defined as a process of answering a question, solving a problem, or addressing a topic that is too broad or complex to be dealt with adequately by a single discipline or

---

[16] Strober, *Interdisciplinary Conversations* 1.

[17] M. Soldavenko, 'The Limits of Interdisciplinarity', in J. Parker, R. Samantrai and M. Romero (eds.), *Interdisciplinarity and Social Justice* (Albany, NY: State University of New York Press, 2010) 208.

[18] Solvadenko, 'The Limits of Interdisciplinarity' 209.

[19] Dalke, Grobstein and McCormack, 'Theorizing Interdisciplinarity'.

profession.'[20] It can be understood as any form of dialogue or interaction between two or more disciplines, focusing on 'the concerns of epistemology – the study of knowledge – and tends to be centered around problems and issues that cannot be addressed or solved within the existing disciplines, rather than the quest for an all inclusive synthesis'.[21] The term can mean a process involving the forging of connections across different disciplines, of establishing a kind of undisciplined space in the interstices between disciplines in an effort to transcend disciplinary boundaries altogether.

Interdisciplinary studies have the potential to do more than simply bring the different disciplines together; they can form part of a more general critique of academic specialisation as a whole in order to expand and transform areas of knowledge. This philosophy and approach is integral to the paradox and contingency of human rights as highlighted earlier. The concept, content and context of human rights are challenging to self-contained academic disciplines because the very nature of human rights involves human experiences that are too complex and intricate for any discipline to fully understand and work with. In particular, the inadequacy of a legal approach to human rights is obvious when we consider the need to understand behaviour that underlies human rights violations, and trying to influence and transform it in order to enhance the agency of the human subject in the implementation of her own human rights, as emphasised earlier.

The assumption underlying belief in law as the primary discipline for human rights is due to the fact the present system for the setting and implementation of human rights norms is founded on international treaties and other documents that are adopted under the general framework of international law. Moreover, the practical application of human rights norms is also dependent on national constitutional and legal systems. However, while international and domestic law may be necessary, they are far from sufficient for sustaining the theory and practice of human rights anywhere in the world. At a most basic level, the discipline of law is incapable of explaining the gap between the promises of international treaties and institutions, on the one hand, and the practical reality of

---

[20]   J. Thompson Klein and W. H. Newell, 'Advancing Interdisciplinary Studies', in W. H. Newell (ed.), *Interdisciplinarity: Essays from the Literature* (New York: College Entrance Examination Board 1998) 3.

[21]   J. Moran, *Interdisciplinarity* (New York: Routledge 2010) 15.

human rights practice around the world, on the other.[22] This requires investigation by the various social sciences of the causes of social conflict and political oppression, and the interaction between national and international politics. A legal approach to human rights cannot adequately analyse the ethical, political, sociological, economic and anthropological dimensions of human rights. The social sciences have substantive interests and research methods that can illuminate the social practice of human rights and therefore contribute greatly to the study of human rights.[23]

Social sciences and the humanities are needed for understanding the international and domestic politics of human rights, and the formal development of human rights through political processes, such as debates and votes at international and domestic institutions. Those disciplines can explain the factors and processes that produce human rights violations, and under which conditions are they more likely to happen. By formulating and empirically testing causal hypotheses, social scientists can contribute to the making and implementation of policies that are conducive to better protection and implementation of human rights norms.[24] Even for the legal dimension of human rights, the social sciences can study how the law is made, interpreted and implemented, at both the international and domestic level.[25] 'Beyond law lies social reality that shapes what the law says, how it is implemented, and who, as a consequence, gets what, why, when and how … The analysis of human rights requires, therefore, the social-scientific analysis of social and political forces that shape and either facilitate or hinder the implementation of human-rights law.'[26] Anthropology can help with understanding how normative systems evolve and interact with state legal systems. It can provide possible analytical opportunities for focusing on particular situations, individual actions, wider structural inequities and systems of meaning.[27] With its experience

---

[22] M. Freeman, *Human Rights: An Interdisciplinary Approach* (Cambridge: Polity 2002) 4.

[23] Freeman, *Human Rights* 78.

[24] K. de Feyter, 'Treaty Interpretation and The Social Sciences', in F. Coomans, F. Grünfeld and M. T. Kaminga (eds.), *Methods of Human Rights Research* (Antwerp/Oxford/Portland, OR: Intersentia 2009) 217–18.

[25] M. Freeman (2005) 'Putting Law in Its Place: An Interdisciplinary Evaluation of National Amnesty Laws', in S. Meckled-Garcia and B Çali (eds.), *The Legalization of Human Rights: Multidisciplinary Perspectives on Human Rights and Human Rights Law* (New York: Routledge, 2005) 52–3.

[26] Freeman, 'Putting Law in Its Place' 54.

[27] S. Merry, 'Anthropology and International Law' (2006) 35 *Annual Review of Anthropology* 99–116.

with traditional normative systems, anthropology can also improve our understanding of how international law works as a de-centralised rule-making system that relies on social pressure, collaboration and negotiations among parties to develop rules and resolve conflicts. 'The contextualization of human-rights discourse may also reveal its class character; access to the world of human-rights defenders is not distributed equally across social classes. The truth-regime of law treats all persons as equal, even though, in relation to social power, they are not.'[28] Contributions of psychology include understanding the mindset of victims and violators, sympathy, empathy and motivation of cruelty, as factors in human behaviour that can affect the status of human rights in different communities.[29]

Granted the various social sciences and humanities can add to our understanding of the theory and practice of human rights, what and how does *inter*disciplinarity add to *multi*disciplinarity?

In theory, a clear distinction can be drawn between *inter*disciplinarity and *multi*disciplinarity. Multidisciplinarity refers to the sum total of knowledge derived from different disciplines on a given subject ... [in contrast] Integration is key to an interdisciplinary approach. This may consist of the use of a methodology that somehow escapes disciplinary limitations, and catches reality more fully, or of the development of a grand theory on a specific issue that is disconnected from any specific discipline, but is based on an amalgam of methods and findings. Real research ventures, educational programmes or strategies may defy easy classification under either label.[30]

Ideally, we would want to retain benefits of disciplines and foster interdisciplinary collaboration. Encouraging interdisciplinary collaboration allows individual researchers to accumulate more information and apply multiple methodologies to their analysis and conclusions. Collaboration increases the likelihood of effective and innovative solutions. As scholars and researchers consider questions from outside their own disciplines, learn other methods and think about possible significance of the findings of other disciplines for their own work they may begin to think about their own disciplines in new ways. However, while it is clear that social scientists have a lot to add to our understanding of human rights and how they work, there

---

[28] Merry, 'Anthropology and International Law' 55.   [29] Freeman, *Human Rights* 90–2.
[30] K. De Feyter, 'In Defence of a Multidisciplinary Approach to Human Rights', in K. De Feyter and G. Pavlakos (eds.), *The Tension Between Group Rights and Human Rights: A Multidisciplinary Approach* (Portland, OR: Hart 2008) 13.

is the risk that they may ignore or misinterpret applicable legal norms.[31] Moreover, it may be true that 'genuine, high quality interdisciplinary research is rare because few researchers are fully qualified in more than one discipline'.[32] This may be true of any field or discipline of study when it first emerges and evolves over time, as none of the disciplines that we now take for granted was born fully fledged and easy to do. In any case, various aspects of such a proposition can be the subject of research. For instance, how do we judge whether interdisciplinary research is of 'genuine, high quality'? What does being 'fully qualified in more than one discipline mean', who is to judge and on which criteria? To confirm, I am not denying the possible validity of that proposition, but only seeking its clarification with a view to redressing the causes and manifestation of the difficulty. After all, that is what happened with all the 'established disciplines' as we have them today.

Further inquiry

Interdisciplinarity can be broadly defined as a mode of research by teams or individuals that integrates information, data, techniques, tools, perspectives, concepts and/or theories from two or more disciplines or bodies of specialised knowledge to advance fundamental understanding or to solve problems whose solutions are beyond the scope of a single discipline or area of research practice.[33] While this philosophy and approach would be, in my view, very useful for the study of human rights for the purpose of promoting effective and sustainable implementation of these rights, as emphasised from the outset, there are some inherent ambiguities and tensions in the concept that need clarification and mediation. For instance, how can interdisciplinarity escape the limitations of disciplinarity by maintaining its flexibility and indeterminacy, while being focused and effective in fulfilling its mandate? How is interdisciplinarity different from multidisciplinarity, and how to achieve its value-added in practice?

I have also highlighted some specific themes or issues that can benefit from further inquiry, such as the question of the mediation of the paradox of global

---

[31] F. Coomans, F. Grünfeld and M. T. Kaminga, *Methods of Human Rights Research* (Antwerp/ Oxford/Portland, OR: Intersentia 2009) 12.

[32] Coomans, Grünfeld and Kaminga, *Methods of Human Rights* 17.

[33] Strober, *Interdisciplinary Conversations* 16.

inclusivity of discourse about the interdisciplinarity of human rights. Is the idea of 'imagining the unimaginable and retrieving the irretrievable', as suggested in the introduction of this chapter, coherent and viable? Can this approach deliver on the promise of mediating the paradox of inclusivity in the post-colonial context? Another theme or set of issues to be addressed relates to the quality of interdisciplinary researching relation to human rights in particular. There also the related question of the 'qualifications' of those who can do truly interdisciplinary human rights research? Is this a question of training and expertise in particular fields, or a matter of philosophical or cultural orientation, perhaps a political attitude as well? In the final analysis, an interdisciplinary approach to the study of human rights may not work well or fail to deliver on its promise, but those who believe, as I do, in the necessity and possibility of the universality of human rights should take this approach seriously. In view of the multiple and complex theoretical and practical challenges facing this visionary project, including its inherent paradox and contingency highlighted earlier, I believe that every possibility should be explored for the theoretical clarification and practical facilitation of the implementation of human rights throughout the world.

Further reading

Baker, J., Lynch, K., Cantillon, S. and Walsh, J., 'Equality: Putting the Theory into Action' (2006) 12 (4) *Res Publica* 411–33

Downing, T. E. and Kushner, G. (eds.), *Human Rights and Anthropology* (Cambridge, MA: Cultural Survival 1988)

Glendon, M. A., 'Interdisciplinary Approaches: Rights in Twentieth-Century Constitutions' (1992) 59 *University of Chicago Law Review* 519–38

Hathaway, O. A., 'Do Human Rights Treaties Make a Difference?' (2001–2) 111 (8) *Yale Law Journal* 1935–2042

Landman, T., *Protecting Human Rights: A Comparative Study* (Washington, DC: Georgetown University Press 2005)

McCamant, J. F., 'Social Science and Human Rights' (1998) 35 (3) *International Organization* 531–52

Messer, E., 'Anthropology and Human Rights' (1993) 22 *Annual Review of Anthropology* 221–49

Simonsen, K.-M. and Tamm, D. (eds.), *Law and Literature: Interdisciplinary Methods of Reading* (Copenhagen: DJØF Publishing 2010)

Slaughter, A. -M., Tulumello, A. and Wood, S., 'International Law and International Relations Theory: A New Generation of Interdisciplinary Scholarship' (1998) 92 *American Journal of International Law* 367–97

Thompson Klein, J., *Interdisciplinarity: History, Theory, and Practice* (Michigan, MN: Wayne State University Press 1990)

Humanities, Culture, and Interdisciplinarity: The Changing American Academy (Albany, NY: State University of New York Press 2005)

Vincent, R. J., *Human Rights and International Relations* (Cambridge University Press 1986)

Washburn, W. E., 'Cultural Relativism, Human Rights, and the AAA' (1987) 89 (4) *American Anthropologist* 939–43

Wilson, R. A. (ed.), *Human Rights, Culture and Context: Anthropological Perspectives* (London: Pluto Press 1997)

6 Atrocity, law, humanity: punishing human rights violators

Gerry Simpson

François de Menthon, one of the French Prosecutors at the Nuremberg war crimes trial in 1945, was assigned the task of defining humanity. The context was a trial in which a more or less new legal category – crimes against humanity – had to be created to encompass the system of abuse and murder instituted by the Nazis in the mid 1930s. This development had a spatial imperative (Nazi crimes committed against Germans in Germany fell outside the category of 'war crimes', a category encompassing only acts committed against foreign soldiers or civilians), a temporal imperative (war crimes applied only to acts committed during war and excluded peace-time offences) and a moral imperative (it was believed that an unprecedented level of baseness had been reached and that the response to it required a new language and new law).

In its delineation of crimes against humanity, de Menthon's opening address to the International Military Tribunal invoked three distinguishable concepts. The first was the idea that certain acts were crimes against human beings regardless of the race, religion, national affiliation or ethnicity of the victims.[1] This was international criminal law in its universalising mode, and it was an inspiration for two 1948 landmarks: The Genocide Convention (in the field of criminal law) and The Universal Declaration of Human Rights (UDHR) (in the field of human rights law).

De Menthon's second version of crimes against humanity advanced an understanding of them as crimes materially affecting one particular group but somehow committed against all human beings. To quote the language of the International Military Tribunal, these were crimes that 'shocked the conscience of mankind', and this shock incited the agents of mankind into adopting a variety of now-familiar responses: universal jurisdiction over war criminals,[2] international tribunals (Milosević in The

---

[1] F. de Menthon, 'Opening Address (January 17, 1946', in M. R. Marrus (ed.), *The Nuremberg War Crimes Trial 1945–46: A Documentary History* (Boston, MA: Bedford/St Martin's 1997).

[2] H. Arendt, *Eichmann in Jerusalem: A Report on the Banality of Evil* (London: Penguin Classics 2006; first published 1963).

Hague) and the concept of 'prosecute or extradite' found in treaties like The Apartheid Convention and The Torture Convention (Pinochet in Piccadilly).[3]

The third, and most radical, concept of humanity saw it as a unified, indivisible and inalienable category that resisted both attempts to divide human beings into 'more or less human' as well as political programmes through which a person's humanity could be forfeited or alienated. Crimes against humanity, then, as Hannah Arendt remarked, had their origins in an effort to abolish humanity through a policy of mass murder, slavery and deportation whose governing principle was the imperative that the Jewish people was to be destroyed and whose governing methods were marked by a combination of industrial murder, savagery, extreme cruelty and relentless humiliation. The Holocaust was a crime, as she put it, against the order of mankind.[4]

The International Military Tribunal charged the high-ranking Nazis with three other separate substantive offences (war crimes, conspiracy and crimes against peace) but, while these are not unconnected to the human rights law project that developed in the wake of the Second World War, it was the prosecution of crimes against humanity that contributed most to the development of human rights in the immediate aftermath of the war and defined the relationship between international human rights law and international criminal law in the decades that followed. And, it is at least arguable that de Menthon's three categories of humanity continue to underpin the two fields today. Each field rotates around a commitment to securing rights to individuals without discrimination ('humanity', not 'Englishness' or 'civilisation', is the presiding category), each appeals to an assumed common sense or shared universal conscience, and each seems, putatively, committed to the *idea* of inalienability (humanity is a project to be protected against those who would deny humanity to particular classes of people on the basis that individuals within these classes – by exercising their creed or by resisting Empire or by committing acts of terror – have taken themselves outside the category of humanity).

But this last commitment is controversial and unstable. The paradox at the heart of this twin project (international criminal law and international human rights law) is that while its core animating idea is the abolition of all

---

[3] A. Beckett, *Pinochet in Picadilly* (London: Faber & Faber 2002).

[4] Arendt, *Eichmann in Jerusalem.*

distinctions within humanity, some of its most energetic practices are dedicated to punishing 'inhumane' acts (acts committed by individuals who have lost their humanity?) and acting on behalf of humanity against those who are deemed to have stepped outside or defied humanity (think of Léon Bourgeois, at the Versailles Peace Conference, insisting on 'penalties to be imposed for disobedience to the common will of civilised nations').[5] Its favoured penalties, indeed, often come in the form of extreme violence applied to these outsiders (historically, the quartering of pirates, the beheading of tyrants; more recently, the hanging of war criminals and the waging of 'humanitarian wars'). But this history of violence does not appear to have unseated or even qualified humanity's self-confidence. Speaking very much in this vein, Raymond Poincaré, the French President, announced, also at Versailles: 'Humanity can place confidence in you, because you are not among those who have outraged the rights of humanity'.[6]

So, the idea of punishing human rights violators using international criminal law sanctions can be thought of as a negotiation between international law's universalist impulse (sometimes represented by the prosecution of those who commit 'crimes against humanity') and its imperial instinct (mostly found in the repression of 'enemies of mankind'). The second part of this chapter will narrate the story of international criminal law through a reading of the origins of humanity in 'enemies of mankind' (pirates, tyrants and aggressors) and 'crimes against humanity' (war criminals) before surveying the five forms of jurisdiction that constitute the contemporary international war crimes scene. In the final section, I track three affinities between international human rights law and international criminal law and the way in which these affinities are defined, partly, by the bargain (see above) between these two defining projects of humanity.

A short history of law and atrocity

This is not the place to engage in genealogies of humanity (for a variety of diachronic readings of human rights and crimes against

---

[5] *Papers Relating to the Foreign Relations of the United States, 1919 The Paris Peace Conference* (1942–7) 185.

[6] 'Commission on the Responsibility of the Authors of War and on Enforcement of Penalties – Report Presented to the Preliminary Peace Conference' (1920) 14 *AJIL* 95.

humanity),[7] but clearly the programme of humanity emerged burdened with a number of contradictions. In the case of human rights, the French Revolution and the rights of man are encumbered by their associations with extreme violence, the US Declaration of Independence is a document about collective rights to self-determination in which the collective rights of others are textually repressed ('savages'), and the effort to outlaw slavery (in the name of humanity) coincides with an intensification in the repressive policies of Empire (this is a short list).

The idea of a humanity against which crimes are committed and in the name of which these crimes can be punished and repressed (international criminal law) has a similarly equivocal history. Three possible origins might be identified here (the final of these origins will serve as an introduction to the modern history of war crimes law).

The first lies in the repression of piracy (more or less throughout the history of the *ius gentium* but particularly during the golden age of Atlantic piracy in the seventeenth and eighteenth centuries). Pirates were the first 'enemies of mankind' against which an international legal regime could be mobilised. But if piracy somehow 'constituted' mankind then it was a severely attenuated form of mankind composed of a tiny fraction of relatively wealthy nations intent on constructing a global (or at least North Atlantic) market in goods. Melodramatic language ('mankind'), invective (heinous crimes) and enraged repression (the public hangings of pirates) produced an unforgiving security order[8] – and bequeathed to international criminal law a rhetorical superstructure (enemies of mankind, crimes against humanity and so on).[9]

A second origin lies in the enlightenment itself. God's overthrow led to the re-grounding of human experience in forms of nature and reason; it provoked an ethical loneliness and it required a sacralisation of the secular. Humanity became an enlightenment project designed to bring reason to the irrational. Enemies of the enlightenment (tyrants in Europe and the Americas) and enemies of civilisation (savages on the world's peripheries)

---

[7] L. Hunt, *Inventing Human Rights: A History* (New York: W. W. Norton 2007); R. Blackburn, 'Reclaiming Human Rights' (2010) 69 *New Left Review* 126–38; S. Moyn, *The Last Utopia: Human Rights in History* (Cambridge, MA: Harvard University Press, 2010).

[8] M. Rediker, *Villans of All Nations: Atlantic Pirates in the Golden Age* (New York: Verso 2004).

[9] E. Kontorovich, 'The Piracy Analogy: Universal Jurisdiction's Hollow Foundation' (2004) 4 *Harvard Journal of International Law* 183; G. Simpson, *Law, War and Crime* (Cambridge: Polity 2007).

become enemies of mankind (two people are beheaded in Europe – Charles I and, a century later, Louis XVI – and, one hundred years after Louis' execution, two million people are beheaded in Leopold's Congo).[10]

The final (legal–technical) origin of humanity is found in the first half of the twentieth century and in the wake of the enlightenment project that had sustained it. And here I begin another synoptic history: this time of the modern project – sometimes called international criminal law, sometimes called the law of war crimes – to hold individuals accountable for violations of fundamental norms of international law and political decency.

The First World War – that final 'abridgment of hope'[11]– gave rise to the first serious effort (at Versailles) to instal humanity as a legal category. During the war, Lloyd George promised war crimes trials for the defeated Germans, and, in tandem with the equally punitive French, he managed to have inserted into the Versailles Peace Treaty provisions calling for the trial of the Kaiser for crimes against 'the sanctity of nations and against international morality' (Article 227) and demanding war crimes trials for his associates (Articles 228–230). Crimes against humanity and crimes against peace thereby were introduced into the lexicon of global politics (indeed, they help cement the whole idea of it).

The transitional document is the *Report of the Commission on the Responsibilities of the Authors of the War*. Meeting at Versailles in 1920 and composed of lawyers and diplomats from the victorious states, this commission was given the task of determining who was to be charged and with what. There was a split between commission delegates wedded to the old ideas of wars as inter-sovereign affairs and sovereignty as a bundle of unchallengeable prerogatives, and those who wished to transform war into a form of police action and state prerogative into sovereign privilege.

---

[10] This figure can only be a guessed at. The figures for deaths in the Belgian Congo caused by induced starvation and massacre vary. Indeed, the variance itself is disturbing. Mark Twain put the figure at 5–8 million. Brian Fawcett has Hannah Arendt quoting a figure of between 15 and 40 million dead. See A. Hochschild, *King Leopold's Ghost* (New York: Houghton Mifflin 1998); B. Fawcett, *Cambodia* (New York: Columbia University Press 1986); M. Twain, *King Leopold's Soliloquy* (Philadelphia, PA: Warren Co. 1905). The most common practice was to cut off the limbs or heads of victims (including many children) in order to prove administrative competence. The photograph (in Hochschild) of a Congolese father sitting next to the severed hand and foot of his five-year-old daughter is horribly illustrative. Only two decades later, the Allies were claiming that Belgian children had suffered the same fate under German occupation. These stories proved to be untrue but they provide a powerful impetus for the first internationally mandated war crimes trials.

[11] L. Strachey, *Literary Essays* (New York: Harcourt, Brace & Co. 1949).

According to the first group (it included the US and Japanese delegations, each of whom appended a 'Memorandum of Reservations' to the final report), it was meaningless, in the midst of a morally pluralistic international order, to speak of 'crimes against humanity' (in any event, they argued, the Kaiser was entitled to immunity in respect of any 'crimes' he might have committed). The Majority disagreed, calling the German elite to account for what Billy Hughes, the Australian Prime Minister, had called 'treason against humanity'.[12] Even the Majority delegates were deeply uncomfortable with the idea of crimes against peace, though, and it was not until Nuremberg that there was consensus on the need to hold violators responsible for crimes against peace and humanity (it is, perhaps, worth noting here by way of partial explanation that Germany was entirely subdued and occupied in 1945 whereas at the end of the First World War, the German Army remained in occupation of foreign territory).[13]

At the same time, the category 'enemies of mankind' was revived through the idea – first found in the League of Nations – of humanity acting as a unified political agent, or concatenation of Great Powers (in the name of the international community) against outlaw or aggressor nations. This transformation, disentangled by Carr[14] and lamented by Schmitt, transformed war into a form of 'pest control'.[15]

The tentative beginnings at Versailles (the peace treaty and crimes against humanity and peace) and Geneva (the League of Nations and collective security) were consummated at Nuremberg (the International Military Tribunal) and San Francisco (the UN Charter and the institutionalisation of a collective security mechanism directed at would-be aggressors) in 1945.

Fifty years after twenty-one Nazi leaders were tried in Germany and forty-two Japanese A Class suspects were tried in Tokyo, and after a recess from 1948 to 1993 when there were only domestic trials – in Lyon (Klaus Barbie), in Jerusalem (Adolf Eichmann), in Frankfurt (the concentration camp guards trial), in Tel Aviv (John Demjanjuk) – international criminal law has become an intensely active institutional field.

I began writing this chapter on the day (27 June 2011) that the Pre-Trial Chamber I of the International Criminal Court (ICC) issued its decision to

---

[12] G. Bass, *Stay the Hand of Vengeance* (Princeton University Press 2000) 68.
[13] R. J. Evans, 'The Scramble for Europe' (2011) *London Review of Books*, 3 February 17–19.
[14] E. H. Carr, *The Twenty Years' Crisis* (Basingstoke: Palgrave Macmillan 2001).
[15] C. Schmitt, *The Nomos of the Earth* (New York: Telos 2003) 123.

issue arrest warrants against Colonel Gaddafi, his intelligence chief, Abdullah Senussi, and his son, Saif.[16] It was also the day that the trial of four senior Khmer Rouge leaders (Case 002) commenced in Phnom Penh. It might be possible, then, to celebrate this as the culmination of a particular moment in the history of institutions. The ICC, itself thought of as a sort of terminus for international law, had finally insinuated itself into the heart of international diplomacy by indicting a major political figure; meanwhile, the Cambodian Extraordinary Chambers was embarking on the last of its trials – perhaps, the final such trial to be heard by a hybrid tribunal (a mixed international and national tribunal) in this era of hybridity. At the very least, all of this, combined with the Security Council's activism in relation to piracy (the original international crime and now a recently revived practice see, for example, Security Council Resolution 1861 (2008) and Resolution 1851 (2008)) and the recent indictments of Hezbollah leaders by the Special Tribunal for The Lebanon (the Hariri Tribunal), is symptomatic of a discipline enjoying its most productive period.

By the beginning of the twenty-first century, then, there were at least five different forms of international criminal jurisdiction. First, the Security Council, perhaps shamed by its inaction in Bosnia and Rwanda, had established two ad hoc tribunals, in The Hague (the International Criminal Tribunal for the Former Yugoslavia, ICTFY) and in Arusha, Tanzania (the International Criminal Tribunal for Rwanda, ICTR) with jurisdiction over crimes against humanity, genocide war crimes and serious violations of the laws of war. These tribunals had limited jurisdiction in one sense (they were temporally and territorially confined) but expansive jurisdiction in another (for the first time, war crimes committed in *non*-international armed conflict violations were tried). Trials arising out of these institutional developments (e.g. *Milosević*;[17] *Krstić*;[18] *Akayesu*,[19] a major trial in which the international humanitarian law of rape and sexual assault was developed and the first genocide conviction in an international war crimes tribunal was achieved; and *Tadić*,[20] applying the laws of war to internal armed

---

[16] *Prosecutor v. Muammar Gaddafi, Said Al-Islam Gaddafi and Abdullah Sanussi* ICC-01/11-01/11 (2011).

[17] *Prosecutor v. Slobodan Milosević (Amended Indictment)* IT-02-54-T (22 November 2002).

[18] *Prosecutor v. Radislav Krstić* IT-98-33-T, Judgment (2 August 2001).

[19] *Prosecutor v. Jean-Paul Akayesu* ICTR-96-4-T, Judgment (2 September 1998).

[20] *Prosecutor v. Duško Tadić* IT-94-1-A, Judgment (15 July 1999).

conflict) produced international criminal law's richest jurisprudence to date. The current (at time of writing) trials of Radovan Karadžić and Ratko Mladić represent the end-game for this ad hoc tribunal process.

The second form of jurisdiction involved hybrid tribunals created by joint action of an international organ and a local or state government. The paradigm case was found in Sierra Leone where a mixed tribunal established pursuant to an agreement between the Secretary-General and the Sierra Leonean government, and composed of international and local judges, applied a mixture of Sierra Leonean law (the law of arson, for example) and international criminal law (crimes against humanity, for example). The hybrid tribunal has, itself, given rise to hybrid forms. Apart from Sierra Leone and Cambodia (where the Tribunal has more of a national emphasis than in other cases), there are forms of internationalised tribunals in Kosovo (the *Resolution 64* courts), in the Lebanon and in Bosnia, each engaged in the prosecution of genocidaires and war criminals.

Of course, alongside all of this are two – perhaps less glamorous – forms of national jurisdiction. In one case, national courts apply a traditional form of territorial or nationality jurisdiction to 'their own' war criminals, e.g. Germany prosecuted large numbers of German war criminals after the war; indeed, this is the default position in international humanitarian law. The Rome Statute (1998) creating the ICC is structured around a preference that local courts will prosecute, and are best able to prosecute, crimes committed by their own nationals or on their own territory. A successful ICC is one that will engage in no prosecutions at all but will, instead, provoke states into indigenous responses to mass atrocity.

In the other case at the local level, national courts are given or adopt a form of universal jurisdiction over crimes committed elsewhere and by the nationals of other states. The trial of Adolf Eichmann at the Jerusalem District Court in 1961 was an example of this form of universality; the Israelis prosecuted Eichmann for crimes committed against Hungarian Jews in Hungary. Universal jurisdiction is the most radical and far-reaching solution to the problem of impunity. Local courts, in effect, act as agents for the 'international community'. But this can lead to tensions. Robust assertions of extra-territorial jurisdiction can bring states into conflict with each other. In 2000 a Belgian magistrate sought the arrest of the then-Foreign Minister of the Democratic Republic of the Congo (DRC), Ndombasi Yerodia, alleging that he had committed the crime of 'incitement to commit genocide'. This act was made criminal in the 1948 Genocide Convention but the striking feature of this case is that extra-territorial genocide had also been criminalised under Belgian law by the War Crimes, Genocide and Crimes against Humanity Acts of 1993 and 1999. These extraordinary statutes made it a crime, *under Belgian law*, to commit genocide anywhere in the world. Belgium was, as it were, acting as an agent for humanity. The DRC sued Belgium successfully before the International Court of Justice (ICJ). The Court accepted that the Belgian action had violated Yerodia's sovereign immunity (and therefore the DRC's sovereignty) though it did not address the question as to whether the initial assertion of jurisdiction was lawful (*Arrest Warrant Case*[21]). These 'sovereignty' concerns are, of course, the very stuff of international criminal law, and have emerged in cases like *Pinochet*[22] (before the UK House of Lords); *Jones* v. *Kingdom of Saudi Arabia*[23] (also before the House of Lords and involving allegations of torture directed against the Saudi state and one of its officials, Colonel Aziz) and *Belgium* v. *Senegal*[24] (at the ICJ and concerning a Belgian claim that Senegal has not met its Torture Convention obligation to try Hissein Habré, the former President of Chad (and someone widely believed to have committed crimes against humanity while in office)) as well as in response to the application to apply for an arrest warrant to be issued against former Israeli Foreign Minister, Tzipi Livni, during her 2011 visit to the UK (on which see now Police Reform and Social Responsibility Act 2011). These competing claims of humanitarian universality and sovereign exclusivity are likely to be a prominent feature of this field for some time. But, of course, humanity is compromised here, too, because of its associations with hegemonic assertions of power.

Finally, of the five jurisdictions, there is the ICC itself. Widely regarded as international criminal law's greatest single achievement, the Court, established in 2002, has jurisdiction over crimes against humanity, war crimes, genocide, and (probably) from 2017, the crime of aggression. This is a relatively small category of crimes, and excludes treaty offences such as drug trafficking, terrorism and people trafficking; emerging crimes such as certain forms of environmental devastation; and other sundry breaches of international law such as intervention.

---

[21] *Case Concerning the Arrest Warrant of 11 April 2000 (Democratic Republic of the Congo v. Belgium) ('Arrest Warrant Case')*, Judgment [2002] ICJ Rep. 3.

[22] *R* v. *Bow Street Magistrate & Or; Ex parte Pinochet Ugarte (No. 3)* [1999] 2 All ER 97.

[23] *Jones* v. *Kingdom of Saudi Arabia* [2006] UKHL 26.

[24] *Questions Relating to the Obligation to Prosecute or Extradite (Belgium v. Senegal)* [2009], www.icj-cij.org/docket/index.php?p1=3&p2=3&code=bs&case=144&k=5e.

But the Court's capacity to hear cases is further constrained by the jurisdictional structure under which it operates. This is constituted by a wholly typical amalgam of sovereignty, humanity and hegemony. The Court has competence over two broad categories of cases. In the first case, either states (typically states parties) make complaints to the Prosecutor about situations in which they believe crimes are being perpetrated or the Prosecutor initiates investigations using her *proprio motu* power. In these instances, the Court acquires jurisdiction only if the territorial state or perpetrator-national state is a party to the Statute (or one of those states (it is often the same state) has ceded jurisdiction to the court though a separate instrument giving such consent). This jurisdiction is grounded in a mixture of 'humanity' (a prosecutor acts on behalf of the international community in bringing cases to the court) and state sovereignty (states act as gatekeepers to the Court). At present, there are several situations (e.g. in the DRC, in Uganda and in the Central African Republic, CAR) and a number of cases (*Bemba*,[25] *Lubanga*[26]) that have come within the court's jurisdiction in this way.

But inserted into the structure of the ICC Statute is what might be thought of as an ad hoc procedure resembling the one that brought the ICTFY and ICTR into existence. Under Article 13 (2) of the ICC Statute the Security Council is given a referral power that allows it (acting collectively) to bring a situation within the court's jurisdiction. This – alongside a provision (Article 16) giving the Council authority to prevent situations being dealt with by the Court – is the Court's hegemonic aspect. These provisions secure the prerogatives of the Great Powers in the face of the potential intrusions of sovereigns (minor states who might be inclined to embarrass the elite powers) and the much-debated possibility of over-zealousness on the part of an independent prosecutor keen to speak humanity to hegemony.

In fact, judging by the Court's current docket, there was little risk of either occurring. Instead, with the indictment of Colonel Gaddafi and his associates, humanity and hegemony are conjoined. Crimes against humanity, it might be argued, can be redefined as indecent acts committed by individuals *who are enemies of mankind*. This would explain why Gaddafi and President Bashir of the Sudan have been indicted following referrals by the Council under Article 13 (2). And it would explain why there is no prospect

---

[25] *Prosecutor v. Jean-Pierre Bemba Gombo* ICC-01/05-01/08.
[26] *Prosecutor v. Thomas Lubanga Dyilo* ICC-01/04-01/06.

of arrest warrants being issued against, say, former Colombian President Uribe or the current Uzbekistan President Karimov. Theirs are crimes against humans, not humanity.

Humanity, then, has its moral face ('crimes against humanity') and its imperial face ('enemies of mankind'). Packaged together, the result is wars fought by agents of humanity (say, NATO acting as the 'international community' in Libya in 2011) on behalf of humanity (to protect the human rights of civilians in Benghazi) and accompanied by judicial interventions against 'enemies of mankind' (the Security Council's referral of the Libya situation to the ICC and the subsequent issuance of arrest warrants (Security Council Resolution 1970)).

International criminal law and human rights law: three intersections

In the rest of this chapter, and as a way of inquiring further into the idea of what Ruti Teitel famously called 'humanity's law',[27] I want to briefly trace these faces of humanity through the doctrine, history and general orientations of the two fields of human rights law and international criminal law in three sets of relations they have *to each other*. These are (1) the idea of the two fields as part of analogous processes of domestication, internationalisation and personalisation, and the associated belief that international criminal law somehow represents the completion of human rights law (because international criminal tribunals might sometimes give meaning to human rights norms or because international criminal law promises the enforcement of human rights aspirations); (2) the way in which international criminal law might be understood as a test of our commitments to human rights standards and; (3) the sense that (and this returns us to the first part of the chapter) international criminal law and international human rights law might share a set of pathologies that emerge from the same trauma (The Holocaust) and are reconstituted in the same institutional moment (the creation of a category of 'crimes against humanity' at Nuremberg or the revival of the category 'enemies of mankind' at Versailles and Nuremberg).

---

[27] R. Teitel, *Humanity's Law* (Oxford University Press 2011).

(1) Individualisation, internationalisation, domestication and completion

It is possible to think of both international criminal lawyers and international human rights lawyers as participants in three broader developments in legal culture. The first is the *individualisation* or personalisation of international law. Prior to 1945, international law largely was devoted to organising relations among sovereign states and between metropolitan colonisers and their colonial outposts. Individuals were not entirely absent of course but in general their status was parasitic on states themselves (e.g. ambassadors or aliens) or they appeared as *sui generis* threats to international order (e.g. pirates). The institutional dynamism present at the end of the Second World War changed all this. At San Francisco (the UN, drawing on some precedents found at the Congress of Vienna (the abolition of slavery) and in the post-First World War minorities' treaties) and at Nuremberg, the individual became a central concern of the international legal regime. The UN Charter contained the first traces of a legal order that was to become the human rights system with individuals having, for the first time, rights exercisable against their governments. At the same time, the International Military Tribunal introduced into international law a form of individual responsibility. As the Tribunal intoned: 'crimes are committed not by abstract entities but by men', and this principle found its way into subsequent legal instruments (The Rome Statute Article 27; the ICTY Statute Article 7). Furnishing individuals with rights and liabilities also was a way of undermining a version of sovereignty that had until then placed the conduct of a state's officials beyond international scrutiny. This explains why international criminal law[28] and human rights law are understood as being somehow in conflict with or contradiction to 'sovereignty'.

A second development concerns the *internationalisation* of national law. This is the now-familiar (and not wholly novel) phenomenon involving the penetration into local legal institutions of international legal norms. International human rights doctrine began as a series of abstractions later made concrete by a human rights bureaucracy (the Human Rights Committee; the Commission for Human Rights (later the Human Rights Council); the European Court of Human Rights, ECtHR), by the activism of

---

[28] R. Cryer, 'International Criminal Law vs State Sovereignty: Another Round?' (2006) 16 *European Journal of International Law* 979.

the human rights movement and by the increasing deployment of international human rights norms in local legal space. This last tendency has inspired a transformation in national legal culture in Europe, Australia and Canada (though much less so in the USA), and was reproduced in international criminal law where local initiatives (the implementation of treaty law into national law) and consequent litigation brought home another set of international legal norms. The *Pinochet* proceedings remain the best example of this: the revolution at Nuremberg in 1945 (eventually) prompts an international treaty (The Torture Convention 1984) that, in turn, gives rise to national legalisation in the UK (Criminal Justice Act 1988, s. 132), which provides for a form of universal jurisdiction over suspected torturers. This model has been emulated in later case law in the UK (*R* v. *Zardad*,[29]) and has some precedents in the USA (Alien Tort Claims Act).

The final development along these lines might be termed the *domestication* of international law. This describes the effort to give international law the appearance or sheen, as well as some of the accoutrements, of a fully functioning national legal system. This process of juridification (and judicialisation, in particular) offers the possibility, too, of a system in which human rights principles – long thought of as vague (the right to decent health care) or contradictory (freedom of expression as against the right to respect for privacy) – might be given subtler or more precise meanings by international tribunals engaged in the concrete application of these norms. Some human rights treaties, of course, are part of international criminal law. To take two obvious examples, the Torture Convention and the Genocide Convention describe egregious breaches of human rights as crimes or demand that states criminalise the conduct in question. But what they do not do such a good job of is defining these offences, and this is where the various criminal courts established in recent times have made a significant contribution. For example, the ICTY has gone some way to defining torture by establishing the requirements for torture (*Furundžija*[30]) and imprisonment (*Kordić*[31]) as crimes against humanity. (Sometimes, of course, this can result in divergent approaches: the Torture Convention requiring official action but *Kunarac* saying torture in armed

---

[29] *R* v. *Zardad* [2007] EWCA Crim 279.
[30] *Prosecutor* v. *Anto Furundžija* IT-9-17/1-T, Judgment (10 December 1998).
[31] *Prosecutor* v. *Dario Kordić and Mario Čerkez* IT-95-14/2-A, Appeal Judgment (17 December 2004).

conflict does not require the presence of an official (*pace* a case such as
Furundžija) (*Prosecutor* v. *Kunarac*,[32] para. 496).)

Something similar can be seen in the various elaborations of war
crimes, crimes against humanity and genocide in the Rome (ICC) Statute
and, in particular, its appendix defining the elements of crimes. In this
sense, international criminal law might be understood as the corollary of
human rights law or as human rights law's enforcement arm. The most
commonly traced narrative arc in international human rights law is of a
legal order that begins as a set of norms that are subsequently managed or
overseen by a system of institutions. This transition from abstract norm to
concrete procedure was a success, of course but it remained the case that at
some basic – almost primitive – level human rights law was perceived as
unenforced or unenforceable. Breaches of human rights might provoke the
engagement of the human rights machinery but these 'breaches' resulted
in a form of state or civil responsibility. The breach by a state official of a
human right elucidated in, say, the International Covenant on Civil and
Political Rights (ICCPR) or the European Convention on Human Rights
(ECHR) gave rise to administrative action (e.g. judicial review of a failure
to provide access to justice), not criminal prosecution. In most human
rights instruments there was no reference to any potential criminal
sanction.

The brute enforcement of human rights norms by international (and
local) criminal courts has been posited, then, as the solution to the problem
of compliance. And these efforts certainly accord with the view that states
ought to provide some sort of accountability mechanism for serious
breaches of human rights standards:[33] UN Commission on Human Rights,
para. 4.[34] Of course, the picture is complicated by two factors. First, compliance in this, and most other areas of social life, is rarely about enforcement as such. It is invariably the case that only a relatively small number of
breaches of law are both detected and punished. Mostly, law is obeyed as a
matter of habit, reciprocity, socialisation and internalisation.

---

[32] *Prosecutor* v. *Dragoljub Kunarac et al.* IT-96-23-T and IT-96-23/1-T, Judgment (22
February 2001).

[33] Evans, 'The Scramble for Europe'.

[34] UN Commission on Human Rights, *Basic Principles and Guidelines on the Right to a Remedy
and Reparation for Victims of Gross Violations of International Human Rights Law and
Serious Violations of International Humanitarian Law* (19 April 2005), http://ap.ohchr.org/
document/E/CHR/resolutions/E-CN_4-RES-2005-35.doc.

Second, when human rights abuses *are* the subject of legal regulation, this will quite often involve overlapping jurisdictions (civil and criminal, national and international, administrative and punitive) and not one single international criminal law 'case'. A good example of this is the case of Baha Mousa, the Iraqi hotel clerk murdered by British forces at a detention facility outside Basra in southern Iraq and later litigated in front of military courts exercising criminal jurisdiction under the terms of the International Criminal Court Act (2001) (criminalising 'inhumane treatment') or under the Army Act (1955) (*R* v. *Payne*[35]) and before civil courts exercising a form of jurisdiction created by the UK's Human Rights Act (HRA 1998) (*Al-Skeini*[36]).

In this way, international human rights law and international criminal law, because they precisely do engage in this sort of system-building, are projects to complete international law.[37] In the case of international criminal law (others in the volume will speak with greater authority about human rights law in this regard), the enhanced enforceability and extended reach of its norms, its institutional fertility, the growing self-confidence of its practitioners and its privileged place in the popular imagination all combine to offer it enormous vitality.

And yet, so much depends on *what* international criminal law is completing. This chapter has argued that international criminal law is split between its innocent pretensions to justice or enforceability or ending impunity ('humanity' in its universalising voice) and a legal practice through which norms are mobilised in order to discipline outsiders or advance particular political projects. Thus, the relatively upbeat story of this section of the chapter could be inverted to produce a narrative of Great Power immunity (in the past fifty years not a single Westerner has stood trial for war crimes before an international criminal court), sovereign resilience (Saudi Arabia's immunity before UK courts) and imperial blitheness (the sense that it is invariably the case that enemies of mankind are other people).

---

[35] *R* v. *Payne* General Court Martial Charge Sheet (20096), www.publications.parliament.uk/pa/ld200506/ldlwa/50719ws1.pdf.
[36] *R (Al-Skeini)* v. *Secretary of State for Defence* [2007] 3 WLR 33.
[37] For a sceptical appraisal, see F. Mégret, 'The Politics of International Criminal Justice' (2002) 13 (5) *European Journal of International Law* 1261–84.

(2) Do enemies of mankind have human rights?

International criminal law, of course, is a test of our commitment to the rights protection due to such enemies (accused war criminals can be thought of as belonging to a particularly vulnerable group). A pervasive concern in the history of international criminal law is the problem of fairness to the accused. At Versailles, the US representatives on the Commission on the Responsibilities of the Authors of the War were anxious to preserve the sovereign immunity enjoyed by heads of state (including the Kaiser); at Nuremberg, the German defence lawyers argued that their clients were being subject to *ex post facto* laws in violation of natural justice;[38] and in Tokyo, Justice Pal, the Indian dissenting judge, described the trial as a hypocritical sham perpetrated on the Japanese leadership by long-time aggressors (i.e. the Western nations).

Later debates and cases continue to reflect these concerns. In the very first proceeding before the ICTY in The Hague (indeed, the first case before an international criminal court since the Nuremberg and Tokyo trials in the 1940s), the defendant, Duško Tadić, raised a whole raft of what turned out to be proto-typical concerns about his trial. At various interlocutory hearings and at the trial itself, his defence lawyers claimed that the new tribunal lacked legitimacy (because it had been created by the Security Council, a political body that lacked the authority to establish criminal courts), that he had been denied rights to a fair trial (because of a lack of 'equality of arms') and that the anonymity of witnesses deprived him of the right to know and cross-examine such witnesses. Such claims have continued to be a staple of jurisdictional proceedings before international tribunals and debates about the structure of new international courts. Partly as a consequence of all this, the Rome Statute for the ICC includes quite elaborate protections for the rights of the accused, e.g. Article 22 ensures that such individuals will not be subject to retroactive or vague laws (the *nullem crimen sine lege* principle).

But, here too, international criminal law remains beholden to a structure in which 'humanity' acts against the inhumane periphery. Rob Cryer has made the distinction between 'safe' and 'unsafe' tribunals as a way of understanding this.[39] According to this view, the Great Powers (acting as the 'international

---

[38] *Trial of the Major War Criminals before the International Military Tribunal, Nuremberg,* Judgment (1 October 1946) (1947) 41 *AJIL* 172.

[39] R. Cryer, *Prosecuting International Crimes: Selectivity and the International Criminal Law Regime* (Cambridge University Press 2005) 233.

community') make a calculation whenever courts are on the point of being established. Where the institution in question is likely to assert legal power over those states or their personnel, the substantive rules to be applied will be narrowly defined, the protections accorded to defendants expansive and the jurisdictional framework limited and tightly constrained. The ICC is a model of this sort of unsafe tribunal. In other cases, where a tribunal is established in order to investigate and prosecute a relatively discrete category of defendants – the various ad hoc and mixed tribunals come to mind – and where there is little prospect of elite states being implicated in the process, the rules tend to be applied more flexibly, the jurisdiction is more assertive and the defendants' rights are more modest (the US Military Commissions are good examples of safe tribunals with seriously restricted defendants' rights).

International criminal law, of course, is enacted in many places and in many different, curial and extra-curial, settings and enemies have been subject to its jurisdiction in a number of different ways. In *Tadić*, the defence cavilled at the prospect of a Security Council empowering itself to establish new criminal courts. Five years after that case, the Council began to act *like* a criminal court. In Resolution 1267, the Council established a Sanctions (Anti-Terrorism) Committee with the task of implementing various resolutions on terrorism. That committee, acting in a quasi-executive, quasi-judicial mode, then placed a number of individuals on its lists of suspected terrorists or terrorist sympathisers. These individuals, whose assets, according to the terms of Resolution 1267 and Resolution 1333, were to be frozen and travel rights suspended, were denied any right of appeal against the decisions of the Council. It seemed as if enemies of mankind did not have human rights after all. Recent case law at the European Court of Justice (ECJ) has reversed this tendency by approaching the problem of 'enemies of mankind' precisely from the perspective of the relationship between a form of international criminal law and human rights law. In *Kadi*,[40] EC regulations implementing the terms of the Security Council measures were challenged for their conformity to EU human rights law. The ECJ found that the rights of individuals within the EU were not dissolved simply by operation of Security Council resolutions or provisions of the UN Charter. As the Grand Chamber put it, in para. 303:

---

[40] *Yassin Abdullah Kadi & Al Barakaat International Foundation* v. *Council & Commission* (Joined cases C-402/05P and C-415/05P) European Court of Justice, Judgment (3 September 2008).

These provisions (of the UN Charter) cannot, however, be understood to authorise any derogation from the principles of liberty, democracy and respect for human rights and fundamental freedoms enshrined in Article 6 (1)EU as a foundation for the Union.

This, we might say, was humanity's universalising impulse striking back against a too-brazen deployment of the resources of the 'international community' against 'enemies of mankind'.

(3) Pathologies of the humanitarian project

As we have seen, human rights law and international criminal law each find their origins in coincident moments of legal innovation at San Francisco and Nuremberg. But humanitarianism's violence is also inaugurated here. The Nuremberg Trial ended with the hanging of eleven leading Nazis. The UN Charter is a desideratum to peace and human rights but it is a manifesto for police violence, too. Nuremberg's great revolutionary gesture was the invention of the category 'crimes against humanity'. The Holocaust had rendered existing law speechless; the only adequate response was new law. This new law was, of course, partly, a law of humanity: it abolished absolutist principles of sovereignty, it inspired one of modernity's greatest social and political movements (the human rights movement) and it introduced a form of legal punishment for political murder. But Nuremberg's three progeny – human rights, collective security, international criminal law – have provoked also, at times, a sort of punitive humanitarianism that conjoins war, humanity and punishment. In particular, international criminal law, properly anatomised, continues to be in most instances the law applied to 'enemies of mankind'.

Further reading

Arendt, H., *Eichmann in Jerusalem: A Report on the Banality of Evil* (London: Penguin Classics 2006; first published 1963)

Bass, G., *Stay the Hand of Vengeance* (Princeton University Press 2000)

Beckett, A., *Pinochet in Piccadilly* (London: Faber & Faber 2002)

Blackburn, R., 'Reclaiming Human Rights' (2011) 69 *New Left Review* 126–38

Binder, G., 'Representing Nazism: Advocacy and Identity at the Trail of Klaus Barbie' (1989) 98 *Yale Law Journal* 1321–83

Carr, E. H., *The Twenty Years' Crisis* (Basingstoke: Palgrave Macmillan 2001)

Convention Against Torture and Other Cruel, Inhuman or Degrading Treatment or Punishment 1984

Cryer, R., *Prosecuting International Crimes: Selectivity and the International Criminal Law Regime* (Cambridge University Press 2005)

'International Criminal Law vs State Sovereignty: Another Round?' (2006) 16 *European Journal of International Law* 979

Douglas, L., *The Memory of Judgment: Making Law and History in the Trials of the Holocaust* (New Haven, CT: Yale University Press 2001

Drumbl, M., *Atrocity, Punishment and International Law* (New York: Cambridge University Press 2007)

Evans, R. J., 'The Scramble for Europe' (2011) *London Review of Books*, 3 February 17–19

Finkielkraut, A., *Remembering in Vain: The Klaus Barbie Trial and Crimes against Humanity* (R. Lapidus, trans.) with S. Godfrey, introduction by A. Y. Kaplan (New York: Columbia University Press 1992)

Fussell, P., *The Great War and Modern Memory* (Oxford: Clarendon Press 1975)

Hunt, L., *Inventing Human Rights: A History* (New York: W.W. Norton 2007)

Af Jochnick, C. and Normand, R., 'The Legitimation of Violence: A Critical Analysis of the Gulf War' (1994) 35 (2) *Harvard International Law Journal* 387–416

Kirchheimer. O., *Political Justice* (Princeton University Press 1960)

Kontorovich, E., 'The Piracy Analogy: Universal Jurisdiction's Hollow Foundation' (2004) 4 *Harvard Journal of International Law* 183

Kraus, K., *The Last Days of Mankind* (play) (1915–19)

Luban, D., 'The Legacies of Nuremberg' (1987) 54 (4) *Social Research* 779–829

Mann, T., *The Magic Mountain* (New York: Vintage Books 1996) (1st edn 1924)

Mégret, F., 'The Politics of International Criminal Justice' (2002) 13 (5) *European Journal of International Law* 1261–84

De Menthon, F., 'Opening Address (January 17, 1946)', in M. R. Marrus (ed.), *The Nuremberg War Crimes Trial 1945–46: A Documentary History* (Boston, MA: Bedford/St Martin's 1997)

Moyn, S., *The Last Utopia: Human Rights in History* (Cambridge, MA: Harvard University Press 2010)

Police Reform and Social Responsibility Act (2011) (UK) s. 153, www.legislation.gov. uk/ukpga/2011/13/part/4/crossheading/arrest-warrants/enacted

Rediker, M. , *Villains of All Nations: Atlantic Pirates in the Golden Age* (New York: Verso 2004)

The Report of the Baha Mousa Inquiry (8 September 2011), www.bahamousainquiry. org/report/index.htm

Röling, B., *The Tokyo Trial and Beyond* (Cambridge: Polity 1991)

Schmitt, C., *The Nomos of the Earth* (New York: Telos 2003)

Schwarzenberger, G., *International Law and Totalitarian Lawlessness* (London: Jonathan Cape 1943)

Shklar, J., *Legalism: Law and Ideology* (Cambridge, MA: Harvard University Press 1964)

Simpson, G., *Law, War and Crime* (Cambridge: Polity 2007)

Steiner, G., *The Death of Tragedy* (London: Faber & Faber 1961).

Strachey, L., *Literary Essays* (New York: Harcourt, Brace & Co. 1949)

Teitel, R., *Humanity's Law* (Oxford University Press 2011)

UN Commission on Human Rights, *Basic Principles and Guidelines on the Right to a Remedy and Reparation for Victims of Gross Violations of International Human Rights Law and Serious Violations of International Humanitarian Law* (19 April 2005), http://ap.ohchr.org/documents/E/CHR/resolutions/E-CN_4-RES-2005-35.doc

7 Violence in the name of human rights

Simon Chesterman[*]

Three months after NATO concluded its seventy-eight-day campaign over Kosovo, Secretary-General Kofi Annan presented his annual report for 1999 to the UN General Assembly. In it, he presented in stark terms the dilemma confronting those who privileged international law over the need to respond to gross and systematic violations of human rights:

> To those for whom the greatest threat to the future of international order is the use of force in the absence of a Security Council mandate, one might ask – not in the context of Kosovo – but in the context of Rwanda: If, in those dark days and hours leading up to the genocide, a coalition of States had been prepared to act in defense of the Tutsi population, but did not receive prompt Council authorization, should such a coalition have stood aside and allowed the horror to unfold?[1]

The hypothetical presented here neatly captured the ethical dilemma as many of the acting states sought to present it. Could international law truly prevent such 'humanitarian' intervention?

The problem, however, is that this was not the dilemma faced in the context of Rwanda. Rather than international law restraining a state from acting in defence of the Tutsi population, the problem in 1994 was that no state wanted to intervene at all. When France, hardly a disinterested actor, decided to intervene, its decision was swiftly approved in a Council resolution (though reference to 'impartiality', a two-month time-limit and five abstentions suggested wariness about France's motivation).

---

[*] This chapter draws upon ideas explored at greater length in S. Chesterman, *Just War or Just Peace? Humanitarian Intervention and International Law*, Oxford Monographs in International Law (Oxford University Press 2001) and 'Military Intervention and Human Rights: Is Foreign Military Intervention Justified by Widespread Human Rights Abuses? No', in P. M. Haas, J. A. Hird and B. McBratney (eds.), *Controversies in Globalization: Contending Approaches to International Relations* (Washington, DC: CQ Press 2009) 188–99.

[1] K. A. Annan, Address to the General Assembly (UN, UN Press Release SG/SM/7136, New York, 20 September 1999), www.un.org/news/Press/docs/1999/19990920.sgsm7136.html.

The capriciousness of state interest is a theme that runs throughout the troubled history of humanitarian intervention. While much ink has been spilt on the question of the legality of using military force to defend human rights, it is difficult to point to actual cases that demonstrate the significance of international law on this issue. States do not appear to have refrained from acting in situations like Rwanda (or Kosovo) simply from fear of legal sanction. Nor, however, do any of the incidents frequently touted as examples of 'genuine' humanitarian intervention correspond with the principled articulation of such a doctrine by legal scholars.

What, then, is the relevance of international law here? This chapter will attempt to answer this question by examining the legal status of humanitarian intervention. The next section will consider 'traditional' international law and arguments that it might entertain a right of humanitarian intervention. This will be followed by an examination of how states dealt with the apparent contravention of such traditional norms in relation to Kosovo, and the impact this has had on subsequent military actions in East Timor, Afghanistan and Libya.

Of particular interest here is the relative importance of ethics and international law in the actual decision-making process of states. From a legal perspective, the question of whether the law may be violated is not itself susceptible to legal regulation. For the ethicist, running beneath the discussion here is the basic question of whether international law itself demands obedience. If international law *per se* is suspect, states (or other actors) might be justified in disregarding it, or at least the more offensive of its provisions. A problem confronting one who would argue such a position is the absence of any situations in which the dilemma has been posed in these terms. It is difficult to point to a case in which international law alone has prevented a state from otherwise acting to protect a foreign population at risk. And, in those incidents usually marshalled as 'best cases', factors other than concern for the population were paramount. (An important – but discrete – area of ethical inquiry is whether states and other actors have an *obligation* to act to protect populations at risk. Such action could, of course, take many forms other than military intervention.[2])

Can ethical demands trump such legal structures? The answer, however unsatisfactory, will be that the question is so unlikely to arise in practice as to be of questionable value answering in theory.

---

[2] See, e.g., ICISS, *The Responsibility to Protect* (Ottowa: International Development Research Centre December 2001), www.iciss.ca.

Humanitarian intervention and international law

The status of humanitarian intervention in international law is, on the face of it, quite simple. The UN Charter clearly prohibits the use of force. The renunciation of war must be counted among the greatest achievements of international law in the twentieth century; that this was also the bloodiest of centuries is a sober warning as to the limits of law's power to constrain the behaviour of states.

The passage agreed to by states at the San Francisco Conference of 1945 was broad in its scope:

All Members shall refrain in their international relations from the threat or use of force against the territorial integrity or political independence of any state, or in any other manner inconsistent with the Purposes of the United Nations.[3]

The prohibition was tempered by only two exceptions. First, the Charter preserved the 'inherent right of individual or collective self-defence'.[4] Second, the newly established Security Council was granted the power to authorise enforcement actions under Chapter VII. Although this latter species of military action is sometimes considered in the same breath as unilateral humanitarian intervention, Council authorisation changes the legal questions to which such action gives rise.

Both exceptions provide examples of the inexorable expansion of certain legal rights. Self-defence, for example, has been invoked in ever-wider circumstances to justify military actions such as a pre-emptive strike against a country's nuclear programme, and in 'response' to a failed assassination attempt in a foreign country. It also provided the initial basis for the USA's extensive military actions in Afghanistan in late 2001. Security Council-authorised actions have expanded even further, mandating actions in Somalia and Haiti in the 1990s that would never have been contemplated by the founders of the UN in 1945. Nevertheless, neither exception encompasses humanitarian intervention, meaning the threat or use of armed force in the absence of a Security Council authorisation or an invitation from the recognised government, with the object of protecting human rights.

A third, possible, exception concerns the role of the General Assembly. Interestingly, it first arose at a time when it was feared that a Russian veto

---

[3] UN Charter, Article 2(4).   [4] UN Charter, Article 51.

would block a Security Council resolution authorising intervention. For some months in 1950 the representative of the USSR boycotted the Council in protest at the UN's continuing recognition of the recently defeated Kuomintang regime in China. In his absence, three resolutions were passed which in effect authorised the USA to lead a military operation against North Korea under the UN flag. The return of the Soviet delegate precluded any further Council involvement. At the initiative of Western states, the General Assembly adopted the *Uniting for Peace* resolution. This provided that the Assembly would meet to recommend collective measures in situations where the veto prevented the Council from fulfilling its primary responsibility for the maintenance of international peace and security. In the case of a breach of the peace or act of aggression, the measures available were said to include the use of armed force.[5] The legal status of the capacity of the General Assembly to do more than authorise peacekeeping is dubious, but a resolution was passed recommending that all states lend every assistance to the UN action in Korea, and it was used again in relation to the Suez crisis in 1956 and in the Congo in 1960. The procedure has subsequently fallen into disuse, however. In particular, it appears not to have been seriously contemplated during the Kosovo crisis – reportedly due to fears that NATO would have been unable to muster the necessary two-thirds' majority support of the member states.

At first glance, then, traditional international law does not allow for humanitarian intervention. There have, however, been many attempts to bring humanitarian intervention within the remit of this body of law. These have tended to follow two strategies: limiting the scope of the prohibition of the use of force, or arguing that a new customary norm has created an additional exception to the prohibition.

The UN Charter prohibits the use of force 'against the territorial integrity or political independence of any state, or in any other manner inconsistent with the Purposes of the United Nations'. It has sometimes been argued that certain uses of force might not contravene this provision. For example, it has been argued that the US invasion of Panama in 1989 was consistent with the UN Charter because 'the United States did not intend to, and has not, colonialised [*sic*], annexed or incorporated Panama'.[6] As Oscar

---

[5] GA Res. 377A(V) (1950).

[6] A. D'Amato, 'The Invasion of Panama was a Lawful Response to Tyranny' (1990) 84 *American Journal of International Law* 520.

Schachter has observed, this demands an Orwellian construction of the terms 'territorial integrity' and 'political independence'.[7] It also runs counter to various statements by the General Assembly and the International Court of Justice (ICJ) concerning the meaning of non-intervention, as well as the practice of the Security Council, which has condemned and declared illegal the unauthorised use of force even when it is 'temporary'. This is consistent with the drafting history of the provision, which the US delegate to the San Francisco Conference (among others) emphasised, left 'no loopholes'.

Is it possible, however, that a new norm might have developed to create a separate right of humanitarian intervention? Customary international law allows for the creation of such norms through the evolution of consistent and widespread state practice when accompanied by the necessary *opinio iuris* – the belief that a practice is legally obligatory. Some writers have argued that there is evidence of such state practice and *opinio iuris*, typically pointing to the Indian action to stop the slaughter in East Pakistan in 1971, Tanzania's actions against Idi Amin in neighbouring Uganda in 1978–9, and Vietnam's intervention in Kampuchea in the same year. In none of these cases, however, were humanitarian concerns invoked as a justification for the use of force. Rather, self-defence was the primary justification offered in each case, with humanitarian (and other) justifications being at best secondary considerations.

Such justifications are important, as they may provide evidence of change in the law. As the ICJ has observed:

The significance for the Court of cases of State conduct *prima facie* inconsistent with the principle of non-intervention lies in the nature of the ground offered as justification. Reliance by a State on a novel right or an unprecedented exception to the principle might, if shared in principle by other States, tend towards a modification of customary international law.[8]

The fact that states continued to rely on traditional justifications – most notably self-defence – undermines arguments that the law has changed.

---

[7] O. Schachter, 'The Legality of Pro-Democratic Invasion' (1984) 78 *American Journal of International Law* 649.

[8] *Case Concerning the Military and Paramilitary Activities in and Against Nicaragua (Nicaragua* v. *United States of America) (Merits)* (International Court of Justice, 27 June 1986) ICJ Rep., hwww.icj-cij.org 109.

The international response to each incident is also instructive. In relation to India's action (which led to the creation of Bangladesh), a Soviet veto prevented a US-sponsored resolution calling for a ceasefire and the immediate withdrawal of armed forces. Tanzania's actions were broadly tolerated and the new regime in Kampala was swiftly recognised, but states that voiced support for the action typically confined their comments to the question of self-defence. Vietnam's successful ouster of the murderous regime of Pol Pot, by contrast, was met with positive hostility. France's representative, for example, stated that

[t]he notion that because a régime is detestable foreign intervention is justified and forcible overthrow is legitimate is extremely dangerous. That could ultimately jeopardize the very maintenance of international law and order and make the continued existence of various régimes dependent on the judgement of their neighbours.[9]

Similar statements were made by the UK and Portugal, among others. Once again, only a Soviet veto prevented a resolution calling upon the foreign troops to withdraw; Pol Pot's delegate continued to be recognised as the legitimate representative of Kampuchea (later Cambodia) at the UN until as late as 1990. Even if one includes these three 'best cases' as evidence of state practice, the absence of accompanying *opinio iuris* fatally undermines claims that they marked a change in the law.

More recent examples of allegedly humanitarian intervention without explicit Security Council authorisation, such as the no-fly zones in protection of the Kurds in northern Iraq and NATO's intervention in Kosovo, raise slightly different questions. Acting states have often claimed that their actions have been 'in support of' Security Council resolutions, though in each case it is clear that the Council did not decide to authorise the use of force. Indeed, it is ironic that states began to claim the need to act when the Security Council faltered in precisely the same decade that the Council's activities expanded so greatly. At a time when there was a far stronger argument that paralysis of the UN system demanded self-help, the ICJ considered and rejected arguments that 'present defects in international organisation' could justify an independent right of intervention.[10]

Interestingly, despite the efforts by some legal scholars to argue for the existence of a right of humanitarian intervention,[11] states themselves have

---

[9] S/PV.2109 (1979, para. 36 (France).

[10] *Corfu Channel (United Kingdom* v. *Albania) (Merits)* (1986) ICJ Rep. 4, hwww.icj-cij.org 35.

[11] See, e.g., F. Tesón, *Humanitarian Intervention: An Inquiry into Law and Morality*, 3rd edn (Dobbs Ferry, NY: Transnational Publishers 2005).

continued to prove very reluctant to embrace such a right – even in defence of their own actions. This is particularly true in the case of NATO's intervention in Kosovo. Such reluctance appears to have stemmed in part from the dubiousness of such a legal argument, but also from the knowledge that if any right were embraced it might well be used by other states in other situations.

Unusually among the NATO states, in October 1998 Germany referred to NATO's threats against the Federal Republic of Yugoslavia as an instance of 'humanitarian intervention'. The Bundestag affirmed its support for the Alliance – provided that it was made clear that this was not a precedent for further action.[12] This desire to avoid setting a precedent was reflected in subsequent statements by NATO officials. US Secretary of State Madeleine Albright later stressed that the air strikes were a 'unique situation *sui generis* in the region of the Balkans', concluding that it was important 'not to overdraw the various lessons that come out of it'.[13] UK Prime Minister Tony Blair, who had earlier suggested that such interventions might become more routine, subsequently retreated from this position, emphasising the exceptional nature of the air campaign. This was consistent with the more sophisticated UK statements on the legal issues.

This trend continued in the proceedings brought by Yugoslavia against ten NATO members before the ICJ. In hearings on provisional measures, Belgium presented the most elaborate legal justification for the action, relying variously on Security Council resolutions, a doctrine of humanitarian intervention (as compatible with Article 2 (4) of the UN Charter or based on historical precedent), and the argument of necessity. The USA also emphasised the importance of Security Council resolutions, and, together with four other delegations (Germany, the Netherlands, Spain, and the UK) made reference to the existence of a 'humanitarian catastrophe'. Four delegations did not offer any clear legal justification (Canada, France, Italy, Portugal). The phrase 'humanitarian catastrophe' recalled the doctrine of humanitarian intervention, but some care appears to have been taken to avoid invoking the doctrine by name. The formulation was first used by the UK as one of a number of justifications for the no-fly zones over Iraq, but no

---

[12] Deutscher Bundestag, Plenarprotokoll 13/248, 16 October 1998, 23129, http://dip.bundestag. de/parfors/parfors.htm.

[13] US Secretary of State Madeleine Albright, Press Conference with Russian Foreign Minister Igor Ivanov, Singapore, 26 July 1999, http://secretary.state.gov/www/statements/1999/990726b.html.

legal pedigree had been established beyond this. (The court ultimately ruled against Yugoslavia for technical reasons concerning its jurisdiction, never discussing the merits of the case.)

Such reticence to embrace a clear legal position was repeated in two major commissions that investigated the question of humanitarian intervention. The Kosovo Commission, headed by Richard Goldstone, concluded somewhat confusingly (from an international legal perspective) that NATO's Kosovo intervention was 'illegal but legitimate'.[14] The International Commission on Intervention and State Sovereignty (ICISS), chaired by Gareth Evans and Mohamed Sahnoun, acknowledged that, as a matter of 'political reality', it would be impossible to find consensus around any set of proposals for military intervention that acknowledged the validity of any intervention not authorised by the Security Council or the General Assembly:

> But that may still leave circumstances when the Security Council fails to discharge what this Commission would regard as its responsibility to protect, in a conscience-shocking situation crying out for action. It is a real question in these circumstances where lies the most harm: in the damage to international order if the Security Council is bypassed or in the damage to that order if human beings are slaughtered while the Security Council stands by.[15]

Key elements of the ICISS report, *The Responsibility to Protect*, were adopted by the UN World Summit in a 2005 resolution of the General Assembly, which acknowledged that a state's unwillingness and/or inability to protect its own population from genocide, war crimes, ethnic cleansing or crimes against humanity may give rise to an international 'responsibility to protect'. This was limited to peaceful means, however, except in extreme circumstances where the provisions of Chapter VII of the UN Charter may be invoked.[16] The report and the UN resolution were carefully silent about what happens if the Council doesn't agree.

What is a lawyer to make of all this? It seems fairly clear that there is no positive right of humanitarian intervention without authorisation by the Security Council. Nor, however, does it appear that a coherent principle is

---

[14] Independent International Commission on Kosovo, *The Kosovo Report* (Oxford University Press 2000) 4.

[15] ICISS, *The Responsibility to Protect* 54–5.

[16] 2005 World Summit Outcome Document, UN Doc. A/RES/60/1 (16 September 2005), www.un.org/summit2005, paras. 138–139.

emerging to create such a right. Rather, the arguments as presented tend to focus on the non-application of international law to particular incidents. The next section will explore the implications of such an approach to international law, and where it might lead.

The exception and the rule

James Rubin provides a graphic illustration of the debates between NATO capitals on the question the legality of the Kosovo intervention:

> There was a series of strained telephone calls between Albright and Cook, in which he cited problems 'with our lawyers' over using force in the absence of UN endorsement. 'Get new lawyers,' she suggested. But with a push from Prime Minister Tony Blair, the British finally agreed that UN Security Council approval was not legally required.[17]

Such equivocation about the role of international law in decision-making processes is hardly new; the history of international law is to some extent a struggle to raise law above the status of being merely one foreign policy justification among others. As indicated earlier, however, most of the acting states appear to have taken some care to present the Kosovo intervention as an exception rather than a rule.

This approach to humanitarian intervention is not new. Various writers have attempted to explain the apparent inconsistency by reference to national legal systems. Ian Brownlie, for example, has likened this approach to the manner in which some legal systems deal with the question of euthanasia:

> [I]n such a case the possibility of abuse is recognized by the legal policy (that the activity is classified as unlawful) but ... in very clear cases the law allows mitigation. The father who smothers his severely abnormal child after several years of devoted attention may not be sent to prison, but he is not immune from prosecution and punishment. In international relations a difficulty arises in that 'a discretion not to prosecute' is exercisable by States collectively and by organs of the United Nations, and in the context of *practice* of States, mitigation and acceptance in principle are not always easy to distinguish. However, the euthanasia parallel is

---

[17] J. Rubin, 'Countdown to a Very Personal War', *Financial Times* (London), 30 September 2000.

useful since it indicates that moderation is allowed for in social systems even when the principle remains firm. Moderation in application does not display a legislative intent to cancel the principle so applied.[18]

Obviously, as the demand for any such violation of an established norm increases, so the need for legal regulation of the 'exception' becomes more important. This seems to be occurring in the case of euthanasia, as medical advances have increased the discretion of doctors in making end-of-life decisions. In many jurisdictions, continued reliance on the possibility of a homicide charge is now seen as an inadequate legal response to the ethical challenges posed by euthanasia. In relation to humanitarian intervention, however, such demand remains low and it is widely recognised that legal regulation of any 'exception' is unlikely in the short term.

For this reason, an alternative analogy is sometimes used: that of a person acting to prevent domestic violence in circumstances where the police are unwilling or unable to act. The analogy is appealing as it appears to capture the moral dilemma facing an intervener, but is of limited value as such acts are typically regulated by reference to the existing authority structures. An individual in most legal systems may defend another person against attack, and in certain circumstances may exercise a limited power of arrest. In the context of humanitarian intervention, this analogy merely begs the question of its legality.

The better view, then, appears to be that humanitarian intervention is illegal but that the international community may, on a case-by-case basis, tolerate the wrong. In such a situation, claims that an intervention was 'humanitarian' should be seen not as a legal justification but as a plea in mitigation. Such an approach has the merits of a basis in international law. In the *Corfu Channel Case*, the UK claimed that an intervention in Albanian territorial waters was justified on the basis that nobody else was prepared to deal with the threat of mines planted in an international strait. The ICJ rejected this argument in unequivocal terms, but held that a declaration of illegality was itself a sufficient remedy for the wrong.[19] Similarly, after Israel abducted Adolf Eichmann from Argentina to face criminal charges for his role in the Nazi Holocaust, Argentina lodged a complaint with the

---

[18] I. Brownlie, 'Thoughts on Kind-Hearted Gunmen', in R. B. Lillich (ed.), *Humanitarian Intervention and the United Nations* (Charlottesville, VA: University Press of Virginia 1973) 146. (Emphasis in original.)

[19] *Corfu Channel Case*.

Security Council, which passed a resolution stating that the sovereignty of Argentina had been infringed and requesting Israel to make 'appropriate reparation'. Nevertheless, 'mindful' of the concern that Eichmann be brought to justice, the Security Council clearly implied that 'appropriate reparation' would not involve his physical return to Argentina.[20] The governments of Israel and Argentina subsequently issued a joint communiqué resolving to 'view as settled the incident which was caused in the wake of the action of citizens of Israel which violated the basic rights of the State of Argentina'.[21]

This is also, broadly, consistent with current state practice. During the Kosovo intervention, some suggested that the action threatened the stability of the international order – in particular the relevance of the Security Council as the Charter body with primary responsibility for international peace and security. In fact, the Security Council became integral to resolution of the dispute (despite the bombing of the Embassy of one permanent member by another). In Resolution 1244 (1999), the Council, acting under Chapter VII, welcomed Yugoslavia's acceptance of the principles set out in the 6 May 1999 Meeting of G-8 Foreign Ministers and authorised member states and 'relevant international organisations' (in other words NATO) to establish an international security presence in Kosovo. The resolution was passed within hours of the suspension of bombing, and was prefaced with a half-hearted endorsement of the role of the Council:

Bearing in mind the purposes and principles of the Charter of the United Nations, and the primary responsibility of the Security Council for the maintenance of international peace and security.[22]

More importantly, Resolution 1244 (1999) reaffirmed the commitment 'of all Member States to the sovereignty and territorial integrity of the Federal Republic of Yugoslavia' even as it called for 'substantial autonomy' for Kosovo. The tension between these provisions has left the province in a legal limbo ever since, and continues to complicate the independence it declared in early 2008.

Later in 1999, military action in East Timor affirmed more clearly the continued role of the Security Council, with authorisation being a condition

---

[20] S/4349 (1960); SC Res. 138 (1960).

[21] Joint Communiqué of the Governments of Israel and Argentina, 3 August 1960, reprinted in 36 ILR 59.

[22] SC Res. 1244 (1999), Preamble.

precedent for the Australian-led International Force for East Timor (INTERFET) action. (This authorisation, in turn, depended on Indonesia's consent to the operation.) Though it was presented at the time as evidence that the international community was prepared to engage in Kosovo-style interventions outside Europe, the political and legal conditions in which the intervention took place were utterly different. The view that they were comparable reflected the troubling assumption that, when facing a humanitarian crisis with a military dimension, there is a choice between doing something and doing nothing, and that 'something' means the application of military force. This narrow view has been challenged by then-UN Secretary-General Kofi Annan, who has stressed that 'it is important to define intervention as broadly as possible, to include actions along a wide continuum from the most pacific to the most coercive'.[23] Similarly, the ICISS has sought to turn this policy question on its head. Rather than examining at length the right to intervene, it focuses on the responsibility of states to protect vulnerable populations at risk from civil wars, insurgencies, state repression and state collapse.[24]

Inhumanitarian non-intervention and the responsibility to protect

Implicit in many arguments for a right of humanitarian intervention is the suggestion that international law currently prevents interventions that should take place. This is simply not true. Interventions do not take place because states choose not to undertake them. On the contrary, states have frequently intervened for a great many reasons, some of them more humanitarian than others. For those who would seek to establish a law or a general ethical principle to govern humanitarian intervention, a central question must be whether it could work in practice. Do any of the incidents commonly marshalled as examples of humanitarian intervention provide a model that should be followed in future? Should Kosovo, for example, be a model for future negotiations with brutal regimes? If so, why were the terms presented to Serbia at Rambouillet more onerous than those offered after a seventy-eight-day bombing campaign?

[23] Annan, September 1999 Address.   [24] ICISS, *The Responsibility to Protect.*

Returning to the analogy made by Kofi Annan, quoted at the beginning of this chapter, the type of problem confronting human rights today is not Kosovo but Rwanda. Put differently, the problem is not the legitimacy of humanitarian intervention, but the overwhelming prevalence of inhumanitarian non-intervention. Addressing this problem requires mobilising the political will of member states as much as it does the creation of new legal rules. In this context, the rhetorical shift adopted by the ICISS – from a *right* of intervention to the *responsibility* to protect – may mark the most significant advance in this contested area of international relations.

The move from right to responsibility is more than wordplay. In particular, shifting the debate away from a simple question of the legality of humanitarian intervention, *stricto sensu*, serves two distinct policy goals. First, the legal debate is sterile. It is unlikely that a clear and workable set of criteria could be adopted on a right of humanitarian intervention. Any criteria general enough to achieve agreement would be unlikely to satisfy any actual examples of allegedly humanitarian intervention. Indeed, it is clear from the statements of NATO leaders during and after the Kosovo campaign that they did not want the air strikes to be regarded as a model for dealing with future humanitarian crises. The alternative – a select group of states (Western liberal democracies, for example) agreeing on criteria among themselves – would be seen as a vote of no confidence in the UN and a challenge to the very idea of an international rule of law.

More importantly, however, the focus on a responsibility to protect (R2P) highlights the true problem at the heart of this ongoing debate. The problem is not that states are champing at the bit to intervene in support of human rights around the globe, prevented only by an intransigent Security Council and the absence of clear criteria to intervene without its authority. Rather, the problem is the absence of the will to act at all.

Responsibility to protect, as a result, has achieved considerable traction in a short time. Nevertheless, the case of Libya suggests the wariness of the Security Council in embracing R2P. This was in many ways a perfect storm. State leaders are usually more circumspect in the threats they make against their population than was Gaddafi; impending massacres are rarely so easy to foresee. Combined with the support of African states and the Arab League for intervention, this left most states on the Council unwilling to allow atrocities to occur – and others unwilling to be seen as the impediment to action.

Even then, Resolution 1973 (2011), which authorised the use of all necessary measures to protect civilians, was vague about what might happen next. As in many previous cases, the commitment of leaders to confining their countries' involvement to air strikes alone and for a limited duration was transparently a political rather than military decision. The commencement of military action, as in many previous cases, swiftly showed that air strikes alone were unlikely to be effective. The potential tragedy of Benghazi soon devolved into farce as the Libyan rebels were revealed to be a disorganised rabble.[25]

Do something, do *anything*, is not a military strategy. At the time of writing, it is far from clear how the Libyan conflict will play out, but that outcome will have consequences that reach far beyond Libya itself. R2P may have made it harder to say 'no', but what happens next will clearly affect the likelihood of whether future leaders will say 'yes'.

Conclusion

Following the 11 September 2001 terrorist attacks on New York and Washington, DC, the USA swiftly sought and received Security Council endorsement of its position that this was an attack on the USA and that action taken in self-defence against 'those responsible for aiding, supporting or harboring the perpetrators, organizers and sponsors of these acts' was justified.[26] Self-defence does not require any form of authorisation (though measures taken should be 'immediately reported' to the Council), but the fact that the UN was involved so quickly in a crisis was widely seen as a welcome counterpoint to the unilateralist impulses of the George W. Bush Administration.

Nevertheless, the decision to seek Security Council approval also reflected a troubling trend through the 1990s. Military action under its auspices has taken place only when circumstances coincided with the national interests of a state that was prepared to act, with the Council in danger of becoming what Richard Falk has described as a 'law-laundering service'.[27] Such an approach downgrades the importance of authorisation

---

[25] See further S. Chesterman, '"Leading from Behind": The Responsibility to Protect, the Obama Doctrine, and Humanitarian Intervention after Libya' (2011) 25 *Ethics & International Affairs* 279.

[26] SC Res. 1368 (2001).

[27] R. A. Falk, 'The United Nations and the Rule of Law' (1994) 4 *Transnational Law and Contemporary Problems* 628.

to the point where it may be seen as a policy justification rather than a matter of legal significance. A consequence of this approach is that, when authorisation is not forthcoming, a state or group of states will feel less restrained from acting unilaterally. This represents a fundamental challenge to the international order established at the conclusion of the Second World War, in which the interests of the powerful would be balanced through the exercise (real or threatened) of the veto.

In the context of humanitarian intervention, it was widely hoped that such a departure from 'traditional' conceptions of sovereignty and international law would privilege ethics over states rights. In fact, as we have seen, humanitarian intervention has long had a troubled relationship to the question of national interest. Many attempts by scholars to formulate a doctrine of humanitarian intervention require that an acting state be disinterested (or 'relatively disinterested'). By contrast, in one of the few articulations of such a doctrine by a political leader, Prime Minister Blair proposed his own criteria, one of which was whether 'we' had national interests involved.[28]

The war on terror has reduced the probability of 'humanitarian' interventions in the short term, but raises the troubling prospect of more extensive military adventures being undertaken without clear legal justification. President Bush's 2002 State of the Union speech in particular, in which he referred to an 'axis of evil', suggested a preparedness to use ethical arguments (and absolute ethical statements) as a substitute for legal – or, it might be argued, rational – justification.

All such developments should be treated with great caution. A right of humanitarian intervention depends on one's acceptance that humanitarian ends justify military means. As the history of this doctrine shows, the ends are never so clear and the means are rarely so closely bound to them. In such a situation where there is no ideal, where Kosovo presents the imperfect model (and lingers today as a testament to NATO's imperfect victory), it is better to hold that humanitarian intervention without Council authorisation remains both illegal and morally suspect, but that arguments can be made on a case-by-case basis that, in an imperfect world, international order may yet survive the wrong.

---

[28] M. Evans, 'Conflict Opens "Way to New International Community": Blair's Mission', *The Times*, 23 April 1999. The five criteria were: Are we sure of our case? Have we exhausted all diplomatic options? Are there military options we can sensibly and prudently undertake? Are we prepared for the long term? And do we have national interests involved?

Further reading

Bellamy, A. J., *Responsibility to Protect: The Global Effort to End Mass Atrocities* (Cambridge: Polity, 2009)

Chesterman, S., *Just War or Just Peace? Humanitarian Intervention and International Law, Oxford Monographs in International Law* (Oxford University Press 2001)

Evans, G., *The Responsibility to Protect: Ending Mass Atrocity Crimes Once and for All* (Washington, DC: Brookings Institution 2008)

Holzgrefe, J. L. and Keohane, R. O. (eds.), *Humanitarian Intervention: Ethical, Legal and Political Dilemmas* (Cambridge University Press 2003)

International Commission on Intervention and State Sovereignty, *The Responsibility to Protect* (Ottawa: International Development Research Centre December 2001)

Lillich, R. B. (ed.), *Humanitarian Intervention and the United Nations* (Charlottesville, VA: University Press of Virginia 1973)

Orford, A., *Reading Humanitarian Intervention: Human Rights and the Use of Force in International Law* (Cambridge University Press 2003)

International Authority and the Responsibility to Protect (Cambridge University Press 2011)

Pattison, J., *Humanitarian Intervention and the Responsibility to Protect: Who Should Intervene?* (Oxford University Press 2010)

Tesón, F. R., *Humanitarian Intervention: An Inquiry into Law and Morality,* 2nd edn (Dobbs Ferry, NY: Transnational Publishers 1997)

Wheeler, N., *Saving Strangers: Humanitarian Intervention in International Society* (Oxford University Press 2000)

8 Reinventing human rights in an era of hyper-globalisation: a few wayside remarks

Upendra Baxi

Too much has been said about human rights; my apologies for adding more verbiage! In at least a partial defence, I must say that the engaging recent talk and action about 'reinventing' human rights may not be entirely diversionary. New human rights frameworks, instruments, norms and standards are constantly invented. Some old human rights frameworks are also being 'dis-invented' in the contemporary conjuncture of neoliberalism and wars of and on terror and in our era of hyperglobalisation. Even as the ascendant forms of primitive accumulation of global capital discredit the hard-won insistence on decency and dignity at workplaces, deny minimum wages and repress associational rights of workers, movements of resistance and counter-power reinvent global solidarity rights. The trinity of invention, disinvention and reinvention calls for some labours of understanding; here, all I aspire towards is an elementary grasp of these three notions.

I think that it is high time that we begin to acknowledge that human rights constitute acts of ethical as well as juridico-political manufacture. The idea of human rights is a remarkable recent ethical invention. It is ethical because human rights enunciate the values of human dignity and freedom; it is juridico-political as a *socio-technical* invention. Human rights are moral (the responsibility that each human owes to the other) and juridical (the responsibility that political authority owes to citizens as well as all subjects within its jurisdiction). Human rights constitute an invention because they generate new signifying systems of values, principles, institutions, movements, practices and languages.

The creativity of human rights

A threshold concern relates to any value-addition that this 'Trinitarian' discourse may provide. In what ways, if any, may this discourse offer yet another critical theory approach to human rights?

Epistemological, ontological and ideological critiques of human rights often render obscure the labours of production of human rights values, norms, standards and the institutional frameworks sustaining them. Furthermore, inventive activity in the sphere of human rights attracts the metaphors offered by Hans Joas for creativity as a form of social action: 'Expression', 'Production', 'Revolution', 'Life', 'Intelligence' and 'Reconstruction.'[1] The labours of invention (as well as of dis-invention and re-invention) offer narratives of human rights as collective ethical – as well as juridico-political – inventions.

This trinity makes considerable moral/ethical sense for a comparative social theory of human rights and further provides a good resource for diverse human rights and social movements, especially practices of sentimental moral reason and insurgent popular action.

Invention

The notion of 'invention'– perhaps, a better coinage is 'fabrication'[2] – has many rich histories. To 'invent' (creating something new) is not the same as to 'discover' (finding out what pre-exists). Yet across various realms the distinction gets complicated. In part, this is so, because creative expression and production in inventions differ – we have material or technological inventions as well as symbolic and semiotic, spiritual or ethical inventions. How these orders/regimes of invention inter-relate is a question of great importance, which I may mention but not fully pursue here. It is clear from recent studies in technology and modernity that all technological inventions remain social productions. All 'infrastructures' and 'technologies' are 'in fact *socio-technical* in nature, entailing not just 'hardware' but 'organizations, socially communicated background knowledge, general acceptance and reliance'.[3]

---

[1] H. Joas, *The Creativity of Action* (J. Gains and P. Keast, trans.) (Cambridge: Polity 1996) Ch 2.

[2] Perhaps, the term 'fabrication' foregrounds the materiality of invention a little better: thus a recent work on law and anthropology privileges the term 'fabrication' 'precisely because it suggests modes of action which are lodged in rich, culturally-specific, layers of texts, practices, instruments, technical devices, aesthetic forms, stylised gestures, semantic artefacts, and bodily dispositions', see A. Pottage, 'Introduction: The Fabrication of Persons and Things', in A. Pottage and M. Mundy (eds.), *Law, Anthropology, and the Construction of the Social: Making Things and Persons* (New York: Cambridge University Press 2004) 1.

[3] P. N. Edwards, 'Infrastructure and Modernity: Force, Time, and Social Organization in the History of Sociotechnical Systems', in T. J. Misa, P. Brey and A. Feenberg (eds.), *Modernity and Technology* (Cambridge, MA: MIT Press 2003) 188.

Non-material inventions – symbolic or normative systems – affect, as well as remain affected by, the technological regimes of invention. We know well by now the digitalised social media networks that today shape the future of human rights across the world. To take even a more powerful example, the Cross was a crude material invention; yet it gave rise to the powerful symbolisation of suffering and sacrifice and to novel redemptive visions.

The order of invention of 'things' and its articulations of materiality remains critical for systems of meaning and representation. The very invention of 'keywords', for example, is a joint production of material and non-material invention. As Eric Hobsbawm reminds us:

WORDS speak louder than documents. Let us consider a few English words which were invented, or gained their modern meanings, substantially in the period of sixty years [1789–1848] constituting an 'age' of 'revolution'... such words as 'industry', 'industrialist', 'factory', 'middle class', 'working class', 'capitalism' and 'socialism'. They include 'aristocracy' as well as 'railway', 'liberal' and 'conservative' as political terms, 'nationality', 'scientist' and 'engineer', 'proletariat' and (economic) 'crisis'. 'Utilitarian' and 'statistics', 'sociology' and several other names of modern sciences, 'journalism' and 'ideology', are all coinages or adaptations of this period.[4]

Somewhere within these coinages lurks an emergent keyword: 'Human Rights.' If the 'Age of Revolution' may not be grasped outside these coinages, neither may the reconstitution of the world order invented by the post-Westphalian regime. The 'Age of Revolution' marks also the birth pangs of the 'Age of Human Rights'.

Through the figure of 'speaking beings' Julia Kristeva reminds us of the symbolic and semiotic signifying practices in which the 'speaking subject at once makes and unmakes himself'[5] marking passages in the 'status of the subject – his relation to the body, to others, and to objects'.[6] Note that Kristeva imagines the 'subject' as always 'embodied' (corporeal), as social (permeated by relationships with the other) and as imbricated in physical nature with its givenness and social nature (as recurrently reproduced/ commoditised 'objects').

One may then perhaps extend Kristeva's insights to the invention of the idea of human with human rights, to refer to histories of meaning and of

---

[4] E. Hobsbawm, *The Age of Revolution: 1979–1848* (London: Random House 1962) 1.

[5] J. Kristeva, *Language, the Unknown: An Initiation into Linguistics* (A. Menke, trans.) (New York: Columbia University Press 1989) 265–72.

[6] J. Kristeva, *Revolution in Poetic Language* (L. S. Roudiez, trans.) (New York: Columbia University Press 1984) 15.

affect as transformative passages/movement in the 'status of the subject'. This construction evokes various narratives of the constitution of a 'desiring subject' of human rights. The status of the subject remains conditioned (if not determined) by material inventions that provide the infrastructures for human rights.

To state the rather obvious, the logics of scientific and ethical inventions differ. Normative ethical inventions/discoveries (such as human rights) carry an overload of justification that techno-scientific orders of invention may not, and almost always do not, bear. Unlike, however, 'material' and 'aesthetic' inventions, critical questions concerning responsibility/answerability surround the work of discovery and invention of human rights. For example, the regimes of creation crystallised variously in the idea of 'art for art's sake', or even art for market's sake, thrive on maximal repudiation of notions about the social responsibility of artistic creation. Much the same may be said about techno-scientific inventions. Indeed, a near-absolute freedom of imagination and invention assumes the form of a basic human right in both discursive forms. To take this away is to impoverish the futures of human rights. Censorship of art forms and prohibition or regulation of certain kinds of scientific research are often thus said to violate the rights to freedom. To whom one may owe responsibility/answerability emerges as a crucial question in the spheres of human rights discovery/invention.

'Dis-invention' and 're-invention'

What may one mean by 'dis-invention'? Technological/material inventions may be seen as dis-invention as desuetude; over time, some inventions cease to have any use and often entail the disappearance of the object of invention as well as of the ways of life associated with these. The quill and the inkpot, the carbon paper from which the typewriter produced many copies and the stencil are decidedly things of an already distant past. The disappearance of these inventions is not mourned but rather fully embraced even by human rights and social movement activists.[7] What matters

---

[7] I do not know whether Mohandas Gandhi had he been with us today used the e-mail or SMS rather than a postcard; in his hands and pen this form of governmental monopoly over the means of communication also becomes an instrument of its subversion; nor do I

therefore is not the disappearance of erstwhile objects but rather the varied histories of the reception of dis-invention.

How may we speak of the dis-invention of signifying/semiotic systems? We currently witness the disappearance of several world-historic human rights languages. They include the 'socialist' languages whose leitmotif of distributive justice informed many human rights conceptions; radical self-determination languages (now said to be exhausted in post-colony and post-Cold War, even post-Westphalian world orderings, poignantly as regards the first world nations and peoples); and the proletarian languages (affirming and celebrating the collective rights of the working classes). In their place and space, we have the new human rights languages of the politics of recognition (the human rights to identity within difference) and to 'participation' within 'representation' (as readers of Nancy Fraser and Alex Honneth know rather well). The differences on display have many, and conflicted, narrative histories.

Forms of 'reception' of disappearance vary of course when some ethical languages or signifying systems fall into disuse. 'Neocons' celebrate the disappearance of the erstwhile languages of redistributive justice even as human rights and social movement campaigners mourn the loss of the social worlds thus signified. Neo-Nazis mourn the human rights induced dis-invention of state-sanctioned racisms, even while seeking their revival; while human rights and social movement activists celebrate the downfall of so many forms of apartheid, remaining anxious about their return in subtler modes. Patriarchs everywhere lament the loss of their worlds caused by the movement of women's rights as human rights. Exponents of the fine arts of predatory globalisation celebrate the dis-invention of utopian socialism, while those who value new approaches to global justice return to it with a melancholic sense of nostalgia. 'Dis-invention' remains a strongly evaluative term of discourse even when it displays languages, logics and paralogics of reversal.

The notion of 'reinvention'– scarcely a term of art – is harder to describe and evaluate. Reinvention often attracts the disdainful phrase that it amounts to the 'reinvention of the wheel'! Of course, 'wheels' are constantly reinvented in the material realm – from the bullock cart to the Boeing

know whether the Mahatma would have critiqued the new technologies in the same way in which he decried the old ones in his famous tract *The Hind Swaraj*: M. Gandhi, *The Hind Swaraj and Indian Home Rule* (1909), www.sscnet.ucla.edu/southasia/History/Gandhi/hind_swar_gandhi.html.

aircraft wheels. Here, I refer to normative and institutional forms of reinvention. The former occurs through the creation of aspirational human
rights normativity; the latter by constant institutional reinventions. Let
me start with a brief exploration of the difference between discovery and
invention.

Discovery rather than invention

One way to explain this distinction is by means of a little bit of God-talk.
The lineages of human rights are often found in the realms of theology and
in particular the nature and limits of pious interpretation. Speaking in ideal-
type terms, the task of a pious interpreter (or the community) comprises
feats of discovery of the meaning of God's Will (theological voluntarism)
and His Reason (theological rationalism.) The difference matters, if only
because it remains possible to think that God endowed the faithful and the
pious with the gift of human reason in order give them a fuller grasp of His
Reason – His 'original intention'. Heretical pious hermeneutics across all
religions have enlarged and often enriched the horizons of human freedom
as an integral aspect of Divine Reason by insisting, in sum, that even as
human reason may not question God's Will, it may not entirely gainsay His
Reason.

Abdullahi An-Na'im reminds us at the level of theory that reading the
Holy Koran entails making choices between the Mecca and Medina schools
of *shari'a*,[8] the latter not merely more compatible with contemporary
human rights enunciations but also prefiguring these. So on the register
of social movements do the acts of pious reading of the Holy Book by
Islamic women. In a different context, Michael Perry urges us to ask
whether or not the notion of human dignity – the cornerstone of contemporary human rights enunciations – remains 'ineliminably religious'
(conceived as the sacredness of the human person).[9] How else, for example,
can we explain the Islamic theologians' critique of the Shiite constructions
of martyrdom (*shahada*) as un-Islamic?[10]

---

[8] See his *Islam and the Secular State: Negotiating the Future of Shari'a* (Cambridge, MA:
   Harvard University Press 2008).
[9] M. J. Perry, *The Idea of Human Rights: Four Inquiries* (New York: Oxford University Press
   1998) 5.
[10] B. K. Freamon, 'Martyrdom, Suicide, and the Islamic Law of War: A Short Legal History'
   (2003) 27 *Fordham International Law Journal* 299–369.

Leaving aside the question of the (im)possibility of non-theological orderings,[11] what we may properly call 'fundamentalism' is the attempt at rendering Divine Will as an absolute imperative, confining theological rationalism to the margins. At stake here is the closure of interpretation by the evocation of God's Will which no form of pious interpretation may ever revisit except sinfully. The problem of radical inconsistency between contemporary human rights values, norms and standards and theological voluntarism resembles what Jean-François Lyotard has called a *Differend*. If for some peoples of faith some human rights mean nothing at all except transgressions of God's Will, the Divine intent and plan, what occurs is a disinvention of the very idea of human rights – a form that may not be fully addressed by voguish talk about tolerance, multiculturalism, 'reasonable pluralism' and the allied secular discourses about freedom of religion and conscience as basic human rights.

Dislocations of the morality of aspiration and duty

It was Lon Fuller who developed this distinction. For Fuller, the morality of aspiration is 'the morality of the Good Life, of excellence, the fullest realization of human powers' and of 'experiment, inspiration, and sponta- neity' presented in contrast with the morality of duty, and with the further thesis that far from being a binary this contrast presents a continuum.[12] Aspirational human rights statements, from the American to the French and the Universal Declaration of Human Rights (UDHR), are paradigmatic of the creative variety of declarations; their moral appeal is world-historical, plotting the collective human sentiment, albeit clearly they reveal a disconnect between their sense of aspiration on the one hand and the power of duty on the other.

Within the UN system, human rights declarations have a special place and status. They often prepare ground for treaty-based obligations, they offer extensions of the idea and doctrine of *ius cogens* and they pave pathways for aspirational statement to become fully fledged normative instruments. Some declarations remain dead on arrival – for example, declarations of a New International Economic Order (NIEO) and the

---

[11] See the provocative analysis by R. Brague, 'Are Non-Theocratic Orders Possible?' (Spring 2006) *The Intercollegiate Review* 3–10.

[12] L. Fuller, *The Morality of Law* (New Haven, CT: Yale University Press, revised edn 1969) 5, 28.

UNESCO-based declaration of a New Informational Order (NIO). In contrast, the UN Declaration of the Right to Development (DRD) has led to sustained endeavours at developing such a right.[13] Furthermore, 'regional' human rights declarations abound; suffering peoples and communities in resistance have also recourse to declarations, the most notable being the recent Zapatista and Ogoni Peoples human rights declarations or the 2010 Cochabamba Draft Declaration of the Rights of Mother Earth.

It is clear that these communicative achievements are considered well worth the labours of arriving at inclusive and consensual statements; they mark a collective growth in ethical sentiment. The high growth curve of human rights declarations can thus be read as a new 'morality of aspiration' that is just as important as the 'morality of duty'.

Human rights aspirational statements can be seen as ways of 'doing things with words' – performative speech-acts deploying language as forms of social action. They carry both the illocutionary force of saying things in specific contexts as well as having perlocutionary effects that often exceed the intention of the speaker.[14] If human rights 'discovery' furnishes an example of the illocutionary effects of human rights declarations, human rights 'inventions' signify the perlocutionary effects of what is said and left unsaid in human rights declarations.

The speech-acts comprising the UDHR – especially its invention of the birth-metaphor (all humans are born with and possess equal respect for their dignity) – far exceed now the original intention of the speaking subjects. The enterprise of domination always aims at reducing the 'speaking subject'; the enterprise of human rights seeks constantly to expand such subjects or extend the future reach of perlocutionary effects. For example, the current waves of the 'Arab Spring' enunciate the future histories of 'doing things with words' neither entirely anticipated nor fully ascribable to the narratives of effect/affect of the UDHR. Their presupposed conversational contexts assume a relatively stable community of meanings; some linguistic philosophers call this effect a '"conversational perspective

---

[13] Not being a critical etymologist is a disability here; even so, I may suggest that if a 'declaration' is a statement about acts of 'discovery', 'covenants' refer to acts of promissory faith (as is indeed the case with the Covenant on Social, Economic and Cultural Rights, ICESCR, for example). Yet both the forms – and human rights Covenants – articulate human rights (discovery) as well as make statements about rights-in-the-making or even human rights 'to come'.

[14] See T. M. Holtgraves, *Language as Social Action: Social Psychology and Language Use* (Mahwah, NJ: Lawrence Erlbaum Associates 2002).

taking" phenomenon in which one's actions, and the meaning of those actions are closely intertwined with the actions and interpretations of others outside which social language use *remain insensible*.[15]

Let me now turn to concerns about the implosion of aspirational statements. These produce human rights weariness among theorists as well as the dominated and the oppressed, leading to varieties of human rights scepticism.[16] Furthermore, there is much talk about 'over-production': on the side of movements, it is argued that there are too few human rights while critics complain that there are far too many. If human rights and social movement activists articulate the deeply felt desire for converting all basic material and non-material needs into aspirational statements of human rights[17] their critics suggest that over-production of such statements fails to take human rights seriously. Onora O'Neill – a Kantian exponent of human rights – suggests:

> If we take rights seriously and see them as normative rather than aspirational, we must take obligations seriously. If on the other hand we opt for a merely aspirational view, the costs are high. For then we would also have to accept that where human rights are unmet there is no breach of obligation, nobody at fault, nobody who can be held to account, nobody to blame and nobody who owes redress. We would in effect have to accept that human rights claims are not real claims.[18]

O'Neill does not suggest that aspirational statements are not necessary or desirable; yet if not translated into norms ('real claims') too many majestic declarations may prove counter-productive. This task is never easy, as she demonstrates with reference particularly to the human right to health and more generally with social and economic human rights. It is not enough to identify the subject of such rights; we need to identify also the agents and institutions that owe determinate obligations in relation to such rights. This endeavour should proceed with great care, given the fact that, unlike the right to freedom and liberty rights, socio-economic rights (such as shelter, housing, or health) are rights to goods and services that must be produced and made available by disaggregated serial entrepreneurs. Evoking Edmund Burke, O'Neill begins and ends her reflections with the imagery of the 'farmer and the physician' whose willing social co-operation constitutes a crucial

---

[15] See Holtgraves, *Language as Social Action* Ch 6.
[16] U. Baxi, *The Future of Human Rights* (Oxford University Press 2008) Chs 3 and 4. This work will be hereafter cited as Baxi, *The Future of Human Rights*.
[17] Baxi, *The Future of Human Rights* Ch 4.
[18] O. O'Neill, 'The Dark Side of Human Rights' (2005) 81 (2) *International Affairs* 430.

prerequisite for any responsible activity of norm-formation around the 'right to life'. This 'Burke-an' narrative of O'Neill offers a veiled critique of socialist approaches to human rights – a message suggesting an egregious error. Such rights depend on the spontaneous miracles of a rational choice-based production of goods and services, a realm of social co-operation outside which the 'progressive realisation' of social and economic human rights may remain indeed chimerical.

For O'Neill, human rights aspiration remains caught in 'a dark and tempting undercurrent of pleasure in blaming'. Wanton articulations of human rights blame-games offer often enough easy and 'cheap pleasures even for complainants whose case is not upheld':

> Those who cast blame can appropriate enjoy and prolong their role and status as victims, can enjoy indignation and a feeling of superiority, even if they cannot quite identify or demonstrate the failings of others. If it proves impossible to identify a blameworthy culprit, they can at least blame the system, that is to say the institutional framework that is failing to achieve 'progressively the full realization of the rights recognized ... by all appropriate means, including particularly the adoption of legislative measures'.[19]

O Neill goes further with the invocation of Nietzsche's dictum that '[s]uffering peoples have horrible willingness and capacity for inventing pretexts for painful emotional feelings', ransacking 'dark and dubious stories in which they are free to feast on suspicion and to get intoxicated on their poisonous anger'.[20] Such readings of Nietzsche however furnish an anachronistic anthropology of human rights. The voices of human and social suffering that demand political responsibility for acts of radical evil scarcely thrive on this ransacking of 'dark and dubious stories' in the way Nietzsche describes. Nor do those who characterise the plight of the world's impoverished peoples as the ultimate global political obscenity constitute an assemblage of 'vengeful subjects'.

Blaming the 'system' for being indifferent to human rights, however, is not always an idle pastime. It assumes dimensions of the collective practice that question the repressive potential of governing others as if they were lesser humans – in whatsoever name, whether 'God', 'Empire', or 'democracy'. Ethical blaming practices (naming and shaming the state and state-like actors who together constitute the 'system') constitute a virtue for those

---

[19] O'Neill, 'The Dark Side' 438.   [20] O'Neill, 'The Dark Side' 439.

who dare imagine alternative institutional frameworks,[21] from the perspective of here-and-now suffering humans. Aspirational human rights statements signify the 'bright' rather than the 'dark' side for human rights futures.[22] Put differently, O'Neill's description of the 'dark side' needs supplementation in terms of the moral status and power of 'victims'.[23]

O'Neill's concern is that contemporary human rights norms, and standards extend and expand state powers too much by 'establishing systems of control and discipline that extend to into the remotest corners of life, leaving them with the consoling pleasures of blame'; she reiterates Bernard Williams' criticism that blame is and remains 'the characteristic reaction of a morality system' in which 'obligations and rights have become the sole ethical currency'.[24] Her caution that this may pave the way for the future demise of the socio-technical invention of human rights languages and action should concern us all. Yet, it remains unclear whether as a matter of observable fact, the pre-eminence of human rights languages renders other languages (such as that of justice) a counterfeit currency.

Reading rights from human contingency

Juridico-political inventions of human rights ascribe their values, norms and standards to acts of human will and reason and, more crucially, the 'politics' of human desire. In this sense the invention of human rights marks the advent of the post-religious era in which all forms of sovereign power (whether of the state or institutionalised religions) are prised open by a new politics of human rights desire. The politico-juridical and socio-technical regime of human rights inventions privilege the passage from divine or natural law necessity to the diverse orders of 'contingent necessity'.[25]

---

[21] Speaking at least for myself having invested more than a quarter of a century in acts of solidarity for the Bhopal-violated humanity (and other engagements with the histories of otherwise lost causes in the Global South), I do not believe that the exuberance of excess of human rights aspirational statements constitute a 'dark side' of human rights.

[22] For a patient and painstaking demonstration of this truth, see B. A. Simmons, *Mobilizing for Human Rights: International Law in Domestic Politics* (Cambridge University Press 2009).

[23] See, in particular, the reflections in L. Thomas, 'Evil and Forgiveness: The Possibility of Moral Redemption', in A. Veltman and K. J. Norlock (eds.), *Evil, Political Violence, and Forgiveness: Essays in Honour of Claudia Card* (New York: Lexington Books 2009) 115.

[24] O'Neill, 'The Dark Side' 439.

[25] J. Butler, E. Laclau and S. Žižek, *Contingency, Hegemony, Universality: Contemporary Dialogues on the Left* (London: Verso 2000).

The idea of being – and remaining – human and having rights is no longer pre-ordained; rather it emerges in and through the specificity of 'politics' and the 'political'. The foundation of human rights is no longer a set of 'eternal' truths but the dis-anchored desires behind the practices of both domination and resistance. The historic reality of aspiration and norm names basic or fundamental human rights as a series of contingent human rights truth-claims based on 'three assumptions: the vulnerability of embodiment, the precariousness of institutions, and the interconnectedness of social life'.[26]

Put differently, what makes us all humans (the universality of human rights) flows from what Quentin Meillassoux calls, in a very different context, the 'necessity of contingency'. For H. L. A. Hart, this necessity flows from elementary social facts: all humans are finite, equally vulnerable to pain and suffering, and remain liable to infirmities of reason and will. This leads to some 'minimal natural law' postulates.[27] I do not know how far this framework may be extended to human rights; yet it is clear that human rights and the 'new' social movements extend a new conspectus not just to the actually existing humans, but also to past humans (for example in reparations for slavery and crimes against humanity) and now to the collective species-being of all born and to be born as humans (the collective affirmation of the dignity of present and future generations of humans as evidenced in sustainable development and climate change claims). These remarkable developments in collective moral sentiment (named as human rights portals) re-conceptualise images of both predation and vulnerability.

Despite difficulties, we need to adapt and expand Meillassoux's notion of 'ancestral truths'[28] into the languages of ancestral 'moral' human rights truths: for example, the idea that God created all humans as equal or the UDHR claim that those born human possess equal dignity and freedom. These human rights truths create here-and-now types of perfect and imperfect duties as well as equally indeterminate orders of future obligations

---

[26] B. S. Turner, 'The End(s) of Humanity: Vulnerability and the Metaphors Membership' *The Hedgehog Review* (Summer 2001).

[27] See H. L. A. Hart, *The Concept of Law* (Oxford: Clarendon Press 1961). I remain aware that I extend Hart a bit here!

[28] See Q. Meillassoux, *After Finitude: An Essay on the Necessity of Contingency* (R. Brassier, trans.) (London: Continuum 2008), which addresses entirely 'ancestral' as any reality anterior to the emergence of the human species – or even anterior to every recognised form of life on earth. Meillassoux is concerned with ancestral statements about the discourse of scientific statements concerning the origins of earth, matter, and human life.

towards generations yet to be born. These obligations are justified by a belief that privileges the continued survival of the earth and its peoples as well as other beings and entities (biodiversity). Take this away, and very little will remain of our impassioned engagement with the future of humanity, environment, and rights! In this way, aspirational human rights statements provide critical impetus towards a wider zone of human rights creativity and inventiveness.

A further remarkable aspect of juridico-political (socio-technical) human rights invention(s) may be grasped by adapting Hegel's three moments of 'abstract universality' (undifferentiated identity of all humans as bearers of universal rights), 'abstract particularity' (all humans are entitled to a certain order of freedom and dignity) and 'concrete universality' (the claims of the right-less to have human rights, or the continued reinvention of the category of the bearers of human rights).[29] Human rights aspirations crystallise the first moment; international or constitutional human rights norms and standards articulate the second; the third moment is continuously happening, through the translation of basic human needs into human rights or through the creation of rights to identity within difference or more crucially through the practices of insurgent human rights reason (currently in the 'Arab Spring'). The logic is not one of linear succession (as for example in the classification of three generations of human rights) but of dialectical play among the three moments. This is particularly pertinent in relation to some extraordinary and historically unreal singular claims about the Euro-American invention of human rights.[30]

Put differently, then, the histories of the three moments go well beyond charismatic stories about the 'regional metaphysic' of the 'great' American and French declarations. Their 'greatness' stands inversely proportional only to the complete irresponsibility towards the non-European others. These others have contested and combated human rights 'essentialism' in its various forms: the denial of human status through violent social exclusion in the old and new forms of human slavery, the subjugation of women and indigenous peoples, and the colonised as well as the treatment of neo-colonial subjects as inferior humans or non-human. The un-making of these justifications constitutes varieties of speech-acts – the deployment of language as a form of social action,[31] which in turn de-legitimise some

---

[29] Baxi, *The Future of Human Rights* Ch 5.

[30] See Baxi, *The Future of Human Rights* Chs 2–6 and the materials cited and discussed therein.

[31] See Holtsgrave, *Language as Social Action* Ch 7.

singular claims of modern/contemporary human rights authorship. Acknowledging fully, as one ought to, the celebrated discourse of the European Enlightenment – the discourse of freedom and rights – remains open to many and at times is exposed to profound internal contestations.[32] It is clear however that this contestation did not go far enough and did not redress its ingrained epistemic racism and its logic of violent social exclusion of the *Indio* by the *Illustrado*, to use a Filipino expression.

The universal human rights thus said to be invented remained the work of the second moment of 'abstract particularity' in which the idea of being 'human' and of 'having' rights signified a human rights subject capable of freedom and reason, attributes denied to the non-European other. This 'regional' human rights metaphysics is presented as a 'universal' one, even today, inviting the indictment of human rights 'imperialism'!

My suggestion is that the world–historical real – the third moment of 'concrete universality' of human rights 'inventions' – began its itinerary in the struggles of the non-European others. The invention of the right of subjugated peoples for self-determination begins with Mohandas Gandhi and his ethic of non-violent struggle against colonialism/imperialism. The invention of a human right against pervasive racial discrimination (apartheid) begins with Nelson Mandela and, in a different setting, with Martin Luther King, Jr. The struggles against universal patriarchy begin their myriad itineraries of resistance for women's rights/human rights everywhere. It needs to be more fully recognised than is the case now that contemporary human rights values, norms, and standards emerged much earlier than the UDHR. We must recognise that its foundational assertion – 'All human beings are born free and equal in dignity and rights'– cannot be understood without the invention of the right to self-determination ushered in by the struggles of the non-European others.

In this sense, 'the' history of human rights still remains to be fully written. Unfortunately, even the progressive vanguard club and hub of human rights critics rarely entertain the notion that the non-European other may be anything other than a mimetic being, at best enacting mere footnotes to

---

[32] See J. L. Israel, *Enlightenment Contested: Philosophy, Modernity, and the Emancipation of Man 1670–1752* (Oxford University Press 2006). As concerns specifically the discourse of the rights of non-European others, see G. Cavallar, *The Rights of Strangers: Theories of International Hospitality, the Global Community, and Political Justice since Vitoria* (London: Ashgate 2002).

the contractarian lineages of a Locke or Rousseau, names and discourses fully unfamiliar to most non-European others.

Pre-committment and negotiability

Accepting that human rights involve a dialectical flow among the three moments of 'abstract universality', abstract particularity' and 'concrete universality', aspirational human rights statements engage the first two moments, while statements about the morality of duty relate to the third. Aspirational human rights enunciations invent and develop pre-commitment strategies; negotiation strategies characterise the translation of aspirations into norms.

Pre-commitment strategies set out certain 'decisions of principle'[33] that Hannah Arendt describes as 'political principles'[34] in relation to human rights. For Arendt, these principles are not so much articulations of moral or natural rights; they are principles of human praxis through which 'our rights and dignity can only be assured by our own efforts and agreements'.[35] Pre-commitment strategies represent histories of effort and agreement that place certain human rights beyond the play of political power seeking to ensure that these may not be the 'playthings of power',[36] or of the counter-power of insurgent social actors. Pre-commitment strategies aspire to disable 'the claims of everything else, of political and economic ideology, of even religion in some instances, and most of all the demands of self-interest'[37] especially when basic human rights values are at stake.

[33] See, R. M. Hare, *The Language of Morals* (Oxford University Press 1952) 56–78. Citing this eminent moral theorist is of course not a good way of remembering him, because he did not hold human rights talk in good esteem and frowned at 'the unthinking appeal to ill-defined rights, unsupported by argument, that does the harm': see Hare, 'What is Wrong with Slavery' (1979) 8 (2) *Philosophy & Public Affairs* 1103–1212.

[34] See the unfortunately little noticed, yet germinal, contribution by J. C. Isaac, 'A New Guarantee on Earth: Hannah Arendt on Human Dignity and the Politics of Human Rights' (1996) 90 (1) *American Political Science Review* 61–73.

[35] Isaac, 'A New Guarantee' 66.

[36] Justice M. Hidayatuallah, in saying this in *Sajjan Singh* v. *State of Rajasthan* [1965] 1 SCR 933; AIR 1965 SC 845 in the context of an overweening power of the Indian Parliament to amend even the basic rights provisions of the Constitution, eventually triggered a fully fledged doctrine of the essential features of the basic structure of the Constitution which may not be amended away: see for a more recent analysis, S. Krishnaswamy, *Democracy and Constitutionalism in India* (Delhi: Oxford University Press 2009).

[37] I derive these words from an incisive analysis by F. J. Murphy, 'The Problem of Overridingness' (1998) 36 (2) *The Southern Journal of Philosophy* 5.

Pre-commitment strategies, at least within national constitutional contexts, seek to render state action ethical, governance just, and power in all its forms accountable. They also address 'non-state' conduct that transgresses basic human rights to freedom. For pre-commitment strategies all aspirational human rights are inter-related. The tasks of negotiation strategies are onerous and complicated.

If aspiration-makers are 'moral realists' who believe that moral reasons for action exist independently of an individual desires or goals,[38] the negotiation strategies of human rights norm-makers are prudential. The term 'prudence' in 'modern virtue ethics' signifies a 'certain skill in making moral distinctions, a skill in realising what, in a concrete and complicated situation, morality requires'.[39] While such skills are necessary for the consensual formations of human rights declarations, prudential skills and competences in negotiation strategies remain directed to the feasible and the realistic.

Both pre-commitment strategies and negotiation strategies vary with time, place, and circumstance, an aspect often overlooked by human rights critics. The negotiation strategies are directed towards: (a) constantly reaffirming and expanding the customary human rights law of *ius cogens;* (b) negotiating human rights treaty obligations; (c) incentivising the naming and monitoring of gross, flagrant, and massive human rights violations; and (d) promoting practices of transnational activist adjudication.[40] Negotiation strategies circulate furthermore a range of socio-technical inventions such as the institutions and networks of UN Human Rights Treaty Bodies, the UN Human Rights Council and the Office of the Human Rights Commission (and allied human rights agencies at regional and national constitutional

---

[38] T. Tännsjö, *From Reasons to Norms: On the Basic Questions in Ethics* (Dordrecht/Heidelberg: Springer 2010) 9 offers a sustained defence of moral realism this way: there exist 'objective normative reasons, existing independently of our conceptualisation' and 'the claim is that there exists only *one* source of normativity. There is, in each situation, one, and only one, truth about what we ought to do, and our moral (normative) reasons explain this obligation.' For the moment the following description by Frederick L. Ware should suffice: 'The project of moral realism is to establish an "objective" morality that all persons are obliged to regard as authoritative and thus bypass the involved and complicated process of moral formation and negotiation of conflicting social interests': see his 'Theology of Nature without Moral Realism: A Response of Jürgen Moltmann', www.andyrowell.net/.../ware_response_to_moltmann_theo logy_of_nature_(date of last access 29 August 2011) 3.

[39] Tännsjö, *From Reasons to Norms* 90.

[40] U. Baxi, 'Public and Insurgent Reason: Adjudicatory Leadership in a Hyper-Globalizing World', in S. Gill (ed.), *Global Crises and the Crisis of Global Leadership* (Cambridge University Press 2011) 161–78.

levels). This means that while human rights negotiators may not be able to ignore or bypass state sovereignty, they are not deterred from trying to circumscribe its prowess. Hannah Arendt speaks to human rights negotiators everywhere when she says that the notion of dignity enshrined in the UDHR needs a 'new guarantee which can be found only in a new political principle, in a new law on the earth, whose validity this time must comprehend the whole of humanity while its power must remain strictly limited, rooted and controlled by newly defined territorial entities'.[41]

Negotiation strategies also remain liable to dis-invention and re-invention. The rise and growth of human rights diplomacy constitutes a remarkable aspect of the 're-invention' of human rights. Distinctions between several forms of human rights diplomacy of course remain essential. I here mention only four distinctions: first, governmental or governance human rights diplomacy; second, the global civil society human rights advocacy; third, human rights diplomacy as practised within the UN system by a variety of special institutions and arrangements;[42] and fourth a whole variety of practices of interpretation developed by international, supranational, regional and national courts and related *fora* of international judicial process. These are immensely varied forms and practices with some shared features and some deep disagreements. A common property for these four forms of human rights diplomacy is 'negotiation'. It remains crucial to acknowledge that what is at play and at war are practices of negotiation. If governance/governmentality human rights diplomacy remains conflict-riven/driven, so do the practices of NGO/human rights diplomacy. It would be astonishing to think that this may be ever otherwise! Further, both the forms articulate strongly held perspectives about what may fall within the domain of 'pre-commitment' and outside it. 'Negotiation' entails both opening and closure, a dynamic scarcely captured by the crude appellation 'tradeoffs'. Global civil society actors cannot but participate in closure as well as openings alongside other human rights diplomats. Where perhaps they differ from these others raises concerns about the kinds of 'politics' at stake. Elsewhere I develop a distinction

---

[41] H. Arendt, *The Origins of Totalitarianism* (New York: Harcourt Bruce 1973) ix.

[42] Such as UNESCO, WHO, the International Labor Organization (ILO), the UN High Commissioner for Refugees (UNHCR), FAO, UNCTAD, WIPO and now the World Trade Organization (WTO); even more crucial remains the intersection of the new human rights diplomacy with specialised institutions within the UN system such as the Human Rights Treaty Bodies, Human Rights Council and the Commissioner on Human Rights.

between politics '*of*' human rights, that is the use of human rights languages to justify the specificity of the political conjuncture or in general the ends of domination and politics '*for*' human rights, that is the deployment of human rights languages for transformative ends.[43] Even as I maintain that contemporary human rights remain unthinkable outside this invention of NGO/human rights diplomacy, its potential to enhance or diminish human rights futures is not always as writ large as many a critic of 'human rights imperialism' or 'hegemony' seems to suggest.

I must however at least summarily mention that in reaching its very own distinctive 'thousand plateaus', global civil society human rights diplomacy via complex interaction with other institutional actors contributes just as much to the dis-invention of human rights. This, at least in my view, occurs most poignantly in acts/feats of global social policy via the expansive domains and platforms partially of the UN Development Programme (UNDP) articulated programmes of 'good governance' and the Millennial Development Goals and targets. The latter certainly and cruelly mock the ideals and attainments of internationally enunciated social and economic human rights obligations by converting these human rights into languages of insensible global social policy.[44] The summits of global civil society human rights diplomacy are not without its shallows! I mention this not with a view to detract from the stunning contributions thus made but merely to suggest that we need encyclopaedic reflexive labours to deal with facile indictments of 'bad faith' in the production of the normative politics of human rights.[45]

The aspirational compass of the UDHR which even today continues to navigate the ship of human rights on stormy voyages may be criticised for its inadequacies – its enunciation of principles remains indicted on several counts: its sources are broadly Euro-American; its state-centred scope leaves outside the pale the agents, managers and networks of global capital; its relative silence concerning rightless peoples, especially refugees, asylum seekers, internally displaced peoples and the masses of impoverished

---

[43] I describe these two kinds of politics severally in Baxi, *The Future of Human Rights.*

[44] See U. Baxi, '"A Report for all Seasons?": Small Notes on Reading *In Larger Freedom*', in C. R. Kumar and D. Srivastva (eds.), *Human Rights and Development: Law, Policy, and Governance* (Hong Kong: Lexis/Nexis 2006) 495–514 and Baxi, 'What May the Third World Expect from International Law?' (2006) 27 *Special Issue: Third World Quarterly* 713–25.

[45] See U. Baxi, 'Politics of Reading Human Rights: Inclusion and Exclusion within the Production of Human rights', in S. Meckled-García and B. Çali, *The Legalization of Human Rights: Multidisciplinary Perspectives on Human Rights and Human Rights Law* (London: Routledge 2006) 179–84.

peoples; its ecological insensitivity (astonishing indeed as the UDHR was composed in the immediate aftermath of Hiroshima–Nagasaki).

The act of writing/reading human rights remains an enterprise that no doubt often poignantly fails,[46] and human rights critiques are justified in demonstrating why and how. Even so, this indictment of 'bad faith' ignores the fact that each and every spectacular failure seems to pave way for fresh articulations of a morality of duty. This was the case with the Rome Treaty establishing the International Criminal Court (ICC) with a wide-ranging universal jurisdiction over war crimes and crimes against humanity, with the development of crimes of aggression in the wings. To be sure, at the present moment the ICC performances symbolise mere 'fictions of justice'[47] and global power asymmetries create no obligations over the veto power of the five permanent members of the UN Security Council, each of which may stifle the criminal prosecution of their kith and kin. Yet, this does not render articulations of the morality of aspiration and movements towards a just world ordering entirely inchoate.

Some critics maintain that the legalisation or juridification of human rights is a form of bad faith, since complex forms of human rights legalisation 'de-politicise' collective social action. Whether this is truly the case is a question that invites labours of understanding comparative social theory of human rights, and not indulgent performatives of critique of the 'ontology' and 'epistemology' of human rights. How else could the morality of duty be translated into practices of arresting the abuse of public power in the moment of 'concrete universality'? Further, more work needs to be done to understand the ways in which social and human rights movements deploy legalised negotiation strategies.[48] Were we to read the myriad forms of counter-hegemonic 'juridicalisation' as expressions of 'bad faith', how can we understand and explain forms of participation by 'global civil society' that pursue negotiating human rights strategies?[49]

---

[46] See, for example, A. Le Bor, 'Complicity with Evil': The United Nations in an Age of Modern Genocide (New Haven, CT: Yale University Press 2006); J. Hagan and W. Rymond-Richmond, Darfur and the Crime of Genocide (Cambridge University Press 2008); and, in a different narrative vein, O. Bartov, Mirrors of Destruction: War, Genocide, and Modern Identity (Oxford University Press 2000).

[47] See K. M. Clarke, The Fictions of Justice: The International Criminal Court and the Challenge of Legal Pluralism in Sub-Saharan Africa (New York: Cambridge University Press 2009).

[48] See Baxi, The Future of Human Rights 207–12.

[49] See Simmons, Mobilizing for Human Rights Chs. 5–8.

Reductionist readings tinged with forms of post-Cold War ideological certitude continue to suggest that both pre-commitment and negotiation strategies are no more or no different than assemblages/appendages in the service of global capital, accentuating an inherent vulnerability to hegemonic appropriation. According to these critiques human rights developments are necessary social illusions, or celebrations of the Lacanian belief of desire as lack.[50] The critique of what may be *wrong* about *rights* remains *now* pervasively exemplified by pioneering thinkers – a meta-ethical discourse far too exuberant and varied to deserve the indignity of summative conversational gestures. Yet, I may not resist saying that the A-to-Z club (from Agamben to Žižek) critiquing contemporary human rights development seems to regard all human rights 'white' swans as 'black' tinted and tainted with the Dark Side of the (Euro) Enlightenment!

I do not deny – who indeed can – the demystification of human rights-talk and even action that manifests its hegemonic appropriation in the service of domination without hegemony (to adopt a withering phrase from Ranajit Guha[51]). This is evident in the cases of 'military humanism', the 'war on terror' or the politics of regime-change which appear as human rights-friendly on the one hand, and on the other hand pointing towards a comprehensive conversion of almost all human rights obligations into mere and fungible languages of global social policy. In contrast, counter-power contests, and reconfigures, the languages, logics and paralogics of human rights and servicing Hannah Arendt's imagery of the 'right to have

---

[50] On a Lacanian analysis, human rights 'legalise desire,' and 'become a phatasmatic supplement that arouses but never satisfies the subjects' desire'. 'Human rights thus ... like the *object petit a* become a phantasmatic supplement that arouses but never satiates the subject's desire. Rights always agitate for more rights; they create new areas of claim and entitlement but these must always prove insufficient. We keep inventing new rights in an endless attempt to fill the lack but this only defers desire.' 'The discourse of human rights thus presents a fantasy scenario in which society and individual are perceived as whole, as non-split. In this fantasy, society is understood as something that can be rationally organized, as a community that can become non-conflictual if it only respects human rights': C. Douzinas, 'Human Rights, Humanism, and Desire' (2001) 6 *Angelaki* 197, quoting R. Saleeci, *The Spoils of Freedom: Psychoanalysis and Feminism After the Fall of Socialism* (London: Routledge 1994) 127; and see also C. Douzinas, *The End of Human Rights* (Oxford: Hart 2000) 312–18.

[51] See R. Guha, in a book entitled *Dominance without Hegemony: History and Power in Colonial India* (Cambridge University Press 2007).

rights'[52] or Jacques Rancière's accentuation of struggles for infinite inclusion.[53]

The past and future human rights temporalities form the stake of this contestation. It has taken more than half a century of imagination and effort to arrive at a socio-technical invention of the morality of duty symbolised now by the ICC.[54] What can the human rights martyrs in Tripoli, Tunis, Damascus and Tehran learn after all from the awesome verity (and litany) of post-metaphysical critiques of human rights?[54] Surely, one may say that the post-revolutionary moment will recompose pre-commitment strategies into 'negotiated strategies' – dividing liberty rights from social and economic rights as dictated by forms, grammars and contexts of the specificity of 'politics' in time, place and circumstance. Granting this fully, one must also ask whether a specific revolutionary moment remains a history of nothingness, illustrating the adage that the more things change the more they remain the same. May it be after all the case that nothing changes when everything seems to transform for a revolutionary moment? Would then the power of political passion for total domination continue its itineraries, as if nothing had ever happened?

Further reading

Betsill, M. M. and Corell, E., *NGO Diplomacy: The Influence of Non-Governmental Organizations in International Environmental Negotiations* (Cambridge, MA: MIT Press 2008)

Caudhill, D., 'Lacan and Legal Language: Meanings in the Gaps, Gaps in the Meaning' (1992) 3 (2) *Law and Critique* 169–210

Goodrich, P., Barshack, L. and Schutz, A., *Law, Text and Terror: Essays for Peter Legendre* (London: Glasshouse Press 2006)

Picciotto, S., *Regulating Global Corporate Capitalism* (Cambridge University Press 2011)

Supiot. A., *Homo Juridicus: On the Anthropological Function of the Law* (London: Verso 2007)

---

[52] P. Birmingham, *Hannah Arendt and Human Rights: The Predicament of Common Responsibility* (Bloomington, IN: Indiana University Press 2006). See also S. Párekh, *Hannah Arendt and the Challenge of Modernity: A Phenomenology of Human Rights* (London: Routledge 2008).

[53] See J. Rancière, 'Who is the Subject of the Rights of Man?' (2004) 103 (2–3) *South Atlantic Quarterly* 307 (a text that requires reiterated reading, with or without further meditations on a text by S. Žižek, 'Against Human Rights' (2005) 34 *New Left Review* 115–31).

[54] See the poignant analysis by Judge N. Ehrenfreund, *The Nuremberg Legacy: How the Nazi War Crimes Trials Changed the Course of History* (London: Palgrave Macmillan 2007).

Part III

Platforms

Reconstituting the universal: human rights as a regional idea   9

Chaloka Beyani

This chapter discusses the reconstitution of the universality of human rights as a regional idea that as a result becomes visible through the lens of regional treaty-based systems of human rights. There are four such initiatives: the European Convention for the Protection of Human Rights and Fundamental Freedoms 1950[1] (European Convention), the American Declaration of the Rights and Duties of Man 1948[2] (American Declaration) read together with the American Convention on Human Rights 1969[3] (ACHR, American Convention), and the African Charter on Human and Peoples' Rights 1981[4] (African Charter). Although these regimes form the pinnacle of regional human rights law, they have crystallised into regional systems in which a corpus of specific human rights regimes have sprouted in relation to, for example, the prevention of torture,[5] the protection of minorities,[6] women,[7] children, and economic, social

---

[1] Council of Europe, CETS: 005 (entered into force 3 September 1953).

[2] OAS, Ninth International Conference of American States, Bogotá, Colombia, 1948. *Basic Documents Pertaining to Human Rights in the Inter-American System*, www.oas.org/en/iachr/mandate/basic_documents.asp.

[3] OAS, OAS, Treaty Series, No. 36, entered into force 18 July 1978.

[4] African Union, African Charter on Human and Peoples' Rights 1981, OAU Doc. CAB/LEG/67/3 rev. 5, 21 I.L.M. 58 (1982) (entered into force 21 October 1986).

[5] See for example, OAS, Inter-American Convention to Prevent and Punish Torture 1985, OAS, Treaty Series, No. 67 (entered into force 28 February 1987); Council of Europe, European Convention for the Prevention of Torture and Inhuman or Degrading Treatment or Punishment 1987, CETS No. 126 (entered into force 1 February 1989).

[6] See for example, Council of Europe, Framework Convention for the Protection of National Minorities 1995, CETS: 157 (entered into force 1 February 1998).

[7] OAS, Inter-American Convention on the Granting of Civil Rights to Women 1948, OAS, Treaty Series, No. 23 (entered into force 17 March 1949); Inter-American Convention on the Granting of Political Rights of Women 1948, OAS, Treaty Series, No. 3 (entered into force 29 December 1954); Inter-American Convention on the Prevention, Punishment and Eradication of Violence against Women 1994, 33 ILM 1534 (1994) (entered into force 3 May 1995); African Union, Protocol to the African Charter on Human and Peoples' Rights on the Rights of Women in Africa, 2000 CAB/LEG/66.6 (S13 September 2000) (entered into force 25 November 2005).

and cultural rights,[8] etc. Such treaty regimes are not the focus of this chapter although they should be acknowledged as belonging to respective regional systems of human rights.

We start our discussion of reconstituting the universal by examining the essential characteristics of universality, the reasons for reconstituting the universal and the place of universality as the flying buttress of regionalism. This discussion is then followed by an examination of human rights protection as a regional idea. Here we consider the reasons behind the establishment of regional regimes of human rights, the essence of regional human rights obligations in the context of universality, and the relative differences between regional human rights regimes. The chapter then examines regional human rights protection mechanisms, and the dynamics that lie behind the development of human rights law by the cross-fertilisation of human rights ideas across regional bodies of human rights. This development is seen as a reinforcement of universality. (The issue of relativism is not directly discussed as it falls outside the compass of the chapter albeit, as is to be expected, it emerges frequently as a point of importance when working through the content of the regional rights' instruments that we will be discussing.)

Reconstituting the universal

In theory the universality of human rights posits the centrality of the human being viewed as a whole over that that suggests a narrower focus on the autonomy of the individual.[9] The underlying assumption of universality is of a universal human nature that is knowable by reason or rationality and which differs from any other reality.[10] This uniqueness of being human or

---

[8] OAS, Additional Protocol to the American Convention on Human Rights in the Area of Economic, Social, and Cultural Rights 1988, OAS, Treaty Series, No. 69 (entered into force 16 November 1999); Council of Europe, *European Social Charter* 1961 (rev. 1996), CETS No: 035 (entered into force 26 February 1965). The European Social Charter is the counterpart of the European Convention for the Protection of Human Rights and Fundamental Freedoms in the sphere of economic and social rights.

[9] C. Gearty, *Essays on Human Rights and Terrorism* (London: Cameron May 2008) Ch 29.

[10] Y. Ghai, 'Universalism and Relativism: Human Rights as a Framework for Negotiating Interethnic Claims' (1999–2000) 21 *Cardozo Law Review* 1096.

'ubuntu'[11] is the universal organising precept of human rights. It is reflected in the formative standards of international human rights law. The Charter of the UN in 1945[12] laid down the concept of human rights as a testament, a strong 'never again', to the atrocities and human horrors that were witnessed in the Second World War. By means of the Charter the world, then and now, reaffirmed faith in the fundamentality of human rights, the dignity and worth of the human person, equal rights of women and men, and established the duty to respect human rights universally without discrimination as to various aspects of human identity.

It is clear that the Charter did portend the universality of human rights by enshrining an international legal obligation to respect human rights, even though admittedly it did not advance the concept further than that. But the immense legal force of the Charter generated an unstoppable impetus that quickly produced the Universal Declaration of Human Rights 1948[13] (UDHR, Universal Declaration), the instrument that symbolises the legal and moral compass of universality in international relations. In the aftermath of the Second World War, that Declaration underscored universality by signalling a shift from the segmented protection of minorities under the Treaty of Versailles in 1919[14] to the protection of all humans on an inclusive basis that was depicted in its preamble as 'a common standard of achievement'. The aim was to secure the 'universal and effective recognition and observance' of human rights the world over.[15]

Reflecting its underlying commitment to universality, the Universal Declaration substantively proclaimed that all human beings are born 'free and equal in dignity and rights, and that they are endowed with reason and conscience' and should act towards one another in a spirit of humanity.[16] So far as establishing the international dimension of universality was concerned, the Universal Declaration built on the foundations of the international legal framework of the UN Charter, but went further to stipulate the entitlement of human rights across the board:

Everyone is entitled to all the rights and freedoms set forth in this Declaration, without distinction of any kind, such as race, colour, sex, language, religion, political or other

---

[11] This term means 'being human' among the Bantu-speaking peoples in Africa. It was given prominence in the decision of the South African Constitutional Court in the death penalty case of the *State* v. *Makwanyane and Another* 1995 (3) SA 391.
[12] 1 UNTS XVI.   [13] Adopted by UN GA Res. 217 A(III) of 10 December 1948.
[14] League of Nations, Paris Peace Conference 1919, League of Nations Treaty series 1919–47.
[15] UDHR Preamble.   [16] UDHR Article 1.

opinion, national or social origin, property, birth or other status. Furthermore, no distinction shall be made on the basis of the political, jurisdictional or international status of the country or territory to which a person belongs, whether it be independent, trust, non-self-governing or under any other limitation of sovereignty.[17]

If international law was the early medium for conveying the universality of human rights, then its positivist consent-based nature in relation to treaties for the most part also set up pitfalls towards the effective realisation of universality. Consent to human rights treaties by individual states as the basis of obligations to protect human rights engendered selectivity as states chose which treaties to accept and which to reject. In addition to the problem of selectivity running against the grain of universal application, positive international law arguably even went so far as to render the universal nature of human rights 'negotiable' through the discussions (and compromises) that inevitably preceded agreement on human rights treaties.

Certain negative consequences ensued as a result. An ideological chasm grew between civil and political rights on the one hand, and economic, social and cultural rights on the other hand; it took from 1948 to 1966 to negotiate and conclude the international human rights standard setting treaties that benchmarked universality in the form of the International Covenant on Civil and Political Rights[18] and the International Covenant on Economic, Social and Cultural Rights[19] (CCPR, ICESCR, International Covenants). The urgency of the momentum set by the Charter of the UN and the Universal Declaration was lost. This meant that the international protection agenda that was driven by the quest for universality was considerably delayed. The International Covenants only came into force in 1976, nearly thirty years after the universal standards had been spelled out in the Universal Declaration. Since then much has come about by way of international human rights instruments and bodies at the level of the UN. But by then regional instruments of human rights had already pushed themselves to the forefront in the pioneering of the protection of human rights as a universal idea.

Establishing the regional

The genesis of regional systems of human rights in Europe, the Inter-Americas, and later in Africa, drew inspiration from the universality of

---

[17] UDHR Article 2.   [18] UN, Treaty Series, Vol. 999 171.   [19] UN, Treaty Series, Vol. 993 3.

human rights that we have just discussed. However due consideration should be given (and often this is ignored) to the fact that the Inter-American human rights system developed contemporaneously with the Universal Declaration. It was indeed the first to formulate a cohesive framework of protecting human rights anchored in the American Declaration, which was adopted by the Organization of American States (OAU) six months *before* the adoption of the Universal Declaration by the UN in 1948. And while the UN struggled to articulate universality in a binding treaty format from 1948 to 1966, the Council of Europe was readily able to do so very early on, in 1950 when it adopted its European Convention on Human Rights (ECHR, European Convention).

It is clear however that the regional reinforcement of universality in the Middle East and Asia is a late idea that has been much preoccupied by debates on values, culture, and religion. In Asia, the Association of South East Nations (ASEAN) declared adherence to human rights and fundamental freedoms in the ASEAN Charter 2007[20] and set up an ASEAN Inter-governmental Commission on Human Rights to prepare a Declaration on Human Rights for the Southeast Asian region that is to be based on the principles of universality. In the Arabic region, it was not until 1994 that the Council of League of Arab States adopted the Arab Charter on Human Rights. The difficulties inherent in embracing human rights as a universal idea became evident when none of the member States of the Council of the League ratified the Arab Charter initially, and a revised Arab Charter was subsequently adopted in 2004, entering into force in 2008. The Arab Charter purports to affirm the idea of human rights in the Charter of the UN and the Universal Declaration, and proclaims that human rights are universal, indivisible, interdependent and inter-related.[21] But what cannot be avoided is that certain aspects of it clearly depart from universality, for example, with regard to the international human rights for women, children and non-citizens, and in addition it poses a specific problem in equating Zionism with racism.[22]

---

[20] ASEAN Treaties Collection Series 341. Article 7 of the Charter seeks to promote and protect human rights and fundamental freedoms.

[21] M. Rishmawi, 'The Arab Charter on Human Rights and the League of Arab States: An Update' (2010) 10 (1) *Human Rights Law Review* 169–78.

[22] Statement by UNHCR on the entry into force of the Arab Charter on Human Rights, Geneva, 30 January 2008, www.pointdebasculecanada.ca/spip.php?article238.

While we acknowledge that hitches in regionalism abounded as obstacles to human rights in the Arab region and in Asia, it is important to acknowledge that the ethical, moral, and legal imperative of human rights has proved to be a testimony to the recognition and endurance of the idea of universality as such, without or within certain qualifications. For despite these difficulties, our argument remains that human rights bodies at regional level breathe life into the notion of universality and that they are vital cogs in it, positioned uniquely between the UN human rights system and national systems of human rights. For instance, the European Court of Human Rights (ECtHR) was the first to produce a radiating effect on the protection of human rights and the development of international human rights law by UN treaty bodies, the Inter-American and African regional systems, as well as national human rights law in most Commonwealth jurisdictions. This pioneering influence shows that regional systems are essentially an integral part of universality and should not be seen as merely reinforcing or being complementary to the UN system of human rights through which universality is commonly, indeed unduly narrowly, construed in international law.

However, as we have seen from the Arab example, the arguments in favour of universality as a regional idea have to be tempered with caution against the propensity of regional localism in relative autonomous regional systems of human rights. This predisposition should not be exaggerated, however, since the manifestation of universality in regional systems is in itself a safeguard against regional localism in the first place. Relative localism is often a product of legal, cultural, or religious pluralism, and regional human rights systems function as a constraint against it within a framework of agreed standards. In this context regional obligations of human rights provide safeguards as they are owed mutually between states parties to regional instruments. Invariably regional states will also be parties to international human rights instruments; these bolster universality and also provide a check on regionalism because of the requirement that regional or other obligations assumed by member states of the UN must be consistent with those of the Charter.

The most recent example of a regional human rights system, the African Charter on Human and Peoples' Rights (1981), is a good case in point. The idea of peoples' rights in the African Charter derives partly from the principle of self-determination of peoples contained in the Charter of the UN and the International Covenants, and partly from the idea of peoples that is to be found in the Universal Declaration. But its usage in the African Charter also encompasses the language of minorities and indigenous peoples. The idea of duties originates in the American Declaration and the Universal Declaration in which it is declared that 'everyone has duties to the community in which alone the free and full development of his personality is possible'. Therefore the notion of duties is not the novelty of the African Charter that many assume. This aspect of the African Charter, along with issues of progressive culture and the duty of African states to promote and protect morals and traditional values recognised by the community, should be determined in light of universality and coherence in an integral framework of human and peoples' rights. Viewed in this way, far from being a threat to universality the document's provisions become concrete expressions of what universality means in specific places.[23]

Regional human rights systems offer the prospect of like-minded states undertaking to respect and to ensure respect for human rights with a common regional will that is bound by a common heritage and bonded by coherent human rights treaty regimes. Their creation owes much to the desire to bring human rights home by means of binding instruments spearheaded by respective regional political bodies, namely (to take the main examples) the Council of Europe, OAS and the African Union.

This idea of a regional shape to human rights that remain universal is firmly embedded in the fabric of regional human rights regimes. When formulating the European Convention in 1950, member states of the Council of Europe paid specific consideration to the weight of the Universal Declaration. In their view, the Universal Declaration aimed at securing the universal and effective recognition and observance of the rights contained in it. The Council of Europe therefore resolved to take the first steps for the collective enforcement of certain of the rights stated in the Universal Declaration. These rights were seen as the foundation of justice and peace after the Second World War in Europe; they were also important to maintaining political democracy as a safeguard against the then very real threat of communism.

For its part, the OAS acknowledged universality in the American Declaration in 1948 as well as in the American Convention (1969) by

---

[23] C. Beyani, 'Toward a More Effective Guarantee of Women's Rights in the African Human Rights System', in R. Cook, *Human Rights of Women* (University of Pennsylvania Press 1994) 285–306.

affirming that American states have on repeated occasions recognised that the essential rights of humanity are not derived from the fact of being a national of a certain state, but are based upon attributes of human personality.[24] Having preceded the Universal Declaration, there is naturally no explicit mention of it in the American Declaration, but the common elements to the two instruments are immediately apparent to readers. The quintessential expression of universality, the principle that 'All men are born free and equal, in dignity and in rights, and, being endowed by nature with reason and conscience, they should conduct themselves as brothers one to another' appears in the preamble to the American Declaration and also forms Article 1 of the Universal Declaration, with only some minor modification. The American Convention of 1969 pays homage to the Universal Declaration and recognises the importance and justification of regional and international instruments of human rights as a mark of universality. The context for these developments was the necessity for regional cohesion, combating the threat of communism and bringing to account dictatorial military regimes in the South American region.

As previously noted, the African Charter is the most recent of the functioning regional systems of human rights. The motivation behind its adoption lay in the exposure of massive violations of human rights by military regimes and one-party self-perpetuating dictatorial systems of government and self-styled emperors on the continent. Upon adopting the Charter, the then OAS (Organisation of African States, now the African Union) drew on the universality inherent in the Inter-American system and recognised that fundamental human rights stemmed from the attributes of human beings, which justified their national and international protection.[25] The African Charter was an effort by African states to promote international cooperation as required by the Charter of the UN and the Universal Declaration. While the notion of peoples' rights was seen as a necessary guarantee of human rights, it was also thought that the enjoyment of rights and freedoms implied the performance of duties on the part of everyone. The Charter also sought to underscore, or perhaps (more nostalgically) to resurrect, virtues of historical tradition and values of African civilisation which would serve to inspire and sharpen reflection on the concept of human and peoples' rights.

---

[24] Preamble, American Declaration, and the American Convention.
[25] Preamble, African Charter.

The substance in the regional

Taken together, the substantive scope of these regional human rights instruments covers civil and political rights generally. In universally binding terms, the CCPR contains the most well known and most widely accepted formulation of civil and political rights. However, relative differences as regards certain civil and political rights exist as between these regional documents, for example, with respect to the family, privacy, freedom of expression and states of emergency. The European Convention protects 'family and private life' with a separate provision on marriage; while both the American Convention and African Charter protect the family as the fundamental group unit of society inclusive of marriage. Just as in the CCPR, the American Convention makes separate provision for the right to privacy while the African Charter omits privacy altogether.

Clearly the family is not depicted as collective unit under the European Convention in the same way it is under the American Convention, the African Charter, and the CCPR. It is clearly the case however that relative differences of this nature signal variation in approach rather than of substance. This argument is reinforced by reference to one case that was decided by both the ECtHR and the Human Rights Committee on the same facts arising from marriage, divorce and family, both bodies reaching a similar decision affirming dissolution of the marriage before each tribunal, and also making similar pronouncements concerning custody, and the responsibilities of the parents towards the religious education of their child.[26]

On matters of homosexuality, the separate provision on 'family life' in the CCPR has influenced a similar provision in the American Convention. In this field the Human Rights Committee has reached decisions that have been in tandem with those of the ECtHR.[27] It is argued that cases of this nature provide real positive tests of universality in regional human rights systems. Regional treaties are considered to be living instruments whose content is enriched with time and subsequent developments in human rights. For example, the conjunctive protection of private and family life by the European Convention has been utilised by the ECtHR to make far-reaching

[26] *Hendricks* v. *Netherlands* 96 *ILR* 603 (ECHR); *Hendricks* v. *Netherlands* 96 *ILR* 633 (Human Rights Committee).
[27] *Toonen* v. *Australia* 1–3 Human Rights Reports (1994) 97.

decisions involving matters of privacy such as homosexuality[28] and gender reassignment,[29] and the quality of life that includes social rights, such as employment[30] and the environment.[31] With certain limitations migrants also enjoy protection from deportation on account of that Convention's commitment to respect for private and family life.[32]

In contrast, it would appear to be the case that private life has been omitted from the African Charter for homophobic reasons. However this did not prevent the African Commission from admitting and considering a complaint arising out of a conviction for sodomy, until the matter was withdrawn after a friendly settlement was reached.[33] The African Charter also omits provisions allowing derogation from human rights during states of emergency because of Africa's unhappy history with dictatorial governments' resort to prolonged derogations from guarantees of human rights under special powers. In place of a derogation clause, the Charter contains clauses allowing restrictions on human rights to be made according to law. The African Commission has required that such restrictions must be consistent with international law, thereby reflecting the analogous universalist positions taken on states of emergency by the European and American regional human rights systems.

With respect to the categories of civil and political rights contained in the European Convention, the American Declaration and the American Convention notably add humane treatment, the right to seek and enjoy asylum, and non-refoulement. Of these, the right to humane treatment under the American Convention is construed as an obligation to respect the inherent dignity of the human person. The scope of this is so broadly formulated that it goes beyond the ambit of similar provisions in the European Convention and the African Charter. It includes the right to respect for physical, mental and moral integrity, prohibition of torture or cruel, inhuman, or degrading punishment or treatment, and lays down specific requirements for the treatment of persons who may be lawfully deprived of liberty based, for example, on the segregation of accused persons from those serving punishment for criminal conviction and the separation of minors from adults in criminal proceedings. The aim of

---

[28] E.g. in *Dudgeon* v. *UK* 4 EHRR 149.
[29] E.g. in *Sheffield and Horsham* v. *UK* (1999) EHRR 163.
[30] *Sidabras and Dziautas* v. *Lithuania* (2004) ECHR 395.
[31] *Budayeva* v. *Russia* (2008) ECHR 15339/02.   [32] *Uner* v. *Netherlands* (2006) ECHR 340.
[33] *S* v. *Banana* 2000 3 SA 885.

punishment is emphasised as having the essential purpose of reforming and readapting prisoners.

Neither the European Convention nor the African Charter spells out humane treatment in quite these terms. But Article 3 of the European Convention encapsulates the essence of humane treatment in its prohibition of torture or inhuman or degrading treatment or punishment. This narrow reading is deceptively simplistic and misses the substantive dynamic reach attained by Article 3 over the years. For a start the prohibition of torture and inhuman or degrading treatment or punishment is absolute. The threshold of the prohibition hinges on the severity of the stigma of torture as such or cumulatively or separately by reference to treatment or punishment that is inhuman or degrading. Although the right to seek and enjoy asylum is not included in the European Convention, the horizontal reach of Article 3 effectively protects asylum seekers and refugees, terrorist suspects and others, from being refouled or extradited to states where there is a risk of being subjected to torture or inhuman or degrading treatment or punishment. All these advances have been achieved by judicial action, through strong judgments from the ECtHR.

The core of what counts as humane treatment in the African Charter revolves around the respect owed to every human in view of the dignity that is inherent in him or her as a human being and the recognition of the legal status that naturally flows from this. The relevant principle extends to the prohibition of all forms of exploitation and degradation of human beings, particularly slavery, the slave trade, torture, cruel, inhuman or degrading punishment and treatment. The African Commission has found denationalisation and subsequent deportation to be contrary to the prohibition of torture, cruel, inhuman or degrading punishment and treatment. Inclusion of exploitation, slavery and the slave trade within the prohibition of torture, cruel, inhuman or degrading punishment and treatment is a variation that is germinated out of specific African historical concerns, but that does not detract from universality: the variation exists in separate provisions in the European Convention and the American Convention. Explicit provisions in the African Charter and the American Convention on the right to seek and obtain asylum mirror those of the Universal Declaration. Under the African Charter the right to seek and obtain asylum implicates non-refoulement, although the American Convention stands out in that the rights concerning humane treatment, asylum and non-refoulement, all provide a separate and/or combined basis for added protection against the unlawful removal of persons contrary to these rights. These regional standards reinforce universality by providing complementary protection to asylum seekers and refugees with respect to the Convention Relating to the Status of Refugees (1951).

In so far as economic, social and cultural rights are concerned, it is evident that the principles underlying their universality have their foundation in the Charter of the UN. It was in the Universal Declaration that these principles were transformed into economic, social and cultural rights alongside civil and political rights. However, prospects for the implementation of an integrated concept of human rights as expressed in the Universal Declaration vanished after 1948 due to ideological differences regarding the protection of economic, social and cultural rights. A distinct proviso was made for these rights in the resulting ICESCR. With the exception of self-determination in common Article 1 to the Covenants, the ICESCR dealt with the subject matter of economic, social, and cultural rights from the perspective of state responsibility whereby the content of those rights had to be derived from the obligations undertaken by states to realise or recognise or ensure them.

Human rights as a regional idea incorporate economic, social and cultural rights by reconstituting them, in varying degrees, alongside civil and political rights. This reconstitution of economic, social and cultural rights in regional systems is notable for rendering them amenable to being determined in the decisions of regional Courts or Commissions. Though the text of the European Convention devotes no space to economic, social and cultural rights, the right to education is a social right that is protected in Protocol 1 to that European Convention. Article 2 of Protocol 1 provides a negative guarantee, i.e. 'no person shall be denied the right to education' and goes on to create an obligation to 'respect the right of parents to ensure such education and teaching in conformity with their own religious and philosophical convictions'.

In one of its landmark decisions, the Grand Chamber of the ECtHR held that the education of Roma children[34] in schools segregated for children with mental disabilities in the Czech Republic was discriminatory and violated the right to education. Besides education, the Court has also been innovative, as was earlier observed, in stretching the right to private and family life to include social and economic rights, such as environmental

---

[34] *D H and Others* v. *Czech Republic* (2007) ECHR 57325/00.

protection and employment. Evidence of further detailed protection of economic and social rights in Europe can be found in the European Social Charter.

In the Inter-American system, the American Declaration establishes a standard quantum of economic, social and cultural rights, over which the Inter-American Commission has the requisite jurisdiction. In contrast, the American Convention merely provides a framework for the application of economic social and cultural rights on the basis of progressive realisation. The substance of these rights is to be found in the American Convention on Economic, Social, and Cultural Rights (ACESCR). The method taken by the African Charter to protect economic, social and cultural rights differs by integrating them in the Charter and by negating the principle of progressive realisation on the premise of mutuality, namely that the satisfaction of economic, social and cultural rights is a guarantee for the enjoyment of civil and political rights.

In taking this approach, the text of the African Charter protects a narrower range of economic and social rights – the right to work, health, cultural life of the community, and education. Despite this narrow latitude, the inclination of the African Charter towards the mutuality of civil and political rights on the one hand and economic, social and cultural rights on the other has led the African Commission to espouse universalism creatively by holding that:

Internationally accepted ideas of the various obligations engendered by human rights indicate that all rights – both civil and political rights and social and economic – generate at least four levels of duties for a State that undertakes to adhere to a rights regime, namely the duty to respect, protect, promote, and fulfil these rights. These obligations universally apply to all rights and entail a combination of negative and positive duties. As a human rights instrument, the African Charter is not alien to these concepts.

As we have already noted, the African Charter adds peoples' rights – to existence and self-determination on an unquestionable and inalienable basis; to freely dispose of their wealth and natural resources in their exclusive interest; to their economic, social and cultural development as part of their freedom and identity – and with these comes the concomitant duty of African states – individually or collectively – to ensure the exercise of the right to development, environment, and international peace and solidarity based on the UN Charter. Within the African Charter, there is a co-relation, whether tenable or not, between these duties of states and the individual duties owed to the family, society, and international community, and the duty owed to respect fellow human beings without discrimination. There are also standards in the African Charter on 'values of African civilisation' and acceptance of the idea of the family as 'custodian of morals and traditional values recognised by the community'. These aspects of the African Charter gravitate towards local regionalism, but a point is once again worth stressing here: the stipulated values and morals stand to be constrained by the human rights framework of the Charter as a whole and of course this is squarely situated within international or universal standards of human rights.

It is tempting to use the now worn out phraseology of 'generations' of human rights to illuminate the path of human rights as a regional idea, taking note of civil and political rights for a start in the European Convention, the addition of economic and social rights in the American Convention, and the subsequent addition of peoples' or solidarity rights in the African Charter. This temptation should be resisted because the typology of 'generations' of human rights is misleadingly superficial. The common standards of human rights achieved in the Universal Declaration provide a statement of the modern concept of human rights that is distinct from, but builds on civil liberties, embodies civil and political rights, economic, social and cultural rights, and refers to 'peoples' in its preamble as the underlying legitimating factor to the rights it enshrines. It is all there in this foundational document.

Enforcing regional rights

Regional human rights treaties not only embody the universality of human rights, but also establish mechanisms for their protection. Indeed the political will to commit to the protection of human rights is easier to harness regionally. Political, social, cultural, and economic cohesion make it more likely that states at regional level will comply with decisions made by regional Commissions or Courts on matters of human rights. Moreover, regional human rights systems are linked to regional political bodies that oversee issues of protection and non-compliance, such as the Council of Europe and Committee of Ministers with regard to the European Convention, the OAU in relation to the Inter-American system, and the

Summit of Heads of State of the African Union in relation to the African Charter. This, however, is not to suggest that problems of non-compliance or resistance to the protective role of regional bodies do not arise in the protection of human rights at a regional level. This issue is outside the scope of this chapter, but the point to take is that there are inbuilt compliance oversight mechanisms in the protection of human rights as a regional idea.

It is useful to provide a brief overview of the nature of regional mechanisms of enforcement of human rights since these now invariably come with the human rights courts that are lacking in the international human rights system. Under the European Convention, the European Commission on Human Rights was established in 1954 and was followed by the ECtHR in 1959. This dual structure was reformed by means of Protocol 11 to the Convention in 1998 when the fact-finding Commission was abolished to cut down on the backlog of cases and enable direct individual access to the Court. The problem of backlog has however persisted, an indication that the Court bears the burden of its own success, a success which must be protected against political intrusion under the guise of reform (as for example in the current debate on proposed reforms to deal with a limited number of more serious cases, leaving the rest to be dealt by national courts).

The difficulty created by at least some of these suggested changes is the failure to appreciate that human rights empower individuals to have their rights protected by regional systems when national legal systems fail, or fail to do so adequately. So the avalanche of cases before the court must show serious dissatisfaction with the performance of some of the national courts in protecting human rights, particularly in light of political problems and issues of human rights posed by the enlargement of the membership of the Council of Europe. This has also presented the court with the problem of functionality. Since each member state of the Council of Europe nominates a judge to the Court, the enlargement of the Council means that the Court has forty-seven judges, corresponding to the enlarged membership of states in the Council of Europe.

Given these developments – further consequences of the court's success – the debate on reform needs to be informed by the legal and administrative reforms already in place. The imperative of ensuring the functionality of the court has led to streamlining the organisation of the court into committees dealing with admissibility, chambers deciding on cases, and the Grand Chamber, which handles cases from the chambers as well as important cases. Protocol 14 (2004) introduced these important reforms and underscored the necessity to expedite cases at the stage of admissibility where there would be no significant disadvantage. A repetitive cases procedure has also been introduced aimed at reaching early friendly settlement. The process of reforming the ECtHR has been underway from meetings held at Interlaken in 2010 and continued at Izmir in 2011 and Brighton in 2012, where a ministerial conference was held to consider, among other matters, proposals for reform made by the UK as the then current Chair of the Council of Europe.[35]

In the Inter-American region, the American Declaration was not only (as we have seen) the precursor of human rights as a regional idea; it also continues to be an active component of it, now side by side side with the American Convention. Dual existence of these instruments is the key to unlocking the overlapping functions of the Inter-American Commission and the Inter-American Court in protecting human rights in the Inter-American region. The Inter-American Commission was established in 1959 under the auspices of the American Declaration and its competence to promote and protect human rights extends to the member states of the OAS.

The Inter-American Court on Human Rights (IACHR) was established under the American Convention in 1979 and has competence on Convention matters in relation to states parties that recognise its jurisdiction. But the Convention also gives expression to the existence of the Commission (Article 33), which makes the Commission competent to exercise promotional and remedial roles with regard to states parties to the Convention. It should be understood that this Commission has an overlapping competence over human rights protected in the Declaration and those protected in the Convention. Leaving aside these differences, the Inter-American system replicates the role of the European Commission played with regard to the Court under the European Convention prior to 1998. Individuals have direct access to the Inter-American Commission and not to the Court, and only the Commission and states parties have access to the Court.

In the African region, the African Commission on Human and Peoples' Rights was established in 1987 to promote and protect human and peoples' rights under the African Charter. The Commission has original competence

---

[35] See Prime Minister David Cameron, Speech on the European Court of Human Rights, 25 January 2012, www.number10.gov.uk/news/european-court-of-human-rights/.

in relation to all states parties to the Charter. In 1998 a Protocol establishing an African Court of Human Rights was adopted. The effect of this was to replicate the dual nature of the Inter-American system, with the difference that there is no treaty-based defined relationship between the Commission and the Court. Both bodies are legally independent of each other. But no sooner had the Protocol entered into force than a decision was made by the African Union to merge the African Court of Human Rights with the African Court of Justice. If this merger brought about difficulties in the co-existence of these courts, then further complications arose when the African Union decided to endow the African Court of Human Rights with criminal jurisdiction. The pace of reform has been so rapid that the Court has not had time to settle, and endowing it with criminal jurisdiction will altogether alter its character as a human rights court whose chamber co-exists ambiguously with the chamber of the African Court of Justice. Reforms that were aimed at strengthening the system have effectively weakened it, leaving the African Commission autonomous and relatively stronger than the Court.

Regional drivers of the universal

It should now be clear that a great contribution to knowledge, understanding, and the protection of human rights as a universal idea has been made by regional human rights systems, individually and collectively. The European system has developed the frontiers of human rights law in such areas as extra-territorial jurisdiction and the application of human rights in armed conflict. Each of these areas has in turn been extended to cover a very great deal, such as (for example) bars to deportation and extradition, the right to life and the 'right to die' by assisted suicide, procedural safeguards applicable in the event of killing by security forces, fairness in criminal proceedings, deprivation of liberty, the scope of private and family life and the manifestation of religious beliefs.

By using a combination of advisory opinions and decisions, the Inter-American system has developed the frontiers of human rights law in such areas as disappearances, extra-territorial jurisdiction and the interception of asylum seekers at sea, application of the laws of armed conflict in human rights, protection of life from moment of conception, human rights guarantees in situations of emergency, the remedy of *habeas corpus* in situations of emergency, body search and violation of human dignity, restrictions to the death penalty, nationality of married women, illegality of prior censorship of publications and freedom of information, and irregular migrants. Development of the frontiers of human rights law by the African Commission is apparent in such areas as peoples' rights to self-determination and to return to ancestral lands, use of force, occupation, and human rights, the African tradition requiring burial of bodies, extra-judicial killing, military coups being contrary to political participation, the role of the press in a democracy, serious and massive violations of human rights arising from deportation of a community, mass expulsion of foreign nationals, effect of torture on detention, nationality and statelessness, asylum and non-refoulement, and economic social and cultural rights.

Viewed collectively, regional human rights systems display a dynamic cross-fertilisation of human rights law. This is the case with regard to state responsibility for human rights, disappearances, fairness in criminal proceedings, human rights and the environment, and human rights and armed conflict. Reconstituting human rights as a regional idea adds significance to universality as a concrete and not abstract concept. Regional human rights systems embody universality as the governing framework of human rights and reinforce it with protection mechanisms. It is mainly the decisions of regional human rights Commissions and Courts that have breathed life into the development of human rights law at both national and international levels.

Further reading

Beyani, C., 'Recent Developments in the African Human Rights System 2004–2006' (2007) 7 (3) *Human Rights Law Review* 582–608

Brighton Declaration on the European Court of Human Rights, www.justice.gov.uk/news/features/brighton-declaration-on-echr-reform-adopted

Chinedu Okafor, O., *The African Human Rights System: Activist Forces and International Institutions* (Cambridge University Press 2007)

Christoffersen, J. and Rask Madsen, M. (eds.), *The European Court of Human Rights between Law and Politics* (Oxford: Clarendon Press 2011)

Goldman, R. K. 'History and Action: The Inter-American Human Rights System and the Role of the Inter-American Commission on Human Rights' (2009) 31 *Human Rights Quarterly* 856–87

Pasqualucci, J. M., *The Practice and Procedure of the Inter-American Court of Human Rights* (Cambridge University Press 2003)

White, R. C. A. and Ovey, C., *The European Convention on Human Rights*, 5th edn (Oxford University Press: 2010)

The embryonic sovereign and the biological 10
citizen: the biopolitics of reproductive rights

Patrick Hanafin

[T]he role of church–state relations ... in laying a particular path for
bioethical governance ... in countries with a strong Catholic influence
at institutional levels ... show[s] the ... difficulties in dealing with the
legacy of the church regarding ... definitions of the embryo.[1]

Italy's soul searching on how to come to terms with [human embryonic
stem cell] research addressed questions about what life is and what it
should be, about who is allowed to speak and act on it, and about the
appropriate places of law and the state in answering these.[2]

[T]he right to life explodes an already ambiguous notion of 'human
rights'.[3]

When individuals in liberal democratic societies attempt to win greater
control over decision-making about their bodies they are engaged in an
unequal power struggle with the state. In order to win more freedom they
must of necessity go before the law in order to assert these rights or
lobby the government for a change in legislation. This active intervention by the individual to win such power has been defined by Nikolas
Rose and Carlos Novas as *biological citizenship*.[4] This term describes the
phenomenon whereby individuals increasingly define their citizenship
in terms of their rights to life, health and cure. This active form of
citizenship also has an ethical dimension for Rose. Rose uses the term

---

[1] O. McDonnell and J. Allison, 'From Biopolitics to Bioethics: Church, State, Medicine and
Assisted Reproductive Technology In Ireland' (2006) 28 (6) *Sociology of Health & Illness*
817–37 at 833.

[2] I. Meltzer, 'Between Church and State: Stem Cells, Embryos, and Citizens in Italian Politics',
in S. Jasanoff (ed.), *Reframing Rights: Bioconstitutionalism in the Genetic Age* (Cambridge,
MA: MIT Press 2011) 105–24 at 107.

[3] L. Bazzicalupo, 'The Ambivalences of Biopolitics' (2006) 36 (2) *Diacritics* 109–16 at 110.

[4] N. Rose and C. Novas, 'Biological Citizenship', in A. Ong and S. J. Collier (eds.), *Global
Assemblages: Technology, Politics, and Ethics as Anthropological Problems* (Oxford:
Blackwell 2005) 439–63 at 440. See also N. Rose, 'The Politics of Life Itself' (2001) 18 (6)
Theory, Culture & Society 1–30.

ethopolitics[5] to define this aspect of biological citizenship. Within this ethopolitical mode individuals 'use their individual and collective lives, the evidence of their own existence ... [to] demand civil and human rights ... They call for recognition, respect, resources ... control over medical and technical expertise.'[6] Rose's notion of *ethopolitics* allows us to visualise the potential of deliberative participative politics within the context of reproductive rights.

Ethopolitics and Italy

In this chapter I take the case of the regulation of artificial reproductive technology in Italy as an example of the complexity of the ethopolitics of reproductive rights-claiming. Italy is both unique and also invokes many questions of enormous current importance for other societies in relation to how one can or should govern the area of assisted reproduction. In 2004 the Italian legislature introduced a law on assisted reproduction that narrowed the scope of reproductive freedom and accorded symbolic legal recognition to the embryo.[7] The Act prohibited the testing of embryos for research purposes, embryo freezing and pre-implantation genetic diagnosis for the detection of genetically transmitted diseases. The legislation also prohibited donor insemination, denied access to assisted reproduction services to single women and provided that no more than three ova be fertilised *in vitro* and that these be transferred to the womb simultaneously. Once couples agreed on the treatment they would not be allowed to withdraw their consent. Any medical professional attempting to carry out procedures prohibited by the legislation would face prison terms or fines, as well as

---

[5] For Rose, *ethopolitics* refers to 'ways in which the ethos of human existence – the sentiments, moral nature or guiding beliefs of persons, groups, or institutions – have come to provide the "medium" within which self-government of the autonomous individual can be connected up with the imperatives of good government. In ethopolitics, life itself, as it is lived in its everyday manifestations, is the object of adjudication ... ethopolitics concerns itself with the self-techniques by which human beings should judge themselves and act upon themselves to make themselves better than they are. While ethopolitical concerns range from those of lifestyle to those of community, they coalesce around a kind of vitalism: disputes over the value to be accorded to life itself, "quality of life", "the right to life" or "the right to choose", euthanasia, gene therapy, human cloning and the like' (Rose, 'The Politics of Life Itself' 18).

[6] Rose, 'The Politics of Life Itself' 19.

[7] Legge 19 febbraio 2004, no. 40, '*Norme in materia di procreazione medicalmente assistita*' (*Gazzetta Ufficiale* no. 45 del 24 febbraio 2004).

suspension from the medical register. This restrictive legislation was the result of a successful campaign on the part of the Roman Catholic Church and lay Catholic interest groups which placed the issue of the sanctity of embryonic life on the legislative agenda, combined with the lack of any ideological commitment on the part of the main political parties in this area, and the continued reliance of politicians on Church support.[8]

The government in introducing this Act refused to see regulation as a form of facilitation for scientific development, and took a dogmatic stance influenced by conservative Roman Catholic social teaching. The Act falls into the model of what Roger Brownsword has called 'regulated prohibition'.[9] The legislation does not attempt to provide an objective legal framework for the governance of assisted human reproduction, but is rather what Roberta Dameno has termed a 'manifesto law' which has for its real objective the upholding of a traditionalist idea of family formation.[10] This prohibitive approach is not unique in Europe and will be encouraged by the recent ruling of the Grand Chamber of the European Court of Human Rights (ECtHR) in *S H and Others* v. *Austria*[11] that widens the margin of appreciation for states in the governance of ART and bizarrely encourages reproductive tourism as a means to securing reproductive liberty. The Court's willingness to hide behind the margin of appreciation in a case where the legislation was discriminatory towards infertile couples demonstrates that institutional rights mechanisms can be no substitute for collective citizen action (ethopolitics) to force legislative change in this area. It is important then within a wider European context to analyse how such prohibitive legislation emerges and more importantly how it can be resisted.

In Italy the restrictive 2004 Act has provoked citizen resistance which has led via a series of judicial reviews, supported by a number of patients' rights groups,[12] to a very gradual rewriting of the Act through judicial

---

[8] For a detailed account of the background to the legislation, see P. Hanafin, *Conceiving Life: Reproductive Politics and the Law in Contemporary Italy* (Aldershot: Ashgate 2007) 49–80.

[9] R. Brownsword, 'Regulating Human Genetics: New Dilemmas for a New Millennium' (2004) 12 *Medical Law Review* 14–39 at 17.

[10] R. Dameno, 'La legge sulla procreazione medicalmente assistita: "una legge manifesto"', in AA. VV., *Un Appropriazione Indebita: L'uso del corpo della donna nella nuova legge sulla procreazione assistita* (Milan: Baldini Castoldi Dalai 2004).

[11] (Application No. 57813/00). Grand Chamber decision 3 November 2011.

[12] Prominent among these are the following patients' rights groups: L'Associazione Luca Coscioni per la liberta di ricerca scientifica; l'Associazione Amica Cicogna; Cerco un bimbo; L'altra cicogna.

intervention. Here we have a parallel writing of law that is also a hollowing out of the law from within. Citizen resistance to the Act demonstrates that the biopolitical imperative to control lives is not a one-way street and can be resisted by the ethopolitical acts of citizens. In such acts of citizen resistance we witness how rights can become something other than dead letters, enunciated but never enacted. Such engagements can be seen as enactments of what Étienne Balibar has called a 'right to politics'. For Balibar a 'right to politics' implies that no one can be emancipated from above but only through one's own acts.[13] In the context of reproductive rights, citizens have engaged in both judicial and political challenges to the legislation. In doing so these citizens mark their lives as valued and valuable. Rights in such a struggle become important weapons in a counter-hegemonic 'tactical biopolitics'[14] where peoples' bodies bear witness to exclusion from full legal citizenship. This resistant biopolitics of living citizens calls for a continuous struggle to maintain and win rights. Indeed as Balibar reminds us: 'the whole history of emancipation is not so much the history of the demanding of unknown rights as of the real struggle to enjoy rights which *have already been declared*'.[15] In this mode of the 'right to politics' the self declares itself not as the subject matter of rights, but as an active participant in the crafting and maintenance of rights. This counter-model refuses, as Linda Zerilli has aptly put it, 'the kind of political thinking that mistakes legal artifacts of freedom for a practice of freedom'.[16]

Investing the embryonic sovereign

The manner in which decisions in relation to the regulation of bioethical matters have been taken in Italy since the foundation of the post-war Republic has been haphazard. Initially the default setting on matters of ethical controversy such as abortion, for example, was the naturalist approach of Roman Catholic theology that coincided with a cultural attachment to patriarchy. Both the secular state and the Church shared a common antipathy to liberalising issues in the area of reproductive

[13] É. Balibar, *Politics and The Other Scene* (London: Verso 2002) 167.
[14] See further B. da Costa and K. Philip (eds.), *Tactical Biopolitics: Art, Activism, and Technoscience* (Cambridge, MA: MIT Press 2008).
[15] Balibar, *Politics and The Other Scene* 6. (Emphasis in original.)
[16] L. Zerilli, *Feminism and the Abyss of Freedom* (University of Chicago Press 2005) 127.

politics.[17] The spur for change came from social movement activism, particularly that of the women's movements in the 1960s and 1970s which put on the agenda the issue of women's reproductive freedom leading to the introduction of legalised abortion in 1978. These changes have been tempered by the persistence within the political culture of a strain of thinking that identifies overtly with Vatican thinking. This cohabitation with the Church spans the political spectrum encompassing both theo-conservatives (*teocons*)[18] and theo-democrats (*teodems*).[19] This has had a detrimental impact on the liberalisation of matters in relation to access to reproductive services in recent years. With the blurring of the lines between the secular and the religious in this regard, a situation has arisen where a true representative politics is not being advanced in matters of bioethical controversy.[20] This has enormous implications for individual freedom, and can be seen clearly in the Italian state's regulation of assisted reproductive technologies (ARTs).

The 2004 Act gave implicit legal recognition to what is termed the *concepito*, literally 'that which is conceived'.[21] The law stands in opposition to the provision in Article 31 (2) of the Constitution of the Italian Republic, which states that no protection independent of the mother shall be accorded to the unborn.[22] Indeed, the Constitutional Court has held that

---

[17] See further L. Caldwell, *Italian Family Matters: Women, Politics and Legal Reform* (Basingstoke: Macmillan 1991) and N. Schiffino, C. Ramjoue and F. Varone, 'Biomedical Policies in Belgium and Italy: From Regulatory Reluctance to Policy Changes' (2009) 32 (3) *West European Politics* 559–85.

[18] To be found broadly on the right of the political spectrum.

[19] To be found among the ranks of centre-left politicians.

[20] See further S. Rodotà, *La vita e le regole: Tra diritto e non diritto* (Milan: Feltrinelli 2006).

[21] Article 1 (1) of the law states:

subject to the conditions and according to the means set out in this Act, which guarantee the rights of all subjects involved, including the *concepito*, access to assisted human reproduction services is permitted in order to facilitate the resolution of reproductive problems caused by human sterility or infertility.

This broad term *concepito* encompasses all stages of pre-natal development including both the embryo and the foetus. The term *concepito* is also used in the 1978 Abortion Act (Legge 22 maggio 1978, no. 194, '*Norme per la tutela sociale della maternita e sull'interruzione volontaria della gravidanza*').

[22] Article 31 states in full:

The Republic furthers family formation and the fulfilment of related tasks by means of economic and other provisions with special regard to large families.

The Republic protects maternity, childhood, and youth; it supports and encourages institutions needed for this purpose.

the welfare of the embryo or foetus does not over-ride a woman's right to health.[23] Under the 2004 Act, access to *in vitro* fertilisation was limited to those categorised as infertile or sterile couples.[24] Couples who were not so defined but who were carriers of a hereditary genetic condition would not have access to assisted reproductive services. Tragically, it is such couples who have no other choice but to seek such services given the risk of transmitting the condition to their offspring if they conceive 'naturally'. This provision interferes both with the couple's right to receive information in relation to making health care decisions, and with their ability to consent fully to such procedures based on a complete knowledge of all the consequences involved in going ahead with the pregnancy. Article 4 of the 2004 Act prohibits donor insemination. The law allows only assisted reproduction using the egg and sperm of the couple involved (*homologous* reproduction) and prohibits the use of genetic material from third parties (*heterologous* reproduction). This reflects a particular ideological narrative, which sees *homologous* reproduction as natural, and *heterologous* reproduction as offending against nature. This was clearly manifested in the debate on the legislation in the Italian Parliament where those who supported the law likened donor insemination to adultery, resulting in the birth of a child that was not that of the husband.[25]

In Article 5, the Act limits access to assisted reproductive services to adult heterosexual couples who are either married or in a stable relationship, are of a potentially fertile age and are both living. Article 6 (3) allows consent to the procedure to be withdrawn only up to the point at which the egg is fertilised, leading to the bizarre result whereby the woman involved could potentially be forced to go through with the procedure once the egg is fertilised. This forced consent measure, as well as going against all principles of autonomy, also breaches Article 32 (2) of the Italian Constitution which states that no person shall be subjected to medical treatment without legal sanction and that the law can in no manner violate the limits imposed by the need to respect human dignity. Article 13 of the law prohibits experimentation on human embryos. Specifically, the law prohibits the production of embryos for

---

[23] See the decision of the Constitutional Court of 18 February 1975, *Corte Costituzionale, sentenza no. 27 of 18 February 1975*. In this decision the Constitutional Court ruled that abortion would be permitted where the physical or mental well-being of the woman required it.

[24] Article 1.

[25] For a detailed analysis of the parliamentary debates on the law on assisted reproduction, see C. Lalli, *Liberta procreativa* (Naples: Liguori Editori 2004) 129–71.

research, all embryo selection for eugenic purposes, cloning and inter-species fertilisation. This aspect of the legislation has curtailed research into genetic illnesses. It also operates in conjunction with Article 12 to prevent pre-implantation genetic diagnosis, as, under a rigid interpretation of the law, such a procedure could be seen as being for 'eugenic' purposes.

During the parliamentary debates on the legislation, it was surprising that delegates from across the party spectrum suspended the reality of the existing constitutional protection provided to those seeking access to assisted reproductive treatment, in the form of the right to health, and voted clearly along the lines of cultural preference. The legislation was passed during the second Berlusconi-led coalition that came to power in 2001. By 2002 the government had secured the approval of a draft of the Bill in the Chamber of Deputies. After its initial approval, the Bill remained in limbo awaiting further discussion in the Senate. The Government did not appear to be in a hurry to speed the Bill through to final approval. However, the Vatican decided to expedite matters and once more exerted its influence on an apathetic Government. In February 2003, on the occasion of the anniversary of the signing of the Lateran Pacts of 1929, representatives of the Government attended a meeting with Vatican officials.[26] On this occasion, the Pope's displeasure at policy in relation to its support for the war in Iraq, the implementation of discriminatory legislation on immigration, and the Government's opposition to the introduction of a system of clemency for prisoners, was communicated to the Government. The Vatican pointed out that the swift approval of a law on assisted reproduction in line with its thinking would go some way to winning back its approval and, more importantly, its political backing.[27] After this meeting the Government's

---

[26] The Lateran Pacts were concluded between the Vatican and the fascist regime on 11 February 1929, and gave official recognition to the special position of the Church in Italian politics. The Pacts recognised Roman Catholicism as the state religion as well as giving many concessions to the Vatican, including, tax exemptions for employees of the Holy See, exemption from jury service for the clergy, and providing for the teaching of Christian doctrine in primary schools. The Pacts were given continued recognition in the post-fascist republic by virtue of Article 7 of the Constitution of 1948 which provides as follows:

The State and the Catholic Church are, each within its own ambit, independent and sovereign. Their relations are regulated by the Lateran Pacts. Such amendments to these Pacts as are accepted by both parties do not require any procedure of Constitutional Revision.

[27] See further C. Valentini, *La fecondazione proibita* (Milan: Feltrinelli 2004) and C. Flamigni and M. Mori, *La legge sulla procreazione medicalmente assistita: paradigmi a confronto* (Milan: Net 2005) 39–42.

lethargic position on assisted reproduction legislation, coincidentally or not, underwent a sea-change. By December 2003, the Government had obtained approval of the draft legislation on assisted reproduction in the Senate, without any significant amendments. The Bill became law on 10 February 2004 after final approval by the Chamber of Deputies.

Significantly, the centre-left opposition did not act to oppose the legislation in spite of its blatantly unconstitutional and anti-liberal nature. In fact, there seemed to be no major difference between the opposition and the Government on the issue when it came to the final vote. They seemed to have a common interest in pushing the law forward based on shared patriarchal values.[28] Francesco Rutelli, then leader of the then main centre-left opposition *Margherita* party,[29] declared that his party members should be allowed to vote according to their conscience on the law. Rutelli's conscience and those of many of his party colleagues led them to vote for the Act, leading to the absence of any effective parliamentary opposition.[30] The matter was complicated by the fact that many of the proponents of the so-called centre-left were also avowed Catholics who had clear views on the sanctity of life of the embryo. This made united parliamentary opposition to the law by the opposition parties unlikely.

Contesting the embryonic sovereign

It is only after seven years of citizen resistance to the Act that it has gradually been reshaped by judicial decisions that have declared unconstitutional many of its provisions. In such a biopolitics of resistance, citizens harnessed their biological lives to once again enter into full citizenship. In doing so they utilised the extant rights to health and equality contained in the Italian Constitution of 1948 which those who passed the Act into law, as

---

[28] There were of course exceptions including the Radical Party, and some dissident voices in the larger parties. See further, E. Cirant, *Non si gioca con la vita: Una posizione laica sulla procreazione assistita* (Rome: Editori Riuniti 2005) 190–204.

[29] Literally 'The Daisy'. The party's full title was *Democrazia e Libertà* (Democracy and Freedom) and was formed as a result of a merger of the Italian Popular Party (PPI), the Democrats, Italian Renewal and the Democrats' Union for Europe.

[30] See further Valentini, *La fecondazione proibita* 123–36, and Lalli, *Libertà procreativa* 163–5. Rutelli's argument was that any legislation, however flawed, was better than none. However, in this case, it was obvious that Rutelli had his eye on the Roman Catholic vote, which remains substantial.

we have seen, ignored as an irrelevance. What we have witnessed in the last seven years is the slow and painful process of the becoming citizen of bare life. In this sense what we see is the gradual winning back of rights via citizen organisation. In order to contest their construction by the law as citizens without reproductive rights, patients' rights groups affected by the legislation engaged in, in Stephen Collier and Andrew Lakoff's term, a 'counter-politics of sheer life', which these same authors went on to define as 'a claim to state resources that is articulated by individuals and collectivities in terms of their needs as living beings'.[31] This praxis of active citizen resistance to claim new rights or to reclaim rights taken from one falls within Rose and Novas' notion of 'biological citizenship'.[32] For Rose and Novas, biological citizenship can 'embody a demand for particular protections, for the enactment or cessation of particular policies or actions . . . claims on political and non-political authorities . . . in terms of the vital damage and suffering of individuals or groups and their "vital" rights as citizens'.[33]

This is an instance of an affirmative biopolitics that opens up the field for political resistance by those categorised as bare life or lives excluded from the human rights protection.[34] Indeed as Joao Biehl has observed, such a development instantiates the figure of the 'patient-citizen'[35] who forces 'a democratization of medical sovereignty and enable[s] alternative health care practices'.[36] Such patient action enacts a form of 'biocommunity'.[37] This community is made up of: 'a . . . group of . . . patients [which] fights the denial of rights and carves out the means to access them empirically'.[38] Rose and Novas have noted that such citizens are:

---

[31] S. J. Collier and A. Lakoff, 'On Regimes of Living', in A. Ong and S. J. Collier (eds.), *Global Assemblages: Technology, Politics, and Ethics as Anthropological Problems* (Oxford: Blackwell 2005) 22–39 at 29.

[32] N. Rose and C. Novas, 'Biological Citizenship', in A. Ong and S. J. Collier (eds.), *Global Assemblages: Technology, Politics, and Ethics as Anthropological Problems* (Oxford: Blackwell 2005) 439–63 at 440.

[33] Rose and Novas, 'Biological Citizenship' 441. As they further note, biological citizenship involves: 'forms of activism such as campaigning for better treatment, ending stigma, gaining access to services, and the like: we might term this "rights bio-citizenship"' (442).

[34] See further G. Agamben, *Homo Sacer: Sovereign Power and Bare Life* (University of Minnesota Press 1999).

[35] J. Biehl, *Will To Live: AIDS Therapies and the Politics of Survival* (Princeton University Press 2007) 135.

[36] Biehl, *Will to Live* 121.   [37] Biehl, *Will to Live* 324.   [38] Biehl, *Will to Live* 324.

'ethical pioneers' – of a new kind of active biomedical citizenship. They are pioneering a new informed ethics of the self – a set of techniques for managing everyday life in relation to a condition, and in relation to expert knowledge . . . they identify an aspect of the person to be worked upon, they problematize that field or territory in certain ways, they elaborate a set of techniques for managing it, and they set out certain objectives or forms of life to be aimed for.[39]

In reaction to the 2004 Act we have seen an instantiation of such an ethopolitics, this time by groups and individuals affected by infertility and genetic illness who see the Act as a major obstacle to gaining access to ARTs and to the development of medical research to identify treatments for genetically inherited conditions. As Ingrid Meltzer has observed: 'Speaking in the name of their physical vulnerability and mobilizing their damaged bodies, they acted as "biological citizens".'[40] Such a praxis of politics allows for a brief glimpse of agonistic 'bioconstitutionalism'[41] in which rights are returned to the scene from which they have been displaced by ideological blindness and indifference. In this sense, we are engaging in a form of biological resistance to biopower.

The first example of such an ethopolitics in the context of the 2004 Act came shortly after the Act was passed into law. There was an attempt spearheaded by the Radical Party to modify the law through the mechanism of the repeal referendum (*referendum abrogativo*). This mechanism requires that the petitioners for a referendum obtain at least 500,000 signatures of citizens with the right to vote. This form of referendum allows the petitioners to outline their proposals for either partial or total repeal of the legislation in question. Once the requisite number of signatures is obtained the referendum proposals are then scrutinised for admissibility by the Constitutional Court.[42] A referendum committee was formed made up of an alliance of the Radical Party, representatives of parties of the centre-left, the Green Party, and other interested parties, including scientists, doctors and patients' groups. The referendum committee called for the total

---

[39] Rose and Novas, 'Biological Citizenship' 450.

[40] Meltzer, 'Between Church and State' 111.

[41] S. Jasanoff (ed.), *Reframing Rights: Bioconstitutionalism in the Genetic Age)* Cambridge, MA: MIT Press 2011) 12, notes: 'bioconstitutionalism . . . stresses the irreducible contingency of life–law relationships and thereby helps restore normative agency to social actors.'

[42] See Legge no. 352 1970, *Norme sui referendum previsti dalla Costituzione e sulla iniziativa legislative del popolo.* See further A. Barbera and A. Morrone, *La Repubblica dei referendum* (Bologna: Il Mulino 2003) 11–27.

abrogation of the legislation. In addition, and in the event that the Constitutional Court would reject this proposal, four proposals, which would partially repeal the legislation, were also proffered. The first of these would partially repeal Articles 12, 13 and 14 of the Act, and thereby remove the ban on embryo freezing and embryo experimentation. The second proposal would lead to the partial amendment of Articles 1, 4, 5, 6, 13 and 14, repealing the limitation on three embryos to be transferred simultaneously, and removing the limitation on access to such procedures to sterile or infertile couples alone. This would allow couples who were carriers of genetic disease access to such services. The third proposal would remove the legal recognition of the embryo. This would have led to the total repeal of Article 1 and partial repeal of Articles 4, 5, 6, 13 and 14. The final proposal would remove the ban on donor insemination. This would lead to the repeal of Articles 4, 9 and 12.

Once the required signatures were obtained the referendum proposals were submitted to the Constitutional Court, as required by the Italian legislation on citizen initiative referenda.[43] The Court decided to allow four out of the five proposed referendum proposals. The proposal that was rejected was that which called for the total repeal of the Act. With the four referendum proposals admitted, the referendum campaign began. The main opposition to the referendum came from the Roman Catholic Church. The Church set up an anti-referendum committee called 'Science and Life' (*Scienza e Vita*) to campaign on its behalf. The anti-referendum campaign instead of calling for a 'no' vote called for voters to abstain so that the required quorum of 50 per cent + 1 of voters would not be reached and the ballot would be declared invalid. This tactic was seen as a far more effective way of allowing the law under question to remain untouched but was also a subversion of the so-called deliberative democratic process. Thus, having used the legislative process to secure their aims, the Church and the conservative right now tried to sabotage the democratic system again because it didn't serve their ends.

The anti-referendum campaign proved to be successful. The quorum was not reached, with only 25.9 per cent of voters turning out.[44] The battle for values in this case was won by default. The reason for the large abstention

---

[43] Legge no. 352 1970, *Norme sui referendum previsti dalla Costituzione e sulla iniziativa legislative del popolo*.
[44] See G. Luzi, 'Procreazione, quorum fallito', (2005) *La Repubblica* 14 June 2.

cannot be attributed simply to the Church's call for a boycott of the polls. The issue of assisted reproduction was not one that excited the enthusiasm of many voters. They saw it as an issue that affected a minority of the population. Moreover, the recent history of referendums in Italy has been marked by a high rate of abstention. Of the eighteen referendums held between 1997 and 2003, none has achieved the required quorum.[45] This might be attributed to fatigue on the part of the electorate in relation to the use of the referendum; for example in 2000 alone there were seven referendums. Notwithstanding the debate over the appropriateness of the referendum as a means of bringing about democratic change, the wider issue of the introduction of a law that erases autonomous reproductive decision-making has demonstrated the success of the Vatican's strategy of engaging explicitly in political action.

The evolution of rights biocitizenship

The draconian implications for couples who sought access to assisted reproductive services of the rigid implementation of the law can be seen clearly in the cases which (quite independently of the referendum campaign) have also challenged the legislation. The first case to test the provisions of the Act was heard in Catania in Sicily in May 2004.[46] In this case, a couple, who were both healthy carriers of the genetic condition *beta thalassaemia*,[47] requested approval of pre-implantation embryo selection to ensure that the child born as a result would not suffer from this condition. The judge ruled that this was not permissible under the Act, and noted that the fertilised eggs be implanted whether or not there is a risk that they may carry this disease. This ruling was based on Article 14 of the Act that

---

[45] See Barbera and Morrone, *La Repubblica dei referendum* 209–51.

[46] *Tribunale di Catania, 1 sezione civile,* 3 May 2004, www.diritto.it/sentenze/magistratord/ trib_ct_40_19_03_04.html. See further R. Fenton, 'Catholic Doctrine Versus Women's Rights: The New Italian Law On Assisted Reproduction' (2006) 14 *Medical Law Review* 73–107 at 100–4.

[47] *Beta thalassaemia* is a blood disorder that reduces the production of haemoglobin, the iron-containing protein in red blood cells that carries oxygen to cells throughout the body. This leads to a lack of oxygen in many parts of the body. Children who suffer from *beta thalassaemia* develop life-threatening anaemia, they do not gain weight and may develop yellowing of the skin and whites of the eyes. Sufferers may have an enlarged spleen, liver, and heart, and their bones may be misshapen. Many have such severe symptoms that they need frequent blood transfusions to replenish their red blood cell supply.

prohibited the creation of a number of embryos greater than that strictly required for one contemporaneous transfer. The number created should be no greater than three. The couple argued that the 2004 Act was incompatible with the rights guaranteed in Article 2 (the guarantee of inviolable human rights) and Article 32 (2) (the right not to be forced to submit to unwanted medical treatment) of the Italian Constitution.[48] The judge dismissed these claims, noting that the obligation to transfer three embryos into the womb simultaneously, did not constitute unconsented medical treatment contrary to Article 32 (2) of the Constitution.

In addition, the judge dismissed the claim that the couple's inviolable human rights were being interfered with, noting that there was no fundamental right to have a child of one's desires.[49] The judge argued that the child in this case is a potential child rather than an actually existing one. Thus, for the judge, the couple are interested not in the health of any child born as a result of the procedure, but in their wish to have the child of their desires, i.e. a healthy child, something which in his reading the Constitution does not guarantee. Here the future child's physical condition is disregarded in the service of the protection of 'Life' itself in the abstract.[50] If the couple were to continue with the implantation and subsequently discover that the future child would suffer from such a condition, the only option left open to them would be a therapeutic abortion.[51] The process would then have to start over again with no guarantee that a similar outcome would not eventuate.

---

[48] Article 2 states:

The Republic recognizes and guarantees inviolable human rights, be it as an individual or in social groups expressing their personality, and it ensures the performance of the unalterable duty to political, economic, and social solidarity.

Article 32 (2) states:

Nobody may be forcefully submitted to medical treatment except as regulated by law. That law may in no case violate the limits imposed by respect for the human being.

[49] This mirrors the 1987 papal instruction, *Donum Vitae*, penned by the then Cardinal Ratzinger, now Pope Benedict XVI, which outlined the Roman Catholic Church's position in relation to artificial reproductive technologies, noting that the legitimate desire for a child should not be seen as a right to have a child at all costs. That would be to treat such a child as merely a means to an end. In the 1995 papal encyclical *Evangelium Vitae*, which called for the protection of life, IVF was seen as contrary to Church teaching because it constituted a danger to the embryo.

[50] See Valentini, *La fecondazione proibita* 139–58.

[51] See further M. Fusco, 'Il "caso" Catania e la legge sulla procreazione assistita: Il referendum e davvero l'unica strada' *Diritto & Diritti*, www.diritto.it/articoli/dir_famiglia/fusco1.html.

A further challenge to the law was heard in Sardinia in July 2005. In this case, Article 13 of the Act was the subject of the challenge.[52] In this case the *Tribunale Civile* of Cagliari referred the question of the constitutionality of Article 13 to the Constitutional Court (*Corte Costituzionale*) for review. Here, a couple, X.Y. and Z.J., who had been refused access to pre-implantation genetic diagnosis by their attending consultant in accordance with Article 13 of the 2004 Act, claimed that this refusal was contrary to Articles 2, 3 and 32 (1) of the Italian Constitution.[53] X.Y. had, on a previous occasion, undergone IVF treatment and had discovered in the eleventh week of her pregnancy that the foetus was affected by *beta thalassaemia*. As a result she decided to undergo a pregnancy termination. On this occasion the couple wanted to make sure that the embryo was not affected by the condition before implantation. They refused to go ahead with the implantation before undergoing a pre-implantation genetic diagnosis. The doctor involved refused this service as it was contrary to Article 13 of the 2004 Act. The judge in this case noted that the question of the constitutional legitimacy of the law was not manifestly without foundation. In referring to decisions of the Constitutional Court in relation to abortion, the judge noted that the Constitutional Court had always declared in favour of the right to health of the woman when it came into conflict with the protection accorded to the foetus. In addition, the judge spoke of the right of a woman in such a case to receive the fullest information on the state of health of the embryo. Thus, in this case the general right to receive information in relation to medical procedures would apply to information obtained via pre-implantation genetic diagnosis in relation to the state of health of the embryo. The judge noted that this was the case in relation to determining the health of a foetus *in utero*. Therefore, if couples in the position of the applicants were to be refused access to pre-implantation

---

[52] For a copy of the decision, see www.lucacoscioni.it/?q=node/5796.

[53] Article 3 provides as follows:

All citizens have equal social status and are equal before the law, without regard to their sex, race language, religion, political opinions, and personal or social conditions.

It is the duty of the republic to remove all economic and social obstacles that, by limiting the freedom and equality of citizens, prevent full individual development and the participation of all workers in the political, economic, and social organization of the country.

Article 32 (1) states:

The republic protects individual health as a basic right and in the public interest; it provides free medical care to the poor.

genetic diagnosis then this would place them in a different position to couples who had a right to obtain access to tests to determine the state of the foetus *in utero*. This raised the question of whether this ban was in accord with the equality provisions in Article 3 of the Constitution, as well as the human rights provisions of Article 2 and the specific provisions in relation to the right to health in Article 32 (1). The judge referred the matter to the Constitutional Court for a consideration of the constitutionality of this aspect of the law.

The matter was duly heard by the Constitutional Court on 24 October 2006.[54] After very little deliberation (and on the same evening as the hearing) the Court declared inadmissible the question of the constitutional legitimacy of Article 13. The written decision was produced on 9 November 2006, and was an even greater affront to justice and to the idea of constitutional adjudication than the initial rushed declaration of inadmissibility had been. The Court, without actually stating why it was doing so, noted that the reference of the lower court in Cagliari to the Constitutional Court was not admissible. The decision merely stated that the Cagliari court's assumption was contradictory in that the constitutionality of the impugned article could be deduced from other articles in the legislation and in the light of the interpretation of the entire law against the background of its stated intent. This highly circular and problematic non-decision merely states, in effect, that 'we cannot review the admissibility of this request because we think the law is constitutional, because of its stated aims'. In other words, the law is intended to protect the embryo and, as such, any procedure that would harm the embryo is not legitimate.

However, the Constitutional Court refused to measure the constitutional validity of Article 13 against the principles of equality and the right to health in the Constitution. It merely stated that the law itself was justified by its legitimating principles. Clearly unwilling to judge the constitutionality of the issue, the Court (in a decision which was not unanimous) stated that

[54] Corte costituzionale, Ordinanza 369/2006, www.cortecostituzionale.it/ita/attivitacorte/pro nunceemassime/pronunce/. For further analysis see L. Trucco, 'La procreazione medical mente assistita al vaglio della Corte Costituzionale' (2006) *Consulta Online*, www.giurcost. org/studi/trucco.html; S. Luca Morsiani, 'A buon intenditor poche parole' (2006) *Forum di Quaderni Costituzionali*, www.forumcostituzionale.it/site/index2.php?option=com_con tent&task=view&tid; and A. Morelli, 'Quando la Corte decide di non decidere. Mancato riorso all'illegitimità conseguenziale e selezione discrezionale dei casi (nota a margine dell'ord. no. 369 del 2006)' (2006) *Forum di Quaderni Costituzionali*, www.forumcostituzionale.it/site/ index2.php?option=com_content&task=view&tid.

the law is legitimate because of its ideological premise. In this case we are faced with the exception in which normal constitutional principles do not apply. The physical and mental well-being of the woman is of no importance in a state in which the key principles (or *criteri ispiratori*) include the protection of 'Life' in the abstract.

This fortunately was not to be the last word by the Constitutional Court on the matter. The phase of judicial deference to the legislators' intent just described gave way to a second phase of judicial interpretation that engaged with the actual constitutional rights that were displaced by the legislators in the 2004 Act. This change of approach became evident first in a number of lower court decisions, one of the most important of which was the decision of the Regional Administrative Tribunal of the region of Lazio in January 2008.[55] This Case was initiated by the World Association for Reproductive Medicine (WARM), a not-for-profit organisation which represents the interests of professionals working in the area of medically assisted reproduction. The action challenged, *inter alia*, the legitimacy of the Code of Practice introduced by Ministerial Decree in 2004, as being *ultra vires* the powers of the Minister of Health, as well as the constitutionality of Article 14 of the 2004 Act. WARM also contested the conflation of the terms sterility and infertility in the Act and the legal status accorded to the embryo in the Act. This challenge, that also had the support of a number of other reproductive rights organisations, was opposed by the Italian government together with a number of conservative civil society organisations, such as the Movement for Life, who intervened *ad opponendum*. The Court in its decision overruled parts of the Code of Practice introduced pursuant to the 2004 Act.[56] The impugned provisions related to Article 13.5 of the Act.[57] The decision also raised doubts over the constitutionality of Article 14.2 of the Act. In effect what the decision did was to over-rule the limitation on pre-implantation genetic diagnosis of embryos for observational purposes only, on the basis that such a provision could not be enacted by delegated legislation. The Minister of Health had therefore exceeded his powers in introducing this measure by ministerial regulations. As a result of this decision, the guidelines on assisted reproduction were revised on 11 April 2008. This was a major

---

[55] Tribunale amministrativo regionale del Lazio, sentenza no. 398 (reg. ord. no.159 del 2008) 21 January 2008.

[56] Ministerial regulations (Explanatory notes on assisted reproductive technology) introduced by Ministerial Decree No. 15165 21 July 2004.

[57] Article 13 of the law prohibits experimentation on human embryos.

victory for medical professionals and patients affected by the prohibitive legislation.

A further major victory for rights biocitizenship came with the decision of the Italian Constitutional Court of 1 April 2009,[58] which reversed the ban in Article 14 of the 2004 Act on the transfer in any one cycle of a maximum of more than three embryos.[59] This case came to the Constitutional Court by way of referral from the Regional Administrative Tribunal of the region of Lazio in its decision of 21 January 2008 discussed above in which it questioned the constitutionality of parts of the 2004 Act. In addition the Court also received two referrals from the *Tribunale Ordinario* of Florence from its decisions of 12 July 2008 and 26 August 2008.[60] In both of these decisions the Florence court questioned the constitutionality of Article 14 of the Act insofar as it prohibited the freezing of spare embryos, the imposition of a maximum limit of three embryos which could be created in any IVF treatment cycle and the need for their simultaneous transfer to the patient's womb. In addition the Court questioned the constitutionality of Article 6 (3) of the Act that decreed that once a woman had consented to the simult-aneous transfer of these three embryos she could not withdraw that consent.

The Constitutional Court in its decision held that Article 14.2 of the Act was unconstitutional and in particular breached Article 3 of the Constitution in relation to equality and Article 32 of the Constitution which upholds the right to health. As a result of this decision, Article 14.2 of the 2004 Act is no longer to be interpreted as placing a limit on the number of embryos to be transferred. The Court held that the number of embryos transferred in any treatment cycle should be based on individual medical opinion based on the facts of each patient's case. The decision also overruled the ban in Article 14 (1) on the freezing of embryos. As a result of the decision, embryos that might not be used in a treatment cycle may now be frozen. The Court, in referring to Article 1 of the Act, noted that the interests of all parties (not just the embryo) should be considered citing the Constitutional Court's jurisprudence on abortion.

Following on from this Constitutional Court ruling there have been a number of subsequent successful challenges to the Act in the lower courts.

---

[58] Corte Costituzionale, sentenza no.151/2009 (1 April 2009).

[59] Article 14 also outlaws cryopreservation, the destruction of embryos and embryo reduction.

[60] See Tribunale Ordinario di Firenze, ordinanza del 12 luglio 2008 (reg. ord. no. 323 del 2008) and Tribunale Ordinario di Firenze, ordinanza del 26 agosto 2008 (reg. ord. no. 382 del 2008).

The *Tribunale Civile* of Florence[61] overturned the ban on *heterologous* IVF with donor eggs or donor sperm in Article 4 of the Act and referred this aspect of the Act to the Constitutional Court for review. On 21 October 2010 the *Tribunale Civile* of Catania made a similar ruling, questioning the constitutionality of the ban on IVF using donor gametes.[62] In the decision of the *Tribunale Civile* of Salerno of 13 October 2010 the limitation in Article 1 of the 2004 Act on access to *in vitro* fertilisation to those categorised as infertile or sterile was successfully challenged.[63] Couples who are not so defined but who are carriers of a hereditary genetic condition cannot have access to assisted reproductive services. The Court ruled in favour of access to pre-implantation genetic diagnosis in the case of a couple who were neither sterile nor infertile. The couple suffer from amyotrophy, which causes the progressive wasting of muscle tissues.

This aspect of the Act is also now the subject of an application to the ECtHR. This case was declared admissible in June 2011 and a First Instance decision is currently awaited.[64] The case concerns a couple, Mr Pavan and Ms Costa, both carriers of a hereditary illness, cystic fibrosis, who wish to prevent this condition being inherited by any second or subsequent child they might have together. In September 2006 they gave birth to a child with cystic fibrosis, only then becoming aware that they were both carriers of the disease. The couple have a one in four chance of having a child born with the condition and a one in two chance that any future child of theirs will be a carrier of the condition. They want to ensure that any further child they have will neither have nor be a carrier of the condition. As we have seen, the 2004 Act prevents access to pre-implantation genetic diagnosis to couples suffering inherited genetic conditions. It only allows access to screening for infertile couples or where the male partner has a viral disease that can be transmitted through sexual intercourse, such as HIV, or Hepatitis B and C. Since these exceptions did not apply to this couple, the only option open to them as the law stood was to have an abortion on discovery via foetal testing that the future child was either a sufferer or carrier of the condition. In fact, Ms Costa conceived a child with cystic fibrosis so decided to undergo an abortion in February 2010. In their application to Strasbourg, the couple are relying on Article 8 in conjunction with Article 14 of the European

---

[61] Tribunale civile di Firenze (6 October 2010).
[62] Tribunale civile di Catania (21 October 2010).
[63] Tribunale civile di Salerno (13 October 2010).
[64] *Costa and Pavan* v. *Italy* (Application No. 54270/10).

Convention on Human Rights (ECHR). Their complaint is that they have suffered discrimination compared to infertile couples or those couples in which the male partner has a sexually transmitted disease.

The portents for the success of this challenge do not look good if previous Strasbourg jurisprudence on challenges to restrictive IVF laws is anything to go by. The most prominent of these is the Grand Chamber decision of 3 November 2011 in *S H and Others* v. *Austria*.[65] In this case it was held that there was no violation of Article 8 ECHR in a case involving a challenge to the provision of the Austrian Assisted Procreation Act that prohibits the use of sperm from a donor for IVF and ova donation in general. The Austrian Assisted Procreation Act only allows IVF with gametes from the couples involved. Even though the Grand Chamber noted that there was a clear trend across Europe in favour of allowing gamete donation for IVF, it added that an emerging consensus was still under development and so was not as yet based on settled legal principles. The Court held by a majority of thirteen votes to four that there had been no violation of the Convention. The Grand Chamber further noted that the Austrian legislation was not disproportionate as it had not banned individuals from going overseas for infertility treatment unavailable in Austria. This assumes, without thinking, that couples are in a position to engage in such reproductive tourism. The decision was entirely at odds with the First Instance ruling in the same case on 1 April 2010.[66] Indeed the majority judgment of the Grand Chamber in this case demonstrates the Court's unwillingness to make the right to reproductive freedom anything more than a mere empty piece of rhetoric which has no possibility of being accessed in reality if one is unfortunate enough to be a citizen of a state (like Italy or Austria, for example) which has restrictive laws on assisted reproduction. The laughable declaration by the majority that the fact that more liberal regimes exist in other Council of Europe states in relation to assisted reproduction would mean that couples like S and H could engage in 'reproductive tourism' to gain access to a technology which they should have access to in their own home state. This blatant inability to uphold reproductive rights by using the highly dubious mechanism of the margin of appreciation and the existence of the possibility of reproductive tourism is a shameful failure to intervene to develop a more pluralist model of reproductive rights protection in Europe. Indeed the

---

[65] (Application No. 57813/00). Grand Chamber decision 3 November 2011.
[66] *S H and Others* v. *Austria* (Chamber judgment) 1 April 2010.

joint dissenting opinion of Judges Tulkens, Hirvela, Lazarova-Trajkovska and Tsotsoria in *S H and Others* v. *Austria* noted as such when it observed:

[T]he Grand Chamber unhesitatingly affirms that there is not yet 'clear common ground between the member states' and that the margin of appreciation to be afforded to the respondent State 'must be a wide one', allowing it to reconcile social realities with its positions of principle. That reasoning implies that these factors must now take precedence over the European consensus, which is a dangerous departure from the Court's case-law considering that one of the Court's tasks is precisely to contribute to harmonising across Europe the rights guaranteed by the Convention . . .

. . . in a case as sensitive as this one, the Court should not use the margin of appreciation as a 'pragmatic substitute for a thought-out approach to the problem of proper scope of review'.[67] Ultimately, through the combined effect of the European consensus and the margin of appreciation, the Court has chosen a minimum – or even minimalist – approach that is hardly likely to enlighten the national courts.[68]

Conclusion: law as a reflection of a shared feeling

In his book *Why I Am Not a Secularist*, political theorist William Connolly[69] argues that rights cannot be created by a top down 'molarpolitics of public officials' but comes instead from a mobilisation of self-styling selves, 'the molecular movements of micropolitics'.[70] We can see the play between the *micropolitics* of movements of individuals in Italy who are attempting to self-style their reproductive choices, and the *molarpolitics* of politicians, who attempt to prevent the creation of this right. This *molarpolitics* is based on rigid moral beliefs and refuses to recognise contrary views. It blocks the dialogic political process and creates stasis. In discussing the concept of *micropolitics*, Connolly uses the analogy of how an individual in working out her position on bioethical issues is confronted with differing sympathies and values. In coming to decide, one is confronted with differing views both

---

[67] Citing the joint dissenting opinion of Judges Turmen, Tsatsa-Nikolovska, Spielmann and Ziemele, annexed to the *Evans* v. *United Kingdom* judgment of the Grand Chamber of 10 April 2007, point 12.

[68] Joint dissenting opinion annexed to *S H and Others* v. *Austria*, points 10 and 11.

[69] W. Connolly, *Why I Am Not A Secularist* (University of Minnesota Press 1999) 147.

[70] Connolly, *Why I Am Not a Secularist* 149.

outside and within oneself. He gives the example of the right to die and of an individual who believes that death must only come when either God or nature brings it.[71] This person is shocked by movements who call for a right to doctor-assisted death for those in severe pain as the result of a terminal illness. However once the initial shock of this claim dissipates the person begins to think of the suffering of terminally ill individuals in a world of high-tech medical care. In such a case Connolly claims, '*one part of your subjectivity now begins to work on other parts.* In this case your concern for those who writhe in agony as they approach death may work on contestable assumptions about divinity or nature already burnt into your being.'[72] Connolly highlights the uncertainties and tension within the self on the issue after such an individual starts to weigh up the many competing interests involved. Indeed having worked on the self:

You continue to affirm . . . a teleological conception of nature in which the meaning of death is set, but now you acknowledge how this judgment may be more contestable than you had previously appreciated . . . What was heretofore nonnegotiable may now gradually become rethinkable. You now register more actively the importance of giving presumptive respect to the judgment of the sufferer in this domain, even when the cultivation of critical responsiveness to them disturbs your own conception of nature, death, or divinity.[73]

Connolly's notion of *micropolitics* allows us to rethink the relation between rights and bioethics. It allows us to focus on the actual desires and interests of the individual who claims a right in the biomedical context. Connolly terms this behaviour on the part of citizens an *ethos of engagement* with existing moral and social givens which may bring about unexpected consequences or transformations in the societal default thinking on bioethical issues. Similar to Rose's notion of *ethopolitics* this active resistance on behalf of citizens affected by prohibitive legislation on bioethical issues leads to a reactivation of rights protection for those deprived of such protection. This process Connolly terms 'an ambiguous *politics of becoming* by which a new entity is propelled into being out of injury, energy and difference'.[74] Micropolitical movements such as the patients' rights groups in Italy which continue to call for more liberal regulation of the ART sector

---

[71] Connolly, *Why I Am Not a Secularist* 146.
[72] Connolly, *Why I Am Not a Secularist* 146. (Emphasis in original.)
[73] Connolly, *Why I Am Not a Secularist* 147.
[74] Connolly, *Why I Am Not a Secularist* 160. (Emphasis in original.)

or those individuals who bring legal challenges to the existing law, 'expose modes of suffering and injury heretofore located below the radar of public discourse. Sometimes the politics of becoming exposes how a list of basic rights that recently seemed complete harboured obscure and inadvertent exclusions inside the sweep of its formulations.'[75] This process of *micro-politics* provokes us to rethink existing modes of addressing bioethical problems. The individual in this case takes responsibility for her own autonomous self and works on the political and legal terrains to bring about real change. This *micropolitics* of rights would see law not as the imposition of a rigid moralistic view but rather as what Italian legal theorist Stefano Rodotà has called 'a reflection of a shared feeling'.[76]

The manner in which reproductive autonomy has been hijacked by a particular ideological view in a country in which pluralist legal values are enshrined in the Constitution is deeply problematic. The series of court challenges to the 2004 Act and the continuing civil society political organisation against it demonstrate the need for continued political organisation on the part of citizens to win back what were once thought to be established rights, such as a right to decide in relation to reproduction. The 2011 decision of the Grand Chamber of the ECtHR in *S H and Others* v. *Austria*, discussed above, alerts all those with an interest in defending reproductive rights to the need to supplement court challenges with other forms of political action such as campaigns to repeal prohibitive legislation using both national and transnational alliances of medical professionals and patients' groups. The example of Italy provides both a warning to those who think reproductive autonomy should be taken for granted and also provides examples of how collective citizen action is essential in the establishment and maintenance of reproductive rights.

Further reading

Bazzicalupo, L., 'The Ambivalences of Biopolitics' (2006) 36 (2) *Diacritics* 109–16

Brownsword, R., 'Regulating Human Genetics: New Dilemmas for a New Millennium' 12 *Medical Law Review* 14–39

Fenton, R., 'Catholic Doctrine Versus Women's Rights: The New Italian Law On Assisted Reproduction' 14 *Medical Law Review* 73–107

[75] Connolly, *Why I Am Not a Secularist* 160.   [76] Rodotà, *La vita e le regole* 16.

Hanafin, P., 'Gender, Citizenship and Human Reproduction in Contemporary Italy' (2006) 14 (3) *Feminist Legal Studies* 329–52

Conceiving Life: Reproductive Politics and the Law in Contemporary Italy (Aldershot: Ashgate 2007)

'Cultures of Life: Embryo Protection and the Pluralist State', in M. Freeman (ed.), *Law and Bioethics* (Oxford University Press 2008) 177–96

'Refusing Disembodiment: Abortion and the Paradox of Reproductive Rights in Contemporary Italy' (2009) 10 (2) *Feminist Theory* 227–44

Jasanoff, S. (ed.), *Reframing Rights: Bioconstitutionalism in the Genetic Age* (Cambridge, MA: MIT Press 2011)

Meltzer, I., 'Between Church and State: Stem Cells, Embryos, and Citizens in Italian Politics', in S. Jasanoff (ed.), *Reframing Rights: Bioconstitutionalism in the Genetic Age* (Cambridge, MA: MIT Press 2011) 105–24

Rodotà, S., *La vita e le regole: Tra diritto e non diritto* (Milan: Feltrinelli 2006)

Rose, N., 'The Politics of Life Itself' (2001) 18 (6) *Theory, Culture & Society* 1–30

Rose, N. and Novas, C., 'Biological Citizenship', in A. Ong and S. J. Collier (eds.), *Global Assemblages: Technology, Politics, and Ethics as Anthropological Problems* (Oxford: Blackwell 2005) 439–63

11 Spoils for which victor? Human rights within the democratic state

Conor Gearty

The two big ethical ideas to emerge victorious from the short twentieth century were human rights and democracy. Initially an old trope revived to rally elite morale during the Second World War, the first of these (human rights) was useful to the designers of the second, the controlled democracies that were then being constructed in the loser-states of Germany, Italy and Japan.[1] After this brief moment centre-stage, however, both rather lost their universalist lustre, with human rights being sidetracked off into an international arena of pious declarations and unenforceable agreements while a respect for state sovereignty that was indifferent to domestic political arrangements fast became the norm at the UN. Their time came again in the 1970s with both being dusted down for use once more, this time in the late Cold War as a convenient stick with which the West felt able to beat its communist rivals.[2] Just as in 1945, the success that flowed from the breakthroughs of 1989 produced democratic/human rights nation-building on a grand scale. Almost to an (ex)-comrade, the post-Soviet and post-Soviet-bloc states chose forms of government that declared themselves to be democratic while at the same time ostensibly respectful of the human rights of all those within their borders. Federal arrangements were carefully designed, bicameral legislatures lovingly re-created from training sessions on Capitol Hill, presidents constituted to embody their states while being simultaneously dependant on the will of their people. And in very many of these schemes, overseeing this tumultuous worker-bee activities in these new hives of democratic freedom were the various Constitutional Courts, given over-riding responsibility for the protection of human rights.[3]

---

[1] M. Mandel, 'A Brief History of the New Constitutionalism, or "How We Changed Everything so that Everything Remained the Same"' (1998) 32 *Israel Law Review* 250–00, is a fascinating account.

[2] S. Moyn, *The Last Utopia: Human Rights in History* (Cambridge, MA: Harvard University Press 2010) is an outstanding account of the growth and decline and then rebirth of human rights.

[3] Moyn, *The Last Utopia* and S. B. Snyder, 'Principles Overwhelming Tanks: Human Rights and the End of the Cold War', in A. Iriye, P. Goedde and W. I. Hitchcock (eds.), *The Human Rights*

Since these successes of the early 1990s, human rights and democracy have become the bywords for constitutional modernity everywhere, underpinning progressive change in the former colonies of Africa as old independence leaderships have died away,[4] in the post-authoritarian states in South America,[5] in the newly unshackled South Africa,[6] and even in those places where the West's remit has most recently run: Afghanistan has a fine constitution[7] and Iraq's, too, is second to none, with its domestic bill of rights and lavish judicial protection for these fundamental guarantees.[8] When the 'Arab Spring' set in train its own momentum towards change in 2011, it was almost inevitable – and certainly it seemed natural – for the opposition and activists alike to call not only for 'democracy' but for 'human rights' as well.

And yet for all its obviousness, surely there is something that a moment's reflection makes unavoidably clear: respect for human rights and democracy do not naturally fit together. In human rights we have an idea that advertises truth as its essence: we are human; we have these rights; they are universal, as much part of us as our breathing, our thinking, our being us; they are ineradicable, inalienable, fundamental and so while they can be breached ('abused') they cannot simply be taken away or removed. Now contrast this with what democracy is primarily about, on any of its many competing theories: community self-government; the will of the people; representative government; the sovereignty of the electorate. All of these require that there can be no prior morality to which the decisions of the people must submit – self-government as a people is not about doing what

Revolution: An International History (New York: Oxford University Press 2012) 265–83 are good on the background. R. Blackburn and J. Polakiewicz (eds.), *Fundamental Rights in Europe: The European Convention on Human Rights and its Member States, 1950–2000* (Oxford University Press 2001) is the standard work on the rights side. See, for the constitutional context past and present, A. Albi, *EU Enlargement and the Constitutions of Central and Eastern Europe* (New York: Cambridge University Press 2005). For a fascinating insight into the thinking of the mid 1990s, see 'Constitutions of Central and Eastern European Countries and the Baltic States' (1995) 2 *Sigma Papers* (Paris: OECD Publishing), www.oecd-ilibrary.org/docserver/download/fulltext/5kml6gf26mvk.pdf? expires=1332858734&tid=id&accname=guest&checksum=28A1D6DC1D01E22D024D38E4 C6042A23 (date of last access 27 March 2012).

4 E.g. The Constitution of Kenya, rev. edn (2010) (National Council for Law Reporting with the authority of the Attorney General).

5 E.g. The Constitution of Brazil (1988).

6 Constitution of the Republic of South Africa (1996).

7 www.afghan-web.com/politics/current_constitution.html (date of last access 27 March 2012). See esp. Ch 2.

8 See www.uniraq.org/documents/iraqi_constitution.pdf (date of last access 27 March 2012).

you are allowed to do; it is about doing what you choose to do. The people are not infants in a playpen with the absolute freedom merely to play with the toys they are given; they are citizens who can design (and as it happens perpetually re-design) the playpen, put things in, take things out, create new games with new rules and entirely fresh ways of conducting themselves. Now of course often there will be little conflict between the two – the democratic players can and often do construct their world in a way that respects the rights of all those caught up in the arena they control. But they do not have to. And when they don't, there is *inevitably* a clash between representative government and human rights. Which should win?

Law's empire[9]

Until recently the answer to this question has always been human rights. This has been largely due to the influence of the USA in shaping democratic discourse in the immediate aftermath of the breakthroughs of the late 1940s and again after 1989. Before the first of these moments, the US constitution of the late eighteenth century had been regarded as irrelevant to state-building by those outside the USA and largely a force for conservatism by those within. True, the document did not at the outset mandate the protection of any kind of individual rights over the (then not democratic) political, but amendments which were almost immediately made (designed to render the settlement more agreeable to the states that had signed up to it) did speak of constitutional rights in an abstract way – freedom of speech and of assembly, freedom from unreasonable search and seizure, and so on. This then made possible and also understandable, sensible even, the later (in 1803) assertion of a judicial power to protect such rights and freedoms, initially against the federal branches of government[10] and later against the state authorities as well.[11] The way in which the US Supreme Court went about discharging its asserted duty to protect rights was one of the many ways in which, through the first 150 years or so of the Republic's existence, progressive ideas were rendered extremely difficult to realise in a legal

---

[9] R. Dworkin, *Law's Empire* (Cambridge, MA: Belknap Press 1986).
[10] *Marbury* v. *Madison* 5 US (1 Cranch) 136 (1803).
[11] For an early example of the process of selective incorporation, see *Adamson* v. *California* 332 US 46 (1947).

shape. Of course there was more to it than the justices' interpretation of the US 'bill of rights', with rulings on separation of powers and the extent of the federal power also playing a part, but the collective impact of the court's judgments over many decades (on slavery; the 'separate but equal' doctrine underpinning segregation; the regulation of business to protect workers; the need to control left-wing speech; etc.) was to make progressive opinion scathing of its role in US society.[12]

This changed in the decades after 1945 in a way that was in due course (as we shall see) to have an effect on the balance between human rights and democracy even in those countries resistant to reshaping in either 1945 (the victorious allies) or 1989 (the established democracies). First the Court itself had received a nasty shock in the 1930s, being made the subject of a vitriolic campaign against it by President F. D. Roosevelt, one which the president lost in an immediate crude political sense (the court went unreformed) but won in the longer term in that the justices backed away from their hostile engagement with his progressive New Deal legislation.[13] In search of a new role, the justices happened upon the protection of civil and political rights (via an obscure footnote which has been elevated by generations of awed American law professors to the status of a Moses-like tablet of stone),[14] producing its proudest moment in 1954, *Brown* v. *Board of Education of Topeka*,[15] a case which in requiring the racial desegregation of schools (overturning a past precedent[16]) seemed to signal a brighter, more progressive future for what were called 'civil rights' but which connected with the notion of human rights that was then unfolding on the international arena (all those pious declarations).

There is no doubt that the US Supreme Court under the leadership of Earl Warren and then (to a lesser extent) Warren Burger produced powerful liberal interventions in a culture that was otherwise dogged (at the state level at any rate) by majoritarian hostility to minorities and by the durability of old-fashioned religious orthodoxies beyond which the democratic system seemed incapable of moving. The years 1954 through to 1973 saw cases on police powers, access to contraceptives, free speech, due process, national security and public protest enter the liberal lexicon

---

[12] A. Cox, *The Court and the Constitution* (Boston, MA: Houghton Mifflin 1987) is a wonderfully told and accessible account.

[13] 'The switch in time that saved the nine': Roberts J's change of position in *West Coast Hotel Ltd* v. *Parrish* 300 US 379 (1937).

[14] *US* v. *Carolene Products* 304 US 144 (1938).   [15] 347 US 483 (1954).

[16] *Plessy* v. *Ferguson* 163 US 537 (1896).

of US culture with the progressive professoriate so pleased with the results that they chose not to think too hard about how they came about. Legal academics in prestigious US law schools fell over themselves to explain why democracy, properly interpreted, needed this kind of judicial oversight. The imposition of the US model elsewhere made more sense in progressive or 'human rights' circles with the US Court itself now also doing good emancipatory work. And since this was at a time when US influence was at its highest in the West, its ways of seeing quickly became the daily panorama of the free world.

If *Brown* marked the start of this phase in the Supreme Court's life, then the equally well-known (notorious even) decision of *Roe* v. *Wade* in 1973 marked its end.[17] Here the Court (by a seven to two majority) ruled in favour of a right to abortion (or in the careful slogan of its supporters a 'right to choose'). The detailed opinion by the lead judge, Blackmun J, resembled more the thoughts of a painfully careful minister introducing a measure into a legislative assembly than they did the authoritative interpretation of a bill of rights drafted nearly two hundred years before which had nowhere mentioned abortion (of course), nor even (perhaps more surprisingly) the right to privacy from which it was said the right could be deduced.[18] In vain did one of the dissentients warn that the ruling 'partakes more of judicial legislation than it does of a determination of the intent of the drafters [of the relevant amendment]', with 'the conscious weighing of competing factors that the Court's opinion apparently substitutes for the established test [being] far more appropriate to a legislative judgment than to a judicial one'.[19] The democratic playpen was being sharply restricted, just as it had been (albeit from a different angle) in the 1930s. What the USA has seen since this fateful decision has been a revolt by conservatives against the unaccountability of the Supreme Court which has been much fiercer than anything attempted by the progressives under Roosevelt: 'original intent' has become the new orthodoxy so far as constitutional interpretation is concerned; the appointment of justices is now highly controversial and nakedly partisan; the Court itself has been dragged into politics. The apotheosis of this failure of law to

[17] 410 US 113 (1973).

[18] The story is told many places of course but for direct interviews with two of the key justices and others involved in the ruling, see C. A. Gearty, 'The Paradox of United States Democracy' (1992) 26 *University of Richmond Law Review* 259–79, reprinted in C. A. Gearty, *Essays on Human Rights and Terrorism* (London: Cameron May 2008) Ch 8 217–37.

[19] Rehnquist J.

stand above politics came in *Bush* v. *Gore*,[20] when the Republican majority on the court delivered the presidency to the Republican candidate, the ever-thinning fig leaf of legal reasoning having fallen away almost completely in the emergency of the moment.

By 2000, however, it was too late for the democracies that had already incorporated the US system of civil rights into their frameworks of government. All such states from Germany, Italy and Japan at the end of the war through the decolonised nations in the 1950s and 1960s right up to the post-Soviet states of today have had to cope with the fact that their passing judgements about what is required are merely contingent assertions about the public interest, capable at any moment of being successfully nullified by the adjudicative referee sitting above the fray. The American difficulties with such an approach have played out across the world. The abortion issue has been the focus of particularly bitter constitutional discussion not only in the USA but in Germany[21] and Ireland[22] as well, and at the supranational European Court of Human Rights (ECtHR).[23] But it has only been one flashpoint among many. And as mention of the ECtHR reminds us, traditional understandings of democracy as popular or at least parliamentary sovereignty have taken a further knock by the move towards human rights ascendency in those parts of the world where regional government has increasingly come to take the place of the local: the ECtHR of the Council of Europe for one, but also the EU with its Charter of Rights and constitutional principles overseen by its European Court of Justice (ECJ).[24] There have been weaker moves along similar lines in both Africa and South America.[25]

Emboldened by success, and (in fairness to the judges) often mandated by the constitutions which it is their duty to apply, courts are increasingly being invited to colonise further parts of the political in the name of the demands of human rights: the enforcement by judges of social priorities under the guise of 'economic and social rights' is becoming more and more what democracy

---

[20] 531 US 98 (2000).

[21] See the decision of the German Federal Constitutional Court at BVerfGE 39,1. There is an English translation at http://groups.csail.mit.edu/mac/users/rauch/nvp/german/german_abortion_decision2.html (date of last access 27 March 2012).

[22] Most infamously *X* v. *Attorney General* [1992] 1 IR 1.

[23] *A B C* v. *Ireland* app. 25579/05 16 December 2010 (Grand Chamber).

[24] A. O'Neill, *EU Law for UK Lawyers* (Oxford: Hart 2011) Ch 6 is particularly good on the EU side.

[25] J. Rehman, *International Human Rights Law*, 2nd edn (Harlow: Longman 2010) Ch 9 (America) and Ch 10 (Africa).

is now supposed naturally to entail.[26] It is hard to know which is worse from the democratic point of view: when courts disappoint litigants by denying seemingly clear human rights out of a sense of deference to the executive (as in, arguably, South Africa) or where the courts happily impose their will at the behest of well-heeled litigants who therefore manage to steal a march on their less affluent (and so less-empowered) fellow citizens, as appears to have happened in Brazil with regard to the right to health, for example.[27] The success of US-style rights standing squarely above elected representatives has seemed to carry with it not only a shift in emphasis away from legislatures to questions about who these judges are and what kind of litigants have the muscle to get before them but also a kind of fatalistic calming of the political, as though its only role is to imagine not a better future but rather what the judges are likely to say.

A different balance

There has always been a set of alternative models available, however, to that offered by the US Constitution. Emerging from the UK as an independent country enjoying Dominion status in the early 1920s, the 'Irish Free State' (or Republic as it became in 1949) offers not one but two such examples, each drawn from the very earliest decades of the country's independent life. First the guarantees of rights in the Free State's foundational instrument were deliberately left open to legislative change in the course of the first eight years of its operation.[28] The idea was for the democratic representatives to be given the chance to perfect these guarantees before they were frozen in form and placed above the law for ever. The clause permitting these alterations could itself be altered. Perhaps inevitably the government and law-makers of the day could not resist the challenge; in 1929 the period of legislative amendment was extended to sixteen years.[29] The 'fundamental rights' in the Constitution became as uncertain and potentially transient as the assertions in law of any 'here today; gone tomorrow'

---

[26] A drift that I criticise in C. A. Gearty, 'Against Judicial Enforcement', in C. A. Gearty and V. Mantouvalou, *Debating Social Rights* (Oxford: Hart 2011) 1–84.

[27] On which country, see O. L. M. Ferraz, 'The Right to Health in the Courts of Brazil: Worsening Health Inequities' (2009) 11 (2) *Health and Human Rights* 33–45.

[28] Constitution of the Irish Free State (Saorstát Eireann) Act 1922, Article 50.

[29] Constitution (Amendment No. 16) Act 1929. See *The State (Ryan)* v. *Lennon* [1935] 1 IR 170.

legislators. This location of rights entirely within the political may appeal to some but it came at a high price in terms of the conceptual integrity of the whole system – basic rights that could change at a majoritarian whim gave constitutional law (and indeed all rights-talk) a bad name. So when the Irish Constitution of 1937 was written and promulgated, a code of untouchable (albeit generally qualified) rights were placed above law in the American style – and this has gone on to produce the usual US-style story of judicial supremacism allied to public controversy.[30] But that Constitution also did something rather fresh.

The second innovation for which Ireland deserves to be remembered was its creation of a set of Directive Principles within its Constitution which were designed to guide law-makers but which were expressly placed beyond the reach of the courts.[31] Now of course the judges have retaliated to some extent, finding in these principles evidence for 'personal rights' that they have then contrived – US-style – to read into the other, justiciable bits of Ireland's bill of rights. But the point of the exercise for present purposes is its ambition – an early effort to square the circle between the moral power of rights language and the inevitably contingent demands of democratic politics. The Indian Constitution of 1949 followed suit, setting out a whole range of goals for future legislators to ponder but for the courts to leave well alone.[32] Judges generally dislike these political manoeuvres, the hanging of juicy morsels of ethical engagement just outside their reach, and in India just as in Ireland the courts have been active in more orthodox fields.[33] The approach seemed over the years to have withered on the vine for lack of nutrition, particularly when the Warren Court was in its pomp and progressive judicial activism the order of the democratic day. But recently, it has made an important come-back, albeit now wearing rather more sophisticated democratic dress.

The impetus for this fresh approach to the relationship between democracy and human rights has come from what has been called the Old Commonwealth, i.e. those states whose colonisation by and practical independence from the UK were early occurrences in that country's imperial history. While the US model has been influential, particularly with those for whom the Warren Court was the paradigm, it never quite took hold as it

---

[30] The standard account is J. M. Kelly, G. Hogan and G. Whyte (eds.), *The Irish Constitution*, 4th edn (Dublin: Bloomsbury Professional 2003).

[31] Constitution of Ireland, Article 45.   [32] Indian Constitution, Part IV, Articles 36–51.

[33] Particularly under Part III, 'Fundamental Rights'.

could among the defeated. In 1960 the Canadians enacted a Bill of Rights, that sought to impose itself on future legislators but in a way so hedged about with qualifications and so immersed in compromise that, advertising its tentativeness to all, it quickly declined into irrelevance.[34] New Zealand went down a not dissimilar route with its Bill of Rights of 1981, a document aimed primarily at the control of executive power in the usual common law way and deliberately choosing to forgo the opportunity to challenge legislative supremacy, more like the Ireland of 1922 than the South Africa of 1994.[35] In 1982 however and faced with a constitutional crisis in the form of Quebec's effort to secede from the country, the then-Canadian Administration of Pierre Trudeau hit upon a formula with which to maintain the integrity of the nation over which he had democratic oversight – a 'charter of rights' bringing all the people together through the guarantee not only of traditional civil and political rights but of various cultural and linguistic entitlements as well. Enacted after a long period of discussion and an extensive debate among legislators and in the country at large, the Charter did empower the courts to strike down primary laws in the American way – but it also quite deliberately allowed for legislative pre-emption of, or retaliation to, such judicial engagements.[36]

This was in the form of what has become known as the 'Notwithstanding' clause, that part of the Canadian charter which allows either the federal or any of the provincial legislatures explicitly to acknowledge the dubiousness of its proposed actions from a charter point of view, but to carry on anyway, regardless of, or 'notwithstanding' as the article puts it, any such Charter complications. The record in Canada has been that of a fairly activist judicial engagement with Charter rights, with however very little legislative use having been made (after an initial flurry by Quebec had died down) of the 'notwithstanding' get-out clause. This is hardly surprising; all democratic assemblies are certain to hesitate before flaunting their defiance of a foundational rights document to which the people (albeit now perhaps those of an old, superseded generation) have committed themselves. The entrenchment of Canadian judicial pronouncements on the Charter has been deeper in practice than the 'notwithstanding' clause had suggested and to some extent (from a legislator's point of view) promised.

---

[34] For a rare outing in the courts see *R* v. *Drybones* [1970] SCR 282.
[35] New Zealand Bill of Rights Act 1990.
[36] Constitution Act 1982, Sched B, Charter of Rights s. 33.

This came to matter a great deal in the UK in the late 1990s when for various reasons, largely of a domestic political nature, the decision was made to import the language of human rights into the 'colonial mother country' itself, one of the last remaining bastions of undiluted legislative sovereignty (albeit one where the edges of parliamentary vitality had already been sapped by commitment to the EU and – to a lesser extent – the European Convention on Human Rights, ECHR).[37] US-style judicial supremacism having been immediately ruled out (the message of the catastrophic post *Roe* v. *Wade* years had got through), the Labour Government which came into office in 1997 after eighteen years of Conservative rule initially believed that it had to choose between the Canadian and New Zealand models. Proponents of a strong judicial role (many of whom might privately have hankered after a US-style solution, warts and all) argued for the first; more traditional parliamentary sovereignty sentimentalists (who would perhaps have preferred no bill of rights at all) pushed for the second. Reconciling these two positions produced the novel approach to the issue that is now to be found in the UK's Human Rights Act (HRA) 1998. The rights themselves are conventional enough, all borrowed from the ECHR and those of the protocols to that agreement to which the UK had already committed itself (and so mainly leaving to one side economic and social rights).[38] A large effort has been made to place their protection within rather than outside the political domain. Section 19 of the Act requires ministers introducing legislation to make statements as to whether or not the bill for which they are responsible is consistent with the Convention rights. A joint committee on human rights (made up of Members of Parliament (MPs) and Lords) was established at around the same time as the Act, and it has been an effective monitor of governmental human rights activity ever since. In the years since enactment of the measure, British politics has become acclimatised to a double debate on human rights, one conducted in general terms about what the idea of human rights requires, necessitates, etc., the other a narrower one about the technical consistency of this or that proposal with the terms of the ECHR. For a country that had had no such discussions to speak of pre-1998, this has been quite a change.[39]

---

[37] For a brief sketch of the background see C. A. Gearty, *Principles of Human Rights Adjudication* (Oxford University Press 2004) Chs 1 and 2.

[38] Human Rights Act 1998, Sched 1.

[39] One that is well mapped by A. Kavanagh, *Constitutional Review under the UK Human Rights Act* (Cambridge University Press 2009).

The true ingenuity of the Act hinges on its treatment of the law. Eschewing the contingent power of the Canadian courts to strike down legislation so long as there is no 'notwithstanding' clause, the HRA specifically preserves the sovereignty of Parliament – and (following the logic of this position) the legality of the acts of public servants which are designed to realise that sovereignty, however preposterous such acts might be (or be thought to be).[40] However – and now rejecting the New Zealand paradigm – the HRA equips the judges to make what it calls 'declarations of incompatibility' where such inconsistencies are thrown up in the course of litigation.[41] The key to understanding these is to grasp that they lack the usual legal force one associates with judicial remedies – they are calls for legislative attention more than they are solutions for specific clients. The Act contains an elaborate set of provisions designed to push such (non)-rulings high up the executive in-tray, and it also (at the time rather controversially) empowers ministers to act to change the law exposed as incompatible but without waiting for parliamentary authority. This is a power not a duty, though, so the government if it is determined enough can reject the court's ethical guidance.[42]

To protect the state from such adverse declarations, however, the Act creates a new and very strong principle of interpretation, demanding of the judges that they give a human rights compatible interpretation to legislation (past and future) whenever this is 'possible' to do.[43] The idea of 'possibility' is a very broad one, an invitation to the judges to push at the boundaries of interpretation in search of human rights consistent readings of statutes. This is not quite a 'Notwithstanding' clause approach – more than express disclaimers by Parliament can get it off the human rights hook – but nor is it the passive search for the intended or plain meaning of words with which English law is so familiar from generations of careful case-law. Faced with the task of applying this test of 'possibility' to cases that have come before them, the courts have done on the whole rather well, seeking first to identify what the original purpose of a statute was, then asking whether the 'possible' change being proposed (and which is necessitated by the relevant human right) goes with or against the grain of that purpose; in other words follows its general thrust rather than does violence to it.[44] Only if the latter is the case, if what the judges are being invited to do is really outside the original act, would

---

[40] See ss. 3 (2) and 6 (2).   [41] S. 4.   [42] For further details see s. 10 and Sched 2.
[43] S. 3 (1).
[44] The leading case is probably *Ghaidan* v. *Godin-Mendoza* [2004] UKHL 30, [2004] 2 AC 557, [2004] 3 WLR 113.

necessitate a kind of 'judicial vandalism',[45] do the judges throw their hands up in the air, admit the thing to be impossible and turn to their power to issue a declaration of incompatibility as a kind of consolation prize for defeat.

As with Canada, however, this has not happened very often, hardly at all. Both the Labour Administration and the Coalition Government that replaced it in 2010 have certainly done their fair share of public nagging about the negative impact of human rights but their engagement with the administrative reality of the HRA has shown a rather different side; definitive court rulings have been accepted and declarations of incompatibility have been acted on, even in situations such as those relating to executive detention after the 11 September attacks (Labour) or the protection of society from child abusers (the Coalition) which have been intensely irritating (or worse) to ministers. So far as the first of these is concerned, a declaration of incompatibility issued in December 2004 by a majority ruling of the appellate committee of the House of Lords (the then-highest court in the country) essentially condemned (but, following the scheme of the Act, without prohibiting) those provisions in the Anti-terrorism, Crime and Security Act 2001 which had allowed the detention without charge not of suspected terrorists as such but only of those of them who were foreign and who could not be expelled from the country in the ordinary way since no place could be found to take them which would not itself threaten their basic rights upon arrival.[46] The judges accepted the executive judgement that the country faced an emergency but condemned as irrational and unacceptably discriminatory the restriction to *foreign* suspects – were there no 'home-grown threats' they asked, a question without the possibility of a negative answer, the point being tragically hammered home in the London bombings six months' later. At the time ministers took grave exception to the challenge to their authority on such a basic issue as that of national security but they nevertheless accepted the ruling, bringing the regime to an end and replacing it with a complex framework of control orders, itself designed to be compatible with human rights law and applicable to British and non-British alike.[47] The UK's commitment to legality is shown by these cases to be deep indeed.

---

[45] *R (Anderson)* v. *Secretary of State for the Home Department* [2002] UKHL 46, [2003] 1 AC 837, para. 30.

[46] *R (A)* v. *Secretary of State for the Home Department* [2004] UKHL 56, [2005] 2 AC 68, [2005] 2 WLR 87.

[47] Prevention of Terrorism Act 2005; these orders have since been replaced by other, similar measures.

Acceptance of the child abuse register case demonstrates the interesting way in which this framework of human rights is bedding down in the UK.[48] A UK prime minister loudly and vocally opposed to the HRA nevertheless found himself arguing in Parliament for the implementation of a declaration of incompatibility issued by the Supreme Court which had insisted on a degree of procedural fairness even for that class of person whose behaviour had become so much the focus of negative attention in recent years, child abusers. Typically the law to force them onto registers had had an adverse impact on individuals out of all proportion to its social worth, and the judges had said so – albeit without (just as in the detention case) having the power to force the government's hand. Blaming the judges in an understandable but still tasteless exercise in political self-protection (insisting wrongly that the judges had required him to act) Mr Cameron nevertheless went along with what human rights deemed necessary.[49] There is a regional dimension to the UK's compromise – the need to adhere to the ECHR – which may yet lead to a ECtHR ruling to the effect that all declarations of incompatibility have to be enforced or the UK will be in default of its promise (under Article 13 of the Convention) to guarantee effective remedies for breaches of the Convention.[50] But the mini-constitutional crisis that this is likely to inspire is not yet on the horizon. For now the internalisation of human rights within democracy that the UK model illustrates is an innovative effort to square the circle between democracy and human rights in a way that retains a degree of integrity for both ideas.

It is also proving to be popular. When the Irish found themselves having to implement the ECHR into their domestic law (as part of their obligations under the arrangements that had brought political violence to an end in Northern Ireland) it was to the British model that they turned – their 2003 European Convention on Human Rights Act replicates the essential features of the 1998 measure. In Australia, the debate about rights has increasingly taken a British shape, with the Australian Capital

---

[48] *R (F)* v. *Secretary of State for the Home Department* [2010] UKSC 17, [2011] 1 AC 331, [2010] 2 WLR 992.

[49] 'David Cameron condemns supreme court ruling on sex offenders' *Guardian* 16 February 2011, www.guardian.co.uk/society/2011/feb/16/david-cameron-condemns-court-sex-offenders (date of last access 27 March 2012). The 'minimum possible changes to the law' were promised, but without any acknowledgement that the minimum possible was none at all.

[50] See *Burden* v. *United Kingdom* app. 13378/05, 12 December 2006 (Chamber); 29 April 2008 (Grand Chamber), para. 43.

Territory having adopted a UK-style law[51] and other states having either followed suit or adapted still more diluted versions of the same set of basic ideas.[52] There are so few such traditional democracies left that there are not many places with the opportunity to create a new set of relationships between democracy and human rights along British lines. But for democrats wedded to the potentially infinite capacity of elected government, but aware of the unavoidability of human rights-talk at the present time, it represents the best way of managing the conflict between these ideas – whose complementarity (I have argued here) is more apparent than real. The cover of cohesion survives only because democracy does not challenge in any kind of radical way the preservation of individual rights (including especially property rights) that is the main *raison d'être* of (and reason for the success of) human rights in the post-1945 era. But what would happen if a domestic democratic polity were determinedly to wrench itself free of the strictures of rights law? It is with this general question that I end this chapter.

The limits of law's empire

Let us suppose two scenarios. In one a radical socialist government has been elected to office in a democracy; in the other a right-wing nationalist party has achieved the same. Neither scenario is perhaps as unthinkable as each once was, with much of the world still deeply affected by the damaging impact of the collapse of the financial markets at the end of the first decade of the twenty-first century. Suppose that the socialist government legislates for the confiscation of much private property, the nationalisation of some profitable industry and a vast increase in the power of the bureaucratic state in the fields of planning and environmental regulation, while our hypothetical nationalist administration leaves the structures untouched but goes after immigrants and asylum seekers in a dramatically aggressive way. In both cases the challenge to

---

[51] Human Rights Act 2004 (ACT).

[52] See, for example, Victoria's Charter of Human Rights and Responsibilities Act 2006. See for a very interesting discussion of the response of Australian politicians to rights-talk, C. Evans and S. Evans, 'Messages from the Front Line: Parliamentarians' Perspectives on Rights Protection', in T. Campbell, K. D. Ewing and A. Tomkins (eds.), *The Legal Protection of Human Rights: Sceptical Essays* (Oxford University Press 2011) Ch 16 329–46.

human rights law would be clear – but what could that law do by way of reply? If the system were one based on the British model just discussed, then the answer would seem to be next to nothing: the government could either ignore all the declarations of incompatibility that followed from their actions or (if these bothered them) use their parliamentary majority to secure repeal of the Act. If rights were protected on the US model then clearly more could on paper be done – laws could be struck down, the Constitution as interpreted by the judges used as a shield against the passing wishes of today's tyrannical majority. But in a democratic system, for how long could this last?

In a famous book, Alexander Bickel called the US Supreme Court 'the least dangerous branch'[53] and by that he meant that its effectiveness was dependant on others, or to put it another way such tribunals are always at risk of President Andrew M. Jackson's famous reputed response to a negative Supreme Court ruling of Chief Justice Marshall in 1832: 'John Marshall has made his decision; now let him enforce it.'[54] In 1940 the then-President of the Irish Free State's Executive Council reacted to an adverse ruling of the Irish Supreme Court by re-enacting the impugned measure with relatively insubstantial changes and contriving to have the matter sent right back for reconsideration (the stratagem worked).[55] And if all else fails the judges can simply be frog-marched out of their offices never to return, as happened – more or less – to Zimbabwe's unfortunate chief justice Anthony Gubbay in 2001. Only the most sheltered of lawyers can believe that words on paper matter entirely independently of the world around them, a world upon which they entirely rely for any substantive impact they might happen to have.

Does this leave, then, the elected branch – however distorted, immoral, misguided or brutal – in the position of guaranteed victor over the human rights ideal as this is realised in judicially guaranteed codes of basic rights? This states the matter too baldly. Our hypotheticals are extreme cases, and the culture of human rights, rooted in legal practice but also in a society's common sense of basic standards, serves to support the ethical status quo against such plunges into extremism. In both the constitutional and UK

---

[53] Reissued in 1986 with a new foreword by Harry Wellington (New Haven, CT: Yale University Press 1986).

[54] *Worcester* v. *Georgia* 31 US (6 Pet.) 515 (1832).

[55] *The State (Burke)* v. *Lennon and the Attorney General* [1940] IR 136 followed by *In re the Offences Against the State (Amendment) Bill 1940* [1940] IR 470.

models, the elevation of the protection of human rights above ordinary politics serves as a kind of 'commitment check', an inhibition against just these kinds of populist plunges into a dark future in which all talk of human rights is rendered irrelevant and/or futile. The term can also defend itself further by re-grouping as a set of particular values rather than simply this over-arching one of human rights: there are many who might think the idea of human rights too vague to be defended but who would go to the barriers to defend the principle of the rule of law or to support the idea of free speech. There is a procedural dimension to each of these that takes them away from policy and into the very machinery of government upon which democracy depends: judgements will be more likely to be successfully received where they can be presented as protective of the democratic and/or constitutional status quo rather than as interventions (under the guise of 'human rights') on this or that policy issue. But even here the judgements do not succeed merely because they have been pronounced. The paradox of judicial reasoning in the field of human rights is that to be successful it must always be sensitive to its political context while seeming utterly to ignore exactly this in all its public utterances.

Further reading

Blackburn, R. and Polakiewicz, J. (eds.), *Fundamental Rights in Europe: The European Convention on Human Rights and its Member States, 1950–2000* (Oxford University Press 2001)

Campbell, T., Ewing, K. D. and Tomkins, A. (eds.), *The Legal Protection of Human Rights* (Oxford University Press 2011)

Cox, A., *The Court and the Constitution* (Boston, MA: Houghton Mifflin 1987)

Fenwick, H., Phillipson, G. and Masterman, R. (eds.), *Judicial Reasoning under the UK Human Rights Act* (Cambridge University Press 2009)

Gardbaum, S., 'How Successful and Distinctive is the Human Rights Act? An Expatriate Comparatist's Assessment' (2011) 74 (2) *Modern Law Review* 195–215

Gearty, C. A., 'The Paradox of United States Democracy' (1992) 26 *University of Richmond Law Review* 259–79

Principles of Human Rights Adjudication (Oxford University Press 2004)

Gilbert, G., Hampson, F. and Sandoval, C., *Strategic Visions for Human Rights: Essays in Honour of Professor Kevin Boyle* (Abingdon: Routledge 2011)

Hoffman, D., *The Impact of the UK Human Rights Act on Private Law* (Cambridge University Press 2011)

Kavanagh, A., *Constitutional Review under the Human Rights Act* (Cambridge University Press 2009)

Klug, F. and Gordon, J. (eds.), '10th Anniversary of the Human Rights Act' (2010) (6) *Special Issue, European Human Rights Law Review* 551–630

Mandel, M., 'A Brief History of the New Constitutionalism, or "How We Changed Everything so that Everything Remained the Same"' (1998) 32 *Israel Law Review* 250–00

Manokha, I., *The Political Economy of Human Rights Enforcement* (Basingstoke: Macmillan 2008)

Meckled-García, S. and Çali, B. (eds.), *The Legalization of Human Rights* (New York: Routledge 2006)

Moyn, S., *The Last Utopia: Human Rights in History* (Cambridge, MA: Harvard University Press 2010)

Devoluted human rights[1] 12

Chris Himsworth

To combine in the same mindscape the separate ideas of human rights protection and of devolution prompts a number of thoughts. Some may be at quite a high level of generality; some much more specific to the arrangements of a particular state. At the most general level one might first have in mind the contribution that the study of devolution might make to an understanding of those processes whereby rights, first formulated and proclaimed at an international level, may 'cascade' down to the level of the nation state and then to regions within that state and perhaps beyond. This might be seen as a process in which there is an increasing degree of specificity of the rights to be applied – perhaps involving an idea of an initial rights baseline which may be enhanced to a higher degree of rights protection (however such a notion is to be understood[2]) or customised to take account of the conditions – political, social or legal – particular first to the state and then to the regions of a state. If such a cascading vision is to be adopted, it has presumably to be routinely assumed that this process is one that will not be wholly unproblematic. Some of the conditions, specific to a state or region, may, at least at first, conflict, either in their substance or their procedures, with the cascaded rights. Rights deriving from prior national or regional (e.g. Europe-level) rights may not chime precisely with existing 'rights' at the devolved level. Judicial procedures for the enforcement of rights (including, for instance, those rules which determine who may seek the enforcement of rights, on what time scale and in the expectation of what remedies) may also adjust only with some difficulty to the enforcement of the newer generation of rights. Rules and procedures may well be necessary for the resolution of uncertainties of hierarchy to decide which rights rules should prevail. Institutions (presumably mainly courts but not exclusively so) need to be empowered to apply these rules of conflict

---

[1] The style 'devoluted' seems better suited than the more familiar 'devolved' to capture the convolutions of the condition of human rights in devolved Scotland.

[2] On the problems of understanding such 'higher' levels of rights protection, see, e.g., J. H. H. Weiler, *The Constitution of Europe* (Cambridge University Press 1999) 102–7.

resolution, an issue which may be of particular concern where there is some expectation of a degree of uniformity in the application of rights and yet also a sensitivity to local conditions.

Injected into these general considerations about tiers of rights and their protection is a more specific concern about the divergence of purpose between the process of devolving power and the process of incorporating rights protection into a devolution settlement. To the person in the devolved street, there may appear to be no conflict between the idea of combining a new form of democratic governance with new protections of human rights. They may be readily linked as simply two perfectly compatible aspects of the same reform project. To the devolved institutions of government, however, whether legislative or executive, the two strands may easily be in conflict. They have received a new set of freedoms to act within their defined areas of competence and yet these new freedoms may appear to be curbed by the restrictions imposed out of respect for the newly defined human rights of the population[3] – in a situation which may appear not too dissimilar to the situation of those former British colonies liberated on independence to legislate and to govern with a new freedom which is suddenly subordinated to obligations to respect the newly defined human rights of their citizens, obligations which the imperial state had never chosen to impose on its own forms of government prior to independence.[4]

Before we move on to consider these questions with greater specificity in relation to devolution in the UK and, in particular, Scotland, an acknowledgement should be made of the importance of the national (i.e. UK-level) dimension of the human rights project. When rights were to be 'brought home'[5] under the Blair government in 1997–8, this was a policy to be implemented across the UK as a whole. It was the UK that was the party to the European Convention on Human Rights (ECHR); it was the UK Government's responsibility to ensure, that the state's obligations under the Convention were observed; and it was the UK Government's view that this would best be done by a form of 'incorporation'[6] of the Convention

---

[3] See, e.g., A. C. Cairns, *Charter versus Federalism: The Dilemmas of Constitutional Reform* (Montreal: McGill–Queen's University Press 1992).

[4] See, e.g., S. A. de Smith, *The New Commonwealth and its Constitutions* (London: Stevens & Sons 1964) Ch 5.

[5] See *Bringing Rights Home* (Cm 3782 1997).

[6] For the argument that the HRA 1998 did not truly 'incorporate' the Convention, see, e.g., the then Lord Chancellor at HL Debs, 585, col. 422 (5 February 1998).

rights by legislation passed by the UK Parliament to apply across the country as a whole. There was an underlying assumption – an assumption which has been sustained during the period since the Human Rights Act (HRA) 1998 was passed – that the international treaty base of the rights demanded a high degree of harmonisation (if not uniformity) of observance and implementation of rights and that the means of achieving this through UK-level judicial supervision was in the form, initially, of the (Appellate Committee of the) House of Lords and the Judicial Committee of the Privy Council (JCPC) and, latterly (since October 2009), of the UK Supreme Court.[7] Prior to the passing of the HRA, there was a much weaker recognition of 'human rights' as a formal element in the UK constitutional order. 'Civil liberties' was the more usual language and, although such liberties might be reinforced by legislation passed by the UK Parliament, there was no insistence that they should have a UK character overall.

But the period since the HRA has been different. The experience of so much ECHR-oriented litigation and so many important issues being propelled into the top courts has inevitably given the human rights project a stronger UK-level character. This has been a position reinforced by the debates generated in the later years of the Labour Governments to 2010 and, since 2010, of the Coalition (Conservative–Liberal Democrat) Government to produce a British or UK Bill of Rights either to replace or to supplement the HRA.

Against that backdrop of the HRA as a UK-level project, we have now to turn to its devolutionary aspects, and with particular reference to Scotland. In doing so, we have to recognise that, as a manifestation of sub-state government, there is indeed something special about devolution – in the form, at least, that it has taken in the UK; and that there is something special – many special things, in fact – about Scotland. By the 'specialness' of devolution is meant that, as opposed to the situation of federalism with the federal–state relationship governed by an overarching written constitution guaranteeing an autonomy protection to both tiers, both devolution and human rights protection were projects of the UK Government and Parliament and remain, in the manner assumed by the underlying doctrine of parliamentary supremacy, formally subject to the overall supervision and regulation of the UK Parliament. This is a familiar (if evolving) feature of the

---

[7] See, e.g., the debate on reforming the law on appeals on human rights grounds to the UK Supreme Court, 240.

UK Constitution. It is not, therefore, surprising to the constitutional observer. But the consequences of both the human rights and the devolution regimes remaining malleable at the hand of the UK Parliament rather than their being protected from unilateral amendment by Parliaments at both levels are of enduring significance.

In the specific case of Scotland, these consequences have three inter-related characteristics. The first is the relationship – which has turned out to be one of considerable technical complexity – between the HRA and the Scotland Act 1998. But, secondly, that relationship has to be understood against a constitutional and political backdrop that has produced conflict about the sustainability of the HRA but, more importantly, concerning also the devolution 'settlement' created by the Scotland Act. The situation has, in particular, been complicated by the election in Edinburgh of a minority SNP Government from 2007, and a majority SNP Government from 2011. And, thirdly, there is an interaction between the combined devolution and human rights projects, sustainable or not, and that other feature of the UK which has made it a country, in ways dating back long before devolution, of three separate legal systems – England and Wales, Northern Ireland and Scotland. Scotland is not only one of the components of the UK's asymmetric devolution arrangements but is also home to a legal system of its own.[8] These three characteristics and the ways in which they interact will be considered in the sections that follow.

The HRA and the Scotland Act 1998[9]

In certain respects, the 'incorporation' of the ECHR by means of the HRA operates to exactly the same effect in Scotland as it does in all other parts of the UK. Thus, for instance, the obligations on public authorities to behave in ways compatible with Convention rights and the obligations of courts to enforce those rights are straightforwardly applicable in Scotland – even if the particular public authorities may be different and the courts are also different. The obligations of Scottish courts in the face of UK legislation found to be incompatible with Convention rights[10] are the same as those of

---

[8] See C. M. G. Himsworth, 'Devolution and its Jurisdictional Asymmetries' (2007) 70 *MLR* 31.

[9] For an early analysis, see S. Tierney, 'Convention Rights and the Scotland Act: Redefining Judicial Roles' (2001) *PL* 38.

[10] HRA s. 4.

courts in other parts of the UK. The superimposition of devolution does, however, make some differences and if, for instance, a court makes a declaration of incompatibility in respect of a provision in a UK Act within a sector of legislative competence now devolved under the Scotland Act to the Scottish Parliament, then any obligation to legislate to remove the incompatibility falls on that Parliament and the power to make a 'remedial order' is available to the Scottish Ministers rather than to a UK-level minister.[11]

But the consequences of devolution go much deeper. In common with the provision made for the other devolved territories,[12] special provision was made in the Scotland Act to impose on the Scottish Parliament and also on the Scottish Executive[13] human rights obligations over and above those imposed by the HRA. In addition to other restrictions on its competence, most notably those which restrain it from legislating on reserved matters such as foreign affairs, tax and social security, the Scottish Parliament is specifically prohibited from legislating in a way which is incompatible with Convention rights.[14] It is beyond its competence to do so. And the same applies to acts of the Scottish Government. In relation to the Scottish Parliament this has the important constitutional consequence that its status as a legislature inferior to the UK Parliament is formally reconfirmed. The Scotland Act provisions reinforce these in the HRA that declare Acts of the Scottish Parliament (ASPs) to be 'subordinate legislation'[15] in contrast with the UK Parliament's 'primary legislation'. Not for the Scottish Parliament the benefit of mere declarations of incompatibility under s. 4 of the HRA. Any provision in an ASP held to be incompatible with Convention rights is 'not law'[16] and invalid. Even if this is a feature that is arguably wholly

---

[11] See, e.g., the Sexual Offences Act 2003 (Remedial) (Scotland) Order 2010 (SSI 2010/370), but see also SSI 2011/45.

[12] See Government of Wales Act 1998 (and the Government of Wales Act 2006), Northern Ireland Act 1998.

[13] For a long time now, and especially since the SNP came into power in 2007, the Scottish Executive has been informally known as the 'Scottish Government'. The Scotland Act 2012 has made it the official term. Throughout this chapter, 'Scottish Government' is used.

[14] S. 29 (2)(d).   [15] S. 21 (1).

[16] Scotland Act s. 29 (1). Until very recently, this had never occurred but, in February and March 2012, provisions in the Criminal Procedure (Scotland) Act 1995 (inserted by the Criminal Justice and Licensing (Scotland) Act 2010) and the Agricultural Holdings (Scotland) Act 2003 were held to be outwith competence. See *Cameron* v. *Cottam* 2012 SLT 173 and *Salveson* v. *Riddell* [2012] CSIH 26, respectively.

consistent with the formal subordination of the Scottish Parliament in the structure of devolution, surely it inevitably gives rise to sensitivities about its status vis-à-vis the courts and the UK Parliament?

Another distinguishing and related feature of the Scotland Act is that it provides special procedural machinery for the determination of questions which arise for resolution by courts as to the competence of either the Scottish Parliament or the Scottish Government. These procedures apply as much to questions involving Convention rights compatibility as they do to competence challenges on any other grounds. Such competence challenges are defined as 'devolution issues'.[17] The detail of the procedures that they attract need not be addressed here. There is mention below, however, of the role of the law officers (at both the Scottish and UK levels) in relation to devolution issues and also of the circumstances in which the provisions permit not only civil law questions but also human rights issues arising in the Scottish criminal courts to be taken to the UK Supreme Court.

Despite these special substantive and procedural rules contained in the Scotland Act, there was a clear intention from the start that the human rights provisions of that Act should operate entirely harmoniously with the provisions of the HRA itself. For this purpose, some obvious precautions were taken and, at relevant points in the Scotland Act, definitions of terms in the HRA were adopted – in relation to 'Convention rights' themselves, 'victims' of violations, and available remedies.[18] Not everything, however, has gone wholly smoothly. Quite apart from the issues of high political and constitutional difficulty relating to the conduct of criminal trials (on which see further below), the interweaving of the two statutory regimes has been far from comfortable. One illustration of this was the explosive confrontation that took place in the *Somerville* Case.[19] In a human rights challenge raised as a devolution issue against the Scottish Prison Service, the most contentious issue was whether the petitioners' case was time-barred. The Scottish Ministers defended the action by claiming that, although the Scotland Act was itself silent on the matter, the twelve-month time bar of the HRA should be read into the Scotland Act as well. In short, this approach was approved by the Inner House of the Court of Session but was then, in a robust critique of the lower court, denied on appeal to the House of Lords. The case involved a conflict between two different visions of the

---

[17] Scotland Act s. 98 and Sched. 6.   [18] See s. 126 (1), s. 100 (1) and s. 100 (3), respectively.
[19] *Somerville* v. *Scottish Ministers* 2008 SC (HL) 45.

relationship between the two Acts.[20] The House of Lords preferred the view that, in contrast with the style adopted in the HRA, the Scotland Act placed Convention rights' compatibility on the same footing as other restrictions on the competence of the Scottish Parliament and Government. In respect of challenges on grounds of lack of competence, there could be no time bar. The consequence of the decision was, after a long delay and much acrimony between the Scottish and UK Governments, that the Scottish Parliament was given the authority to establish a time bar by Act of the Scottish Parliament.[21]

If *Somerville* (and its aftermath) illustrates some of the problems inherent in the operationalisation in tandem of the two reforming projects contained in the HRA and the Scotland Act, other questions can arise about how the two projects interact. Two broad areas will be considered in what follows. First, there is the question of how devolution impacts on any possible further reform of human rights law. Secondly, we shall consider the vexed issue of how human rights law has impacted on the conduct of criminal trials in Scotland. Beyond examination of the current rules applicable to devolution and to human rights protection, these two case studies illustrate rather vividly some of the questions generated by the current politics of Scottish devolution.

A new UK Bill of Rights?

In two broad senses, the passing of the HRA was never likely to be the last word on the development in the UK of human rights protection by law. In the first place, there could be institutional innovation designed to promote the cause of human rights, either in direct support of the HRA initiative or at least to make a contribution in a complementary field. Secondly, there have been proposals to replace or substantially to modify the HRA regime, whether in the direction of strengthening or amplifying its existing provision or in the direction of weakening its impact, in particular by disengaging the regime to a greater or lesser degree from its Convention roots and from the authority of the Strasbourg Court. Both of these projects raise

---

[20] See C. M. G. Himsworth, 'Conflicting Interpretations of a Relationship' (2008) 12 *Edinburgh Law Review* 321.

[21] The Scotland Act 1998 (Modification of Schedule 4) Order 2009, SI 2009/1380 enabled the passing of the Convention Rights Proceedings (Amendment) (Scotland) Act 2009.

important devolution-related questions because of the division of competences that the Scotland Act and the other devolution Acts have produced.
This is neatly illustrated, in relation to post-1998 institutional developments by the creation, on the one hand, of the Equality and Human Rights
Commission,[22] and, on the other, of the Scottish Human Rights Commission
(SHRC).[23] The first is a UK-level Commission (with an outpost in Glasgow)
with a general responsibility to promote and monitor human rights, and to
protect, enforce and promote equality. The SHRC also has the task of
promoting human rights. The parallel existence of the two institutions
reflects the terms of the devolution settlement. Although the HRA itself is
a UK measure and is protected from amendment by the Scottish
Parliament,[24] 'human rights' are not, in terms, reserved under the
Scotland Act and it was, therefore, seen as wholly competent for the
Scottish Parliament to legislate to establish the SHRC. On the other hand,
the Scotland Act *does* exclude from the Parliament's competence the power
to legislate on equal opportunities[25] and the UK-level Equality Commission
has correctly been given powers in those areas by the UK Parliament. That
Commission is expressly prohibited from straying into areas within the
SHRC's own remit.[26]

When one turns to the ways in which the HRA regime might itself be
reformed or replaced, two principal projects fall to be considered. One was
the proposal in 2007 of the Labour Government for the introduction of a
new Bill of Rights[27] and, in 2009, a Bill of Rights and Responsibilities.[28]
More recently, and still at the time of writing, there has been the
Conservative–Liberal Democratic Government's establishment, in accordance with its Coalition Agreement of May 2010,[29] of a Human Rights
Commission with a remit to investigate the case for a UK Bill of Rights.
Although very different in their underlying political motivations and in
their intended objectives, these projects have had the common feature that

---

[22] Equality Act 2006, Part I.   [23] Scottish Commission for Human Rights Act 2006.
[24] Scotland Act, Sched. 4, para. 1 (2)(f). It is understood that the (Westminster) Health and
Social Care Act 2008 was viewed as 'modifying' the HRA (although not amending its actual
text) and thus, in relation to Scotland, beyond the legislative competence of the Scottish
Parliament. That Parliament passed no legislative consent motion.
[25] SA Sched. 5 Part II, S L21.   [26] Equality Act 2006 s. 7.
[27] *The Governance of Britain*, Cm 7170.
[28] *Rights and Responsibilities: Developing our Constitutional Framework*, Cm 7577.
[29] Coalition Programme for Government Ch 3.

they are conducted, quite deliberately, at the UK level. They have had a shared concern to customise in a British way the ECHR-oriented HRA.

Under the conditions of devolution these projects inevitably create sensitivities in the devolved parts of the UK. In Northern Ireland, not only the current mechanisms of devolution but also the condition of peace itself may depend upon the continued honouring of the Belfast Agreement 1998, and the Northern Ireland Human Rights Commission has, within that framework, been consulting on a proposal for a Northern Ireland Bill of Rights.[30] The disruptive intrusion of a 'British' – the terminology itself inevitably creates antagonisms – initiative might be very damaging.[31] But, even in the less precarious conditions of Scotland, questions are raised. These have a combined technical and constitutional character.

Towards the technical end of the scale are questions of competence under the Scotland Act. Of course, both on the strength of the general theory of UK parliamentary supremacy and the terms of s. 28 (7) of the Scotland Act, the UK Parliament can legislate on *any* matter – the feature that principally distinguishes devolution from federalism. But in a constitutional context in which there has been an acknowledgement that, in terms of the 'Sewel Convention' (whose obligations, although devised by a Labour Government, appear to have been seamlessly inherited by the Coalition Government), where devolved sectors of competence are encroached upon, the consent of the Scottish Parliament (by a legislative consent motion) must be obtained, difficulties may arise. An extension of 'rights and responsibilities' into devolved fields such as education, health or criminal or administrative procedure would certainly be problematic if any doubts arose as to whether a legislative consent motion would be forthcoming. Because 'human rights' themselves are not formally reserved, even if the current HRA *is* protected under Sched. 4 to the Scotland Act, there might well be a need for a legislative consent motion if the HRA were to be repealed and replaced.

But, quite apart from technical issues of legislative competence, a British Bill of Rights project is also a matter of constitutional sensitivity in Scotland. The Labour Government's original initiative in 2007 made the error of simply ignoring any devolutionary aspect of the project. Following

---

[30] *Belfast Agreement: Rights, Safeguards and Equality of Opportunity*, para. 4.
[31] *Devolution and Human Rights* (JUSTICE) 2010. The Northern Ireland Commission on Human Rights has submitted very guarded suggestions to the Commission on a UK Bill of Rights.

criticism,[32] their 2009 document did include a chapter on devolution. The Coalition's Commission does, at least, contain two very distinguished Scottish members in Sir David Edward, former Judge in the European Court of Justice (ECJ), and Baroness Kennedy of The Shaws. The Commission is also assisted by an advisory panel which has a Welsh and Scottish membership. But the problem is not merely one of procedural inclusivity. It derives also from the sharp division within Scotland about the country's constitutional future. In that context, *any* explicitly 'British' constitutional project is potentially controversial. Since the launch of devolution and especially since the formation of the first Scottish National Party (SNP) Government in 2007, views on Scotland's future have been sharply divided between, on the one hand, the Unionist parties' vision of a UK to be strengthened by the Scotland Act 1998 and reinforced by the Scotland Act 2012 and, on the other, the SNP's commitment to an independence referendum.[33] Inevitably, any proposal for a new *British* Bill of Rights is a contentious issue. Certainly, there has been virtually no enthusiasm in Scotland for a British Bill.

Competence challenges, especially in relation to criminal proceedings

One of the principal effects of the human rights restrictions imposed by the Scotland Act upon the Scottish Parliament and Government must be that felt by members of the Scottish Government and their legal advisors as they routinely seek to ensure that executive action to be undertaken, subordinate legislation, and the content of Government Bills in the Scottish Parliament conform with the Convention rights and all other constraints on competence. Such activity is largely hidden from public view, although its consequences are seen, in summary terms, when, for instance, ministers certify Bills as within competence on their introduction into the Parliament.[34] Opportunities

---

[32] See, in particular, the Report of the Joint Committee on Human Rights, *A Bill of Rights for the UK?* (2007–8) HL 165, HC 150, vol. I Ch 3.

[33] See *Scotland's Future: Draft Referendum (Scotland) Bill Consultation Paper* (February 2010); First Minister Salmond, SPOR, 26 May 2011, col. 67.

[34] Scotland Act s. 31 (1). In addition, under s. 31 (2) the Presiding Officer must pronounce upon the competence of all Bills. Another public point at which human rights compatibility is discussed is where the Scottish Law Commission comments on legislative competence in relation to draft Bills it has prepared.

are also available during the passage of Bills for the discussion of human rights aspects.

But the highest-profile public debate on the Convention rights compatibility of measures taken by the Government or Parliament may be observed in the circumstances of challenge in the courts. In general, however, the level of such challenges has been very low. In relation to legislation, there have, thus far, been no references of enacted legislation by law officers prior to Royal Assent.[35] The number of ASPs challenged after Royal Assent can almost be counted on one hand[36] and there have been only the two recent successful challenges noted above.[37] Earlier, *Anderson* v. *Scottish Ministers*[38] was a challenge to the Parliament's first ASP, the Mental Health (Public Safety and Appeals) (Scotland) Act 1999. *Adams* v. *Scottish Ministers*[39] was one of several challenges to the Protection of Wild Mammals (Scotland) Act 2002. In *AXA General Insurance Ltd, Petitioners*,[40] the Inner House rejected a challenge by various insurance companies to the validity of the Damages (Asbestos-related Conditions) (Scotland) Act 2009 and that decision was upheld by the UK Supreme Court.[41] In general, there has also been very little by way of legal challenge to the executive action of the Scottish Ministers. Thus, if there had ever been a fear that the Scottish Government and Parliament would find themselves routinely subject to court action on the grounds of straying beyond the limits of their competence, this is a fear that has not been substantially realised in practice.

There is, however, one major qualification to this general proposition. Challenges to the acts of the Lord Advocate, taken as head of the system of criminal prosecution in trials in Scotland, have loomed very large, whether measured in terms of the significance of the issues raised or in terms of their volume. The Lord Advocate is a member of the Scottish Government. He or she must act in a Convention-compatible way – a position that derives, in particular, from s. 57 (2) of the Scotland Act that provides that a member of the Scottish Government has no power to do anything incompatible with

---

[35] Scotland Act s. 31 (2).

[36] The only significant cases so far decided on the reserved/devolved borderline (as opposed to human rights grounds) have been *Martin* v. *HMA* 2010 SC (UKSC) 40 and *Imperial Tobacco Ltd, Petitioner* 2010 SLT 179. *Sinclair Collis Ltd* v. *Lord Advocate* 2011 SLT 620 was decided on grounds of EU competence.

[37] See n. 16.   [38] 2002 SC 1.   [39] 2003 SLT 366.   [40] 2011 SLT 439.

[41] [2011] UKSC 46, 2011 SLT 1061.

Convention rights. An alleged breach of s. 57 (2) gives rise to a 'devolution issue'.[42]

A number of related effects have flowed from this positioning of the Lord Advocate under the Scotland Act. Some of the challenges based on the Lord Advocate's role as prosecutor have raised very significant issues in the conduct of the Scottish criminal justice system. Important cases have included *Starrs* v. *Ruxton*[43] in which the procurator fiscal's prosecution before a temporary sheriff was successfully challenged – on the grounds that the prosecutor could not prosecute in a court held not to be reliably 'impartial' for Article 6 ECHR purposes – and led to the abolition of the office of temporary sheriff. *R* v. *HM Advocate*[44] explored the human rights consequences of delay in criminal trials – although to different effect from the English case of *Attorney General's Reference (No. 2 of 2001)*.[45] And, most notably, in the recent cases of *Cadder* v. *HM Advocate*[46] and in *Fraser* v. *HM Advocate*[47] to be discussed further below, it has been held by the UK Supreme Court that the absence of a solicitor during pre-trial questioning and a failure to disclose information to the defence were, respectively, incompatible with the Convention.

The volume of devolution issues arising in relation to criminal prosecutions has been very substantial. One indication has been that some 10,000 had been notified to the Advocate General for Scotland (the UK Government's Scottish law officer) in the period to 2010.[48] Although only a very small proportion of these challenges have been successful, they have had, it is claimed, a delaying effect on proceedings in the courts.[49]

This situation is one that has attracted much high-profile criticism – criticism that falls broadly into two strands. The first focuses on the arguably cumbersome and delay-inducing operational aspects of the devolution issue procedures just mentioned. The second, however, derives from issues much more deeply embedded in Scottish legal culture, or at least in one version of that culture. Triggered by conditions introduced by devolution under the Scotland Act and the intersection of human rights and criminal procedure, there has been, for the first time in the 300-year period since the Union

---

[42] Discussed, e.g., in *Montgomery* v. *HMA* 2001 SC(PC) 1.   [43] 2000 JC 208.
[44] 2003 SC(PC)21.
[45] [2004] 2 AC 72. And see C. M. G. Himsworth, 'Jurisdictional Divergencies over the Reasonable Time Guarantee in Criminal Trials' (2004) 8 *Edinburgh Law Review* 255.
[46] 2010 SLT 1125.   [47] 2011 SLT 515.
[48] See para. 3.13 of the report of the Expert Group (n. 65).   [49] *Ibid.*, para. 3.12.

between Scotland and England an exposure of the top criminal appeal court in Scotland – the High Court of Justiciary – to review by a London-based court – first the JCPC, and now the UK Supreme Court. While *civil* appeals were taken to the House of the Lords from the very early days of the Union, all *criminal* appeals were disposed of finally in Edinburgh. At many points in the history of its evolution the civil appellate jurisdiction of the House of Lords has been controversial in Scotland but, at the time of the creation of the UK Supreme Court, the asymmetry was retained. There has been strong opposition from some quarters in Scotland to allowing a 'non-Scottish' court to meddle with distinctively Scottish criminal law and procedure.[50]

Although some interventions by the JCPC occurred from the early days of devolution, matters came to a head in the *Cadder*[51] case where a seven-judge UK Supreme Court overturned the decision of a seven-judge High Court in Edinburgh[52] on the issue of the Convention compatibility of practice under the Criminal Procedure (Scotland) Act 1995 in relation to the police questioning of suspects and specifically on the force of the Strasbourg Court's judgment in *Salduz* v. *Turkey*.[53]

The *Cadder* decision had three significant consequences. The first was the need for an immediate adjustment to police procedures that was achieved by the passing of an emergency Bill in the Scottish Parliament.[54] The effect of the Criminal Procedure (Legal Assistance, Detention and Appeals) (Scotland) Act 2010 was to amend the law on access to a solicitor. What was most interesting about its passage, however, was not the content of the Bill itself

---

[50] See, e.g., Lord Hope of Craighead in *R* v. *Manchester Stipendiary Magistrate, ex p Granada Television Ltd* [2001] 1 AC 300 at 304.

[51] *Cadder* v. *HM Advocate* [2010] UKSC 43, 2010 SLT 1125.

[52] *HM Advocate* v. *McLean* 2010 SLT 73.

[53] (2009) 49 EHRR 19. While the High Court had taken the view in *HMA* v. *McLean* 2010 SLT 73 that other procedural guarantees in the Scottish system were sufficient to satisfy the demands of Article 6, the Supreme Court decide that that could no longer survive the specific decision in *Salduz* on access to a lawyer.

[54] Even before the announcement of the Supreme Court decision, deliberately delayed from the hearing in May 2010 to its announcement in October, new provisional guidance was issued by the Lord Advocate. In addition to introducing the new legislation, the Government established a more wide-ranging review of criminal procedure was established under a Court of Session judge (Lord Carloway). In November 2011 Lord Carloway reported with a long list of recommendations including the abolition of the corroboration rule in Scots law. In the meantime, a series of post-*Cadder* ('sons of *Cadder*') judgments (*Ambrose* v. *Harris* [2011] UKSC 43, *HMA* v. *P* [2011] UKSC 44, *McGowan* v. *B* [2011] UKSC 54, *Jude* v. *HMA* [2011] UKSC 55) had been spelling out some of the consequences of the decision in other cases referred to it.

but the tenor of the debate in the Parliament. That debate took place on 27 October 2010[55] and it provided an opportunity for the venting of many human rights frustrations and resentments. Kenny MacAskill MSP, the Cabinet Secretary for Justice, had two principal complaints. In the first place, the devolution arrangements left the Scottish Government and Parliament open to challenge 'on each and every thing'.[56] As the First Minister put it: 'In a normal country . . . [i]f the Court of Session ruled against a person, they would have recourse to the Strasbourg Court and we would be able to argue a case in front of that court. The reason why Scotland is uniquely vulnerable is that the system in Scotland does not even allow us the right to argue the case in front of the court in whose name we are required to make the changes to Scots law.'[57] Secondly, it was, instead, the UK Supreme Court which was empowered to decide the issue and, as the Cabinet Secretary said, that court had decided in *Cadder* that Scottish practice was contrary to the ECHR – 'overturning an earlier Scottish appeal court ruling by our highest court of criminal appeal just last year . . . I will make clear to the UK Government our view that the centuries-old supremacy of the High Court as the final court of appeal in criminal matters must be restored'.[58]

The indignation was carried further by other SNP MSPs. Stewart Maxwell MSP said: 'There should be no UK Supreme Court, as we simply do not have a single legal system within the United Kingdom.'[59] He had more confidence in the decision of seven judges (including the Lord Justice General and the Lord Justice Clerk) with a lifetime of experience in the law of Scotland than in a decision of the UK Supreme Court sitting in London with a majority of English judges.[60] Dave Thompson MSP regretted that the UK Supreme Court had not respected the position and decision of the Scottish criminal appeal court of seven senior and highly respected Scottish High Court judges, 'each with a strong grasp and deep understanding of Scottish law'.[61] Although the debate also provoked in some MSPs a broader antipathy to the status of the ECHR in Scotland and the UK,[62] SNP Members confined their attention to the problems created for the Scotland by the powers of the UK Supreme Court under the Scotland Act. One particular problem they had to confront, of course, was that, for all the Supreme Court's predominantly English

---

[55] The Bill was introduced as an emergency Bill, following approval of a motion to that effect, and all stages of the Bill were taken in the one day – see SPOR (27 October 2010) cols. 29553–29585; 29611–29679.
[56] Col. 29555.   [57] Col. 29571.   [58] Col. 29557.   [59] Col. 29567.   [60] Col. 29568.
[61] Col. 29572.   [62] See, e.g., Bill Aitken MSP at cols. 29669–29670.

membership, in *Cadder*, it was the two Scottish judges who had led the attack on the Scots law rule.[63]

In consequence not only of *Cadder* but also the longer-standing criticisms of the devolution issue procedure in criminal matters,[64] the Advocate General for Scotland set up a review of the working of s. 57 (2) of the Scotland Act. The group of experts entrusted with the review was chaired by Sir David Edward, and its investigations and report[65] are significant for the wide range of views attracted in submissions to the group and then for the middle line steered in its principal recommendations. While the Scottish Government, the Scottish judiciary[66] and also the Scottish Law Commission were in favour of terminating human rights appeals to the Supreme Court, the Faculty of Advocates and the Law Society of Scotland were among those who favoured retention. The group itself recommended that alleged failings of the Lord Advocate as prosecutor should cease to be treated as 'devolution issues', but that a new form of statutory appeal to the Supreme Court on human rights (and EU) grounds should be set up in its place. These recommendations were accepted by the Advocate General and amendments to the Scotland Bill to implement them were introduced by the UK Government at the House of Commons report stage on 21 June 2011.[67]

By that time, however, the other side in the great human rights turf war was mobilising its response. Invigorated by its return to power with an overall majority on 5 May 2011, the SNP Government in Edinburgh declared its outrage at a new decision by the Supreme Court in *Fraser*.[68] In that case, the Supreme Court unanimously overturned a decision of the Appeal Court in Edinburgh to declare the conviction of the appellant unsafe on the grounds that evidence had been withheld from the defence. Indignantly and accompanied by acutely personal interventions by the First Minister and the Justice Secretary,[69] the Scottish Government declared

---

[63] See John Lamont MSP at col. 29563; Robert Brown MSP at col. 29565 and David McLetchie MSP at col. 29672.

[64] The discontents of the Scottish judges had earlier been recorded in the report of the (Calman) Commission on Scottish Devolution: *Serving Scotland Better* (2009) paras. 5.29–5.37, www.commissiononscottishdevolution.org.uk/uploads/2009-06-12-csd-final-report-2009fbookmarked.pdf.

[65] 11 November 2010, www.oag.gov.uk/oag/files/Expert%20Group%20report(1).doc.

[66] The judiciary of the Court of Session and the High Court of Justiciary.

[67] HC Debs col. 275.   [68] *Fraser* v. *HMA* 2011 SLT 515.

[69] Both were flamboyant in their criticism of current arrangements. For the First Minister, see *Holyrood Magazine* 10 June 2011. The Justice Secretary was reported to have threatened a reduction in spending on the UKSC – 'he who pays the piper calls the tune!' *Scotsman*, 2 June 2011 8.

its renewed hostility to all Supreme Court appeals in criminal matters. Its response to the Edward expert group was the setting up of a new review group under the chairmanship of former judge Lord McCluskey.[70] An interim report was demanded from the group in time for debate in the Scottish Parliament before its summer recess,[71] with a final report to follow later in the summer. Interestingly, the group stuck to the middle ground in its interim report and then in its final report[72] with a renewed recommendation that appeals to the Supreme Court should be retained – although with the rider that, seeking a degree of symmetry with English procedure,[73] appeals should reach that Court only if certified by the Appeal Court in Edinburgh as of general public importance, or following a new form of reference by the Lord Advocate or the Advocate General. It became wholly unclear how the battle between the two Governments was to be played out – whether in the initial context of the then Scotland Bill (subject, as it was, to renewed scrutiny by the Scottish Parliament under the Sewel Convention) or in the longer term. In a debate in the Scottish Parliament on 27 October 2011 on 'Scots Criminal Law (Integrity)' the antagonisms over the appellate mechanisms were once again exposed and on 15 December the Scotland Bill Committee of the Scottish Parliament reported (SP Paper 49) with recommendations that any legislative consent motion should be conditional on amendments to the Bill, including amendment of the Supreme Court provisions in line with the McCluskey recommendation.[74] In the meantime, Lord Hope responded robustly to his critics (including Lord McCluskey) in a public speech.[75] Ultimately, a compromise negotiated between the Scottish and UK Governments provided the basis of a legislative consent motion

---

[70] An interesting choice of chairman: Lord McCluskey is a retired Court of Session judge (and, earlier, a Labour Solicitor General for Scotland. He is well known for his scepticism about the reception of the ECHR into UK law (*Law, Justice and Democracy*, London: BBC 1986) and, for one consequence of views he later expressed, see *Hoekstra* v. *HM Advocate* 2000 JC 391). In a more recent article, he has expressed the view that the Supreme Court's decision in *Cadder* was 'flawed, mistaken and misconceived' ((2011) 15 *Edinburgh Law Review* 276).

[71] SPOR, 30 June 2011 col. 1226.

[72] *Examination of the Relationship between the High Court of Justiciary and the Supreme Court in Criminal Cases* (2011), www.scotland.gov.uk/Resource/Doc/254431/0120938.pdf.

[73] A symmetry contested by others. See, e.g., the submission by Sir David Edward and other members of his Expert Group to the Scotland Bill Committee of the Scottish Parliament, www.scottish.parliament.uk/S4_ScotlandBillCommittee/Inquiries/Edward_McMenamin_Boyd_Mullen.pdf.

[74] SP Paper 49.

[75] 'The Role of the Supreme Court of the United Kingdom' (19 November 2011), www.supremecourt.gov.uk/docs/speech_111119.pdf.

passed by the Scottish Parliament on 18 April and the Scotland Act 2012 was enacted. It includes[76] a series of amendments to the Scotland Act 1998 and other legislation that provide a new framework within which Scottish criminal cases may be reviewed by the UK Supreme Court on human rights grounds. Prosecution decisions by the Lord Advocate will cease to trigger 'devolution issues'.

Conclusion

It will be apparent from the debate just outlined that there are no clear conclusions to be drawn. Scotland finds itself in a highly *unsettled* devolution settlement. Far from providing a stable environment in which human rights protection might take its place alongside other opportunities for diversity in subsidiarity, the conditions of constitutional autonomy defined by the combination of devolution under the Scotland Act with the much longer-standing separateness of the Scottish legal system have produced a fluidity and antagonism which have come to be most prominently characterised by the iconic lightning conductor of human rights adjudication. It is true that this is a field that has also been one of some technicality as the precise relationship between the HRA and the Scotland Act has come to be played out, but it has, above all, become a focus for the mobilisation of disputes within the political and the judicial communities. The constitutional future of Scotland is being debated by reference to the contested authority of the Supreme Court of the UK over the human rights of accused persons in the criminal courts of Scotland and the equally contested prospect of a UK Bill of Rights.

Further reading

Boyle, A. et al. (eds.), *Human Rights and Scots Law* (Oxford University Press 2002)

Himsworth, C., 'Human Rights at the Interface of State and Sub-State: The Case of Scotland', in T. Campbell, K. D. Ewing and A. Tomkins (eds.), *The Legal Protection of Human Rights: Sceptical Essays* (Oxford University Press 2011)

'Rights versus Devolution', in T. Campbell, K. D. Ewing and A. Tomkins (eds.), *Sceptical Essays on Human Rights* (Oxford University Press 2001)

Murdoch, J., 'Protecting Human Rights in the Scottish Legal System', in A. McHarg and T. Mullen (eds.), *Public Law in Scotland* (Edinburgh: Avizandum 2006)

---

[76] Ss. 34–38.

O'Neill, A., 'Limited Government, Fundamental Rights and the Scottish Constitutional Tradition' (2009) 85 *Juridical Review* 85–128

'Human Rights and People and Society', in E.E. Sutherland *et al.* (eds), *Law Making and the Scottish Parliament* (Edinburgh University Press 2011)

Reed, R. and Murdoch, J., *A Guide to Human Rights Law in Scotland*, 3rd edn (London: Bloomsbury 2011)

Tierney, S., 'Convention Rights and the Scotland Act: Redefining Judicial Roles' (2001) 38 *Public Law* 38–49

Constitutional Law and National Pluralism (Oxford University Press 2004)

Walker, N. (ed.), *MacCormick's Scotland* (Edinburgh University Press 2012)

Does enforcement matter? 13

Gerd Oberleitner

With the adoption of the Universal Declaration of Human Rights (UDHR) in 1948, a continuing process of human rights standard-setting was set in motion, which has produced a remarkable breadth of human rights norms, standards and principles. Their importance, the changes they have introduced in the relationship between governments and individuals and the impact they exercise on the development of international law are beyond doubt, despite critical comments on the very process of creating these standards and on the future of human rights standard-setting.[1] Enforcing these norms is, however, a different story. Decades of attempts to reduce human suffering through the creation of human rights supervisory and enforcement mechanisms have dishearteningly few results to show. Despite an elaborate institutional framework for protecting these rights, gross human rights violations continue to occur and all too often seem to make a mockery of the proliferation of procedures, committees and commissions on human rights.[2]

As a consequence, human rights activists together with supportive political leadership and scholarly voices keep on calling for the strengthening of human rights enforcement. They are motivated by the realisation that there is little value in abstract rules which do not lead to visible change and that allowing states to consistently ignore human rights obligations derides and damages these very standards, discourages co-operative states and alienates civil society. Enforcing human rights is seen as important beyond the immediate effects on victims of human rights violations as it touches upon the legitimacy of the rules and the stability of the human rights system.

[1] See M. wa Mutua, 'Standard Setting in Human Rights: Critique and Prognosis' (2007) 29 *Human Rights Quarterly* 547–630, and International Council on Human Rights Policy, International Commission of Jurists and International Service for Human Rights, *Human Rights Standards: Learning From Experience* (Geneva: International Council on Human Rights Policy 2006).

[2] See G. Oberleitner, *Global Human Rights Institutions. Between Remedy and Ritual* (Cambridge: Polity 2007) 23–40.

The move from standard-setting to enforcement (or from rhetoric to action) is usually perceived as decisive for the success of human rights.

Yet the preconditions, the ways and means as well as the consequences of practically ensuring observance of international human rights norms, remain ill understood and vividly debated.[3] Even the very term 'enforcement' means different things to different people. There is disagreement on what enforcement mechanisms *ought* to achieve and there is remarkably scarce evidence as to what they *do* achieve, i.e. why human rights enforcement mechanisms succeed and fail and how we can quantitatively and qualitatively measure success. While agreement on the importance of human rights enforcement – as a general proposition – is easy enough to reach, legal and policy analysis soon reveals the obstacles, potential and paradoxes of human rights enforcement. Their better understanding is crucial so as neither to remain complacent in light of the political, legal, economic, social and cultural barriers to enforcing human rights nor to fall into the trap of becoming utopian in our expectations and endeavours. The following sections of this chapter will trace the steps that lead states from committing to human rights towards compliance with international obligations and assess how the respective means and mechanisms of enforcing human rights fare in light of the complex challenge of realising human rights in a given state and society.

Commitment, compliance, coercion

Despite all the rhetoric on the enforcement of human rights, considerable terminological confusion persists. Enforcement differs from the implementation of human rights, which describes the process of translating international obligations into the domestic sphere of nation states. It presupposes some form of commitment by states, expressed in terms of policy (e.g. through political promises) or law (e.g. through the ratification of a human rights treaty). In contrast, enforcement means ensuring observance of existing legal obligations by states, a process that is guided by international law. In a narrow sense, and by analogy with domestic law, enforcement would

---

[3] Consequently, human rights practice has now become a field of research in its own right, see P. Gready and B. Phillips, 'An Unfinished Enterprise: Visions, Reflections, and an Invitation' (2009) 1 (1) *Journal of Human Rights Practice* 1–13.

necessitate (at least potential) non-compliance with an international obligation or an actual breach of a norm, leading to retroactive remedial measures.[4] In the strict sense, this excludes assistance, advice and guidance in implementing norms (which all presuppose that there is the will to comply with a norm accompanied by the inability to do so) as well as preventive measures (which are geared towards avoiding the breach of a norm in the first place). In light of the complexities of translating international norms into the domestic sphere and the limited means available under international law, which will be discussed later on, such a narrow understanding of enforcement seems problematic in terms of human rights.

Enforcement also differs from compliance control. The former is a feature of (international) law and describes how law seeks to ensure compliance with norms by various means and methods. The latter is a construct of international relations theory that aims to shed light on the causes of non-compliance and on the management of such situations within and beyond the law.[5] While international relations theory is at hand to provide some explanations for states' commitment to and compliance with international norms in general, the situation is more puzzling when it comes to human rights. The international human rights system rests on the assumption that governments faithfully implement human rights obligations in their domestic sphere and that international procedures and institutions step in where such implementation is found to be lacking – but both of these are dubious premises. Neither is it fully understood why states feel bound by international law nor why it should be so readily assumed that international law is a framework fully suited to the task of substituting domestic processes.[6] In addition, adherence to human rights seems to offer fewer direct benefits for states than, for example, entering into trade agreements or disarmament arrangements, and is thus less open to rational arguments in favour of compliance.[7]

---

[4] See C. J. Tams, 'Enforcement', in G. Ulfstein (ed.), *Making Treaties Work: Human Rights, Environment and Arms Control* (Cambridge University Press 2007) 392–3.

[5] See J. Brunné, 'Compliance Control', in G. Ulfstein (ed.), *Making Treaties Work: Human Rights, Environment and Arms Control* (Cambridge University Press 2007) 374, with reference to the respective literature.

[6] See D. Donoho, 'Human Rights Enforcement in the 21st Century' (2006) 35 (1) *Georgia Journal of International and Comparative Law* 12.

[7] On the questions associated with the creation of international (human rights) institutions, see M. N. Barnett and M. Finnemore, 'The Politics, Power and Pathologies of International Organizations' (1999) 53 (4) *International Organization* 699–732 and Oberleitner, *Global Human Rights Institutions* 6–22.

In practice states usually see it as their prerogative to take the final decision on whether or not to follow decisions of international bodies, including those that are legally binding. And where they do accept such decisions, they usually reserve for themselves the precise manner and method of giving effect to them under domestic law.[8] A realist might thus dismiss the idea of human rights enforcement straight away and argue that occasional instances of compliance with human rights norms are not the result of legal arrangements but a response to the exercise of external power so that human rights are perhaps occasionally complied with but not consistently enforced on the international level. Such a view does not, however, do justice to the complex process of implementing international human rights norms in nation states. Harold H. Koh has termed such a transformation of international norms a 'transnational legal process'[9] in which states interact with the international legal system, interpret the respective norms and finally internalise them, to varying degrees, in their legal system. Compliance may thus take different forms, from coincidence to convenience (so as to cash in on potential incentives), obedience (so as to avoid sanctions) or internalisation (when attitudes and beliefs change in line with international norms and become constitutive behaviour).[10]

Explanations for states' adherence to human rights norms focus on rationality, legitimacy and communitarianism. Rational choice theory would grant states the freedom to decide, out of self-interest and in a cost-benefit analysis, whether to comply with them or not, so as to avoid undesired transaction costs involved with non-compliance. In a liberal sense, compliance would rather express the legitimacy of a rule, which in turn pushes states towards compliance, or it would flow from the acknowledgement of political identity rooted in liberal democracy. A communitarian view would instead emphasise the persuasive force of core values (including human dignity) and the accompanying peer pressure that drives states to respect rules.[11] Contrary to realist perceptions, it has also been argued that states, in general, enter into international commitments with the intention of complying and that non-compliance results not from an

---

[8] See Donoho, 'Human Rights Enforcement' 15–17.
[9] H. H. Koh, 'How is International Human Rights Law Enforced? (1999) 74 *Indiana Law Journal* 1399.
[10] *Ibid.*, 1400–1.
[11] See on these approaches in greater detail, B. A. Simmons, *Mobilizing for Human Rights: International Law in Domestic Politics* (Cambridge University Press 2009) 57–154.

explicit political will to break the rule but rather occurs as a result of ambiguities in the relevant norms, conflicts with other political priorities or international obligations and constraints on the capacity to comply.[12]

There is, however, more disagreement than evidence on such processes of human rights implementation. While some remain unconvinced that formal implementation (such as treaty ratification) leads to change,[13] others argue to the contrary[14] or maintain that even where norm internalisation remains on the surface, subsequent processes of acculturating human rights into societies have beneficial effects on the overall human rights situation.[15] As a consequence, enforcing international rules is thus less a question of sanction and compulsion so much as calling for managing norm-compliance through a variety of measures designed to identify and overcome its causes. A narrow understanding of human rights enforcement as coercion – in strict analogy to domestic law with its rules and institutions, i.e. parliaments, courts and police forces – misses the requirements and challenges of enforcing international obligations as well as the nature of international human rights law.

International human rights law

Enforcing human rights in the framework of international law meets with additional challenges inherent in the characteristics of this legal regime. To start with, not all of international (human rights) law has the quality of legally binding 'hard' law. Rather, varying degrees of 'hardness' of international law exist, from legally binding treaties all the way down to resolutions, guidelines, principles and bilateral and multilateral diplomatic understandings and arrangements. Indeed, the bulk of international commitments are expressed in 'soft' law, the 'enforcement' of which is (by definition) not suited to coercive measures.[16] More specific to international

---

[12] See A. Chayes and A. Handler Chayes, *The New Sovereignty: Compliance with International Regulatory Agreements* (Cambridge, MA: Harvard University Press 1995) 1–28.

[13] See O. Hathaway, 'Do Human Rights Treaties Make a Difference?' (2001–2) 111 (8) *Yale Law Journal* 1935–2042.

[14] See E. Neumayer, 'Do International Human Rights Treaties Improve Respect for Human Rights?' (2005) 49 (6) *Journal of Conflict Resolution* 950–1.

[15] See R. Goodman and D. Jinks, 'Incomplete Internationalization and Compliance with Human Rights Law' (2008) 19 (4) *European Journal of International Law* 747–8.

[16] See in detail D. Shelton, *Commitment and Compliance: The Role of Non-Binding Norms in the International Legal System* (Oxford University Press 2003).

human rights law, the continuing debate over the most appropriate forms of enforcing civil and political rights on the one hand and social, economic and cultural rights on the other necessitates an in-depth analysis of what is meant by 'enforcing' different types of norms.[17] Furthermore, the limited means of compelling states to adhere to norms under international law call for a cautious approach to enforcement, lest one creates expectations that will go unfulfilled. International bodies, including international human rights courts and criminal courts, have no enforcement agents other than co-operating states that they can turn to for getting hold of individual perpetrators or securing the respect of governments for their judgements.

Conceptually, international law understands enforcement, to a large extent, as dispute-settlement.[18] This reflects the specific nature of international law as a state-driven and state-owned framework that assigns scarce space to the individual human being (both as victim and perpetrator) but sees human rights violations primarily as disputes between states over the non-compliance with previously agreed rules. The general character of international law as an assortment of consensus-oriented treaty-type arrangements between sovereign nation states, the rudimentary participation rights of civil society actors, the missing accountability of non-state actors and the absence of a central enforcement authority together with specific rules for the protection of state sovereignty (such as the principle of non-intervention in domestic affairs[19]) all combine to promote a less than encouraging environment for the effective implementation of human rights.

Understanding the complex challenge of effectively enforcing human rights thus necessitates borrowing from the ideas of law enforcement, compliance control and dispute-settlement. In addition, the application of various possible means of enforcement depends on the specific aims pursued and necessitates answers to these questions: what do we seek to achieve when we 'enforce' human rights? Is it the protection of individual victims from violence? Or financial damages for victims of past violations?

---

[17] See M. Ssenyonjo, *Economic, Social and Cultural Rights in International Law* (Oxford: Hart 2009) 3–48.

[18] See A. L. Paulus, 'Dispute Resolution', in G. Ulfstein (ed.), *Making Treaties Work: Human Rights, Environment and Arms Control* (Cambridge University Press 2007) 359.

[19] Article 2 (7) Charter of the UN: 'Nothing contained in the present Charter shall authorize the United Nations to intervene in matters which are essentially within the domestic jurisdiction of any state.'

Or long-term changes in domestic laws and practice? Or the eradication of extreme poverty? Or the creation of a just social order, perhaps? These are just a few potential goals over the appropriate pursuance of which considerable dispute is likely to occur.

Specific means have been, and will continue to be, developed to reach these and other goals. In what follows here, these will be clustered, ascending from 'soft' forms of enforcement to 'hard' forms (although they may well blend into each other). They comprise persuasive means of human rights diplomacy, international monitoring mechanisms, responses to individual complaints, the use of international (human rights and criminal) courts, resort to incentives and sanctions, and the use of military force. Any such ranking remains, however, sketchy, as it assumes that enforcement takes place in a 'vertical' way (where sovereign states as the primary subjects of international law assert their will) whereas the reality of international affairs is increasingly characterised by a 'horizontal' approach where other stake-holders – civil society actors, non-state groups and business corporations – play a potentially powerful role. Such new governance structures within which various stake-holders are assigned rights and duties under international law are only beginning to emerge, with considerable impact on the future enforcement of human rights.[20]

Enforcing human rights is thus no mechanical imposition of rules by coercion but rather a multifaceted process of ensuring that international obligations are translated into domestic law and administration in a realistic way within the framework of international law. In addition, and perhaps more importantly and more challenging, the superior goal of enforcement should be the effective realisation of human rights in a given society at large; in other words, the building of a culture of human rights. At its very broadest, enforcement is thus aimed at internalising human rights norms and principles through processes of acculturation, adaptation, education and human rights learning in communities, above and beyond coercive and facilitative measures under international law.[21] This

---

[20] See R. McCorquodale, 'An Inclusive International Legal System' (2004) 17 (3) *Leiden Journal of International Law* 477–504. On the particularly important role of NGOs in securing compliance with human rights see, e.g., W. Korey, 'Human Rights NGOs: The Power of Persuasion' (1999) 13 (1) *Journal of Ethics and International Affairs* 151–74.

[21] See W. Benedek, 'Human Rights Education', in R. Wolfrum (ed.), *Max Planck Encyclopedia of Public International Law* (Oxford University Press 2008), www.mpepil.com (date of last access 23 December 2011).

corresponds with the vision of the UDHR that was, after all, adopted as a common standard of achievement to which not just governments but everyone should strive.[22]

Diplomacy and persuasion

Notwithstanding the creation of international institutions and mechanisms specifically dedicated to enforcing human rights, direct interaction between states continues as a means for the promotion and protection of human rights. The central provision of the UN Charter that states have to co-operate, *inter alia*, in matters of human rights[23] means that bilateral and multilateral diplomatic negotiations, international conferences, human rights dialogues and institutionalised forms of exchange of information and discussion on human rights are not only constantly at the disposal of states but – given the specific context – may be an obligation under international law.[24]

While non-confrontational and non-coercive in character, many of these consultation processes are motivated by the desire to ensure adherence to existing human rights norms. They may be convened either ad hoc in response to specific crises and human rights concerns or conducted regularly between states or groups of states. This may be the case in the framework of specific legal arrangements (such as the talks between the EU and the African, Pacific and Caribbean (APC) countries on human rights clauses in the Cotonou Agreement on development cooperation[25]) or as bilateral human rights dialogues. The EU–China human rights dialogue is a prime example for this format. Starting in 1997 and, since 2011, based on the EU Guidelines on Human Rights Dialogues,[26] it is held on the level of high

---

[22] See the Preamble of the UDHR, GA Res. 217A (III) of 10 December 1948.

[23] Article 1 (3) Charter of the UN: 'The purposes of the United Nations are ... to achieve international co-operation in solving international problems of an economic, social, cultural, or humanitarian character, and in promoting and encouraging respect for human rights and for fundamental freedoms for all without distinction as to race, sex, language, or religion.'

[24] See B. G. Ramcharan, *Contemporary Human Rights Ideas* (London: Routledge 2008) 98–114.

[25] See, e.g., S. R. Hurt, 'Co-operation and Coercion? The Cotonou Agreement between the European Union and ACP States and the End of the Lomé Convention' (2003) 24 (1) *Third World Quarterly* 161–76.

[26] EU Guidelines on Human Rights Dialogues, Council of the European Union, 13 December 2001, www.consilium.europa.eu/uedocs/cmsUpload/14469EN_HR.pdf (date of last access 23 December 2011).

political officials and is a structured question-and-answer session on mutually agreed topics. An assessment of the output of this and other dialogues shows, however, that in the absence of mutually agreed goals, appropriate impact assessment tools and meaningful linkages with other policy areas, their value for securing adherence to international obligations remains limited.[27]

Monitoring

Human rights monitoring, often referred to as human rights supervision, comprises a variety of means and mechanisms. It is the gathering of relevant information (through the provision of data, ascertaining of facts and comparative analysis) with a view to critically assessing the human rights situation in general and/or assessing the implementation of specific international human obligations by states, scrutinising and measuring their performance against the demands of international human rights law and providing recommendations for improvement. Third-party, or external, monitoring (where independent international bodies are mandated to examine states' performance) may be distinguished from peer-review processes (whereby states monitor states, for example in the Universal Periodic Review (UPR) of the UN Human Rights Council). Monitoring may be carried out as a regular and institutionalised process (such as the examination of state reports by human rights treaty bodies) or on an ad hoc basis (e.g. by Commissions of Inquiry into specific events).

Monitoring comprises different activities, none of which is aimed at coercion. Monitoring bodies engage in processes geared towards promoting human rights through consultation, justification, recommendation and persuasion. Human rights treaty bodies, for example, resort to the examination of state reports or conduct inquiry missions. Despite its shortcomings (in the form of overdue and inadequate reports) the state reporting procedure formalises consultations on human rights, links them to concrete treaty obligations and forces states to justify their actions or inaction publicly in an international arena. In the absence of any sanctions this usually works

[27] See A. Würth and F. L. Seidenstricker, *Indices, Benchmarks and Indicators: Planning and Evaluating Human Rights Dialogues* (Berlin: Deutsches Institut für Menschenrechte 2005) 39–41.

with co-operative states with a good human rights situation but is unlikely to persuade others.[28] Inquiries and fact-finding missions, such as those carried out by the European Committee for the Prevention of Torture and Inhuman or Degrading Treatment or Punishment in places of detention, are examples of a more forceful intrusion into the domestic affairs of states. The Committee's inquiry, which ends with the publication of a report, weaves together prevention, investigation, public pressure and cooperation with domestic institutions and demonstrates that meaningful supervisory mechanisms can be developed despite the limits of international law.[29]

The special procedures of the UN Human Rights Council (Special Rapporteurs, Independent Experts, Working Groups and Special Representatives of the Secretary General) are also investigative in nature. They perform a range of functions centred on studying a given human rights situation ('country procedures') or human rights issue ('thematic procedure').[30] With the creation of the UN Human Rights Council in 2006, the UPR was introduced as a peer-review process in which all UN member states are subjected to scrutiny on a regular basis. In the words of General Assembly Resolution 60/251 (which set up the Council), the Council shall 'undertake a periodic review, based on objective and reliable information, of the fulfilment by each State of its human rights obligations and commitments in a manner which ensures universality of coverage and equal treatment with respect to all States; the review shall be a co-operative mechanism, based on an interactive dialogue, with the full involvement of the country concerned and with consideration given to its capacity-building needs; such a mechanism shall complement and not duplicate the work of the treaty bodies'.[31] Despite its ambitious mandate, the first cycle of the review has demonstrated the shortcomings of such peer-review processes which allow states to escape close scrutiny more easily than other monitoring procedures.[32]

---

[28] See J. Donnelly, *International Human Rights* (Boulder, CO: Westview 2006) 88.

[29] See R. Kicker, 'The European Convention on the Prevention of Torture Compared with the United Nations Convention against Torture and its Optional Protocol', in G. Ulfstein (ed.), *Making Treaties Work: Human Rights, Environment and Arms Control* (Cambridge University Press 2007) 91–111.

[30] See Oberleitner, *Global Human Rights Institutions* 54–63.

[31] UN GA Res. 60/251, UN Doc. A/RES/60/251 of 3 April 2006, para. 5.

[32] For an analysis of the first cycle of reviews see UPR Info, *Analytical Assessment of the Universal Periodic Review 2008–2010* (2010), www.upr-info.org/IMG/pdf/UPR-Info_Analytical_assessment_of_the_UPR_2008–2010_05-10-2010.pdf (date of last access 23 December 2011).

Complaints and remedies

The process of identifying and remedying structural human rights problems is supplemented by the responses that are made to individual human rights violations. While such individual cases may be part of monitoring processes (e.g. as examples for persistent patterns of violations), the respective mechanisms do not adequately respond to the demands of victims of human rights violations for facts to be established, victims to be named and remedies to be provided. Individual complaints procedures offer such redress. Given that – legally speaking – a human rights violation is a breach of a treaty provision the observance of which has been promised to the other state parties to the treaty, such complaints are the exception to the rule as they allow individuals to directly access an international body with a claim against a state. This is where they differ from inter-state complaints, which have never been used in the UN human rights system and only rarely under the European Convention on Human Rights (ECHR),[33] as no state is easily willing to sacrifice its relations to another state for the sake of responding to individual human rights violations.

Individual complaints procedures appear more rigorous than other monitoring procedures as they seem to produce a judgement-like result where monitoring procedures merely ask for justifications. This analogy is, however, misleading. Following the exhaustion of domestic remedies, individuals submit information to treaty bodies rather than file a court case, and while the decision on a violation of specific treaty provisions is accompanied by recommendations for remedies, their precise contours are left to the state. The conclusions of treaty bodies are not legally binding for state parties; nor can their implementation be enforced. Despite the importance such decisions can have for the development of international human rights law, the immediate effects for the victims may be disappointing. Calls for reform thus include, first and foremost, a more consistent follow-up of treaty body decisions to exert pressure on states to comply with the respective findings.[34]

---

[33] See M. E. Villiger, 'The European Convention on Human Rights', in G. Ulfstein (ed.), *Making Treaties Work: Human Rights, Environment and Arms Control* (Cambridge University Press 2007) 79.

[34] See M. O'Flaherty, 'Reform of the UN Human Rights Treaty Body System: Locating the Dublin Statement' (2010) 10 (2) *Human Rights Law Review* 319–35.

Complaints may also be filed to political bodies such as the UN Human Rights Council. The lessons learned by the precursor of the Council, the Commission on Human Rights – that it cannot restrict itself merely to adopting standards and remain unconcerned with actual human rights violations – led to two procedures, the so-called 1235 and 1503 procedures, named after resolutions of the Economic and Social Council (ECOSOC). While the former provided the basis for human rights monitoring of all countries the latter allowed for communications on consistent patterns of gross human rights violations to be sent to the Commission. Despite a heavy critique of among other matters the rigid filtering mechanism that was deployed (allowing for only a handful of states to be considered every year), the confidential nature of the process and its questionable impact,[35] the procedure has been carried over to the Human Rights Council. Effectively, it represents an 'information-petition system'[36] as it uses petition-like submissions by different sources to ascertain information on systematic human rights violations rather than providing remedies for individuals.

International courts

Resorting to international courts and tribunals to adjudicate human rights violations seems, *a priori*, the most promising means of enforcing human rights and one that is true to a coercive understanding of enforcement. Again, however, one should not fall into the trap of a misleading analogy with the legal systems of nation states and the ways in which domestic courts ensure (with the assistance of law enforcement agencies) respect for the law. International courts are of a different nature, as they adjudicate on state responsibility under international law and as such are – with the exception of specifically created human rights courts – not accessible to victims of human rights violations. This is true, first and foremost, for the International Court of Justice (ICJ). The Court's Statute allows only states to be parties in cases before it; individuals, judicial persons and non-governmental organisations (NGOs) are excluded, and even state

[35] See Z. Kedzia, 'United Nations Mechanism to Promote and Protect Human Rights', in J. Symonides (ed.), *Human Rights: Protection, Monitoring, Enforcement* (Aldershot: Ashgate 2003) 65–6.
[36] J. Rehman, *International Human Rights Law*, 2nd edn (London: Longman 2010) 54.

parties have specifically to consent to their cases being brought before the Court.[37] While the Court has taken decisions on human rights, most prominently in the Advisory Opinion on the *Legal Consequences of the Construction of a Wall in the Occupied Palestinian Territory* Case in 2004,[38] it is far from a human rights court.

In contrast, the regional human rights courts in Europe, Africa and in the Inter-American human rights system provide for legally binding judgments and remedies for individual human rights violations that may include financial damages. They differ in their remit and functions, with the European Court of Human Rights (ECtHR) leading in terms of its jurisdiction (covering more than 800 million individuals in 47 states) and more than 10,000 binding judgments rendered since 1959.[39] In light of this success, it is tempting to see the Court as the ultimate form of human rights enforcement and a blueprint to be followed everywhere. This would, of course, neglect the problems it faces. Over the years, the enormous increase in applications has brought the Court to its knees and necessitates constant reform; a reform in which the *raison d'être* of international human rights courts is at stake: should they be supreme court-types of institutions with jurisdiction over only the most important cases or should they be accessible to all as a final appellate body on human rights?[40] And lest we forget: even the Court's legally binding decisions need to be finally executed by, and within, nation states in a process which is driven by the same tension between power, law and politics which other human rights institutions experience.

Replicating the Court elsewhere in the hope of a mechanical improvement of the human rights situation would also mean ignoring the intricate link between the success of human rights enforcement mechanisms and the environment in which they function. It is a general lesson to be learned: while success and failure of human rights enforcement mechanisms may well be attributed to their institutional design, legal framework and political legitimacy (in all of which the ECtHR may well be considered above average), the close link between the successful implementation of human rights and

---

[37] Article 34 (1) Statute of the International Court of Justice.

[38] Legal Consequences of the Construction of a Wall in the Occupied Palestinian Territory. Advisory Opinion. ICJ Reports 2004 136.

[39] See ECtHR, *50 Years of Activity: The European Court of Human Rights. Some Facts and Figures* (Strasbourg: Council of Europe 2010) 4–6.

[40] See L. Wildhaber, 'Rethinking the Future of the European Court of Human Rights', in J. Christoffersen and M. R. Madsen (eds.), *The European Court of Human Rights Between Law and Politics* (Oxford University Press 2011) 205–30.

democratic and economic development necessitates a careful consideration of the context. This is, after all, what makes both the design of human rights institutions and the measurement of their success and failure so difficult.

Notably, there is no international court of human rights with a global reach. Despite suggestions to create such an institution in 1946, there have never been concerted calls and even less sustained efforts to create such an institution – the idea of a global human rights jurisprudence has seemed too utopian in light of the political and legal obstacles. Even though the creation of such a court seems legally possible (for example through an international treaty just as in the case of the International Criminal Court, ICC),[41] politically feasible (in light of the principled readiness of a great number of states to subject themselves to international human rights jurisprudence and monitoring) and practically possible, there is currently little support for such a move.[42]

Finally, where human rights violations are attributable to individual persons, international criminal justice may be used, by analogy to domestic criminal law, to hold perpetrators to account. The creation of the ICC, the jurisdiction of which covers war crimes, crimes against humanity and genocide,[43] has been a major step in enforcing respect for core human rights obligations. While the ICC, as well as the International Criminal Tribunals for the Former Yugoslavia (ICTY) and for Rwanda (ICTR), deal with 'human rights crimes',[44] they are no human rights courts. Important as international criminal justice is for providing redress to the victims of most serious crimes, the remit of international criminal courts is limited, they depend on the co-operation of states, their response is retroactive and their deterrent force may be elusive. Without downplaying the important developments in international justice there is thus no place for a 'judicial romanticism'[45] that over-values the role of courts in enforcing human rights.

---

[41] See M. Nowak, 'The Need for a World Court of Human Rights' (2007) 7 (1) *Human Rights Law Review* 251–9.

[42] See G. Oberleitner, 'Towards an International Court of Human Rights?', in M. A. Baderin and M. Ssenyonjo (eds.), *International Human Rights Law: Six Decades after the UDHR and Beyond* (Farnham: Ashgate 2010) 359–70.

[43] See Articles 6, 7 and 8 Rome Statute of the ICC, 2187 UNTS 90 (entered into force 1 July 2002).

[44] W. Schabas, 'Criminal Responsibility for Violations of Human Rights', in J. Symonides (ed.), *Human Rights: Protection, Monitoring, Enforcement* (Aldershot: Ashgate 2003) 281.

[45] D. P. Forsythe, *Human Rights in International Relations*, 2nd edn (Cambridge University Press 2006) 90.

Sanctions and incentives

Given how difficult it is to pressure states to obey human rights, resorting to incentives may seem a more promising approach. Economic incentives, in particular, appear as potentially powerful tools for securing compliance with international human rights norms, provided states are viewed as rational actors willing to calculate the costs and benefits of their behaviour. Examples of such an approach, however, dampen expectations. While preferential trade agreements and human rights conditionality have been found to play a role in inducing states to comply with human rights standards, evidence demonstrates that success depends on a number of factors decoupled from economic incentives, and that additional efforts are needed to translate lip-service into tangible improvements of the human rights situation.[46] In a similar way, reaching out to multinational business corporations in an attempt to encourage them to comply voluntarily with human rights norms (to which they are not party) bets on the attraction of human rights as an economic incentive. The continuing debate on whether self-imposed ethical standards are sufficiently motivating or a normative framework with rules and sanctions is more appropriate shows, however, the extent of the persistent disagreement in this area.[47] In Europe, human rights conditionality is also part and parcel of pre-accession negotiations to the EU. Political and economic benefits combined motivate candidate states to change domestic law and administrative practice, including in the field of human rights, but yet again success may not only be short-lived and wane after accession negotiations are concluded, but the very process of asking for human rights improvements in return for economic and political benefits is a complex process with an uncertain outcome, as has been demonstrated in case-studies.[48]

---

[46] See E. M. Hafner-Burton, 'Trading Human Rights: How Preferential Trade Agreements Influence Government Repression' (2005) 59 (3) *International Organization* 593–629.

[47] See A. Rasche and G. Kell, 'Introduction: The United Nations Global Compact – Retrospect and Prospect', in A. Rasche and G. Kell (eds.), *The United Nations Global Compact: Achievements, Trends and Challenges* (Cambridge University Press 2010) 1–19, and Report of the Special Representative of the Secretary-General on the issue of human rights and transnational corporations and other business enterprises, J. Ruggie, *Guiding Principles on Business and Human Rights: Implementing the United Nations 'Protect, Respect and Remedy' Framework*, UN Doc. A/HRC/17/31 (21 March 2011), paras. 1–16.

[48] See, for example, A. Albi, 'Ironies in Human Rights Protection in the EU: Pre-Accession Conditionality and Post-Accession Conundrums' (2009) 15 (1) *European Law Journal* 46–69.

When incentives represent the facilitative approach to enforcement then sanctions are their repressive counterpart. They are, however, themselves a human rights problem for the way in which communities in targeted states are victimised twice, first by human rights violations and then by the consequences of sanctions. Even in its softest form – publicly 'naming and shaming' human rights violators in international arenas or the media – their impact has been found to be questionable and even counter-productive.[49] This is also true for 'hard' forms of sanctions, such as trade sanctions or the withdrawing of economic privileges.[50] The dubious and unpredictable outcome of sanctions and their imposition with no consideration for due process make them an unlikely candidate for achieving goals in line with human rights considerations. Another form of sanctions – excluding states from international organisations – is equally problematic, as excluding wrongdoers lessens rather than enhances their incentive to play by the rules. Similarly, excluding states from the respective human rights treaty to which they are party (by analogy with the practice of withholding the benefits of a trade agreement) is equally undesirable given the nature of international human rights treaties as protective frameworks for individuals.

Use of force

The application of military force for humanitarian purposes continues to pose a challenge to the very concept of human rights, despite ideas such as the responsibility to protect (R2P), which seek to ascertain that the use of force is only employed as a last resort to protect civilians caught in immediate danger.[51] The role of the Security Council as enforcer of human rights obligations – while potentially powerful given the Council's mandate to use coercive measures against states[52] – remains troubled by inconsistency and double standards. While its mandate does not explicitly

---

[49] See E. M. Hafner-Burton, 'Sticks and Stones: Naming and Shaming the Human Rights Enforcement Problem', (2008) 62 (4) *International Organization* 689–716.

[50] See K. Tomasevski, 'Sanctions and Human Rights', in J. Symonides (ed.), *Human Rights: International Protection, Monitoring, Enforcement* (Aldershot: Ashgate 2003) 303.

[51] See ICISS, *The Responsibility to Protect* (2001), www.iciss.ca/pdf/Commission-Report.pdf (date of last access 23 December 2011).

[52] Articles 41 and 42 of the UN Charter allow the Council to apply economic sanctions and military force, respectively.

refer to human rights, the Council has, over the past decades, overcome its ignorance of human rights and now considers the linkage between peace, security and human rights as vital to its functioning. In many of its resolutions, the Council refers directly to human rights by integrating them into peace operations, using human rights language to support democratisation or protect civilians in armed conflict and denounce violations of international humanitarian law.[53] The Council's failure to prevent genocide in Bosnia and Herzegovina and in Rwanda has led to efforts to improve peace operations with a view towards their role for preventing and responding to human rights violations, a process which still meets with many obstacles.[54]

The unilateral use of military force without authorisation of the Security Council remains even more disputed. Waging 'humanitarian wars', with or without the involvement of the Security Council, is caught in the dilemma of reconciling the moral imperative to save strangers and the unpredictable consequences of military action, haunted by selectivity and open to the abusive imposition of political goals.[55] While the robust enforcement of human rights, including the use of armed force and interventions on humanitarian grounds, cannot be ruled out as a last resort, such missions may serve as tools for protecting core human rights in greatest peril and restore security but are ill suited to stand in for the lack of more graduated and legitimate enforcement mechanisms.

Conclusion

While international law remains the only legitimate framework for enforcing human rights, its limits are obvious. International human rights institutions lack the authority and the means to compel states to comply with human rights norms (with the exception of the Security Council, whose suitability as a human rights enforcement agent remains questionable).

---

[53] See J. Mertus, *The United Nations and Human Rights: A Guide for a New Era* (London: Routledge, 2009) 98–123.

[54] See K. Mansson, 'Integration of Human Rights in Peace Operations: Is There an Ideal Model?' (2006) 13 (4) *International Peacekeeping* 547–63.

[55] See, for example, J. L. Holzgrefe, 'The Humanitarian Intervention Debate', in J. L. Holzgrefe and R. O. Keohane (eds.), *Humanitarian Intervention: Ethical, Legal and Political Dilemmas* (Cambridge University Press 2003) 15–52.

Nuanced coercive methods, modelled along domestic law enforcement lines, are not available. Enforcing human rights means largely relying on persuasion and appeals to morality and legitimacy, on occasion and inconsistently supported by political and economic incentives, sanctions or pressure. Even at its strongest – when international courts adjudicate on human rights – the international human rights system cannot escape from this reality.

This is a sobering, albeit unsurprising, diagnosis. It is mitigated by a number of factors, though. A narrow focus on coercion obscures the complexity of translating international human rights obligations into the domestic sphere of nation states, which may include determining and addressing the causes for non-compliance and responding to states' capacity limits. It also under-estimates the role of soft forms of compliance management. Not only are they characteristic for the international legal order but states have found to be, in principle, willing to make use of, and often abide by, the decisions of international bodies.[56] In order for such means of justification, rationalisation, recommendation and persuasion to work, however, some core criteria must be fulfilled. Deliberations and decisions of the respective bodies need to be legitimate, non-selective, consistent, backed by a larger political organisation and coherent with other initiatives, and the institutions need to be credible as for their mandate, composition, funding and expertise.[57] International human rights and criminal courts pave the way in this respect and need continued support. Furthermore, the debate on enforcement, as it stands, still rests very much on traditional patterns of vertical enforcement that puts the state and its institutions at the core. At the same time, new forms of global governance, the increased engagement of civil society (fostered by the use of communication technology) and enhanced accountability of non-state actors begin to provide new avenues for effectively realising human rights beyond traditional top-down enforcement models.

In order to strengthen existing enforcement mechanisms and develop new ones it seems imperative to better understand their (potential) impact. Devising indicators for measuring the effects of enforcement is thus another

[56] See D. Shelton, 'Normative Hierarchy in International Law' (2006) 100 (2) *American Journal of International Law* 319 and J. E. Alvarez, 'International Organizations: Now and Then' (2006) 100 (2) *American Journal of International Law* 329.

[57] See Donnelly, *International Human Rights* 108 and Donoho, 'Human Rights Enforcement' 27–31.

challenge ahead.[58] This is a particularly difficult task given that the improvement of the human rights situation is not an isolated process but is closely linked to larger economic and democratic developments in a given state. And finally, it is equally imperative that an expansion of enforcement mechanisms does not conceal human rights as the larger political and societal project that they are. Conor Gearty has rightly cautioned of the 'dangerous triumph of legal enforceability'[59] of human rights that loses sight of human rights as a political agenda for societal change beyond the limits of law. At the end, any enforcement of human rights is only as good as it changes behaviours and attitudes and configures social life in line with universal standards of dignity.

Further reading

Benedek, W., Gregory, C., Kozma, J., Nowak, N., Strohal, C. and Theuermann, E. (eds.), *Global Standards – Local Action: 15 Years Vienna Conference on Human Rights* (Vienna: Intersentia 2009)

Boyle, K. (ed.), *New Institutions for Human Rights Protection* (Oxford University Press, 2009)

Claude, R. P. and Weston, B. H. (eds.), *Human Rights in the World Community: Issues and Action*, 3rd edn (Pennsylvania University Press 2006)

Fassbender, B. (ed.) *Securing Human Rights? Achievements and Challenges of the UN Security Council* (Oxford University Press 2012)

Goldstone, R. J. and Smith, A. M., *International Judicial Institutions: The Architecture of International Justice at Home and Abroad* (London: Routledge 2009)

Hannum, H. (ed.), *Guide to International Human Rights Practice*, 4th edn (Ardsley, NY: Transnational Publishers 2004)

Kaleck, W., Ratner, M., Singelnstein, T. and Weiss, P., *International Prosecution of Human Rights Crimes* (Berlin: Springer 2006)

Kälin, W. and Künzli, J., *The Law of International Human Rights Protection* (Oxford University Press 2010)

Landman, T. and Carvalho, E., *Measuring Human Rights* (London: Routledge 2010)

Moeckli, D., Shah, S. and Sivakumaran, S., *International Human Rights Law* (Oxford University Press 2010)

---

[58] See, for example, M. Kirby, 'Indicators for the Implementation of Human Rights', in J. Symonides (ed.), *Human Rights: International Protection, Monitoring, Enforcement* (Aldershot: Ashgate 2003) 325–46 and T. Landman, *Measuring Human Rights* (London: Routledge 2010).

[59] C. A. Gearty, *Can Human Rights Survive?* (Cambridge University Press 2006) 62.

Neier, A., *International Human Rights Movement: A History* (Princeton University Press 2012)

Oberleitner, G., *Global Human Rights Institutions: Between Remedy and Ritual* (Cambridge: Polity 2007)

O'Flaherty, M., Kedzia, Z., Müller, A. and Ulrich, G. (eds.), *Human Rights Diplomacy: Contemporary Perspectives* (Leiden: Martinus Nijhoff 2011)

Ramcharan, B. G., *The UN Human Rights Council* (London: Routledge 2011)

Rehman, J., *International Human Rights Law: A Practical Approach*, 2nd edn (London: Longman 2006)

Shelton, D., *Regional Protection of Human Rights* (Oxford University Press 2010)

Simmons, B. A., *Mobilizing for Human Rights: International Law in Domestic Politics* (Cambridge University Press 2009)

Symonides, J. (ed.), *Human Rights: Protection, Monitoring, Enforcement* (Aldershot: Ashgate 2003)

Ulfstein, G. (ed.), *Making Treaties Work: Human Rights, Environment and Arms Control* (Cambridge University Press 2007)

Ulfstein, G. and Kelly, H. (eds.), *UN Human Rights Treaty Bodies: Law and Legitimacy* (Cambridge University Press 2012)

Part IV

Pressures

Winners and others: accounting for international law's favourites[*]   14

Margot E. Salomon

In the latter half of the twentieth century developing countries hitched their demands for economic justice to the potential of international law. Their efforts from the 1960s onwards sought to inaugurate a New International Economic Order (NIEO), to delineate a body of 'international development law', and to institute a human right to development with a far-reaching set of corresponding duties. However the economic reality of today indicates that international law has failed the poor of the world and begs the question as to what interests it has served in their stead.[1]

In 1976 the developed market economy countries, with 20 per cent of the world population, enjoyed 66 per cent of total world income. By contrast, the developing countries – excluding China – with about 50 per cent of the world population, received 12.5 per cent of the total world income;[2] with China included, 70 per cent of the world's people accounted for only 30 per cent of world income.[3] By the twenty-first century, 20 per cent of the world population is receiving approximately 85 per cent of income, with 6 per cent going to 60 per cent of the population.[4] In absolute terms, 40 per cent of the

[*] I would like to thank Danny Bradlow, Ali Kadri and Gus Van Harten for their very helpful comments on a draft of this text. As ever, responsibility for the views presented herein rests solely with the author.

[1] This chapter uses the terms 'developed states or countries', 'industrialised states or countries' and 'the North' largely interchangeably. Similarly, the terms 'developing states or countries' and 'the South' are used. References to 'the West' and the 'third world' are used where necessary to capture the sentiment or language of the period.

[2] K. Hossain, 'Introduction', in K. Hossain (ed.), *Legal Aspects of the New International Economic Order* (London: Frances Pinter 1980) 1–44 at 3.

[3] GA Res. 3201 (S-VI), Declaration on the Establishment of A New International Economic Order, 1 May 1974, preambular para. 1.

[4] R. Wade and M. Wolf, 'Are Global Poverty and Inequality Getting Worse?', in D. Held and A. McGrew (eds.), *The Global Transformations Reader*, 2nd edn (Cambridge: Polity 2003) 440–6 at 441. In terms of global wealth distribution, 10 per cent of adults account for 85 per cent of the world total of global assets, with half the world's populations – concentrated in developing countries - owning barely 1 per cent of global wealth. J. Davies, S. Sandstrom, A. Shorrocks and E. Wolff, *The World Distribution of Household Wealth*, World Institute for Development Economics (Helsinki: UN University 2006).

world population is today living on incomes so low as to preclude fully participating in wealth creation.[5] One in four people (1.4 billion) in the developing world live in extreme poverty, attempting to survive below the international poverty line of USD 1.25 a day.[6] If world poverty has decreased since the early 1990s, it is largely due to poverty-reduction figures in a very small number of populous countries.[7] As for global inequality, it is widening rapidly between states; inequality between countries weighted by population has shrunk since 1980 only when we factor in the fast growth in China and India, and inequality among households is probably increasing.[8] Moreover, while the global gap between the richest and the poorest people has been expanding, there is little evidence of actual improvement in the absolute position of the poorest since the 1980s (when the latest wave of globalisation began).[9] These dire figures unfold alongside the growth of international law dedicated to economic regulation and to the ascent of international human rights law in the area of socio-economic and development rights.

To be sure, there are a range of domestic factors from inadequate economic policies, to corruption, to geography that help to account for the current state of inequity, but it does not follow from the existence of local variations that these must be the only causally relevant factors, and that external factors are irrelevant.[10] Recognising the existence of a state's duties domestically to address poverty and development failures, including by

---

[5] UN Development Programme (UNDP), *Human Development Report 2005: International Cooperation at a Crossroads: Aid, Trade and Security in an Unequal World* (New York: UNDP 2005) 38.

[6] World Bank, www.worldbank.org (Poverty Net). The World Bank uses reference lines set at USD 1.25 and USD 2.00 a day 2005 purchasing power parity (PPP) terms.

[7] See S. G. Reddy and C. Minoiu, 'Has World Poverty Really Fallen?' (2007) 3 *Review of Income and Wealth* 484–502.

[8] The position that there has been a decline in world-wide inequality among households looks to the fast growth of China and to a lesser extent of India to provide the chief explanation. Wade and Wolf [debate], 'Are Global Poverty and Inequality Getting Worse?' 440–6 at 440–1. The World Bank economist Branko Milanović has helpfully analysed global inequalities in terms of three concepts: inequality between states, inequality between countries weighted by population, and income distribution between individuals (or households) in the world, termed 'true world inequality': B. Milanović, 'Global Income Inequality', in D. Ehrenpreis (ed.), *The Challenge of Inequality* (Brasilia: UNDP International Poverty Centre 2007) 6.

[9] T. Lines, *Making Poverty: A History* (London: Zed Books 2008) 25.

[10] See T. Pogge, 'The First United Nations Millennium Development Goal: A Cause for Celebration?' (2004) 5 (3) *Journal of Human Development* 377–97 at 391.

complying with its human rights obligations, does not preclude a full investigation into the ways in which international actors can be deeply implicated in the deprivation of almost half the global population.

The limits to the sovereign equality of states

The two well-established principles of the sovereign equality of states and of non-intervention[11] can be said to comprise three elements when it comes to claims for a just international economic order: the right of states to choose freely their economic system; permanent sovereignty by states over their natural wealth and resources; and the equal participation of developing countries in international economic relations.[12] In the 1960s and 1970s as much as today, developing countries believed that the principle of state sovereignty represented an important legal protection for economically and politically vulnerable states against interference by more powerful foreign states, initially and largely those in the North.[13] At a practical level, its use as a defence has been questionable, just as the commitment to sovereign equality has always been historically inadequate to ensure an international legal order that would *actively* contribute to the development of the weakest sections of the international community. Legal equality and functional equality are not coextensive and sovereign equality was also advanced by developing countries as capable of allowing for 'affirmative action': a means by which substance would be given to the principle of sovereign equality.[14]

---

[11] Charter of the UN (adopted 26 June 1945, entered into force 24 October 1945), 1 UNTS XVI, Article 2; GA Res. 2625 (XXV) of 24 October 1970, Declaration on Principles of International Law concerning Friendly Relations and Co-operation among States in accordance with the Charter of the UN.

[12] The right of every state freely to choose its economic system as an aspect of the (economic) sovereign equality of states was introduced in the Declaration on Principles of International Law concerning Friendly Relations and Co-operation among States. See further, Report of the Secretary-General, *Progressive Development of the Principles and Norms of International Law Relating to a New International Economic Order*, UN Doc. A/39/504/Add.1, 23 October 1984, para. 3.

[13] See D. D. Bradlow, 'Development Decision-Making and the Content of International Development Law' (2004) 27 *Boston College International and Comparative Law Review* 195–217 at 205.

[14] Hossain, 'Introduction' 1–44 at 5–6; Bradlow, 'Development Decision-Making' 195–217 at 206.

The traditional negative requirement to respect each state's fundamental sovereign prerogative by refraining from intervening in its internal or external affairs likewise has offered only a derisory legal methodology in a world of sovereign states with dramatically differing power, wealth and influence. The principle of sovereign equality, that offers merely a normative defence against unwelcomed commercial influence, has failed to embed any positive requirements to advance a comprehensive system of equitable benefit-sharing internationally. That the liberalisation of trade, investment and finance – apart from any harms caused – has not yet accommodated in any significant way the 'non-market governance' of poverty reduction, presents a stark example of the weak redistributive capacity of the international legal system.[15] In the early decades of the UN, as now, this blatant vacuum has initiated no global redistributive mechanism to address the existence of wide-scale deprivation.[16]

Standing in opposition to the traditional interpretation of these two core principles, has been that of international co-operation. As a purpose of the UN's economic and social mandate,[17] as one of the UN's basic principles,[18] and subsequently as a human rights obligation corresponding to socio-economic and development rights,[19] this ideal has sought to provide the foundation upon which positive action in securing these benefits globally would be advanced. Unsurprisingly, international co-operation has offered an important basis upon which the demands for a just international economic order, then and

---

[15] On trade, see J. P. Trachtman, 'Legal Aspects of the Poverty Agenda at the WTO: Trade Law and "Global Apartheid"' (2003) 6 (1) *Journal of International Economic Law* 3–21 at 4 and 10–1; S. Prowse (DfID), *Trade and Poverty Panel, Does International Law Mean Business?: A Partnership for Progress*, International Law Association, British Branch Annual Conference (London) May 2008.

[16] Robert Wade rightly makes this point in the context of contemporary international arrangements generally, in R. H. Wade, 'Globalization, Growth, Poverty, Inequality, Resentment, and Imperialism', in J. Ravenhill (ed.), *Global Political Economy* 2nd edn (Oxford University Press 2008) 373–409 at 403.

[17] UN Charter, Articles 1 (3) 55, 56.

[18] UN Charter, Article 2 (5) in this provision the duty is to co-operate with the Organisation itself in the maintenance of peace and security.

[19] UDHR, GA Res. 217A (III), 10 December 1948, UN Doc. A/810 Article 28; International Covenant on Economic, Social and Cultural Rights (1966) (entered into force 3 January 1976), GA Res. A/RES/2200A (XXI), 993 UNTS 3, Article 2 (1); Declaration on the Right to Development, GA Res. 41/128, Annex, UN GAOR, Forty-first session, Supp. No. 53 at 186, UN Doc. A/41/53 (1986); Convention on the Rights of the Child (1989) (entered into force 2 September 1990), GA Res. A/RES/44/25, Annex 44, UN GAOR Supp. (No. 49) at 167, UN Doc. A/44/49 (1989), Article 4.

now, have been based. The Covenant of the League of Nations took the initial step of laying down that its members should make provisions to secure and maintain 'equitable treatment for commerce'.[20] The UN Charter goes much further, providing as one of the purposes of the organisation the goal of achieving 'international co-operation' in solving international problems of an economic, social character, and in promoting and encouraging respect for human rights for all;[21] and stating that the UN shall promote conditions of economic and social progress and development, and human rights.[22] The Charter frames the lack of economic and social opportunity as detrimental to international relations, and recognises its reversal as dependent upon the co-operation of the international community of states. The UN provided an institutional set-up to support these objectives, in particular through its establishment of the Economic and Social Council (ECOSOC), a principal organ mandated to initiate studies and reports with respect to international economic, social, cultural, educational, health and related matters, and to make recommendations to the General Assembly and UN Specialised Agencies.[23] The Charter also anticipated a central role for the relevant UN specialised agencies in this area[24] that were to be brought into the UN family through relationship agreements with ECOSOC.[25] Obligations of 'international assistance and co-operation' were subsequently included in human rights instruments addressing economic, social and cultural rights and development.[26]

Such was the state of international law when neoliberalism arrived, making it increasingly unlikely that there would be any further advance of this agenda for redistributive action. Neoliberalism has been the dominant economic model since the 1980s, its most recent ascent to the ruling economic orthodoxy taking place with the 1989–90 collapse of communism in the Soviet Union and Central Europe and the 'triumph of capitalism'. Under this ideology, the efficiency of self-regulating markets generates optimum wealth (that will, in theory, trickle down and be helpful to the living standards of the poor over time),[27] and any growth in material

---

[20] Covenant of the League of Nations, 225 Consolidated Treaty Series (CTS) 195, Article 23(e).

[21] UN Charter, Article 1(3).   [22] *Ibid.*, Article 55.   [23] *Ibid.*, Article 62.

[24] *Ibid.*, Article 57.   [25] *Ibid.*, Article 53.

[26] For a comprehensive study, see M. E. Salomon, *Global Responsibility for Human Rights: World Poverty and the Development of International Law* (Oxford University Press 2007).

[27] See J. E. Stiglitz, 'Is there a Post-Washington Consensus?', in N. Serra and J. E. Stiglitz (eds.), *The Washington Consensus Reconsidered: Towards a New Global Governance* (Oxford University Press 2008) 41–56 at 47.

inequality should on this account best be understood as incentivising, thus driving productivity and spurring the economy – a far cry from any kind of manifesto for collective justice.

The new international economic order (NIEO)

Developing states, in particular newly decolonised states, began early on – well before the arrival of neoliberalism – to confront the structural biases of international law and their ensuing development problems by pushing for the creation of a new international economic order. The Latin American states were the early agitators in the 1950s prior to the major wave of post-war decolonisation. In the 1960s and 1970s developing countries mobilised under the auspices of the 'Group of 77' and advocated a reform of the laws governing international economic relations that reflected their post-colonial demands: for control over economic activity within their own borders; for participation in the governance of the globalising economy; for fair access to technology, international trade, finance, and investment; and for international co-operation from industrialised states – with the status of a legal obligation – towards their development aspirations.[28] In the early 1970s, many formerly dependent African and Asian countries attained political independence that bolstered their voices in the General Assembly where developing countries already held the majority of seats. The 'third world' was rebelling against what it recognised as the sanctioning by law of a relationship between 'exploiters and the exploited'.[29] As is well known, the political self-determination of decolonisation highlighted the absence of the 'economic self-determination' of developing countries, nationally and internationally. Their political independence and responsibility for their own economic affairs exposed just how dependent they were on other states and how vulnerable they were within the existing economic system.

The NIEO process resulted in the adoption of several resolutions, most notably the UN Declaration on Permanent Sovereignty over Natural

---

[28] For a useful overview, see M. E. Ellis, 'The New International Economic Order: The Debate Over the Legal Effects of General Assembly Resolutions Revisited' (1985) 15 (3) *California Western International Law Journal* 647–704 at 658.

[29] M. Bedjaoui, *Towards a New International Economic Order* (Paris: UNESCO/New York: Holmes & Meier 1979) 24.

Resources,[30] the Declaration on the Establishment of a New International Economic Order, along with a Programme of Action, and the Charter of Economic Rights and Duties of States.[31] None of these resolutions or declarations was formally binding, and while the representatives of developed states with market economies allowed the Declaration on the Establishment of a NIEO to be adopted by consensus they did so with reservations.[32] As for the Charter of Economic Rights and Duties of States, concerns regarding the standard of treatment for their investors abroad, especially the provisions related to expropriation and compensation, resulted in developed states voting against it.[33] The strong opposition of these industrialised states meant the large convergence of states on the substance of new standards necessary for the formation of customary international law was lacking:[34] any general support within the UN was to remain at the level of broad principle.[35]

As a matter of normative status, there was one success which is often said to have emerged from the efforts by developing states to shape the evolving rules of international economic law: the general acceptance by the international community of the principle of permanent sovereignty over natural resources (PSNR). The General Assembly had decided as early as 1952 to include a right of all peoples and nations to self-determination in a human rights treaty and mandated the Commission on Human Rights to prepare a draft on the subject.[36] In 1955 the General Assembly adopted a draft article

---

[30] GA Res. 1803 (XVII) of 14 December 1962, Permanent Sovereignty over Natural Resources.

[31] GA Res. 3281 (XXIX) of 12 December 1974, the Charter on the Economic Rights and Duties of States, 120 votes in favour; 6 against; 10 abstentions. Those states that voted against the resolution were Belgium, Denmark, German Federal Republic, Luxembourg, UK and the USA.

[32] USA, West Germany, France, Japan and UK. M. Bulajić, *Principles of International Development Law*, 2nd edn (Dordrecht: Martinus Nijhoff 1993) 271.

[33] See further, S. P. Subedi, *International Investment Law: Reconciling Policy and Principle* (Oxford: Hart 2008) 26; D. E. Veilleville and B. S. Vasani, 'Sovereignty over Natural Resources versus Rights Under Investment Contracts: Which one Prevails?' (2008) 5 (2) *Transnational Dispute Management* 1–21 at 4–5.

[34] A. Cassese, *International Law*, 2nd edn (Oxford University Press 2005) 507.

[35] M. Bennouna, 'International Law and Development', in M. Bedjaoui (ed.), *International Law: Achievements and Prospects* (Paris: UNESCO/Dordrecht: Martinus Nijhoff 1991) 619–31 at 621; Cassese, *International Law* 509.

[36] GA Res. A/Res/545 (VI) of 5 February 1952, Inclusion in the International Covenant or Covenants on Human Rights of an Article Relating to the Right of Peoples to Self-Determination, paras. 1–2.

as part of the self-determination provisions in the two Human Rights Covenants, the second paragraph of which subsequently appeared as Common Article 1 (2), and states: 'All peoples may, for their own ends, freely dispose of their natural wealth and resources without prejudice to any obligations arising out of international economic co-operation, based upon the principle of mutual benefit, and international law. In no case may a people be deprived of its own means of subsistence.' The groundwork for the adoption in 1962 by the General Assembly of Resolution 1803 declaring a right to permanent sovereignty over natural resources stemmed from the draft Human Rights Covenants supplied by the Commission on Human Rights to the Third Committee of the General Assembly.[37]

The principle of self-determination in the UN Charter underpinned formal sovereignty, and the post-1945 international order saw the principle of non-intervention in the domestic affairs of other states rendered applicable not just to European states but to all states. The principle of permanent sovereignty over natural resources was motivated by the concern among developing states that orthodox international law on foreign investment undermined the effective exercise of their sovereignty in the economic realm by favouring the interests of capital-exporting states and their corporations.[38] PSNR was thus an attack on established tenets of international law that developing non-self-governing peoples had had no meaningful role in formulating,[39] and on customary international law, in this case in the area of a compensation standard for the expropriation of property, that had been set to reflect the interests of developed states and their international private sector.[40]

---

[37] For a concise summary of the drafting history, see I. Brownlie, *Principles of Public International Law*, 7th edn (Oxford University Press 2008) 539–41.

[38] See D. P. Fidler, 'Revolt Against or from Within the West: TWAIL, the Developing World, and the Future Direction of International Law' (2003) 2 (1) *Chinese Journal of International Law* 29–76 at 41.

[39] See A. Anghie, *Imperialism, Sovereignty and the Making of International Law* (Cambridge University Press 2004) 213 and 212–16.

[40] Sundhya Pahuja provides a summary of the polarised positions on compensation during the NIEO debates when she writes: 'In essence, the West was arguing for the Hull formula of "prompt, adequate and effective", or market-based compensation, determinable internationally. For its part, the Third World was arguing that the relevant compensation should be "appropriate", economically contextual, historically sensitive and determinable nationally': S. Pahuja, *Decolonising International Law: Development, Economic Growth and the Politics of Universality* (Cambridge University Press 2011) 149.

Insofar as the principle of PSNR represented a victory for the developing world, it advanced the notion that sovereign states had the right to expropriate or nationalise the assets of foreign companies under certain conditions, including 'public utility', with the owner being paid 'appropriate' compensation. It seemed to balance the competing priorities of developing states for control over their natural wealth and resources with the interests of developed states whose concern was with ensuring protection for their corporate nationals investing abroad. PSNR presented a statement of the law that was acceptable to the interests of both sides.[41] The story does not, however, end there.

A critical observer will argue that the principle of PSNR represents a questionable victory for developing states in that, first, the *assumptions* that underpin the Declaration reflect their capitulation to the economic ideology of the advanced capitalist world and its unabated commitment to strengthening the rights of foreign capital.[42] Second, whatever normative gains can be said to have emerged in the area of PSNR, the rules in Bilateral Investment Treaties (BITs) today closely approximate or even exceed such old customary rules favoured by industrialised states as the international minimum standard of treatment for aliens (over the national standard of treatment)[43] and the Hull formula requiring 'prompt, adequate and effective' (full) compensation for the expropriation of foreign investments (over 'just' or 'appropriate' compensation).[44] Third, while in the 1970s and 1980s disputes on direct expropriation mainly related to the nationalisation of

---

[41] Resolution 1803 on PSNR did not deny the relevance of international law as a factor in determining appropriate compensation, however nor did it limit the legal basis for the determination of compensation to international law. The legislative language – incomplete as it is – clearly reflects a compromise between the interests of capital-importing and capital-exporting countries. See Subedi, *International Investment Law* 21–3 and M. Sornarajah, *The International Law on Foreign Investment*, 3rd edn (Cambridge University Press 2010) 445 *et seq.*

[42] B. S. Chimni, 'The Principle of Permanent Sovereignty over Natural Resources: Toward a Radical Interpretation' (1998) 38 (2) *Indian Journal of International Law* 208–17 at 213–14.

[43] 'Protagonists of national treatment point to the role the law associated with the international standard has played in maintaining a privileged status for aliens, supporting alien control of large areas of the national economy, and providing a pretext for foreign armed intervention': Brownlie, *Principles of Public International Law* 525.

[44] 'The claim to full or adequate compensation is supported by the majority of capital-exporting states, for the obvious reason that it affords the best protection for the capital which leaves these states as foreign investment.' The concept of 'full compensation' includes consideration of future profits the investment would have made. Sornarajah, *The International Law on Foreign Investment* 412, 414.

foreign property, today the central concern is that concepts such as indirect expropriation may be applied to *bona fide* regulatory measures taken by the host government and aimed at protecting the environment, health and other welfare interests of society, giving rise to claims for compensation.[45]

Concerns over the *application* of the principle of PSNR were highlighted in the years following the adoption of the NIEO declarations, along with wider criticisms over the power differentials embedded in the international investment regime more generally. These concerns endure to date. They include the dependence of many developing countries on financial and technological assistance in order to exploit those natural resources from an international private sector motivated by profit generation. The deeply unsatisfying choices of a poor developing country, then as now, were often to accept a deal offered by the companies or to leave their resources untapped.

Disquiet over a range of other problems existed, including that of stabilisation clauses by which the host state, for instance, agrees not to alter the terms of an investment contract it has undertaken with the foreign investor except with the consent of both parties.[46] Similar concerns are raised today in that stabilisation clauses 'stipulate that the law prevailing at the time the decision was taken by foreign investors to invest in the host country would be applicable to them, and such laws would not be altered to the detriment of the investor'.[47] While under a BIT between the investor country and the investor-receiving country (as distinct from an investment contract between the host government and the foreign investor) a host state is not *per se* prevented from taking new legal or administrative measures in order to govern the country and (ideally) to comply with its treaty obligations under other international legal regimes (for example, human rights or in the area of environmental protection), under customary international foreign investment law the host state would be expected to compensate the investor for economic losses if they amount to 'indirect expropriation'.[48] Certain

---

[45] See 'Indirect Expropriation' and the 'Right to Regulate' in International Investment Law, *OECD Working Papers on International Investment* No. 2004/4 2.

[46] E. Jiminez de Arechaga, 'Application of the Rules of State Responsibility to the Nationalization of Foreign-Owned Property', in K. Hossain (ed.), *Legal Aspects of the New International Economic Order* (London: Frances Pinter 1980) 220–33 at 229–30.

[47] Subedi, *International Investment Law* 104.

[48] *Ibid.* The direction of the case law is yet unfolding on the matter of whether *bona fide* regulatory measures which nonetheless significantly impact the commercial interests of foreign investors should be compensable.

investment contracts go even further than BITs 'and require compensation for *any* interference by the host state that increases the cost of the project'.[49] While foreign investment may bring certain beneficial impacts to the developing country societies, then as now, the subordination of the fundamental right of a state to regulate so as to advance public welfare – as well as its fundamental human rights *obligation* to do so – over the interests of foreign investors remains a sustained point of contention.[50] Other issues along the North–South political cleavage regarding the international law on foreign investment have persisted for decades in one form or another, such as concerns over procedural fairness and a lack of adjudicative independence when it comes to the settlement of investment disputes.[51]

Historically the aim of BITs, it is said, has been to strengthen the protection afforded foreign investors, especially in developing and transitional markets, *in return* for increased inward foreign investment flows. With the rise of globalisation in the 1990s, developing countries courted foreign investors offering incentives and legislative protection.[52] However, in so far as we are prepared to accept that some form of mutual benefit was meaningfully foreseen, the sum of empirical evidence cannot be said to demonstrate incontrovertibly that BITs have contributed even to the targeted objective of economic development in the host states.[53] Moreover, a commitment to social development as part of the foreign

---

[49] *Ibid.* (Emphasis in original.)

[50] 'We have a shared concern for the harm done to the public welfare by the international investment regime, as currently structured, especially its hampering of the ability of governments to act for their people in response to the concerns of human development and environmental sustainability': The *Public Statement on the International Investment Regime*, 31 August 2010. The Statement is available in English, French, Spanish, and Russian, www.osgoode.yorku.ca/public_statement/.

[51] See G. Abi-Saab, 'Permanent Sovereignty over Natural Resources', in M. Bedjaoui (ed.), *International Law: Achievements and Prospects* (Paris: UNESCO/Dordrecht: Martinus Nijhoff 1991), 597–617 at 613–14; G. Van Harten, *A Case for an International Investment Court*, Society of International Economic Law Working Paper No. 22/08 (2008); see further, G. Van Harten, 'Investment Treaty Arbitration, Procedural Fairness, and the Rule of Law', in S. W. Schill (ed.), *International Investment Law and Comparative Public Law* (Oxford University Press 2010) 627–60.

[52] M. Sornarajah, *The Clash of Globalisations and the International Law on Foreign Investment*, The Simon Reisman Lecture in International Trade Policy, Centre for Trade Policy and Law (Ottawa 2002) 4–5.

[53] P. Muchlinski, 'Holistic Approaches to Development and International Investment Law: the Role of International Investment Agreements', in J. Faundez and C. Tan (eds.), *International Law, Economic Globalization and Development* (Cheltenham: Edward Elgar 2010) 180–204 at 186.

investment objectives remains all but absent from BITs,[54] as does a proper calibration of the balance between the rights and obligations of all stakeholders in the investment process, which would include host countries, investors and their home countries, as well as local communities.[55] The obstacle to change is not a lack of solutions, including to the legal investment regime, but is due instead to a lack of political will.[56] In short, the international law that we have is the international law that the powerful want.

Commenting in 1991, Abi-Saab concluded that the real impact and significance of the principle of PSNR was less at the level of concrete technical rules than as regards the 'structure, parameters and basic assumptions' of the international legal system itself. In particular, the principle 'proceeds from the affirmation of the permanent sovereignty of the State and its freedom of action as a general rule, any limitation or obligations attaching to the exercise of this freedom being the exception that has to be demonstrated'.[57] This orientation in international law is manifested in the idea of third-generation human rights, notably a peoples' rights to self-determination which includes sovereignty over their natural resources, along with economic self-determination, also framed as the human right to development, a point to which we will return.[58] But whether in terms of general international law or international human rights law, legal movements that have sought to bolster the economic and social upward mobilisation of developing countries and their people have remained subordinated to the interests of capital-exporting states and their transnational corporations, and to the structures, including judicial, that prioritise the protection of the property and economic interests of foreign investors over the right to regulate of states and, ultimately, the right to political and economic self-determination of their people.[59]

---

[54] *Ibid.*, 181–2.   [55] *Ibid.*, 190.

[56] For a thoughtful overview of how International Investment Agreements (IIAs) could be recalibrated, see Faundez and Tan, *International Law* 180; for a proposed new model for IIAs with rights and obligations for investors, home states, and host states, see H. Mann, K. von Moltke, L. Peterson and A. Cosbey, *IISD Model International Agreement on Investment For Sustainable Development*, Article 1: 'The objective of this Agreement is to promote foreign investment that supports sustainable development, in particular in developing and least-developed countries.'

[57] Abi-Saab, 'Permanent Sovereignty over Natural Resources' 614–15.

[58] See The Declaration on the Right to Development, Article 1 (2).

[59] See the *Public Statement on the International Investment Regime*, para. 5.

There were other key elements of the original NIEO agenda, including the establishment of special and differential treatment under international trade law[60] and demands for access to the exploitation of resources of the deep-sea bed for the benefit of developing countries.[61] But if the 'changes made in the General Agreement on Trade and Tariffs [GATT] law and practice constitute a substantive shift in international law towards basing the application of important international legal rules on a state's level of economic development rather than on the traditional approach of all sovereign states bearing equal and identical obligations under international law',[62] its formal success cannot mask serious doubts as to whether the international trading system has delivered net benefits to developing countries in the form of faster growth and poverty reduction.[63]

Developing states, at least initially, did impact on the contours of international law when it came to the law of the sea, most notably regarding access to non-living resources on or beneath the ocean floor in an area beyond national jurisdiction. Fidler highlights the fact that the common heritage of mankind (CHM) concept – by introducing ideas about the management of global economic resources into the UN Convention on the Law of the Sea (UNCLOS) – instilled in international law a scheme of distributive economic justice.[64] But this was not to last. CHM replaced the 'freedom of the high seas' principle that allowed any state to exploit those resources (for example the mineral-rich deposits) for their benefit, which *de facto* meant those states with the technological capabilities.[65] CHM as such undermined the advantage traditionally afforded developed states and remained a matter of intense controversy even after the adoption of UNCLOS in 1982, with developed states refusing to ratify the treaty. UNCLOS itself did not enter into force for over a decade in part as a result of the CHM element, and in 1994 the

---

[60] Charter on the Economic Rights and Duties of States, Ch II, Article 18.
[61] Charter of Economic Rights and Duties of States, Ch III (Common Responsibilities Towards the International Community), Article 29.
[62] Fidler, 'Revolt Against or from Within the West' 44.
[63] See J. P. Trachtman, 'The Missing Link: Coherence and Poverty and the WTO' (2005) 8 (3) *Journal of International Economic Law* 611–22 at 619; Trachtman, 'Legal Aspects of the Poverty Agenda at the WTO' at 10–11; F. Ismail, *Mainstreaming Development in the WTO: Developing Countries in the Doha Round* (Jaipur: CUTS/Geneva: FES 2007) iii.
[64] Fidler, 'Revolt Against or from Within the West' 46; see also J. T. Gathii, 'Third World Approaches to International Economic Governance', in R. Falk, B. Rajagopal and J. Stephens (eds.), *International Law and the Third World: Reshaping Justice* (Routledge–Cavendish 2008) 255–67 at 260–1.
[65] Fidler, 'Revolt Against or from Within the West' 44–6.

provision was amended to reflect the interests of developed countries as to how those resources should be exploited.[66]

The real reasons the NIEO failed

The NIEO's overall lack of success has been attributed in part to developing countries not having presented a unified platform and an agreed set of concrete objectives.[67] Further, the impact of the debt crisis of the 1980s which devastated developing countries and shifted the attention of the international community from the international economic order to development in individual countries, overshadowed the demands for a NIEO.[68] But the central failure to establishing a NIEO was due to the fact that industrialised states didn't want any such thing. It is not surprising to hear suggested that they were unwilling to enter into genuine global negotiations;[69] and then, as now, were unwilling to see rules created that didn't serve their economic interests well.

Opposition to the spirit if not the letter of calls for a new international economic order continue today with vociferous attempts by industrialised states to keep matters of economics and finance outside of the UN where they are in the minority and instead firmly situated in the organisations where they hold the bulk of power, be it formally such as in the Bretton Woods Institutions under its system of weighted voting,[70] informally as per the G-20,[71] or on the basis of influence as played out in the World Trade Organization (WTO).[72] Sweden, speaking on behalf of the EU, said as much

---

[66] *Ibid.*, 54–5; Chimni. 'The Principle of Permanent Sovereignty' 215.

[67] Bennouna, 'International Law and Development' 621. Developing countries were also accused of 'excessive politicisation' of problems within international organisations and of being irresponsible in the examination of world problems. See Bedjaoui, *Towards a New International Economic Order* 144.

[68] Bradlow, 'Development Decision-Making' 198.

[69] Bennouna, 'International Law and Development' 621.

[70] The NIEO demands included a strong and effective voice for developing countries in the decision-making of international economic institutions as per the Charter on the Economic Rights and Duties of States, Ch II, Article 10.

[71] 'Norway Takes Aim at the G20: One of the Greatest Setbacks Since World War II', *Der Spiegel* Interview with the Norwegian Foreign Minister, 6 June 2010; and see R. H. Wade and J. Vestergaard, 'G20 + 5 Reinforces the Problem of Arbitrary Mechanisms' *Financial Times (International)*, 18 April 2011.

[72] See among others, F. Macmillan, 'The World Trade Organization and the Turbulent Legacy of International Economic Law-Making in the Long Twentieth Century', in J. Faundez and

at the UN Social Forum in August 2009, a meeting convened to discuss the impact of the economic and financial crisis on poverty alleviation and the exercise of human rights globally. Another example comes by way of a Commission mandated by the President of the General Assembly and headed by the former World Bank economist Joseph Stiglitz. The Commission submitted a report to the General Assembly on the crisis in late 2009 calling for an independent body within the UN to analyse the global economy including its social and environmental aspects. The report recommended, *inter alia*, the establishment of a principal organ of the UN – a Global Economic Coordination Council (on a par with Security Council and General Assembly) – to provide high-level leadership at the interface of economic, social, and environmental issues.[73] Little is likely to come about as a result of these recommendations: as is their practice the lead industrialised states are working to make sure that no meaningful action is taken that would give the UN a role as co-ordinator on issues that involve the Bretton Woods Institutions and the WTO.[74] This strategy is predictable: it ensures that the dominant position of industrialised states is maintained (with some space for 'emerging economies'), and that poorer countries continue to be suitably marginalised from influencing international economic affairs. This is convenient because, as Koskenniemi lucidly points out: 'once one knows which institution will deal with an issue, one already knows how it will be disposed of.'[75]

An international development law?

The moniker 'international development law' is, as such, an over-statement. What its proponents sought to achieve by its deployment remains deeply

C. Tan (eds.), *International Law, Economic Globalization and Development* (Cheltenham: Edward Elgar 2010) 158–79; R. Howse, *Mainstreaming the Right to Development into International Trade Law and Policy at the World Trade Organization*, UN Doc. E/CN4/Sub2/2004/17 (2004), paras. 37–9.

[73] *Commission of Experts of the President of the General Assembly on Reforms of the International Monetary and Financial Systems*, 19 March 2009, UN Doc. A/63/XXX.

[74] See, for example. R. H. Wade, *From Global Imbalances to Global Reorganizations: Steps Towards a More Stable and Equitable International Financial System*. Conference on Reforming the Bretton Woods Institutions (Danish Institute for International Studies September 2009) (on file with author).

[75] M. Koskenniemi, 'The Fate of Public International Law: Between Technique and Politics' (2007) 70 (1) *Modern Law Review* 1–30 at 23.

important, but it is best understood as an attempt at reading particular values – including more recently, those derived from other areas of international law such as socio-economic rights – into existing legal frameworks.[76] What has been referred to by some commentators in the recent past as the 'new international law of development'[77] is really an effort to render international law alive to the plight of the poor and to highlight attempts by developing states to see redressed its biases and lacunae. As we have seen, the UN Charter provides the first legal source of the modern era requiring the collective effort of its members in the promotion of economic and social development and human rights. But this does not in itself indicate the existence of an international development law; it merely provides a directive to have one fleshed out.

By fashioning legal arguments drawn from existing international legal doctrine, the NIEO sought to expose the development implications of various sets of international economic rules and, more broadly, to provide a marker against which those rules could be evaluated for being just, procedurally and substantively. The aim of international development law – to imbue existing international economic law with an emphasis on equity and participation – was in many ways shaped and bolstered by the ascent of standard-setting in international human rights law in the decades following the establishment of the UN, in particular in the area of peoples' rights. Developing countries are still agitating for a treaty that captures their development aspirations – today it is under the auspices of the UN Working Group on the Right to Development.[78] It remains an elusive demand.

There is no separate international legal development regime the standards of which can be said to have been breached as a result of egregious global disparities in income and opportunity that pass for the status quo. 'International development law' is not 'the law regulating the relations among sovereign but economically unequal States';[79] it is more amorphous

---

[76] Variations on this view include P. Peters, 'Recent Developments in International Development Law', in S. R. Chowdury, E. M. G. Denters and P. J. I. M. de Waart (eds.), *The Right to Development in International Law* (Dordrecht: Martinus Nijhoff 1992) 113–38 at 113 and R. Sarkar, *International Development Law: Rule of Law, Human Rights, and Global Finance* (Oxford University Press 2009) 77.

[77] J. C. N. Paul, 'The United Nations and the Creation of an International Development Law' (1995) 38 *Harvard International Law Journal* 307–28 at 319.

[78] *Report of the High-Level Task Force on the Implementation of the Right to Development On its Sixth Session* (14–22 January 2010), UN Doc. A/HRC/15/WG2/task force/2, para. 77; see further S. P. Marks, *The Politics of the Possible: The Way Ahead for the Right to Development* (Berlin: Friedrich Ebert Stiftung June 2011), Executive Summary.

[79] Bulajić, *Principles of International Development Law* 43.

and less effective than this: its vitiated impact can be found instead here and there, for example in the preferential and non-reciprocal treatment of developing countries in international trade law, in the language of technology transfer (relevant also to current climate change negotiations),[80] in the content of the human right to development, and in development assistance. At best we might conclude that developing states have succeeded only in this very limited way in harnessing international law.

There are, however, at least two important over-arching contributions to be made by the ideas advanced as international development law that do not depend on it constituting a body of law in the way just described. First, international development law exemplifies precisely why different legal regimes cannot exist in complete isolation and, second, the preoccupations that inform it bring to light the core implication of a rights-based approach to development.

On the first point, the fact that international development law does not in fact form a discrete set of rules may point up its most valuable contribution: the importance of better cross-fertilising the international legal regimes, of trade, investment, finance, human rights, environment, and perhaps others (also) to the ends of justice. This may represent something far more significant than the claim to a new branch of international law by drawing on *existing* areas of international law to show how they impact on and are relevant for human welfare, in particular, of the most disadvantaged globally.

The second, perhaps inadvertent, contribution of international development law is to highlight the link between human rights and development. While it is true that there is still traction for the idea that development is coterminous with economic development and even more narrowly with economic growth, a holistic, human-centred view of development may yet take hold. On this 'modern' account, economic aspects of development cannot be disassociated from social, political, environmental and cultural

---

[80] '[D]espite decades of debate, there has been very little practical movement on technology transfer. There are many reasons for this, but the main one has to do with the international protection of intellectual property (IP) rights ... Here it is enough to point out that the long debate over IP rights has itself become an obstacle to technology policy. Indeed, the argument over IP rights is largely a distraction from the main problem – which is simply *a failure to systematically pursue the technology provisions of the UNFCCC.*' (Emphasis in the original.) *Beyond Technology Transfer: Protecting Human Rights in a Climate-Constrained World* (International Council on Human Rights Policy 2011), Summary and Recommendations.

aspects.[81] In a way that is contrary to economic orthodoxy this approach sees people not only as the primary beneficiaries of development but also as agents of change.[82] The focus is on a process shaped by human rights principles and standards, and not only outcomes, with a key assumption therefore being that capital accumulation does not represent development, but instead 'development ... becomes the articulation of the social forces that shape capital accumulation'.[83]

The tentative contribution of the human right to development

Under the terms of the Declaration on the Right to Development (DRD), it is each person, and not the state *per se*, that is the central subject of development, and as such the person should be the active participant and beneficiary of the right to development.[84] While the focus shifted to the person, this human right in international law represents a set of claims borne of the NIEO. That the DRD offers a posthumous reiteration of NIEO aspirations is unambiguous, even if the US government under the Reagan Administration sought to make it clear to the other members of the UN Commission on Human Rights in 1981 that the DRD they were about to draft should not be used as a means of resuscitating the NIEO.[85] Adopted in 1986, the General Assembly included in the Preamble its awareness 'that efforts at the international level to promote and protect human rights should be accompanied by efforts to establish a new international economic order'.[86] The principles that underpinned the NIEO were articulated in Article 3 (3) of the Declaration whereby: 'States should realize their rights and fulfil their duties in such a manner as to promote a new international economic order based on sovereign equality, interdependence, mutual interest and

---

[81] Bradlow, 'Development Decision-Making' 207; and see R. Danino *Legal Opinion on Human Rights and the Work of the World Bank*, Senior Vice President and General Counsel, World Bank, 27 January 2006, para. 7.

[82] S. Fukuda-Parr, *Global Partnerships for Development*, paper delivered at '25 Years of the Right to Development: Achievements and Challenges', Friedrich Ebert Stiftung/OHCHR (Berlin 24–25 February 2011) (on file with author).

[83] A. Kadri, 'An Outline for the Right to Economic Development in the Arab World' (2011) 56 (2) *Real-World Economics Review* 2–14 at 2.

[84] DRD, Article 2 (1).

[85] S. P. Marks, 'The Human Right to Development: Between Rhetoric and Reality' (2004) 17 *Harvard Human Rights Journal* 137–68 at 143.

[86] DRD, Preambular para. 15.

co-operation among all States, as well as to encourage the observance and realization of human rights.'

The Preamble and the first Article of the DRD reaffirm the centrality of the principle of PSNR in stating that: 'The human right to development also implies the full realization of the right of peoples to self-determination, which includes, subject to the relevant provisions of both International Covenants on Human Rights, the exercise of their inalienable right to full sovereignty over all their natural wealth and resources.'[87] The duties necessary to give effect to the elements that constitute the right to development are of significant note. Uncharacteristically for a human rights declaration (adapted as it was from the Charter of Economic Rights and Duties of States), the DRD provides not only for a 'duty' on the part of the state to formulate national development policies that improve the well-being of its people and that are participatory and oriented towards ensuring a fair distribution of the benefits of any such policies, but it also provides for a 'right' of states.[88] Motivated by the NIEO preoccupations of developing countries with the workings of the international economic system, the formulation implies that the state can assert the right of its people to development against other states and actors. Similarly, while the DRD confirms that the right to development is 'an inalienable human right', it simultaneously asserts that 'equality of opportunity for development is a prerogative both of nations and of individuals who make up nations'.[89]

Effective international co-operation as 'an essential factor for the full achievement of [a state's] development goals' is key to the NIEO's Charter of Economic Rights and Duties of States[90] just as advancing a duty of international co-operation in ensuring world-wide arrangements conducive to human-centred development provides the object and purpose of the DRD. Article 3 (3) refers to the duty of all states to co-operate with each other in ensuring development and eliminating obstacles to development. Article 4 (1) refers to the duty of all states to take steps individually and collectively to formulate international development policies in order to facilitate the full realisation of the right to development. In Article 4 (2) of the DRD provides

---

[87] *Ibid.*, Article 1 (2); see also DRD, preambular para. 7. See also N. Schrijver, *Sovereignty over Natural Resources: Balancing Rights and Duties* (Cambridge University Press 1997) 369–71.

[88] DRD, Article 2 (3), Preambular para. 2; Charter on the Economic Rights and Duties of States, Ch II, Article 7.

[89] DRD, Preambular para. 16.

[90] Charter of Economic Rights and Duties of States, *inter alia*, Preambular para. 10.

that 'effective international co-operation is essential' as a 'complement to the efforts of developing countries' and 'in providing these countries with appropriate means and facilities to foster their comprehensive development'. Like the NIEO instruments that had come before it, the Declaration was a further response – this time harnessing the language and moral authority of human rights – against an international environment largely conducive to the further accumulation of wealth by the wealthy through the expansive tendencies of global capital. In response, the right to development demanded international co-operation under law for the creation of a structural environment favourable to the realisation of basic human rights, for everyone.[91]

As a so-called 'third-generation right', the right to development has the developing state as both a right-holder and duty-bearer, with the individual as the ultimate beneficiary whose human rights can only be secured, in the words of Bedjaoui, by 'liberat[ing] the State from certain international arrangements that siphon off its wealth abroad'.[92] The Charter on the Economic Rights and Duties of States may have built on the insight that the obstacles to bringing welfare to the people of the developing world are not only internal but often external, but it was the DRD that placed people, not states, at the heart of the endeavour to dismantle the mechanisms of economic subjugation, making a just international economic order a human rights matter.

Ian Brownlie concluded in the years following the DRD's adoption that 'the right constitutes a general affirmation of a need for a programme of international economic justice'.[93] There are strong arguments that it makes a distinctive normative contribution to international law: the Declaration gave legal expression to the notion that the ability of states to develop and to fulfil their human rights obligations are constrained by the structural arrangements and actions of the international community.[94] As the drafting of the DRD highlights, it was meant to give substance to the human right to a just international order as recognised in the Universal Declaration of

---

[91] M. E. Salomon, 'Legal Cosmopolitanism and the Normative Contribution of the Right to Development', in S. P. Marks (ed.), *Implementing the Right to Development: The Role of International Law* (Boston, MA: Harvard School of Public Health/Geneva: Friedrich Ebert Stiftung 2008) 17–26 at 17.

[92] M. Bedjaoui, 'The Right to Development', in M. Bedjaoui (ed.), *International Law: Achievements and Prospects* (Dordrecht: Martinus Nijhoff 1991) 1177–1203 at 1180.

[93] I. Brownlie, 'The Human Right to Development' *Commonwealth Secretariat* (1989) 1 at 8.

[94] Salomon, *Global Responsibility for Human Rights* 50–6.

Human Rights (UDHR) in 1948.[95] The juridical re-imagining of the role and parameters of a contemporary international law of human rights that the right to development asserts in the interest of global justice are not to be dismissed lightly. However like the NIEO claims which had come before, it seems that it will only ever be part of an unfinishable story.

Conclusion

In the 1960s developing countries saw the General Assembly and the shaping of international law as important vehicles through which to press their claims for economic justice. The use of these outlets continues to date, even if the range of 'developing countries' today have economic interests along diverse lines.[96] Yet, while we would be careless to ignore the early contribution of those countries to international law, not least in elevating the 'law of nations' to include a 'law of peoples',[97] the NIEO story and its present-day equivalent offer us reasons to be cynical. An audit of development and international law over fifty years points to stark conclusions: that international law in this area serves certain interests and not others and that the nature and scale of poverty and under-development globally are in large part a result of the choices of those states at the top.[98] That international law has favourites is no accident, and an account of the use and in particular the failures of it over decades to advance the development efforts of developing countries shed light on precisely why.

---

[95] Indeed, as a draft of the DRD and the consensus of the drafting committee of intergovernmental experts reflect, the right to development is 'based upon Article 28 of the Universal Declaration of Human Rights'. *Report of the Working Group of Governmental Experts on the Right to Development* (4th session, 9 December 1982) UN Doc. E/CN4/1983/11 Annex IV, Part I, Section II, Article 1.

[96] See B. S. Chimni, 'ECOSOC and International Economic Institutions', in R. Wilde (ed.), *United Nations Reform Through Practice*, Report of the International Law Association's Study Group on UN Reform (December 2011) 48–55.

[97] U. Baxi, 'What May the "Third World" Expect from International Law?', in R. Falk, B. Rajagopal and J. Stephens (eds.), *International Law and the Third World: Reshaping Justice* (London: Routledge–Cavendish 2008) 9–21 at 16.

[98] See generally A. Gewirth, 'Duties to Fulfil the Human Rights of the Poor', in T. Pogge (ed.), *Freedom from Poverty as a Human Right: Who Owes What to the Very Poor?* (Oxford University Press/Paris: UNESCO 2007) 219–36 at 228; T. Pogge, 'Introduction', in T. Pogge (ed.), *Freedom from Poverty as a Human Right: Who Owes What to the Very Poor?* (Oxford University Press/Paris: UNESCO 2007) 1–9 at 6; S. Marks, 'Human Rights and the Bottom Billion' (2009) *European Human Rights Law Review* 37–49 at 48.

Further reading

Abi-Saab, G., 'Permanent Sovereignty over Natural Resources', in M. Bedjaoui (ed.), *International Law: Achievements and Prospects* (Paris: UNESCO/Dordrecht: Martinus Nijhoff 1991) 597

Bedjaoui, M., *Towards a New International Economic Order* (Paris: UNESCO/New York: Holmes & Meier 1979)

'The Right to Development', in M. Bedjaoui (ed.), *International Law: Achievements and Prospects* (Paris: UNESCO/Dordrecht: Martinus Nijhoff 1991)

Bradlow, D. D., 'Development Decision-Making and the Content of International Development Law' (2004) 27 *Boston College International and Comparative Law Review* 195

Chimni, B. S., 'The Principle of Permanent Sovereignty over Natural Resources: Toward a Radical Interpretation' (1998) 38 (2) *Indian Journal of International Law* 208

De Schutter, O., Eide, A., Khalfan, A., Orellana, M., Salomon, M. E. and Seiderman, I., 'Commentary to the Maastricht Principles on the Extraterritorial Obligations of States in the Area of Economic, Social and Cultural Rights' 34 (4) *Human Rights Quarterly* (forthcoming 2012)

Fidler, D. P., 'Revolt Against or from Within the West: TWAIL, the Developing World, and the Future Direction of International Law' (2003) 1 *Chinese Journal of International Law* 29

Hossain, K. (ed.), *Legal Aspects of the New International Economic Order* (London: Frances Pinter 1980)

Muchlinski, P., 'Holistic Approaches to Development and International Investment Law: The Role of International Investment Agreements', in J. Faundez, and C. Tan (eds.), *International Law, Economic Globalization and Development* (Cheltenham: Edward Elgar 2010) 180

Pahuja, S., *Decolonising International Law: Development, Economic Growth and the Politics of Universality* (Cambridge University Press 2011)

15

Resisting panic: lessons about the role of human rights during the long decade after 9/11

Martin Scheinin

What the world has seen since the atrocious terrorist attacks of 11 September 2001, and the counter-terrorism measures states have taken by way of their response, can be characterised as the worst-ever backlash[1] against the promotion and protection of human rights since their post-Second World War emergence in the UN Charter (1945)[2] and the Universal Declaration of Human Rights (UDHR, 1948).[3] In this sense, the 'long decade' has meant the winding back of the clock by sixty years. As many of the challenges posed by states in relation to the normative code of legally binding human rights relate to what was a major achievement in 1976, namely the entry into force as legally binding international treaties of the twin Covenants,[4] one could equally well say that in legal terms the reversal that began in 2001 was of twenty-five years of human rights protection. But if we focus on practices that have reduced the human person to a mere means, such as in the idea of torturing one individual in the expectation of a benefit to a large group of persons, we can speak instead about turning back the clock by 200 years, to times before the wide approval of Immanuel Kant's moral philosophy with its imperative of treating every human being as an end in him- or herself.[5]

The backlash described

One account of what happened during the years following 9/11 is provided by the International Commission of Jurists, in a report entitled *Assessing*

---

[1] See M. Scheinin, 'Terrorism', in D. Moeckli, S. Shah and S. Sivakumaran (eds.), *International Human Rights Law* (Oxford University Press 2010) 583–601.

[2] Charter of the UN, 1 UNTS XVI (entered into force 24 October 1945).

[3] UDHR, GA Res. 217A (III), UN Doc. A/810 at 71 (1948).

[4] ICESCR, 993 UNTS 3 (entered into force 3 January 1976); CCPR, 999 UNTS 171 (entered into force 23 March 1976).

[5] I. Kant, *Groundwork of the Metaphysic of Morals* (1785) (Cambridge University Press 1997).

Damage, Urging Action.[6] This report resulted from three years of work by a panel of eight eminent jurists who conducted sixteen hearings in different countries throughout the world. Among the adverse effects enhanced counter-terrorism measures have had upon the enjoyment of human rights the report maps, *inter alia*: the use of torture and other forms of inhuman treatment, in particular for the gathering of information; resorting to various forms of exceptionalism that avoid well-established institutions and procedures, including through the application of emergency regimes or special counter-terrorism powers; the use of military courts or tribunals and the wide use of preventive measures such as permanent or long-term detention without criminal charges or sanctions against suspected terrorists without trial; new discriminatory practices such as the 'profiling' of potential terrorists; the increased use of intelligence and intelligence co-operation, resulting in the wide use of secret or generally inadmissible information as the basis for the measures by authorities; and a general erosion of legality through certain governments contesting the applicability of human rights law and also international humanitarian law, all this coupled with a manifest lack of accountability.

Much of the massive wave of human rights violations committed in the name of countering terrorism can be attributed to the George W. Bush administration 2001–9 in the USA. The graphic images of prisoner abuse in Abu Ghraib prison in Iraq and the military detention facility in Guantanamo Bay have become symbols of a broad scope of measures through which the Bush Administration sought to escape domestic and international law and to use whatever means they could in combating what it depicted as a 'war' against a global terrorist organisation Al Qaeda, operating under the leadership of Osama bin Laden. Secret detention, extraordinary rendition, torturous interrogation methods and denial of a trial before an ordinary court were some of the key components in the design of the aggressive response by the Bush Administration to the attacks of 11 September.[7]

There are problematic dimensions also in the collective response by states to new waves of international terrorism. For instance, Security Council

---

[6] *Assessing Damage, Urging Action*. Report of the Eminent Jurists Panel on Terrorism, Counter-Terrorism and Human Rights (London: International Commission of Jurists 2009).

[7] For the role of the UK in what the Bush Administration depicted as a 'global war on terror', see R. Brown, *Fighting Monsters: British–American War-Making and Law-Making* (Oxford: Hart 2011).

Resolution 1373 (2001),[8] adopted less than three weeks after 9/11, resulted in a semi-permanent transfer of powers from the General Assembly as the developer of international law to the much smaller Security Council, under the justification that the 9/11 terrorist attacks, 'like any act of international terrorism, constitute a threat to international peace and security'. Resolution 1267 (1999) had already resulted in UN-imposed sanctions against individuals before 2001, and such terrorist listing was greatly expanded after the attacks, particularly through Resolution 1390 (2002) that transformed targeted sanctions against the Taleban in Afghanistan into a regime without geographical or temporal limitations.[9] These sanctions involve primarily travel bans and the freezing of assets, and have been deployed against hundreds of individuals named by a Committee of the Security Council, without due process and without effective recourse to judicial review.[10] Sadly, in resolution 1530 (2004), the Security Council exercised its authority under Chapter VII of the UN Charter wrongly to condemn the Basque terrorist organisation ETA for the Madrid bombings of 11 March 2004.[11] At least the last-mentioned resolution must be categorised as a panic reaction.

Some positive trends?

This author has elsewhere[12] argued that despite this post-9/11 backlash, the 'long decade' from 2001 onwards, after the terrorist attacks of 11 September 2001 has also brought about positive trends and promising potentials.

---

[8] S/RES/1373 (2001). For a criticism of the usurpation of legislative powers by the Security Council through this Resolution, see Report of the Special Rapporteur on the promotion and protection of human rights and fundamental freedoms while countering terrorism, UN Doc. A/65/258.

[9] S/RES/1390 (2002).

[10] S/RES/1267 (1999). For a criticism of the usurpation of quasi-judicial powers by the Security Council through this Resolution, see Report of the Special Rapporteur on the promotion and protection of human rights and fundamental freedoms while countering terrorism, UN Doc. A/65/258. For the current version of Resolution 1267, see S/RES/1989 (2011).

[11] S/RES/1530 (2004): 'Condemns in the strongest terms the bomb attacks in Madrid, Spain, perpetrated by ETA on 11 March 2004, in which many lives were claimed and people injured, and regards such act, like any act of terrorism, as a threat to peace and security.'

[12] M. Scheinin, 'Human Rights and Counter-Terrorism: Lessons from a Long Decade', in D. Jenkins, A. Henriksen and A. Jacobsen (eds.), *The Long Decade: How 9/11 Has Changed the Law* (Oxford University Press 2012).

In order better to explain them, these positive potentials can be condensed into ten partly overlapping trends that will be summarised here:

(1) Over the years since 9/11, there has been a shift in the response by the human rights community, from generalised concerns over human rights abuses to a much more focused and structured debate about the role of human rights law in countering terrorism. Today, the discourse about human rights and counter-terrorism is not merely a moral protest against the backlash as such but covers a wide and rich substantive agenda.

(2) The development of a substantive agenda for voicing human rights concerns in the counter-terrorism context has also meant a move from seeing just the tip of the iceberg of the gravest human rights abuses to assessing the total phenomenon of the human rights consequences of the full range of counter-terrorism measures.

(3) While initially human rights groups may have, because of focusing on the gravest abuses, given rise to an image that they were devoting too much of their attention to the human rights of real or suspected terrorists, a broader agenda and a move to an holistic view of all the human rights consequences of counter-terrorism measures has also brought about a discourse that addresses the enjoyment of human rights by broad strata in society. What has resulted is a new emphasis on focusing not only (or even primarily) on the human rights of 'terrorists' to caring for the human rights of everyone, including stigmatised minorities, members of the mainstream population and victims of terrorism.[13]

(4) The war rhetoric by the Bush Administration resulted for a while in a fairly fruitless situation, as human rights groups devoted much of their energy to contesting the war paradigm and defending the continued applicability of human rights law. This debate was necessary but has gradually moved to a more nuanced assessment of applicable law, so that also human rights lawyers need to understand international humanitarian law and be prepared to address also situations where there is overlap between terrorism and armed conflict.[14]

[13] For substantiation of the first three trends, see the series of thematic reports by the UN Special Rapporteur on human rights and counter-terrorism, www.ohchr.org/EN/Issues/Terrorism/Pages/Annual.aspx.

[14] M. Scheinin and M. Vermeulen, 'Unilateral Exceptions to International Law: Systematic Legal Analysis and Critique of Doctrines to Deny or Reduce the Applicability of Human Rights Norms in the Fight against Terrorism' (2011) 8 *Essex Human Rights Review* 20–56.

(5) At the UN level and more broadly in international co-operation, counter-terrorism and human rights were far too long treated as separate subjects, discussed by different people in their own *fora*. For instance, the Committees of the Security Council that dealt with counter-terrorism matters were fending off human rights concerns by attributing them to separate human rights bodies within the UN structures. Over the years, there has been a slow but steady shift towards looking instead for increasing co-ordination between counter-terrorism efforts and human rights bodies, not least through the creation and operation of the UN Counter-Terrorism Implementation Task Force (CTITF), an inter-agency co-ordination body.[15]

(6) There has been a transformation in the mindset of well-informed policy-makers and counter-terrorism professionals, from viewing human rights as an unfortunate obstacle to counter-terrorism to understanding their positive role in building successful and sustainable counter-terrorism strategies.[16] Today, compliance with human rights is seen both as one pillar of a counter-terrorism strategy and as an ingredient in all other pillars.

(7) The recognition of human rights compliance as an element in a sustainable and successful counter-terrorism strategy has also helped in moving from what has been a merely defensive human rights advocacy, based on the idea of human rights being legally binding minimum standards, to a more offensive use of human rights. Rather than treating them as a set of inconvenient but mandatory minimum standards their scope has been expanded beyond such minimum requirements, as 'best practices' that will pay off even when implemented beyond what is strictly required by law.[17]

(8) The methods developed by the Bush Administration, as well as individual problematic solutions in the national laws of other countries, have been used by authoritarian regimes for bad-faith copycatting across borders, to the effect that ill treatment as part of interrogation methods or detention without trial have been legitimised by reference to Western countries. Over time, such copycatting has given way to more genuine forms of

---

[15] For the CTITF, see www.un.org/en/terrorism/ctitf/index.shtml.

[16] For the Global Counter-Terrorism Strategy, see GA Res. A/RES/60/288 (2006).

[17] Report of the Special Rapporteur on the promotion and protection of human rights and fundamental freedoms while countering terrorism, Martin Scheinin. Ten areas of best practices in countering terrorism. UN Doc. A/HRC/16/51.

learning from experience, including by acknowledging that good human rights lessons learned elsewhere can be part of a strategic response to terrorism.

(9) One of the ill-advised metaphors in the early unfocused discourse on human rights and counter-terrorism was the idea of an abstract 'balance' between security and individual rights. The effect of such rhetoric has tended to always be the same, the forsaking of human rights in the name of presumed benefits for security. Gradually, there has been a move to restricting the scope of any 'balancing' by insisting on the absolute nature of some human rights, such as the prohibition against torture, and by locating any remaining need for 'balancing' to one step in the application of an analytical permissible limitations test, with a carefully defined space for proportionality assessment ('better law approach').[18]

(10) Finally, the discourse of human rights and counter-terrorism has been one of the areas where a need has been identified to shift the focus from the legal obligations of the territorial state in relation to its inhabitants (human rights as vertical norms) to protecting the human rights of the individual irrespective of the actor (transnational law). Hence, counter-terrorism has been one of the issues that has triggered a discussion and elaboration of new concepts and theories about how to make also other actors than the territorial state accountable for action that results in non-enjoyment of human rights – such as other states, international organisations and private actors, including transnational corporations (TNCs) and armed groups.[19]

Post-9/11 panic and human rights as resistance to it

The obstacles against the improvements that have just been described should not be underestimated. One feature of the counter-terrorism hype during the long decade has been that policy-makers have often been reacting to media reports and their expected consequences for the

---

[18] Scheinin and Vermeulen, 'Unilateral Exceptions'.

[19] See M. Scheinin, 'Monitoring Human Rights Obligations and the Fight against Terrorism: Whose Obligations? And Monitored How?', in G. Alfredsson *et al.* (eds.), *International Human Rights Monitoring Mechanisms. Essays in Honour of Jakob Th. Möller*, 2nd rev. edn (Dordrecht: Martinus Nijhoff 2009) 407–20.

formation of public opinion. Acts of terrorism have frequently received disproportionate media attention, for instance in comparison to other causes for the loss of life, and politicians have therefore been challenged by the media to come forward with clear and decisive responses to acts of terrorism.

When this happens politicians can respond in panic, just wanting to be seen as 'doing something'. When the international community wants to 'do something' in respect of an identified threat to international peace and security, this can mean the use of force, even when nobody is quite sure about what consequences this will have. In the counter-terrorism context, 'doing something' on the national level, can involve granting of new powers to the police and the intelligence services, or enacting legislation that is merely symbolic, designed not as proven to be effective but rather to demonstrate the will of politicians to act. In the post-9/11 world, no politician wants to be seen as being 'soft' on terrorism.

When legislation is driven by panic, the outcomes may be quite problematic. These can go beyond such inaccuracies as the Security Council wrongly attributing blame for the Madrid bombs to ETA mentioned above to include such initiatives as the discriminatory 'profiling' of ethnic or religious communities that are perceived as including terrorists; the broadening of police powers, including for detention, without adequate judicial and other safeguards; the mandatory detention of unwanted foreigners; and so on.

In relation to these and similar examples of counter-terrorism measures introduced in panic, it is surely justifiable to say that during the long decade, human rights law has been the *main* source of resistance to such developments, pushing back or at least delaying many of these measures. Defenders of human rights have fought against prevailing assumptions and negative trends to achieve the positive or promising changes that we have earlier catalogued. Investigative journalism has also made a tremendous contribution by revealing and documenting human rights abuses committed in the name of countering terrorism, such as torture, extraordinary rendition, secret detention and detainee abuse.[20] Mention should be made as well of the proponents of professionalism among the counter-terrorism operators such

---

[20] To name one example, the role of *The Washington Post* was remarkable in revealing the practices of secret detention, extraordinary rendition and torturous methods of interrogation applied by the US Bush Administration.

as the police, intelligence services and the military.[21] But in the opinion of this writer, human rights law has been in the vanguard of the resistance.

Human rights and power

This 'long decade' after the terrorist attacks of 11 September 2011 provides ample evidence that human rights have retained their critical potential in respect of inhuman practices such as torture and in relation to the abuse of power. When human rights defenders make a claim about human rights being *law*, *international* law, or *higher* law, they are at the same time making a normative assertion based on the moral dimension of human rights, and in doing so they are utilising the qualities of law as an instrument of power. They are making a claim about how power should be exercised in society and objecting to the whims of those who for expected short-term advantages are willing to trash some of the conventions and guarantees achieved and consolidated into law over centuries. They are insisting on the nature of human rights as black-letter law, and on full compliance with it, as a 'conservative' attempt to resist panic and to defend some of the most valuable achievements of human society.

Where human rights are a tool in the exercise of power, they should be seen primarily as a device for empowerment and emancipation. Human rights were born from the recognition of imbalanced vertical power relationships between the state and the individual. They have retained their critical potential in respect of the exercise and abuse of power. Also with the evolution of law towards legal pluralism and multi-level governance, human rights law has retained its potential as a critical strand within the law itself. Insistence upon compliance with human rights can provide a coherence-building tool in the application of the seemingly incoherent multitude of valid sources of law.

Somewhat paradoxically, efforts to broaden the reach of human rights norms, as societal value choices and also in respect of diagonal and horizontal relationships[22] run the risk of compromising their emancipatory

---

[21] Reference can be made to intelligence agents and interrogation specialists who during the Bush Administration objected to the use of torture and other ill treatment in the interrogation of terrorism suspects.

[22] While the relationship between a state and its individual citizen is clearly a vertical one, the reference to horizontal relationships covers relations between equal private parties, such as

potential. If the state is seen not merely as a *threat* to human rights but as a *guarantor* of human rights within society, as has been said on a number of occasions by the European Court of Human Rights (ECtHR) (including in relation to horizontal relations within ethnic or religious groups[23]) then human rights law may have a double role as both a tool for individual emancipation and as a device for increased state control over the internal life of a community. And if human rights are transformed into a normative project about how humans should lead their lives, they run the risk of losing their empowering capacity in the support of freedom and choice.

Despite this counter-current that gives rise to caution in respect of the last positive trend mentioned earlier in this chapter, the long decade after 9/11 shows that human rights have retained their critical and emancipatory function. We will revisit this theme at the end of this chapter, after first mapping a number of critical challenges to human rights.

Critiques of human rights law and responses to them

The above discussion has already revealed some of the responses by the current author to various critiques of human rights law or of human rights scholarship. The argument that human rights law, as any effort to emphasise the role of *law* in organising a society, will end up transforming human rights into a *tool of power*, potentially even of oppression, was fended off by asserting that the power dimension of human rights is not about supporting the already powerful but rather is concerned with empowerment and emancipation. Yes, human rights law can be used as a tool of power – but as a transformative tool that helps to overcome inequalities and oppression.

Critiques of human rights law as a tool of power fall within a broader family of critiques that instrumentalise human rights or assume their instrumentalisation, by presuming that human rights serve, or should serve, a *function*, and then judging how human rights law does in the delivery of that function. As an example, minority rights may be required to serve the function of integration in society, and then criticised if they sometimes do not perform well in working towards that goal. Or human

---

two individuals. And a diagonal relationship would exist between an individual and a centre of power other than the person's own state.

[23] See, e.g., *Refah Partisi and Others* v. *Turkey*, ECtHR, Grand Chamber Judgment of 13 February 2003, para. 119 (endorsing para. 70 of the Chamber Judgment).

rights in general may be subordinated to their background value of human dignity by seeking to restrict the protection afforded to human rights by arguing that some of them, or some dimensions of them, would not bear a sufficient connection with human dignity.[24] The general answer by this author to these critiques is simply to assert that within the sphere of law or, more generally, human normativity, *every human right is an end in itself.* This expression may be an over-simplification in the sense that ultimately it is the human being, the natural person in flesh and blood, who is the end. Human-created normative categories, such as moral values or legal rights, are social constructs even if deeply embedded, and in that sense just means towards serving living humans. When I assert that human rights should, within the sphere of law, be treated as ends in themselves, this simply means that they do not need any deeper normative justification, such as some unitary background value, which typically would be human dignity.

The requirement that each human right be treated as an end in itself should form part of the definition of human rights, and if this approach were followed, it would surely follow that it would at the same time be necessary to establish a rather demanding test for candidates for the status of a human right. We are back to a concern voiced earlier about adopting too broad an approach to the question of what is a human right.[25] But taking the approach suggested here would free us to be able to dismiss any requirement of a further normative justification behind a human right. This chapter is not the place to develop this position in full but a good occasion to flag it as the author's position.

This approach helps us to deal with some other efforts to undermine human rights. The critiques offered by proponents of cultural relativism and cultural imperialism tend to assume that human rights are a Western innovation without true universal legitimacy. While cultural relativism tries to carve out space for competing interpretations of human rights, or competing alternatives to human rights, the critique against cultural

---

[24] As a prime example of a general functionalist human rights critique, reference may be made to D. P. Forsythe, 'Human Rights Studies: On the Dangers of Legalistic Assumptions', in F. Coomans and M. Kamminga (eds.), *Methods of Human Rights Research* (Oxford: Intersentia 2009). In his Conclusion, Forsythe is explicit in stating: 'One should be prepared to conclude, on the basis of careful research, that human rights law is misguided or not working, . . . Human rights are a means to human dignity; as means, they should not be confused with the desired end' 75.

[25] See also P. Alston, 'Conjuring up New Human Rights: A Proposal for Quality Control' (1984) 78 (3) *American Journal of International Law* 607–21.

imperialism seeks to delegitimise human rights by, once again, attributing to them an assumed function. It is true that the UN was a relatively small club of independent states in 1945 and 1948 when the UN Charter and the UDHR were adopted and the notion of human rights was introduced and crystallised into a catalogue. Nevertheless, since then every single state in the world has through its voluntary decision ratified at least two, usually more, of the central UN human rights treaties,[26] hence committing themselves as a matter of international law to the human rights catalogue of the UDHR. As a matter of law there is, therefore, no question about human rights not being universal. And as a matter of politics one should not ask the authoritarian leaders of some less human rights-friendly states whether human rights are universal. Rather one should ask the oppressed living in those countries, those in search of the empowering and emancipatory potential of human rights.

There are two further and quite different critiques of human rights that deserve as a common response the 'better law' approach that was referred to above when setting out the ten positive trends that have been seen during the long decade. The indeterminacy critique assumes that human rights, perhaps because of their links to morality or because of the fairly abstract formulation of some provisions in human rights treaties, suffer from substantive vagueness to the degree that they can be used to justify anything, even diametrically opposite positions. The proponents of the indeterminacy critique have often failed to study the discourse of human rights law and its institutionalised practices of interpretation. Because of its consolidated lines of interpretation, human rights law is far less vague or unpredictable than an uninformed reader might assume merely on the basis of examination of the text of this or that treaty provision. Expert level command of institutionalised practices of interpretation under human rights treaties results in the transformation of human rights law into 'better law' that is as strict and predictable as to its methodology as any other branch of law.

This said, what was just described as 'better law' may give rise to another form of critique, namely the attacks that are levelled against human rights

---

[26] In all except two cases, one of the human rights treaties ratified by a state would be the Convention on the Rights of the Child, GA Res. 44/25, in itself already covering the whole normative scope of the human rights catalogue. For a visual demonstration of how universal human rights have developed through the voluntary ratification by all states of human rights treaties, see the Human Rights Theme Maps produced by the Raoul Wallenberg Institute of Human Rights and Humanitarian Law, www.rwi.lu.se/tm/ThemeMaps.html.

lawyers for their apologeticism. The expert-level command required for transforming human rights law into better law risks resulting in an uncritical state of mind where the interpretive authority of bodies such as the ECtHR is always seen as beyond any criticism and the role of the scholar is thereby reduced to the mere systematiser of case law. It is true that much of legal human rights research is methodologically simplistic and results in descriptive and uncritical compendia of case law. The answer to these critiques lies in the recognition that in human rights scholarship, as in any other serious scholarship, the true scholar will always retain a critical mind. Hence, the requirement of 'better law' must come together with a call for 'better scholarship' in order to secure that the discourse of human rights law is at the same time based on expertise and committed to creativity, originality and the critical role of the scholar.

Finally, three critiques can be grouped together under what was earlier characterised as a counter-current. As has already been noted, the effort to expand the reach of human rights norms from vertical relationships between the state and the individual to diagonal and horizontal relationships with also private entities and individuals as duty-bearers may carry the risk of diluting the emancipatory potential of human rights law. This development is linked to recent tendencies to re-evaluate the role of the state so as to see it no longer merely as the main threat to human rights but also as their guarantor, particularly in relations between private parties. A related tendency is a renewed emphasis on the duties of the individual, with the proclaimed aim of securing respect for human rights in interpersonal relationships. These positions are being all too easily transformed into the use of human rights norms to dictate how people should lead their lives rather than protecting their right to choose exactly this. Once again, the answer given here lies in the combination of 'better law' and 'better scholarship'. We should elaborate doctrines of positive state obligations under human rights law but without losing our analytical mind and critical attitude in relation to the consequences that might follow.

Conclusion: human rights law as critique

It was already stated above that in respect of the panic reactions that followed 9/11, human rights law provided the *main* form of resistance. Together with the position that the power dimension of the human rights discourse is all about emancipation and empowerment, this justifies the conclusion that the practice of human rights law is a form of critique.

Human rights law represents a critique of inhuman practices such as torture and arbitrary detention. This critique can be defensive in nature, for example when directed against the abuse of power and more generally against imbalanced power relations. Or it can be more offensive, outlining in positive terms normative prescriptions as to how power should be exercised in society.

Furthermore, as human rights law has one leg within the realm of the law itself, and another leg in the sphere of morality, it opens up the possibility of a normative assessment of the law. Human rights function as a critical strand within law. Through its ratification of a number of human rights treaties, a state has chosen to subject itself to a law-based assessment and criticism as to how its practice and legal system conform to the norms of this voluntarily adopted catalogue of human rights law. This assessment may be performed within the sphere of law but at the same time it is conscious of the moral foundation of human rights. Hence, human rights norms are a substantive coherence-building element in any legal system, and also in relation to efforts to secure coherence between overlapping systems of law, such as international law, regional supranational law, private transnational regulation, national (federal) law, local law, or traditional law of natural communities.

'Give me a place to stand on, and I will move the Earth', said Archimedes. In physics, this idea of a fixed fulcrum where a person can stand in order to use a mighty lever to move the whole earth is doomed to fail, as there is no other place to stand but on the earth itself. For a social phenomenon such as law, the fallacy does not apply. One can stand on the moral foundations of human rights and nevertheless use them as a fulcrum within the sphere of law itself, in order to put the whole legal system into motion. This is the critical potential of human rights law.

Further reading

Assessing Damage, Urging Action, Report of the Eminent Jurists Panel on Terrorism, Counter-Terrorism and Human Rights (London: International Commission of Jurists 2009)

Doswald-Beck, L., *Human Rights in Times of Conflict and Terrorism* (Oxford University Press 2011)

Essex Human Rights Review, Special Issue (2011) 8

Jenkins, D., Henriksen, A. and Jacobsen, A. (eds.), *The Long Decade: How 9/11 Has Changed the Law* (Oxford University Press 2012)

Scheinin, M., 'Terrorism', in D. Moeckli, S. Shah and S. Sivakumaran (eds.), *International Human Rights Law* (Oxford University Press 2010) 583–601

Thematic Reports by the UN Special Rapporteur on human rights and counter-terrorism, www.ohchr.org/EN/Issues/Terrorism/Pages/Annual.aspx

What's in a name? The prohibitions on torture and ill treatment today

Manfred Nowak

16

Torture constitutes one of the most serious human rights violations and a direct attack on the core of the dignity and integrity of human beings. As a consequence, the prohibition of torture has been recognised as one of the very few absolute and non-derogable rights in a variety of global and regional human rights treaties. It also has been accepted as a rule of *ius cogens* under international law, in times of both peace and armed conflict. Nevertheless, after having carried out the mandate of UN Special Rapporteur on Torture for six years and having conducted fact-finding missions to eighteen countries in all world regions as well as three joint studies with other special procedures, I have come to the conclusion that *torture is practised in more than 90 per cent of all countries and constitutes a widespread practice in more than 50 per cent of all countries*. In addition, I have found highly deplorable conditions of detention in most countries that often amount to cruel, inhuman or degrading treatment. I was so alarmed by these findings that I have spoken of a *global prison crisis* and have called for a UN Convention on the Rights of Detainees.[1]

In reaction to the systematic practice of torture in Latin American military dictatorships the UN in 1984 adopted the special Convention against Torture and Other Cruel, Inhuman or Degrading Treatment or Punishment (CAT) aimed at strengthening the prohibition of torture and ill treatment through a number of positive obligations to prevent torture, to criminalise torture and bring the perpetrators of torture to justice, and to provide torture survivors with an effective remedy and reparation for the harm suffered.[2] State compliance

---

[1] *Report of the Special Rapporteur on Torture and Other Cruel, Inhuman or Degrading Treatment or Punishment: Study On the Phenomena of Torture, Cruel, Inhuman or Degrading Treatment or Punishment in the World, Including an Assessment of Conditions of Detention*, UN Doc. A/HRC/13/39/Add.5 of 5 February 2010.

[2] For a detailed analysis of each obligation under the Convention, see M. Nowak and E. McArthur, *The United Nations Convention against Torture: A Commentary* (Oxford University Press 2008); for a short summary of the various obligations, see M. Nowak, 'Torture and Enforced Disappearance', in M. Scheinin and C. Krause, *International Protection of Human Rights: A Textbook* (Turku/Åbo: Åbo University Institute for Human Rights 2009), 151–82.

with these obligations is monitored by an independent expert body, the UN Committee against Torture, by various means, including by *ex officio* investigations of systematic practices of torture under Article 20 CAT. A total of 149 states from all regions are today parties to CAT but the situation of torture and ill treatment has not improved since then – this is because of a lack of political will. We know exactly what needs to be done in order to eradicate and prevent torture. If police custody were kept to a maximum of forty-eight hours and involve a thorough judicial review, if all persons arrested by the police were to have a right of prompt access to lawyers, doctors and family members, if all allegations of torture were to be promptly investigated by an independent body and by a forensic expert, if the police were trained in modern interrogation and criminal investigation methods and if confessions extracted by torture were routinely rendered inadmissible in courts, then torture could easily be eradicated.

But in reality, the opposite is done. In many countries of the world, persons suspected of having committed a crime are arrested by the police and kept in police custody for many weeks, months or even years without any effective control. Prosecutors and judges put pressure on the police to 'solve' crimes by means of extracting confessions rather than by fulfilling their function of keeping oversight of police custody. The right to *habeas corpus* is often reduced to a simple telephone call between a police officer and a judge, with the detainee having no effective access to any external control mechanism, a judge, a lawyer, or a doctor. Confessions are still regarded as the 'queen of evidence', and confessions extracted by torture are regularly used by prosecutors and courts to convict a suspect.

In 2002, a new and very promising method of preventing torture and of improving conditions of detention was introduced by the adoption of the Optional Protocol to the Convention against Torture (OPCAT): regular preventive visits to all places of detention by an independent international monitoring body, the UN Subcommittee for the Prevention of Torture, and by so-called national preventive mechanisms (NPMs), i.e. commissions of independent experts with different professional backgrounds (lawyers, doctors, psychologists, sociologists, criminologists, prison experts, social workers, etc.). OPCAT builds upon the experience of the European Committee for the Prevention of Torture (CPT), an expert body regularly visiting places of detention in all forty-seven member states of the Council of Europe and developing minimum standards of detention. But by requiring all states parties to establish independent and professional domestic inspection bodies with the right to carry out unannounced visits to all places of detention (including police lock-ups, psychiatric institutions and special detention facilities for migrants, children, drug users etc.), OPCAT has the potential to become more effective than its European counterpart. In reality, however, many States tend to undermine OPCAT by entrusting the function of NPMs to bodies which do not fulfil the necessary requirements of independence and professionalism and which often lack the financial resources necessary to carry out their important work. Nevertheless, OPCAT is one of the most important and promising new developments aimed at the prevention of torture as it strives at opening up places of detention to scrutiny and at introducing transparency into police, prison and health management.

The most important innovation of CAT was the obligation of states parties to a human rights treaty to use criminal law in order to *fight impunity* as one of the major root causes of torture. All 149 states parties have an obligation under Article 4 CAT to establish the crime of torture, as defined in Article 1, under domestic criminal law with adequate penalties (long-term imprisonment as with other violent crimes), and to subject this crime to the broadest possible jurisdiction (territorial, flag, national and even universal jurisdiction) aimed at avoiding safe havens for perpetrators of torture world-wide. The obligation, rather than the mere possibility of states to establish universal jurisdiction for the crime of torture in accordance with Article 5 (2) CAT was a revolutionary step in international human rights law and, at that time, prompted high expectations for a new era of fighting impunity for one of the worst crimes against human rights. The reality, almost thirty years later, looks totally different. Although torture continues to be widespread in the majority of states, the number of convictions of perpetrators of torture on the basis of the principle of universal jurisdiction can be counted on the fingers of one hand. Governments simply lack the political will to arrest, prosecute and punish heads of state and Government, Ministers of Interior, police officers, soldiers, intelligence agents and prison guards of other countries for the 'mere' crime of torture. But most states have failed even to create a proper crime of torture with adequate penalties under their domestic criminal codes for their own perpetrators: this is because they simply deny the existence of torture and often regard torture as a misdemeanour which might better be dealt with by means of disciplinary measures, such as non-promotion for half a year.

In addition, most states continue to resist any independent mechanism for the prompt and effective investigation of allegations or suspicions of torture in accordance with Articles 6, 12 and 13 CAT. Usually, the police are vested with the monopoly of criminal investigation of all crimes, including crimes committed by the police themselves. It is not difficult to understand that most police officers in the world are not particularly eager to investigate (much less take action against) their own colleagues. Since torture always takes place behind closed doors without independent witnesses and is regularly denied by all actors involved, it is one of the most difficult crimes to investigate. It is, therefore, crucial that torture allegations and suspicions are investigated by an independent and professional body outside the police structure, but with all the powers of a criminal investigation, including those of arrest, search and seize. Only very few states around the world have the political will to establish an effective 'police-police' which means in effect that only very few perpetrators of torture have been subject of a thorough criminal investigation in their own countries, let alone been indicted, prosecuted for (much less convicted of) the crime of torture. As a consequence, impunity as one of the major root causes of torture persists in most of the countries of the world.

In addition to the prevention of torture and the fight against impunity, CAT also provides victims of torture with the *right to an effective remedy and adequate reparation* for the harm suffered (Articles 13 and 14). As already mentioned, remedies in most countries are not effective as allegations of torture by detainees and former detainees are not properly investigated. But even when torture has been proven, survivors of torture only rarely receive any kind of reparation from those responsible. The type of reparation most torture survivors are in need of is medical, psychological, social and legal rehabilitation for the harm suffered. Many victims of torture suffer from post-traumatic stress disorder (PTSD) and other long-term psychological effects for the rest of their life and need rehabilitation treatment for many years. If torture survivors are lucky and enjoy access to such treatment, then this will usually be not in their own countries but in a privately run torture rehabilitation centre in a country that provides them with asylum or other form of protection. The financial resources for these torture rehabilitation centres usually come from private donors, development agencies or international organisations, such as the EU or the UN Voluntary Fund for Victims of Torture, but not from those states or individuals responsible for the practice of torture. In times of economic and financial crisis, many privately run torture rehabilitation centres lack the financial means to provide the services they would wish to provide to torture survivors.

In the following, I will not provide any greater overview of the various obligations of states (under CAT and other human rights treaties) to respect, protect and fulfil the prohibition of torture and ill treatment, referring the interested reader instead to the relevant literature and case law.[3] Similarly, I will not describe the reality of torture and ill treatment in the world as this is covered by the respective reports of the UN Special Rapporteur on Torture and other fact-finding bodies. I will rather discuss some of the more controversial issues related to the definition of torture on the one hand, and other forms of cruel, inhuman or degrading treatment or punishment (CIDT), on the other. This includes the questions of corporal and capital punishment and other challenges to the full enjoyment of the right to personal integrity and human dignity.

Definition of torture, cruel, inhuman or degrading treatment or punishment

Most human rights are formulated in a positive way and then add certain acts that states are prohibited to undertake as well as certain measures that states may take in order to limit the right in question. For example, Article 9 of the International Covenant on Civil and Political Rights (CCPR) and Article 5 of the European Convention on Human Rights (ECHR) first guarantee the right to personal liberty and security and then prohibit arbitrary arrest or detention while the ECHR even contains an exhaustive list of non-arbitrary, i.e. legitimate types of arrest and detention. Articles 19 CCPR and Article 10 ECHR stipulate the right to freedom of expression and then add a specific limitation clause with a number of purposes for legitimate state interference. Similarly, Articles 6 CCPR and 2 ECHR recognise the right to life and then provide for specific exceptions relating to the death penalty and, in case of the ECHR, to the legitimate use of force by law enforcement bodies.

Only a few human rights lack a positive formulation and are expressed only in negative terms. The prohibitions of torture and slavery constitute

---

[3] See Nowak and McArthur, *The United Nations Convention*; H. Burgers and H. Danelius, *The United Nations Convention against Torture: Handbook on the Convention Against Torture and Other Cruel, Inhuman or Degrading Treatment or Punishment* (Dordrecht: Martinus Nijhoff 1988); C. Ingelse, *The UN Committee against Torture: An Assessment* (The Hague/London/Boston, MA: Kluwer Law 2001); A. Boulesbaa, *The UN Convention on Torture and the Prospects for Enforcement* (The Hague: Martinus Nijhoff 1999).

the most prominent examples. The negative formulation of Article 5 of the Universal Declaration of Human Rights of 1948 (UDHR): 'No one shall be subjected to torture or to cruel, inhuman or degrading treatment or punishment') was literally taken over in Article 3 ECHR 1950 (with the exception of the prohibition of cruel treatment or punishment) and Article 7 CCPR 1966 (with the addition of the prohibition of medical or scientific experimentation). Article 5 of the American Convention on Human Rights 1969 (ACHR) is the first human rights treaty which puts this prohibition in context with a positive right: the right to physical, mental and moral integrity and the right to humane treatment. Article 5 of the African Charter on Human and Peoples' Rights 1981 (African Charter) promulgated the 'right to the respect of the dignity inherent in a human being and to the recognition of his legal status' and then prohibited 'all forms of exploitation and degradation of man', including the prohibition of slavery and torture. Similarly, the EU Charter of Fundamental Rights 2000 (EU Charter) created a first chapter entitled 'Dignity' which comprises the right to human dignity, the right to life, the right to the integrity of the person (relating primarily to the fields of medicine and biology), the prohibition of torture and inhuman or degrading treatment or punishment (Article 4), and the prohibition of slavery and forced labour. Finally, Article 8 of the Arab Charter on Human Rights 2004 (Arab Charter) returned to the purely negative formulation that 'No one shall be subjected to physical or psychological torture or to cruel, degrading, humiliating or inhuman treatment'. A combined reading of these provisions in global and regional human rights treaties shows that torture and other forms of ill treatment, as well as slavery, slave trade and forced labour, constitute the most important violations of the *right to personal integrity and human dignity*. Secondly, none of these provisions contains any definition of the concepts of human dignity, personal integrity, nor of the concepts of torture or CIDT. Furthermore, none of these provisions seem to permit any restrictions or limitations of torture or other forms of ill treatment.

The first *definition of torture* was developed in Article 1 CAT: the term 'torture' means 'any act by which severe pain or suffering, whether physical or mental, is intentionally inflicted on a person for such purposes as obtaining from him or a third person information or a confession, punishing him for an act he or a third person has committed or is suspected of having committed, or intimidating or coercing him or a third person, or for any reason based on discrimination of any kind, when such pain or suffering is inflicted by or at the instigation of or with the consent or acquiescence of a public official or other person acting in an official capacity. It does not include pain or suffering arising only from, inherent in or incidental to lawful sanctions.' In Article 16, each state party undertakes to prevent 'other acts of cruel, inhuman or degrading treatment or punishment which do not amount to torture as defined in Article 1, when such acts are committed by or at the instigation of or with the consent or acquiescence of a public official or other person acting in an official capacity', without, however, further defining the concept of CIDT.

The definition of torture in Article 2 of the Inter-American Convention to Prevent and Punish Torture of 1985 is broader than the one in Article 1 CAT. It does not require the involvement of a public official or the threshold of 'severe' pain or suffering, and torture can be inflicted for any purpose. Torture does not even have to cause any physical pain or mental anguish when it is used upon a person 'intended to obliterate the personality of the victim or to diminish his physical or mental capacities'. Article 7 (2)(e) of the Rome Statute of the ICC defines torture in the context of crimes against humanity as 'the intentional infliction of severe pain or suffering, whether physical or mental, upon a person in the custody or under the control of the accused'. It adds the lawful sanctions clause, but does not require the involvement of a public official or any purpose.

In my capacity as Special Rapporteur on Torture, I based myself primarily on the definition of torture in Article 1 CAT. But this definition and the distinction between torture and other forms of ill treatment is definitely in need of further interpretation, which I based on a thorough analysis in the CAT Commentary,[4] taking also into account the other definitions cited above. Torture constitutes an aggravated and, without doubt, the most serious form of ill treatment with a particular stigma attached which means that this term should not be used in any inflationary manner. In principle, two different schools of thought emerged. The first one was developed by the European Court of Human Rights (ECtHR) in the Northern Ireland case[5] and is, despite certain inconsistencies, still relied upon by the European Court and those scholars who follow its jurisprudence. In their opinion, the intensity of the pain or suffering inflicted upon the victim is the decisive criterion in distinguishing torture from CIDT. As a

---

[4] Nowak and McArthur, *The United Nations Convention* 66–86 and 557–76.
[5] ECtHR, *Ireland* v. *United Kingdom*, judgment of 18 January 1978, Ser. A, No. 25.

consequence, inhuman or degrading treatment or punishment requires a lower threshold than severe pain or suffering. Whether degrading treatment requires an even lower threshold than inhuman treatment remains an open question, but degrading treatment means a particularly humiliating conduct. The second school of thought regards the intention of the perpetrator and the purpose of the act, rather than the intensity of the pain or suffering, as the decisive criteria distinguishing torture from CIDT. I added the element of powerlessness of the victim as another distinguishing criterion, following in this respect the definition in the Rome Statute. In my opinion, the *essential elements of torture* are, therefore, the following: the involvement of a public official; the infliction of severe pain or suffering; the intention of the perpetrator and a specific purpose; and the powerlessness of the victim.

According to the explicit wording of both Articles 1 and 16 CAT, torture and CIDT must be committed by or at least with the acquiescence of a *public official*. But this traditional state-centred understanding of torture and CIDT has been eroded in the meantime to a great extent. Both the Inter-American Convention and the Rome Statute no longer require the involvement of a public official. Similarly, the jurisprudence of the International Criminal Tribunals for the former Yugoslavia and Rwanda (ICTFY and ICTR) has applied the crime of torture to non-state actors.[6] Under human rights law, the term 'acquiescence' has been interpreted in a fairly extensive manner based on the due diligence test. In my mission reports and general reports to the UN Human Rights Council I referred to domestic violence against women and children, female genital mutilation and similar traditional practices against women as typical examples of torture or CIDT committed with state acquiescence if governments fail to take effective measures to prevent such practices.[7]

In my opinion, we must distinguish between *three different types of ill treatment*: torture as the most serious form, followed by cruel or inhuman treatment or punishment, and degrading or humiliating treatment or punishment as the least serious manifestation. Only the last of these requires a lower threshold than severe pain or suffering. Any use of physical or mental force on a human being, such as pulling, pushing or verbal abuse, including light

[6] Cf. W. A. Schabas, 'The Crime of Torture and the International Criminal Tribunals' (2005) 37 *Case Western Reserve Journal of International Law* 349–64.
[7] See, in particular, UN Doc. A/HRC/7/3 of 15 January 2008.

forms of corporal punishment, if committed in a particularly humiliating manner, may constitute *degrading treatment or punishment*.[8] Both torture on the one hand, and cruel or inhuman treatment or punishment on the other, require the infliction of severe pain or suffering. If we apply the ordinary meaning of the term '*cruel or inhuman treatment*', it is a very severe form of ill treatment, and it would be strange to require for torture a level of pain or suffering which is even stronger than cruel or inhuman. Such an interpretation was made by the Bush Administration in its attempts to restrict torture to the infliction of excruciating pain or suffering, similar to organ failure, death or lasting mental impairment.[9] But these flawed legal interpretations did not convince the international community, and the practices of the Bush Administration, in particular certain 'enhanced interrogation methods', clearly amounted to torture and violated the respective US obligations under the CCPR, CAT and international humanitarian law.[10]

If a certain treatment inflicts *severe pain or suffering* and cannot be justified in the particular circumstances of the case (non-excessive use of force by law enforcement officials outside detention or direct control), it qualifies as cruel or inhuman treatment. If the additional requirements of powerlessness of the victim, intention and purpose are fulfilled, it also qualifies as torture. Whether the pain or suffering is severe depends on both objective and subjective criteria. But the typical methods of torture, such as severe beatings for a prolonged time, the infliction of electric shocks, burnings, extended hanging, rape or water torture usually are severe enough to qualify as torture. *Intention* means that severe pain or suffering is deliberately inflicted on the victim for a certain *purpose*, as explicitly listed in Article 1 CAT, usually the extraction of a confession or other information. One cannot torture simply by being reckless or negligent. If detainees are forgotten without food or water or prison conditions are so bad that detainees experience severe anguish and suffering, this 'only' amounts to cruel or inhuman treatment despite the fact that detainees

---

[8] Cf., e.g., ECtHR, *Tyrer* v. *United Kingdom*, judgment of 25 April 1978, Ser. A No. 26.

[9] See, e.g., the infamous torture memos by John Yoo and Jay Bybee. Cf. M. Nowak, 'What Practices Constitute Torture? US and UN Standards' (2006) 28 (4) *Human Rights Quarterly* 809–41.

[10] Cf., e.g., *Report of Five Special Procedures On the Situation of Detainees at Guantánamo Bay*, UN Doc. E/CN.4/2006/120, 27 February 2006; *Concluding Observations of the UN Human Rights Committee*, UN Doc. CCPR/C/USA/CO/3/Rev 1 of 18 December 2006; *Concluding Observations of the UN Committee against Torture*, UN Doc. CAT/C/USA/CO/2 of 25 July 2006.

have often told me that the daily suffering in overcrowded, dirty and violent prisons without sufficient air, light, food and medicine is much worse than the torture inflicted during the first days of interrogation. The additional requirement of *powerlessness* means that the victim is in the custody or under the direct control of the perpetrator.[11] The typical situation of torture is in a closed interrogation room when the victim is handcuffed or shackled, perhaps even held incommunicado, stripped naked, blindfolded and suspended in a painful position. It is the use of force and coercion against a powerless human being that makes torture so reprehensible, because it dehumanises the victim and constitutes a direct attack on human dignity.

The *'lawful sanctions' clause* in Article 1 CAT, Article 2 of the Inter-American Convention to Prevent and Punish Torture and Article 7 (2)(e) of the ICC Statute was inserted on the insistence of the USA and certain Islamic states for the purpose of justifying corporal and capital punishment. But a more thorough interpretation in light of modern jurisprudence related to corporal and capital punishment leads to the conclusion that it has no meaningful scope of application.[12] If the term 'lawful sanctions' refers to domestic law, any method of corporal and capital punishment, such as stoning a woman to death according to Shari'a law in certain Islamic states, would have to be regarded as justified simply because it is authorised by domestic law. If it refers to international law, even light forms of corporal punishment are today regarded at least as degrading punishment[13] and are, therefore, violating state obligations under Article 16 CAT that does not contain any 'lawful sanctions' clause. It would be a contradiction to qualify a certain punishment as inhuman or degrading punishment, which is absolutely prohibited under international law, and at the same time as a 'lawful' and, therefore, 'justified' form of torture.

Is the right to personal integrity and human dignity an absolute and non-derogable human right?

The prohibition of torture and CIDT is *absolute*, because the relevant provisions in international and regional human rights treaties do not

---

[11] Cf. Article 7 (2)(e) of the ICC Statute.
[12] See Nowak and McArthur, *The United Nations Convention* 79–84.
[13] Cf., e.g., ECtHR, *Tyrer* v. *United Kingdom*, judgment of 25 April 1978, Ser. A, No. 26.

provide any legitimate limitation clauses as most other human rights do (even including the right to life). The prohibition of torture and CIDT is *non-derogable*, because even in times of war, terrorism, natural disasters and other emergency situation, states parties to the respective general human rights treaties are prevented from derogating from their obligations in relation to this right.[14] On the other hand, Article 2 (2) CAT, which provides that 'No exceptional circumstances whatsoever, whether a state of war or a threat of war, internal political instability or any other public emergency, may be invoked as a justification of torture', only relates to torture, not to CIDT. Does this mean that states parties to CAT may derogate from their obligation not to inflict CIDT on suspected terrorists, as the Bush Administration argued in the context of its 'war on terror'? In my function as UN Special Rapporteur on Torture, lawyers of the US Government tried to challenge me by asking the following question: If a police officer is allowed under international law to go so far as to kill a suspected criminal, and if such use of force is absolutely necessary to defend another person from unlawful violence,[15] then why should a police officer not be allowed to use some coercion ('enhanced interrogation methods', not amounting to torture) against a detainee in order to extract the code of the 'ticking bomb' which otherwise would kill many innocent human beings? On first sight, international human rights law indeed seems to be contradictory in this respect. It is interesting to note that it was the US delegation that succeeded in the early 1980s in the then-UN Commission on Human Rights to delete the reference to CIDT from Article 2 (2) CAT. Such reference had still been included in Article 2 of the original Swedish proposal that was drafted on the basis of Article 3 of the UN Declaration on the Protection of All Persons from Being Subjected to Torture of 1975.[16]

In my opinion, the answer to the question raised by the US Government is as follows: The right to personal integrity and human dignity is not an absolute right, but a non-derogable right. The *mistake of pretending that the right to personal integrity and human dignity was an absolute human right* occurred already during its drafting with a purely negative formulation in Article 3 ECHR and Article 7 CCPR. The right to personal integrity and human dignity should have been drafted in positive terms with a

---

[14] Cf. Articles 4 (2) and 7 CCPR, 15 (2) and 3 ECHR, 27 (2) and 5 ACHR.
[15] Cf. the explicit limitation clause in Article 2 (2)(a) ECHR.
[16] See Nowak and McArthur, *The United Nations Convention* 131–46.

respective limitation clause, similar to Articles 2 and 4 ECHR or Articles 6 and 8 CCPR. The correct formulation of Articles 3 ECHR or 7 CCPR should, in my view, read as follows:

1 Everyone has the right to personal integrity and human dignity.
2 No one shall be subjected to torture.
3 No one shall be subjected to cruel, inhuman or degrading punishment.
4 (a) No one shall be subjected to cruel, inhuman or degrading treatment.
  (b) For the purpose of this paragraph the term 'cruel, inhuman or degrading treatment' shall not include any use of force which is no more than absolutely necessary:
    (i) in defence of a person from unlawful violence;
    (ii) in order to effect a lawful arrest or to prevent the escape of a person lawfully detained;
    (iii) in action lawfully taken for the purpose of quelling a riot or insurrection.

This formulation would not only have the advantage of first expressing a positive human right and only then stipulating which type of conduct would amount to an interference with or violation of this human right. It would also make clear that only torture, or cruel, inhuman or degrading punishment are absolutely prohibited, similar to the prohibition of slavery and servitude in Articles 4 ECHR and 8 CCPR. On the other hand, the prohibition of cruel, inhuman or degrading treatment is subject to limitations, similar to the prohibition of forced or compulsory labour in Articles 4 (3) ECHR and 8 (3)(c) CCPR.

In reality, the police and other law enforcement officials are, of course, allowed to intentionally inflict even severe pain or suffering on a person for certain legitimate law enforcement purposes, such as self-defence, defending a third person from violence, effecting a lawful arrest, preventing the escape of a detainee, quelling a riot, insurrection or violent assembly. But this use of force must be no more than absolutely necessary to achieve any of these legitimate law enforcement purposes. This means that the *principle of proportionality* applies, as in relation to the right to life and other relative rights. But in view of the fact that the right to personal integrity and human dignity is formulated in international and regional human rights treaties as an absolute right, the principle of proportionality is not applied in order to assess whether a legitimate state interference is justified but in order to establish the scope of application of this right. In other words: if a police officer shoots into the legs of a convicted or suspected criminal in order to prevent his escape or uses tear gas to dispel a violent demonstration, the respective treaty monitoring body should first assess whether this use of force constitutes an interference with the right to personal integrity and human dignity, and in the affirmative, then assess whether the police force was lawful under domestic law, was used for a legitimate purpose and was proportional in the particular circumstances of the case. If all three questions are answered in the affirmative, the use of force should be qualified as a justified interference with the right to personal integrity and human dignity and, therefore, not as a human rights violation. In reality, human rights treaty bodies do apply the same test, but in the context of determining the scope of application of the right. If severe pain or suffering was inflicted for a legitimate purpose of policing, and if the use of force was proportional, then as the current case law stands, such conduct does not reach the threshold of CIDT. If the use of force is, however, deemed excessive, the European or Inter-American Court of Human Rights, the UN Human Rights Committee or the Committee against Torture would find a violation of the right not to be subjected to CIDT.

Having reached the conclusion that the right not to be subjected to CIDT should be explicitly and is in effect a relative right subject to the principle of proportionality, the question of the US Government remains: why does preventing the escape of a suspected criminal or dispelling a violent demonstration constitute a legitimate purpose of policing that allows proportional use of force, while using 'enhanced interrogation methods' for the purpose of extracting the code of the 'ticking bomb' from a suspected terrorist is absolutely prohibited. Is the prevention of a terrorist attack not as legitimate a purpose of law enforcement as the arrest of a suspected criminal? The answer to this question can be found by reflecting on the concept of *powerlessness* as a definition criterion distinguishing torture from CIDT as outlined above. If a police officer wishes to arrest a suspected criminal or terrorist, proportional use of force, including the deliberate infliction of severe pain or suffering if absolutely necessary, is permitted. As soon as the person is arrested, handcuffed and, therefore, powerless, i.e. under the direct control of the police officer, no further use of force is permitted. To inflict pain or suffering for the purpose of humiliating the person concerned is to be qualified as degrading treatment, any infliction of severe pain or suffering as cruel or inhuman treatment. If such severe pain or suffering is inflicted to extract a confession or information, or for any other purpose listed in Article 1 CAT, such treatment against a powerless person, above all during detention and interrogation, amounts to torture. In other words: the prohibition of torture constitutes an absolute right, the prohibition of CIDT constitutes only a relative right subject to legitimate limitations. But under general human rights treaties, both rights are non-derogable even under exceptional circumstances. Article 2 (2) CAT only underlines the non-derogable nature of the prohibition of torture but this does not mean that the prohibition of CIDT may be suspended in times of armed conflict or of a 'war on terror'. This conclusion is underlined by the absolute prohibition of torture and CIDT under international humanitarian law, including Article 3 of the four Geneva Conventions.[17]

Do corporal and capital punishment constitute a violation of the right to personal integrity and human dignity?

In the context of the right to personal integrity and human dignity, international human rights law not only prohibits torture and other forms of cruel, inhuman or degrading *treatment*, but also cruel, inhuman or degrading *punishment*. One of the purposes of torture explicitly listed in Article 1 CAT is punishment. The question, therefore, arises as to which type of punishment falls under this prohibition. The most common types of contemporary criminal punishment, i.e. fines and imprisonment, are usually not considered as cruel, inhuman or degrading.[18] Most people would primarily think of violent punishments, such as capital and corporal punishment, when asked about the notion of cruel, inhuman or degrading punishment. But when I raised these questions in my reports to the Human Rights Council and the General Assembly of the UN, I was strongly attacked by certain Islamic and other

---

[17] Cf. M. Nowak, 'The Crime of Torture', in M. Odello and G. L. Beruto (eds.), *Global Violence: Consequences and Responses* (Milan: Franco Angeli 2011) 157–63, www.iihl.org/Default. aspx?pageid=page5424.

[18] But see certain developments in relation to the compatibility of life imprisonment without any chance of earlier release with human rights: See, e.g., Article 37(a) of the UN Convention on the Rights of the Child (1989) and the judgment of the German Constitutional Court of 21 June 1977 (BVerfGE 45, 187).

states and accused of having overstepped my mandate as Special Rapporteur on Torture.[19] This shows how sensitive this issue has become in contemporary international relations and in the international human rights discourse among states. But the political sensitivity and hypocrisy of these discussions should not prevent us from addressing this issue from an academic point of view by interpreting relevant human rights law.

At the time of the drafting of the UDHR and the ECHR in the late 1940s, only very few states had already abolished capital and corporal punishment. Since the death penalty also interferes with the right to life, special exceptions for the death penalty were inserted in most legal provisions relating to the right to life.[20] But *corporal punishment* only interferes with the right to personal integrity and human dignity, and the drafters of these provisions preferred not to add any special limitation clause to this important human right. They definitely wished to prohibit some of the most inhuman, unusual and degrading methods of execution and types of corporal punishment, but where to draw the line was deliberately left to interpretation. The ECtHR was the first international treaty monitoring body that addressed this delicate issue in the judgment of *Tyrer v. United Kingdom*. The Court considered that the ECHR is a living instrument which 'must be interpreted in the light of present-day conditions. In the case now before it the Court cannot but be influenced by the developments and commonly accepted standards in the penal policy of the member States of the Council of Europe in this field.' It held that even three strokes on the naked buttocks of a juvenile on the Isle of Man was no longer compatible with the prohibition of degrading punishment: 'The very nature of judicial corporal punishment is that it involves one human being inflicting physical violence on another human being. Furthermore, it is institutionalised violence that is in the present case violence permitted by the law, ordered by the judicial authorities of the State and carried out by the police authorities of the State. Thus, although the applicant did not suffer any severe or long-lasting physical effects, his punishment – whereby he was treated as an object in the power of the authorities – constituted an assault on precisely that which it is one of the

---

[19] E.g. during the Sixtieth Session of the General Assembly in October 2005 in response to my report, A/60/316 of 30 August 2005 and during the interactive dialogue during the Thirteenth Session of the Human Rights Council in March 2010 in response to my report A/HRC/13/39 of 9 February 2010.

[20] See, in chronological order, Articles 2 (1) ECHR, 6 (2, 4–6) CCPR, 4 (2–6) ACHR, 6 and 7 Arab Charter on Human Rights.

main purposes of Article 3 to protect, namely a person's dignity and physical integrity.'[21] In later judgments this reasoning was also extended to corporal punishment in British schools.[22]

Most importantly, the UN Human Rights Committee and the Inter-American Court of Human Rights followed this jurisprudence in more recent cases related to former British colonies in the Caribbean region.[23] Even the UN Committee against Torture, which originally was hesitant to address this delicate issue, has increasingly criticised Islamic states for corporate punishment provided by Shari'a law.[24] This means that, according to the jurisprudence of relevant international and regional treaty monitoring bodies, all forms of corporal punishment are today considered as cruel, inhuman or at least degrading punishment and are, therefore, absolutely prohibited under modern international law. But certain, primarily Islamic states that still practice corporal punishment as a domestic judicial punishment, strongly disagree with this jurisprudence and respective reports of different UN Special Rapporteurs on Torture.[25]

Even more controversial is the question of *capital punishment*. For many years, a systematic method of interpretation was applied to the relevant provisions on the right to life and the right to personal integrity and human dignity. Since the death penalty was explicitly accepted as a legitimate interference with the right to life, it could not at the same time, so the argument was running, be regarded as a cruel punishment and, therefore, as a violation of the right to personal integrity and human

---

[21] ECtHR, *Tyrer* v. *United Kingdom*, judgment of 25 April 1978, Ser. A, No. 26, paras. 31, 33.

[22] ECtHR, *Campbell and Cosans* v. *United Kingdom*, judgment of 25 February 1982, Ser. A, No. 48; ECtHR, *Y* v. *United Kingdom*, judgment of 29 October 1992, Ser. A, No. 247-A; ECtHR, *Costello Roberts* v. *United Kingdom*, Ser. A, No. 247-C.

[23] See, in particular, the decision of the UN Human Rights Committee in *Osbourne* v. *Jamaica* of 15 March 2000 (Comm. No. 759/1997) and the decision of the Inter-American Court of Human Rights of 11 March 2005 in *Winston Caesar* v. *Trinidad and Tobago*, Ser. C, No. 123. Cf. M. Nowak, *UN Covenant on Civil and Political Rights: CCPR Commentary*, 2nd edn (Kehl/Strasbourg/Arlington, TX: N. P. Engel Publisher, 2005), 167 *et seq.*; Nowak and McArthur, *The United Nations Convention* 561 *et seq.*; see also the Special Rapporteur on Torture, *Study on the Phenomena of Torture, Cruel, Inhuman or Degrading Treatment or Punishment in the World, Including an Assessment of Conditions of Detention*, UN Doc. A/HRC/13/39/Add.5 of 5 February 2010.

[24] Cf. *Concluding Observations of the UN Committee against Torture*, UN Doc. CAT/C/CR/28/5 of 12 June 2002; *Concluding Observations of the UN Committee against Torture*, UN Doc. CAT/A/48/44 of 24 June 1993.

[25] Cf. UN Doc. E/CN.4/1997/7 of 10 January 1997, paras. 3–11; UN Doc. A/54/426 of 1 October 1999; UN Doc. A/HRC/13/39/Add.5 of 5 February 2010, para 228.

dignity. But certain aspects in relation to capital punishment were considered as CIDT. For example, the so-called 'death row phenomenon', i.e. extended periods of detention in a violent atmosphere, and particularly cruel methods of execution were considered as CIDT.[26] In 1989, the UN Convention on the Rights of the Child (CRC) was adopted which, for the first time in an international human rights treaty, did address the question of capital punishment, not in the context of the right to life but, more appropriately, in the context of the right to personal integrity and human dignity. In addition to the prohibition of torture and CIDT, Article 37(a) CRC provides that neither 'capital punishment nor life imprisonment without possibility of release shall be imposed for offences committed by persons below eighteen years of age'. Since all states of the world, with the only exception of the USA and Somalia, are parties to the CRC, and since the US Supreme Court in a more recent judgment also prohibited the death penalty for crimes committed by children,[27] the prohibition of capital punishment for persons under the age of eighteen today constitutes a rule of customary international law and even *ius cogens*. The more recent adoption of Article 7 (1) of the Arab Charter on Human Rights in 2004 does not change such a rule.[28] One of the most sophisticated judgments on the non-compatibility of the death penalty with the prohibition of CIDT in general, i.e. also with respect to adults, was delivered by the South African Constitutional Court in 1995.[29] After carefully reviewing more recent developments in international law and practice, the Court concluded that the death penalty as such amounts to CIDT and is, therefore, absolutely prohibited under the post-Apartheid Constitution of

---

[26] See, e.g., ECtHR, *Soering* v. *United Kingdom*, judgment of 7 July 1989, Ser. A, No. 161; UN Human Rights Committee, *Ng* v. *Canada*, Decision of 7 January 1994 (Comm. No. 469/ 1991); Judicial Committee of the Privy Council, *Pratt and Morgan* v. *The Attorney General for Jamaica*, judgment of 2 November 1993.

[27] See Supreme Court of the United States, *Roper* v. *Simmons*, 543 US 551 (2005), decision of 1 March 2005.

[28] Article 7 (1) of the Arab Charter reads as follows: 'Sentence of death shall not be imposed on persons under 18 years of age, unless otherwise stipulated in the laws in force at the time of the commission of the crime.' This provision is flawed in two respects: It only refers to the imposition of the death sentence 'on persons under 18 years of age' rather than on persons who were under 18 years of age at the time when the crime was committed. Secondly, the exception in the second part of the sentence contradicts a rule of *ius cogens* and can, therefore, not be invoked as a valid excuse by any state party to the Arab Charter.

[29] Constitutional Court of South Africa, *State* v. *Makwanyane and Mchunu* (Case No. CCT/3/ 94), judgment of 6 June 1995.

South Africa. Other supreme domestic courts have adopted a similar approach.[30] But no international or regional human rights treaty monitoring body, including the ECtHR, has adopted this approach, presumably because of the strength of the argument for the systematic interpretation of international treaty law, as outlined above.

In my opinion, the time has come to change this approach. The fact that the death penalty may still be regarded as not necessarily violating the right to life should not be misused as a barrier to the dynamic interpretation of the term 'cruel, inhuman or degrading punishment' in light of present-day circumstances. If even light forms of corporal punishment are today considered as at least degrading punishment, it seems difficult to argue that the ultimate form of corporal punishment, namely capital punishment, should not amount to degrading or inhuman punishment. When the amputation of the hand of a thief constitutes inhuman punishment, how can the amputation of the head of a murderer under the guillotine then be considered as humane punishment? This is simply inconsistent. At a time when two-thirds of the states in the world have abolished capital punishment either *de iure* or *de facto*,[31] when most general human rights treaties have been amended by additional or optional protocols aimed at the abolition of the death penalty,[32] and when the General Assembly of the UN has repeatedly called on all states to abolish this cruel and inhuman punishment and at least to impose a moratorium on executions,[33] the time has surely come to rethink this systematic but misleading interpretation of international human rights treaty law. The death penalty is not opposed by the clear majority of all states because it leads to the death of a human being but because it constitutes a cruel and inhuman punishment and, therefore, violates the human right to personal integrity and human dignity. In my opinion, the death penalty as such and in whatever form must be regarded as torture and has no longer any place in the global society of the twenty-first century.

---

[30] Cf., e.g., Constitutional Court of Hungary, Decision No. 23/1990 (X31) AB of 24 October 1990; Human Rights Chamber of Bosnia and Herzegovina, *Damjanović* v. *Federation of Bosnia and Herzegovina* (Case No. CH/96/30), judgment of 16 March 1998.

[31] Cf. Amnesty International, *Death Sentences and Executions 2010*, 28 March 2011.

[32] See the 6th and 13th Additional Protocols to the ECHR of 1983 and 2002, respectively; the 2nd Optional Protocol to the CCPR of 1990, and the Protocol to the ACHR of 1990.

[33] Cf. UN GA Resolutions: Moratorium on the use of the death penalty: A/RES/62/149, 18 December 2007 and A/RES/63/168, 18 December 2008 and A/RES/65/206, 21 December 2010.

Conclusions

The right protected by the prohibition of torture, cruel, inhuman or degrading treatment or punishment under international human rights law is the *right to personal integrity and human dignity*, which is also closely related to the prohibition of slavery. Although the prohibition of torture and ill treatment contains no limitation clause and, therefore, is considered as an absolute human right, a closer analysis shows that one should distinguish in this respect between the different aspects of the right to personal integrity and human dignity. The prohibition of *torture*, on the one hand, defined as the intentional infliction of severe pain or suffering on a powerless person for a certain purpose, such as the extraction of a confession or information, is an absolute right and permits no balancing with other human rights or state interests, including national security interests in the fight against terrorism.

Outside the situation of detention and direct control, i.e. *powerlessness*, law enforcement officers are, however, vested with the power to exercise physical and other types of force in order to enforce the law, to prevent and combat crime, to maintain public order and safety. In order to arrest a person suspected of having committed a crime, to defend a person from unlawful violence, to prevent the escape of a dangerous person, to dispel a violent demonstration or quell a riot, the police may use force and, thereby, even deliberately inflict severe pain or suffering on human beings. If the force used is reasonable and proportional in the particular circumstances of the case, it does not reach the threshold of *cruel, inhuman or degrading treatment.* If it is excessive, i.e. not proportional to the legitimate aim pursued, it constitutes cruel or inhuman treatment and, thereby, violates the right to personal integrity and human dignity. If the person concerned is humiliated, this may amount to degrading treatment according to the particular circumstances of the case. The need to apply the *principle of proportionality* for the purpose of assessing whether a human rights violation occurred or not shows that the prohibition of CIDT in fact is not an absolute human right.

More difficult to answer is the question whether the prohibition of *cruel, inhuman or degrading punishment* is an absolute right or not. It was inserted into international human rights law in order to eradicate types of punishments under domestic criminal law that are considered to violate the personal integrity or human dignity of the person concerned. But since the application of criminal law is regarded by many states as a typical example of domestic jurisdiction and national sovereignty, any outside interference in this regard is strongly rebutted. This makes the question of corporal and capital punishment a highly sensitive and controversial political issue, as we have seen. This in turn puts a heavy burden on international human rights monitoring bodies, and in fact prevents any rational discourse regarding this highly emotional issue. In my opinion, the prohibition of cruel, inhuman or degrading punishment is an absolute right which does not permit any balancing with other human rights (such as the 'right' of the victim of a particularly brutal crime to revenge) or state interests (such as punitive and retributive policies of combating crime). Consequently, the principle of proportionality does not apply. It is only a matter of interpretation which type of punishment is considered as cruel, inhuman or degrading. According to relevant international and regional human rights case law, any type of *corporal punishment* and certain aspects of *capital punishment* (particularly brutal methods of execution or the 'death row phenomenon') amount to cruel, inhuman or at least degrading punishment and are, therefore, absolutely prohibited. In my opinion, the death penalty is nothing but a particularly harsh form of corporal punishment. Therefore, all forms of corporal and capital punishment fall under the category of cruel, inhuman or at least degrading punishment and constitute a violation of the right to personal integrity and human dignity. But it will still need some time until this interpretation is accepted and applied by all states as a general rule of customary international law.

Finally, I wish to add a few personal thoughts, based on my experience as Special Rapporteur on Torture, on why it is so difficult to eradicate torture and CIDT. In my opinion, the main reasons for this tremendous implementation gap between the noble aspiration to protect human dignity and the sobering reality on the ground are retributive philosophies of criminal justice, a lack of empathy for those behind bars (detention is in most countries a 'privilege' of the poor, the marginalised and the oppressed), corruption in the criminal justice system (police, prosecutors, judges and prison officials), and a lack of access of the poor to justice.

The roughly 10 million prisoners around the world lack any political lobbying power to fight for their human rights. If we wish to address these root causes of torture and CIDT, we need to fight for the legal empowerment of the poor and for replacing retributive philosophies of justice by concepts of restorative justice.

Further reading

Boulesbaa, A., *The UN Convention on Torture and the Prospects for Enforcement* (The Hague: Martinus Nijhoff 1999)

Burgers, H. and Danelius, H., *The United Nations Convention against Torture: Handbook on the Convention Against Torture and Other Cruel, Inhuman or Degrading Treatment or Punishment* (Dordrecht: Martinus Nijhoff 1988)

Cohen, M. (ed.), *The United States and Torture: Interrogation, Incarceration, and Abuse* (New York University Press 2011)

Dewulf, S., *The Signature of Evil: (Re)Defining Torture in International Law* (Oxford/ Antwerp/Portland, OR: Intersentia 2011)

Dunér, B. (ed.), *An End to Torture: Strategies for its Eradication* (London: Zed 1998)

Evans, M. D. and Morgan, R. (eds.), *Protecting Prisoners: The Standards of the European Committee for the Prevention of Torture* (Oxford University Press 1999)

Ingelse, C., *The UN Committee against Torture: An Assessment* (The Hague/London/ Boston: Kluwer Law 2001)

Jaffer, J. and Singh, A., *Administration of Torture* (New York: Columbia University Press 2007)

Kriebaum, U., *Folterprävention in Europa: Die Europäische Konvention zur Verhütung von Folter und unmenschlicher oder erniedrigender Behandlung oder Bestrafung* (Vienna: Verlag Österreich 2000)

Langbein, J. H., *Torture and the Law of Proof: Europe and England in the Ancien Régime* (Chicago University Press 2006)

McCoy, A. W., *A Question of Torture: CIA Interrogation, from the Cold War to the War on Terror* (Basingstoke: Macmillan 2006)

Nowak, M., *UN Covenant on Civil and Political Rights – CCPR Commentary*, 2nd edn (Kehl/Strasbourg/Arlington, TX: N. P. Engel 2005)

'What Practices Constitute Torture? US and UN Standards' (2006) 28 (4) *Human Rights Quarterly* 809–41

'The Crime of Torture', in M. Odello and G. L. Beruto (eds.), *Global Violence: Consequences and Responses* (Milan: Franco Angeli 2011) 157–63, www.iihl. org/Default.aspx?pageid=page5424.

'Torture and Enforced Disappearance', in M. Scheinin and C. Krause, *International Protection of Human Rights: A Textbook* (Turku/Åbo: Åbo University Institute for Human Rights 2009)

Nowak, M. and McArthur, E., *The United Nations Convention against Torture: A Commentary* (Oxford University Press 2008)

Report of the Special Rapporteur on Torture and other cruel, inhuman or degrading treatment or punishment, *Study on the Phenomena of Torture, Cruel, Inhuman or Degrading Treatment or Punishment in the World, Including an Assessment of Conditions of Detention*, UN Doc., A/HRC/13/39/Add.5 of 5 February 2010

Rodley, N. S., *The Treatment of Prisoners under International Law* (Oxford University Press 2009)

Schabas, W. A., 'The Crime of Torture and the International Criminal Tribunals', (2005) 37 *Case Western Reserve Journal of International Law* 349–64

    The International Criminal Court: A Commentary on the Rome Statute (Oxford University Press 2010)

Do human rights treaties make enough of a difference?

Samuel Moyn

In recent years, one of the most intense and interesting debates among mainstream scholars of international law has been whether human rights treaties 'make a difference'. Oona Hathaway kicked off these controversies with a pathbreaking and subversive article suggesting that indeed they do make a difference – sometimes for the worse.[1] Hathaway did not mean to bring a defeatist realism to scholarship, along the lines of the conservative scholars with whom liberals perpetually struggle.[2] Instead, in documenting how easy it has been for states to gain the expressive benefits of treaty ratification without taking legal obligations to heart, with sometimes negative consequences for rights outcomes, Hathaway hoped to prompt a more sophisticated international regime. For example, she suggested, making ratification tougher or probationary for states would filter out or at least pose barriers to the 'insincere ratifiers' and thus make aggregate positive outcomes more likely.

Hathaway's modest scepticism – though offered for the sake of the progressive realisation of human rights by means of international treaty law – seemed scandalous to some. In any case, now Beth Simmons is regarded as having 'settled' the debate about whether human rights law has positive effects. As one reviewer noted of her well-received book, *Mobilizing for Human Rights*, it 'has closed the chapter on whether human rights treaties can make a difference.'[3] More broadly, it has been

---

[1] O. A. Hathaway, 'Do Human Rights Treaties Make a Difference?' (2001–2) 111 (8) *Yale Law Journal* 1935–2042; compare R. Goodman and D. Jinks, 'Measuring the Effects of Human Rights Treaties' (2003) 14 (1) *European Journal of International Law* 171–83 and O. A. Hathaway, 'Testing Conventional Wisdom' (2003) 14 (1) *European Journal of International Law* 185–200.

[2] See, for instance, O. A. Hathaway and A. N. Lavinbuk, 'Rationalism and Revisionism in International Law' (review of J. L. Goldsmith and E. A. Posner, *The Limits of International Law* (Oxford University Press 2005)) (2006) 119 (5) *Harvard Law Review* 1404–43.

[3] B. A. Simmons, *Mobilizing for Human Rights: International Law in Domestic Politics* (Cambridge University Press, 2009); E. Hafner-Burton, review, (2010) 104 (3) *American Journal of International Law* 541.

widely recognised as the most significant work in the field in many years. It is supposed not only to put the concern about insincere ratifiers in its place and thus to clamp down on the potentially creeping worry Hathaway introduced. It also provides a useful contemporary example of the defence mainstream scholarship offers not simply of international human rights treaties but of human rights politics as a general matter. And it is most of all from this perspective that Simmons' book turns out to be of great interest.[4] It shows the sort of hope – a pessimistic reformist hope, I shall claim – that now undergirds mainstream scholarly enthusiasm for international human rights. It is in virtue of its great prominence as an entrant in this largest of all of the debates about human rights law that *Mobilizing for Human Rights* deserves a careful look. But beyond its intrinsic significance it is also a specimen of a general phenomenon that is otherwise difficult to talk about because it is so abstract: how international human rights law understands its mission. Since the book concerns why international human rights law is a morally uplifting and politically crucial project in a disheartening world, it provides a window on the soul of the field.

A mixed message

Simmons brings impressive quantitative acumen to the topic of whether several human rights treaties make a difference. Indeed, the book has been celebrated – unlike Hathaway's more nerve-wracking essay that deployed a novel empiricism but reached a disconcerting answer – in part because it definitively moves international legal scholarship towards a rigour it had sometimes lacked in the past.[5] Though Simmons can only assert correlation and is generally very cautious about the impact of human rights treaties like the International Covenant for Civil and Political Rights (CCPR), the Convention for the Elimination of All Forms of Discrimination against

[4] Compare Eric Posner's rather different focus in his criticisms of Simmons' empirical work: E. Posner, 'Some Skeptical Thoughts on Beth Simmons's *Mobilizing for Human Rights*' University of Chicago Law School Working Paper No. 369 (2012). For further instances of this specific empirical debate, see J. Ron and E. Hafner-Burton, 'Seeing Double: Human Rights Impact Through Qualitative and Quantitative Eyes?' (2009) 61 (2) *World Politics* 360–401 or E. Hafner-Burton, *The Triage Strategy: Reconciling the Promise and Practice of International Human Rights Law* (Princeton University Press forthcoming 2012).

[5] G. Shaffer and T. Ginsburg, 'The Empirical Turn in International Law Scholarship' (2012) 106 (1) *American Journal of International Law* 1–46.

Women (CEDAW), the Convention against Torture (CAT) and the Convention on the Rights of the Child (CRT), her main finding – that they are very likely a positive thing for the world – is surely persuasive and significant.

But Simmons' book is also deeply normative in how it frames its inquiry. In this chapter, therefore, I want to assess how fundamentally its findings depend on debatable political assumptions about the availability of alternative reform. Especially in a large global space in which international human rights will continue to face competition – certainly more than they have faced in what now strongly looks like an interlude between a bipolar world and a multipolar one beset by American and European decline – the analytical emphasis on alternatives will surely seem more and more pressing. Just as the geopolitics of the last two decades opened a relatively opportune space for international human rights, the coming geopolitical era will demand more emphasis on their comparative and competitive relevance than has lately obtained. The end of the Cold War foreclosed old mistakes, but the era that has already begun will place the premium not simply on criticising bad new alternatives in the name of international human rights norms but on seeking a more uplifting political agenda than they have prompted. In this regard I argue that Simmons restores hope in human rights treaties, showing that they make a difference, at a price that is as high politically as it is analytically.

A feature of Simmons' book is its success in its own terms, in other words, is how it enacts a politics and strategy in its own right – in spite of the dispassionate social scientific analysis clothing the book and accounting for its prominence in its discipline. As a proposed model for how to best conceptualise the topic, *Mobilizing for Human Rights* explicitly competes with other views both within and beyond political science that posit that human rights politics may not provide enough positive benefits.[6] And outside more narrowly academic contention, Simmons' approach has definite implications for where to look for moral progress, and the forms it could plausibly take, and thus how to pursue it now. Implicitly, by showing there are grounds for hope in human rights treaties, it assumes in advance a fatalistic limit to how much hope is legitimate.

---

[6] See esp. D. Kennedy, *The Dark Side of Virtue: Reassessing International Humanitarianism* (Princeton University Press 2004), which charges, according to Simmons, that international human rights law 'overpromises' (6, 365–66). In contrast, especially after Simmons's defence against this accusation, my concern is that it now 'underpromises'.

Yet it is just here – as a revealing document of the desperate resignation that has understandably descended upon so many others – that Simmons' book is not fully persuasive. By and large, my worry is that the politics and strategy of the book work as much to marginalise more radical ventures as to give credit to international law where it is due. For Simmons, beneath the good news that human rights treaties serve a purpose lies the bad news that there is no other way to change the world. A justifiable call to recognise the occasional help international human rights treaties provide ends up making it analytically very difficult, and politically fruitless, to imagine help from anywhere else. It is this pessimism that critical scholarship must continue to reject. Simmons may have decisively put to rest Hathaway's query whether human rights treaties make a difference. With that matter settled, the next scholarly step is to ask is whether they make enough of one.

The static international realm

Simmons is refreshingly honest about how limited her defence of international human rights ultimately is. At the end of her study, she persuasively suggests that the modest differences that she claims international treaties regimes provide still matter, even if they do not 'solve all problems'.[7] 'Only the most cycloptic individuals', Simmons writes in one of the most spirited passages in her otherwise staid book, 'see only problems that the law addresses and view law as the only tool to deal with them'.[8] Yet the fact remains that Simmons is so intent on vindicating the limited relevance of human rights treaties that her analysis can't help but bear implications about what alternatives to them are available, whether as a supplement or a substitute.

I begin with Simmons' pessimism about international political transformation, as a prelude to a look at the instability of her argument about the relationship between human rights and local norms and the success of her claim that domestic politics provides the fund of optimism for international human rights law that the international forum itself does not. There is a significant sense in which her approach speaks to a general concern in the whole field. For that reason, it is important beyond the parameters of this book that pessimism is what turns out to pervade her account, and nowhere

[7] Simmons, *Mobilizing* 366.   [8] Simmons, *Mobilizing* 368.

in so open and unambiguous a way as in her views about the unalterability of international politics.

Among other things, Simmons' pessimistic realism shows that the enthusiastic days of the 1990s are long gone, and indeed her book helps the field transcend the mistaken optimism of that time when it was common to repose millennial hopes in human rights. On close inspection, her book is premised on the nearly phobic avoidance of any grandiose assurance that human rights politics might fundamentally transform international politics soon or ever. In this sense, Simmons's book returns the field to the minor claims for improvement with which international human rights mobilisation began – what one observer memorably called 'salvation in small steps'.[9] Yet there is no salvation, even in small steps, to be found in international affairs. Startlingly, Simmons is as much of a realist with respect to the international order as she is a constructivist with respect to domestic politics. Like many in the afterglow of the 1990s who struggle to find relevance for international human rights in a world in which national interest self-evidently persists, Simmons' praise for human rights treaties proceeds based on a large amount of overlap with conservative realists who see nothing else but national interest in world affairs.

Actually, her realism leads Simmons to a generally canny and sometimes surprising cynicism about the realities of a world order in which great powers rule the UN Security Council and states make up international governance organisations. Her view of the impact of human rights treaties and indeed human rights politics in the international sphere is unremittingly negative. Of all the attempts to 'depoliticise' human rights monitoring and enforcement at the UN in the last twenty years – in particular, through the move to the Human Rights Council, the drastic expansion of so-called special procedures, and the proliferation of expert bodies that most international human rights treaties bring about – Simmons concludes that they are by and large unworthy of much respect. Ultimately, she thinks, the UN is an organisation created of, by, and for states. Simmons is blunt: 'Globally centralized enforcement is a chimera.'[10] Given the fact that states behave as realists predict in their external affairs, even causes with the patina of moral legitimacy are best explained according to realist principles. Thus in another passage, Simmons predicts why international human rights

---

[9] B. Simms, 'Salvation in Small Steps' *The Wall Street Journal*, September 10, 2010.
[10] Simmons, *Mobilizing* 154.

enforcement if it takes place will occur only when compelling national interests are not at stake or when they concur in the results (hence recent Middle Eastern history). 'The targets of . . . enforcement efforts', Simmons writes, 'are generally small countries whose sanctioning imposes no important costs for the would-be enforcer'.[11] She claims that 'the interstate vantage point does not provide a lot of reason for optimism', but it is fairer to say that, from the global vantage point, her book provides no reason for optimism at all.[12]

Yet it is still a serious question why, when she breaks with this pessimistic realism in order to hope international human rights norms have traction nonetheless, Simmons looks exclusively to domestic politics. Human rights offer 'a real politics of change', in her phrase, just not in the international order. Her descriptive claim is that human rights, at least through treaties, create 'stakeholders' only or 'almost exclusively' domestically.[13] In saying so, she makes an implicit political judgement about the past and possible constituencies for transnational politics. As far as I can tell, Simmons never defends this judgement.

When it comes to domestic politics, of course, Simmons drops her realism and becomes a constructivist who thinks the legal obligation that treaties layer over moral norms is worth studying and highlighting. It is never spelled out, however, why Simmons assumes staunchly realist premises for the sake of international order even as she regards the domestic forum as a much more promising space for moral norms to recast identity and interest. Accordingly, Simmons ignores the role that alliances of states have played, including at particularly promising moments in post-Second World War history, in reshaping the international order as it has been inherited, or the role that such alliances could play in the future. And she only acknowledges in passing the part played by transnational justice movements, reducing their role to a tutelary one as they intercede to abet domestic politics. The place to look for hope, Simmons says, is in domestic transformation along the lines of the US civil rights movement (even though it went unaided by the international treaties her book is about). Meanwhile, though many have lionised it for bringing about a global human rights movement, Simmons unceremoniously dismisses the transnational Helsinki network as 'much vaunted' – perhaps because it doesn't fit the story

---

[11] Simmons, *Mobilizing* 122.   [12] Simmons, *Mobilizing* 114.
[13] Simmons, *Mobilizing* 126.

Simmons wishes to tell about the exclusively domestic effects of strictly binding international human rights treaties.[14] (To be fair, Simmons does mention in passing elsewhere in the book the transnational alliances that other scholars have covered, restricting their relevance to the isolation of highly repressive regimes.)[15]

I don't mean to defend historical or existing transnational movements for the great difference they have already made. Instead, the point is that Simmons accepts the existing interstate order as the set framework for any available optimism, leading her then inside states in search of the last available forum for progress. Put differently, Simmons' turn to domestic politics as the place where international human rights treaties might providentially matter after all takes place on the basis of her acid scepticism about international affairs. It presupposes a decision that international politics can be reshaped, if at all, solely through the internal politics of each individual domestic forum. In this sense, it seems as if Simmons' constructivism proceeds on the basis of a prior realism. Optimism is snatched from the jaws of a more basic defeatism.

This conclusion matters because it establishes an insufficiently motivated turn to the domestic implications of international human rights treaties, regarded as the sole and slim basis for hope that international human rights politics might profoundly improve the human condition. As I now want to show, Simmons is genuinely undecided about how much difference human rights treaties make with respect to the prior identities and interests of domestic constituencies that turn to them as political tools. And then I will suggest that, when it comes to that social mobilisation, the net effect of Simmons' analysis is to obscure its historical conditions and ideological variety. As a result, I will worry, her impressive book saves the relevance of international human rights treaties at the very high price of obfuscating the historical forces that in fact lead to progressive change – as well as its alternative possible and imaginable forms. This danger goes beyond the perspective of a single author to confront the field as a whole as it seeks to work out what form of progress to entertain – notably in its relationship with domestic political activism.

---

[14] Simmons, *Mobilizing* 7; compare S. B. Snyder, *Human Rights Activism and the End of the Cold War: A Transnational History of the Helsinki Network* (Cambridge University Press 2011).
[15] Simmons, *Mobilizing* 372.

Indigenous self-liberation

When she turns to the domestic forum, Simmons lays out a tripartite structure for how domestic actors can make use of the new tool of international treaties – at any rate, more than they could make of the hazy moral norms of natural law, or their clarification in written form in the Universal Declaration of Human Rights (UDHR, 1948). For Simmons, the political relevance of international treaties depends on the fact that where states are unified for the purposes of their external interstate relations, they are usually sites of at least mildly divisive conflict in their internal politics. And so treaties provide tools for domestic constituencies in competition with each other.

First, Simmons says, treaties empower executives relative to legislatures, on the premise that the former normally have more power over the formulation, ratification and enforcement of treaties than they do over ordinary domestic law. Second, treaties allow for litigation, at least where treaties become part of domestic law, and where independent judges are prepared to enforce their provisions. Finally, treaties offer a supplemental tool for social mobilisation on the ground. The second and third categories clearly work together for, as Simmons points out, litigation is not simply an attempt to vindicate rights in specific cases; sometimes, it is also a political device to raise consciousness and enhance the power of social movements.

Simmons runs into trouble, however, when she theorises how international treaties interact with local meanings – including pre-existing local ideologies and causes. And it is interesting to see how.

Obviously it can't be the case that groups and individuals formulate their demands in terms precisely matching those of international treaties they had no part in writing. Elsewhere in her book, in fact, Simmons once again shows herself a wholly honest observer, willing to acknowledge forthrightly that those who work on international human rights, no matter where they are from, have to be trained to do so outside their own locales. Commenting on the Human Rights Committee, for instance, she observes that most of its members at the relevant time were products of North Atlantic universities, so that 'it can reasonably claimed that this committee – and arguably the oversight committees associated with other multilateral human rights agreements – is the torchbearer for Western rights notions and a conduit for Western values globally'.[16]

---

[16] Simmons, *Mobilizing* 370.

But the same can't be true of the domestic uses of international norms her book is about. Simmons is most worried about a certain neocolonialist critique of human rights, and her view of treaties as enabling local movements in fact is intended to allow her a very strong response to that critique. Opposing Makau wa Mutua's famous theory of the international human rights movement as a system of Western saviours swooping in for the succour of savage victims, Simmons is indignant.[17] '*Treaty commitments*', she insists in response, '*are directly available to groups and individuals whom I view as active agents as part of a political strategy of mobilizing to formulate and demand their own liberation*'.[18]

This heady stuff – active agents formulating their own liberation – shows graphically how emancipatory Simmons wants international human rights, and her scholarship, to be. Indeed one might analyse Simmons' approach as a kind of liberal third-worldism. In the old days, Marxists assumed a perfect match between the ideas and interests their theory attributed to humanity and the third-world movements that were seen as the likely agents of the resistance to capitalist and imperialist oppression. It was therefore not an interesting question whether Marxism might be a Western theory foisted upon local populations. Rather, the assumption was that the ultimate identity of human needs and universal character of the desire for human emancipation across the world guaranteed the coincidence of Marxist theory and indigenous rebellion. Simmons clearly has a similar view, only now it is universal human rights not Marxism that is viewed as the tool of universal emancipation whose role is simply to allow local populations to help themselves. Though it comes from abroad and above, it already matches their interests. Is this what she really believes?

Before investigating this question, let's add that Simmons clearly doesn't want the recourse to the human rights norms in treaty law to be a matter of elites alone – as her first two mechanisms of elite politicians and lawyers might suggest. It is important that the liberation that international law affords through domestic politics is not simply self-liberation but also popular in character. In defence of the supposition that it could be, Simmons writes as follows (again in an entirely italicised sentence): '*Rights treaties affect the welfare of individuals*. If there is any issue area

---

[17] M. wa Mutua, 'Saviors, Victims, and Survivors: The Metaphor of Human Rights' (2001) 42 (1) *Harvard International Law Journal* 201–45.

[18] Simmons, *Mobilizing* 7. (Emphasis in original.)

in which socialization at the non-elite level is important, this should be it.'[19] In my translation, because human rights treaties are about what everyone wants, everyone should respond to their promises.

Offhand, however, one might wonder which facts fit the supposition of mass interest in international human rights norms. After all, other universalisms went global, and penetrated into exotic global locales, before human rights treaties became popular, including Christianity, capitalism, nationalism, and socialism – and it is pretty obvious that all did better at reaching non-elite actors and sometimes inspiring them than international human rights so far. The point is comparative in our era too: students of Pentecostalism have shown that it has boomed massively amongst 'the wretched of the earth' across the same period as the relative ascendancy of international human rights norms, whose inroads into grassroots moral cultures have in fact been relatively minor so far.

Of course, Simmons might respond that her claim is that international human rights treaties have been relevant to popular self-emancipation at all. But in Simmons' compliance chapter, it turns out that self-emancipation (however popular) isn't all there is to the instrumentalisation of treaty law by activist movements. To avoid the critique of human rights imperialism, local movements making use of international treaties in domestic politics have to be self-emancipating in some fundamental sense. She is offering, she says, 'a bottom-up account of treaty effects'.[20] Yet given the rebarbative character of treaties and the high degree of legal literacy required for their use – for unlike Marxists, international lawyers have so far come up with no anthems, slogans, or catchphrases to give their technical doctrines grassroots traction – intermediaries must play a crucial role in making self-emancipation possible. To begin with, 'potential litigants must be aware – or made aware – of their rights under international law'.[21] And activist legal advisers typically matter, Simmons points out, especially when litigation strategies drawing on the authority of treaty norms come into play.[22]

In view of the almost necessary role of external elites – external at the very least in the sense that they bring literacy in human rights law to the mix – in the self-emancipation of the otherwise untutored masses, it is pretty unclear how much to believe in the exact match between the international treaty norm and the framework of local and non-elite grievances. Often Simmons

---

[19] Simmons, *Mobilizing* 139.   [20] Simmons, *Mobilizing* 138.
[21] Simmons, *Mobilizing* 132.   [22] Simmons, *Mobilizing* 135.

speaks more cautiously of clarity a treaty norm might provide to otherwise inchoate local desires, and there is probably something to that argument. But cutting across and running athwart her desire to refute the neocolonialist critique, Simmons also wants to be a constructivist, showing how international treaty law *transforms* local identities and interests more than simply serving as a tool for pre-existing grievances. As she puts it at one point: 'Some citizens may not have thought of a particular practice in rights terms at all.'[23] Her brief against the realism she respects much more in international affairs is that 'moral/legal talk cannot be assumed to be costless, for it risks changing the values, ideas, and interests of potential beneficiaries'.[24] Simmons explicitly insists that this view of 'treaty effects' goes beyond the informational or enlightening role of international law and intermediaries in bringing its good news to specific places. It contributes 'ideas' and 'conceptual frames' that 'animate'.[25]

So which is it? Is the picture one of self-emancipation based on already local values and identities thanks to a new device (thus circumventing the anxiety about neocolonialist imposition) or one of reshaped values and identities thanks to a new framework (thus undercutting the scepticism towards eternal interests)? Are international treaties a source of tools or transformation?

In passing, Simmons relies on anthropologist Sally Engle Merry's work to cut the Gordian knot.[26] According to Simmons, Merry contributes the proposition that 'transnational programs and ideas are translated into local cultural terms by [non-local] agents, but ... "retain their fundamental grounding in transnational human rights concepts of autonomy, individualism, and equality"'.[27] If this story is right, it demonstrates 'the possibility of converting cultural resistance' to what seem like external norms brought by outside actors 'into a rights framework potentially pursuable in courts'.[28] Of course, the story is not right: no translation is perfect, and if this approach were to work it would have to assume an implausible one-to-one adequacy of translation – as if different languages were simply vessels for meanings independent of and transferable among them.

But even were adequate translation possible, it would make for a theoretically untenable picture. For it would mean – again, much as Marxists

---

[23] Simmons, *Mobilizing* 141.   [24] Simmons, *Mobilizing* 143.
[25] Simmons, *Mobilizing* 143–4.
[26] S. E. Merry, *Human Rights and Gender Violence: Translating International Law into Local Justice* (University of Chicago Press 2005).
[27] Simmons, *Mobilizing* 142.   [28] Simmons, *Mobilizing* 132.

once assumed – an identity of interests across humanity merely expressed in a post-Babel confusion of tongues. In rebuilding the tower, international human rights law allows people to understand that they already share in its values – no matter how alien the latter may seem at first. Much as in her realist bent when it comes to the international system, Simmons would have to disclaim her constructivist feints at the domestic level, for ultimately humans cannot help but share the same needs. They do not need new ideas.

To be clear, I myself have no stake in saving local meanings from the imperialist influence of 'Western values'. If it was ever worth doing so, it is too late. If there is values convergence in the world, it is because the homogenisation and interpenetration of values brought about by history started long ago. By the late date that international human rights treaties began to proliferate, there were no pre-contact tribes left anywhere, and everywhere in the world was already subject to prior Western values, notably thanks to colonial rule. That does not mean, however, that ideological competition is over, let alone that everyone has the same fundamental needs everywhere.

The comparative frailty of international human rights norms to serve as popular tools for indigenous self-liberation matters because there are presumably alternative tools, and in fact there were long before international human rights movements began their work. Thus, my worry is that Simmons' account of the emancipatory force of universal values brought from abroad in international treaties but perfectly matching local values takes the focus off the still-raging competition among alternative belief systems and practical movements of possible use to humanity. Even were historically discarded or currently attractive alternatives found wanting, Simmons' focus obscures the imperative to seek better future options. Though her official point is to show simply that international human rights treaties might make a difference, her framework ends up inhibiting the question whether other things might make more of one. Or, to put the worry in a way that reaches past this book into international human rights law as a whole: is the price of relevance to be slim relevance alone?

Social mobilisation and the US civil rights movement

Where did the enterprise of international human rights come from? Simmons offers a summary in an early chapter, which restates the standard assumptions of a burgeoning literature.[29] But Simmons' account of origins doesn't matter to her argument. To be sure, historians like Steven Jensen are hard at work on the political origins of the human rights covenants in the 1960s and archivally rooted studies of those and later treaties are likely to be highly illuminating.[30] But for the purposes of Simmons' core argument about domestic compliance, the human rights treaties she is studying could have fallen from the sky at a recent date and her empirical claims about their impact through domestic politics would still stand.

In this last section, I don't want to doubt those claims – I frankly don't have the competence to do so. For the sake of argument, and in deference to the powerful quantitative methods her book puts on display, I accept Simmons' conclusion that, under a certain set of assumptions and therefore in restricted circumstances, human rights treaties have contributed marginally and thus can contribute in the future to human betterment. As she says, she may even have under-estimated the impact of human rights law.[31] Instead I am interested in how Simmons theorises the relationship between treaties and social movements, in pursuit of my worry that her very demonstration that international law makes a difference obscures how politics might allow for that difference – and for more of it than international treaty law provides.

Unlike in the early part of her book, it really does matter when it comes to social movements that Simmons draws on history to lend credence to her approach. For partly because it has been the topic of so much prior discussion, the US civil rights movement is the model she uses to get her theory of domestic compliance through social mobilisation going.

In her discussion of domestic mobilisation, Simmons claims that the prior ratification of human rights treaties potentially adds value to the agenda of domestic groups for four distinct reasons: it pre-commits government to be receptive to claims based on the treaty or its norms; it may enlarge the movement base to include those who sign on because of government signals; it may provide intangible resources in various forms; and it may

---

[29] Simmons, *Mobilizing* Ch 2. For an alternative view see my *The Last Utopia: Human Rights in History* (Cambridge, MA: Harvard University Press 2010); for a restatement see also my 'Substance, Scale, and Salience: The Recent Historiography of Human Rights' (2012) 8 *Annual Review of Law and Social Science* (forthcoming).

[30] See, e.g., S. Jensen, 'From Jamaica with Law: UN Diplomacy and the Breakthrough for International Human Rights, 1962–1968' (forthcoming 2012).

[31] Simmons, *Mobilizing* 365.

offer additional tools, prominently including new claims in litigation. Simmons then goes on in her empirical chapters to infer that some combination of these hypothetical effects must obtain, supplementing statistical inference with a few narrative interludes.

Yet it is highly illuminating that in her theoretical chapter on compliance Simmons highlights the value of law to the civil rights movement in American history. The problem in doing so is not just, as she acknowledges briefly, that so many recent analyses of the civil rights movement beginning with Gerald Rosenberg's celebrated study have suggested – albeit controversially – that legalisation added little or nothing to, or even interfered with, the mobilisational agenda.[32] Even if it did contribute, which seems likely, it was in relation to displaced alternatives that, of course, no one can now empirically evaluate.[33] And it is also significant, as Simmons doesn't mention, that the US civil rights movement abjured appeal to the very supranational principles whose potential role in domestic mobilisation Simmons wants to vindicate in the present day.[34] Indeed it succeeded precisely on condition of abjuring such appeal: the conditions of movement success, when the productive intersection with law occurred at all, very prominently involved isolation of movement goals from a transnational frame, in favour of patriotic appeal to constitutional principle as part of Cold War struggle. And this isolation powerfully facilitated but also seriously hobbled the ultimate accomplishments of the movement (notably with respect to economic rights or the intersection of race and class). The 'domestication' of the US civil rights movement, according to a series of scholars, accounted for its short-term successes, but is also to blame for some of its long-term and persisting limitations.[35]

And yet Simmons simply relies on the civil rights movement as the prime example of the value of law (and *a fortiori* the extra tools provided by international law) in mobilisational struggle. Is the most interesting feature

---

[32] G. N. Rosenberg, *The Hollow Hope: Can Courts Bring About Social Change?* (University of Chicago Press 1991); Simmons, *Mobilizing* 133–4 and 146 n.

[33] R. L. Goluboff, *The Lost Promise of Civil Rights* (Cambridge, MA: Harvard University Press 2007).

[34] C. A. Anderson, *Eyes off the Prize: The United Nations and the African American Struggle for Human Rights, 1944–1955* (Cambridge University Press 2003).

[35] P. von Eschen, *Race against Empire: Black Americans and Anticolonialism, 1937–1957* (Ithaca, NY: Cornell University Press 1997); M. L. Dudziak, *Cold War Civil Rights: Race and the Image of American Democracy* (Princeton University Press 2000); N. Singh, *Black Is a Country: Race and the Unfinished Struggle for Democracy* (Cambridge, MA: Harvard University Press 2004).

of the US example, in view of the literature, that the law added something –
if Simmons is right to follow Rosenberg's critics in supposing that it did? Or
should that example prompt a fascinating inquiry into what strategies of
mobilisation and what kinds of rival legal strategies (if any) work best in
specific circumstances and over the long term? In other words, it may well
now be beyond doubt that, in some aggregate sense, human rights treaties
'make a difference' through domestic social mobilisation that turns to them.
But compared to what? Doing nothing? Or doing something else? Simmons
herself says that international treaties 'enable and constrain' social movements but then, as I read her, she focuses solely on the positive side of the
ledger. The scholarship on the US civil rights movement hardly seems to
validate this approach.[36]

A yet more serious worry with Simmons' intensive agenda to vindicate
the importance of international human rights law in some absolute sense is
that focusing so doggedly on the value added by treaties takes the emphasis
off the conditions for the prior existence of the very social movements
required to potentially make good use of them. To put this most bluntly, it is
obvious that social mobilisation can do just fine – and achieve great things –
without international law. In fact it is arguable that domestic movements
operating purely under their own power or in solidaristic alliance with
foreign compatriot movements have done more good in the world so far
than those operating under the colour of the additional authority provided
by human rights treaty ratification. I myself interpret the rise of international human rights politics in our own time as connected in some
mysterious way that no one yet understands to the withering of the local
solidarities that once powered social movements – until, that is, they so
notoriously migrated right in US history. In short, for anyone who cares
about progressive change, the socio-historical conditions under which
mobilisation occurs obviously need not include the availability of international human rights instruments. More important, the analytical turn to
international treaties as a last-ditch source of hope that movements will
have new tools if and when they coalesce distracts from addressing the
(very possibly weakening) conditions in which they might do so.

None of this, again, contradicts Simmons' analysis on its own terms. A
marginally useful tool with few actors to use it is still marginally useful to
the extent there are any actors. Simmons ultimately concedes that

---

[36] Simmons, *Mobilizing* 144.

international law is no 'magic bullet'. It simply does what it does.[37] Yet these reflections may still have severe consequences for the overall importance of her point that international law potentially provides modest gains. Her book leads Simmons to the banal conclusion – though usefully linked to a surprisingly vigorous attack on cross-border military intervention for the sake of human rights compliance – that the upshot of studying these treaties is to illustrate the importance of domestic ownership of politics.[38] In response one might ask: why wasn't this obvious already? A focus on treaties might matter supremely if it was felt that some places or some people weren't able to get social movements going under their own power, as African-Americans and their allies in US history were able to do. But of course, Simmons should want to avoid this assumption; as I explained earlier, she is properly afraid of the implication so frequently haunting international human rights that 'they' need 'us' to achieve the basic formal liberties while we didn't need them – or need international law – to obtain these freedoms.

In the end, then, Simmons' approach diverts attention from the task of figuring out how social mobilisation coalesces – in spite of her passing supposition that treaty ratification might expand the movement constituency. And the anxiety about distraction is, indeed, redoubled when it comes not to the civil and political liberties on which Simmons' book largely though not exclusively focuses but to the economic and social conditions that have long been seen as the circumstances for the enjoyment of rights. There have already been many local and global movements, and there could be more, with respect to those conditions.

This fact does not at all mean, obviously, that there is some past, existing, or future alternative to the current human rights treaty regime that Simmons' analytical focus on that regime simply obscures. If that were true, the threadbare hope that human rights treaties provide would pale in comparison to something else worth celebrating. It does mean, however, that the analytic premium must fall on the preservation of space for options,

---

[37] Simmons, *Mobilizing* 350. I thus take the self-understanding of human rights activists and scholars to be contributing the minimally available amount of progress by staving off evil as the real essence of the movement. In contrast, Wendy Brown provocatively indicts 'the old ruse of liberal reformers, in pursuing agendas that have significant effects in excess of the explicit reform, to insist that all they are doing is a bit of good or holding back the dark'. W Brown, '"The Most We Can Hope For . . .": Human Rights and the Politics of Fatalism' (2004) 103 (2–3) *South Atlantic Quarterly* 451–63 at 461.

[38] Simmons, *Mobilizing* 374, 378.

from lost alternatives to new schemes. Their analytical marginalisation in Simmons' book is an especially serious concern when empirical investigation can risk ratifying the exclusive importance of what it is possible to count.

Conclusion

While insisting on the necessity of homegrown mobilisation, Simmons' focus on treaty law surely does imply a political role for global elites accorded the task of making tools available for mass local struggles elsewhere. But one might well believe that 'they' do need 'us' even more, to convince powerful and wealthy states and societies to change their relationships to nations and movements in other places in the world. The gravest criticism to make of Simmons' book, however, is that it is an unconvincing response to a crisis of our own political self-confidence – and not simply in our global role.

In this view, the debate about the difference international human rights treaties make turns out to be not, or not solely, about our relation to the suffering world and where to look for hope for it. *De te fabula narratur:* beneath the regard for others treaties are ostensibly studied for marginally helping, Simmons is implicitly writing about the prospects there are for helping ourselves. And in this regard, there is nothing new or special in the set of basic spiritual assumptions that frame Simmons' intellectual agenda.

According to Roberto Unger, the prime objection to contemporary legal thought is not that it lacks progressive aspirations. Instead, it is that it is wedded to a 'pessimistic reformism' that accepts historical defeat as the necessary context of the minor change it considers feasible. Horrified by the way of the world but convinced there is no real alternative to it, this scholarship turns to 'humanize the inevitable'.[39] If this description is right, the plausibility of the dominant approach is utterly dependent on its premise that there is no other available option but marginal improvement, which then needs to be passionately defended for its redemptive vocation for good in a world in which evil is otherwise comprehensively victorious. Put bluntly, then, pessimistic reformism must be convincing about its pessimism for its reformism to be worth pursuing.

---

[39] R. M. Unger, *What Should Legal Analysis Become?* (New York: Verso, 1996), esp. 78–105.

Unger's remarks clearly dealt with American constitutionalism, which is the field in which the fatalist's smile became so widespread and ingrained in the middle of the twentieth century and until surprisingly recently. But perhaps nowhere is his diagnosis more apt today than when it comes to contemporary scholarship about the politics of international law and human rights. Simmons' book helps think about why. The globe, indeed, is where progressive hopes often seem to have moved since liberals at long last gave up on American constitutional politics in the teeth of insuperable obstacles, serial disappointments and perpetual defeats. If it is remarkable for reasons other than bringing methodological finesse to a contested field – no mean achievement by any measure – Simmons's *Mobilizing for Human Rights* stands out mainly as a symbol of this reactive transfer upward, in an age of much scholarly talk about international, transnational, or even global constitutionalism. No one would claim that global politics are not morally pressing or potentially inspiring, but the rise of interest in them also followed the crisis of the first-best of our own indigenous self-liberation. As a result, it can sometimes seem as if the prominence of international human rights in the contemporary world fulfills Franz Kafka's well-known maxim: 'there is hope, no end to hope – only not for us.'[40]

If that is so, it is perhaps valid to wonder if the scalar move to the globe, even when it is merely supposed to provide new tools for local change, provides grounds for optimism after all. It might, instead, show when probed that pessimism continues to worsen about what people can achieve on their own and with their own tools – most definitely including ourselves. Simmons' book too provides the occasion to ask whether human rights are primarily significant as a breakthrough to utopia or as a symptom of its decline or even departure. In short, *Mobilizing for Human Rights* is not only a window on the world but also a mirror of our own profound depression.

But the fact that Simmons' book might accurately if unintentionally capture the emotional state of many elite observers of global politics, finding a way to accentuate the positive in the midst of otherwise unremitting gloom, does not mean that its intellectual agenda is the right one. For anyone who reads it this way, the lesson it inadvertently teaches is how great the challenge is of convincing people, after years of local and global defeats, that room for greater hope in politics could be won – and through it,

[40] M. Brod, *Über Franz Kafka* (Frankfurt: Fischer, 1966) 71.

room for more of a difference than human rights treaties have so far allowed. It is not obvious how to face that challenge. One thing is sure: how much to hope is not a question any empirical investigation can answer.

Further reading

Brown, W., '"The Most We Can Hope For …"': Human Rights and the Politics of Fatalism' (2004) 103 (2–3) *South Atlantic Quarterly* 451–63

Hafner-Burton, E., *The Triage Strategy: Reconciling the Promise and Practice of International Human Rights Law* (Princeton University Press forthcoming 2012)

Goldsmith, J. L. and Posner, E. A., *The Limits of International Law* (Oxford University Press 2005)

Goodman, R. and Jinks, D., 'Measuring the Effects of Human Rights Treaties' (2003) 14 (1) *European Journal of International Law* 171–83

Hathaway, O. A., 'Do Human Rights Treaties Make a Difference?' (2001–2) 111 (8) *Yale Law Journal* 1935–2042

   'Testing Conventional Wisdom' (2003) 14 (1) *European Journal of International Law* 185–200

Kennedy, D., *The Dark Side of Virtue: Reassessing International Humanitarianism* (Princeton University Press 2004)

   'The International Human Rights Movement: Still Part of the Problem?', in R. Dickinson *et al.* (eds.), *Examining Critical Perspectives on Human Rights* (Cambridge University Press 2012)

Moyn, S., *The Last Utopia: Human Rights in History* (Cambridge, MA: Harvard University Press 2010)

   'Substance, Scale, and Salience: On the Recent Historiography of Human Rights' (2012) 8 *Annual Review of Law and Social Science* (forthcoming)

Mutua, M. wa, 'Saviors, Victims, and Survivors: The Metaphor of Human Rights' (2001) 42 (1) *Harvard International Law Journal* 201–45

Ron, J. and Hafner-Burton, E., 'Seeing Double: Human Rights Impact Through Qualitative and Quantitative Eyes?,' (2009) 61 (2) *World Politics* 360–401

Shaffer, G. and Ginsburg, T., 'The Empirical Turn in International Law Scholarship' (2012) 106 (1) *American Journal of International Law* 1–46

Simmons, B. A., *Mobilizing for Human Rights: International Law in Domestic Politics* (Cambridge University Press 2009)

Smith-Cannoy, H., *Insincere Commitments: Human Rights Treaties, Abusive States, and Citizen Activism* (Georgetown University Press 2012)

Snyder, S. B., *Human Rights Activism and the End of the Cold War: A Transnational History of the Helsinki Network* (Cambridge University Press 2011)

Stein, J. von, 'Do Treaties Constrain or Screen? Selection Bias and Treaty Compliance' (2005) 99 (4) *American Political Science Review* 611–22

Index